Alfred Kingston

East Anglia and the Great Civil War

The rising of Cromwell's Ironsides in the associated counties of Cambridge,

Huntingdon, Lincoln, Norfolk, Suffolk, Essex, and Hertford

Alfred Kingston

East Anglia and the Great Civil War
The rising of Cromwell's Ironsides in the associated counties of Cambridge, Huntingdon, Lincoln, Norfolk, Suffolk, Essex, and Hertford

ISBN/EAN: 9783337012335

Printed in Europe, USA, Canada, Australia, Japan

Cover: Foto ©ninafisch / pixelio.de

More available books at **www.hansebooks.com**

EAST ANGLIA

AND THE

GREAT CIVIL WAR.

THE RISING OF CROMWELL'S IRONSIDES IN THE ASSOCIATED
COUNTIES OF CAMBRIDGE, HUNTINGDON, LINCOLN, NORFOLK,
SUFFOLK, ESSEX, AND HERTFORD.

With Appendices and Illustrations.

BY

ALFRED KINGSTON, F. R. HIST. S.,

AUTHOR OF

"*Hertfordshire during the Great Civil War,*" "*Fragments of Two Centur*"

LONDON:
ELLIOT STOCK, 62, PATERNOSTER ROW, E.C.
1897.

HERTFORD
PRINTED BY STEPHEN AUSTIN AND SONS.

PREFACE.

IN the following pages I have endeavoured to show, not so much what was the part of each individual member of the Eastern Counties Association in the Civil War, as what was their general contribution to the War, and what were the temper and the experience of the people of these Eastern Counties. To have told the story of each of the seven counties separately would have required as many volumes, and, besides, would have been inconsistent with the unity of this famous area of East Anglia, which, stirred by one common impulse, and having sufficient in common in situation and surroundings, assumed a distinctive character of its own, such as no individual county and no other part of the country could show. Nor will the reader find any attempt to compile a history of families and places concerned in the Civil War within the Eastern Counties. Frequent references of this character there will be, but my aim has been rather to present, in as interesting a form as a regard for historical accuracy of detail will allow, the main features of the remarkable story of that East Anglian unity which gave so sturdy an account of itself in the great Puritan Revolution under Cromwell. If, as I believe to be the case, something of that unity still survives in the feeling which prompts old East Anglians, wherever they may be, to cherish, like 'brither Scots,' the traditions of their clan, then perhaps this chapter in their past history, which is here placed on record for the first time, may have an interest both for present inhabitants of, and for those who may be otherwise connected with, these counties which played so famous a part in a great crisis of our history. Whether there may be the like interest in the book for those not so connected with these Associated Counties, will depend upon the degree of success which has attended the author's efforts. Nothing short of failure on his part in telling the story can limit its interest to the counties which gave it birth, for Oliver Cromwell and his Ironsides and East Anglia with its Puritan protest are vital and inseparable parts of the history of England.

The materials for this book are derived almost exclusively from contemporary sources. Among the chief authorities consulted have been the State Papers in the Public Record Office; various manuscript collections and the famous collection of King's Pamphlets, and Civil War Tracts, in the British Museum Library; manuscript and other collections in the University Library, Cambridge, the Bodleian, Oxford, and other Libraries; the Historical MSS. Commission Reports, the Journals of Parliament, and numerous contemporary authorities referred to in the text.

For courteous assistance and facilities for research amongst College papers, and for valuable suggestions, my thanks are especially due to members of the University and the principal Colleges of Cambridge—to Mr. W. Aldis Wright (Vice-Master) and the Rev. Dr. Sinker (Librarian), of Trinity; to Mr. J. Bass Mullinger (Librarian), Mr. Scott (Bursar), and to the Library Committee of St. John's; to Mr. Oscar Browning and Mr. W. H. Macaulay (Bursar), of King's; to Dr. Courtney Kenny, of Downing; and to Mr. Jenkinson and staff at the University Library. To Mr. W. M. Palmer I am especially indebted for much valuable assistance in connection with Puritanism in Cambridgeshire, as well as for the list of ejected Royalist clergy in that county, the result of much labour and research, which appears as Appendix IV. My thanks are also due to Mr. Hamon le Strange, of Hunstanton Hall, Norfolk; to Mr. Alexander Peckover, Lord-Lieutenant of Cambridgeshire; to the Rev. Canon Raven, of Fressingfield, Suffolk; to the Rev. C. H. Evelyn White, Editor of *East Anglian Notes and Queries*; the Rev. W. D. Sweeting, Editor of *Fenland Notes and Queries*; to the Ven. Archdeacon Vesey, of Huntingdon; the Rev. W. M. Noble, Rector of Wistow, Hunts; to Mr. W. B. Redfern, Mr. Robert Bowes, and Mr. T. D. Atkinson, of Cambridge; to Mr. Joseph Phillips, of Stamford; Dr. Perry, President of the Spalding Gentlemen's Society; Mr. C. P. Tebbutt, of Bluntisham, St. Ives; and other correspondents whose kind interest is none the less valued though not individually mentioned. While I am conscious that so much good-will deserved a better return than that which is here presented, I venture to hope that the result, such as it is, may not be altogether without interest for the general reader, or some small claim upon the indulgence of those who best know the nature of my task.

ALFRED KINGSTON.

ROYSTON, HERTS.
September, 1897.

CONTENTS.

CHAPTER.	PAGE
I.—INTRODUCTION—CROMWELL AND HIS NEIGHBOURS AT HUNTINGDON, ST. IVES, AND ELY	1
II.—SHIP-MONEY RIOTS—STRANGE SCENES IN THE CHURCHES—PETITIONS AND PROTESTATIONS	18
III.—THE KING DEPARTING FROM HIS PARLIAMENT — RIVAL PROCLAMATIONS	33
IV.—CROMWELL AND THE COLLEGE PLATE—RAISING THE KING'S STANDARD—TUMULTS IN EAST ANGLIA—THE BATTLE OF EDGEHILL	55
V.—A GREAT HISTORIC UNITY—THE EAST ANGLIAN COMPACT—CROMWELL AND THE ROYALISTS—THE FORTIFICATION OF CAMBRIDGE	76
VI.—THE FIRST SIEGE OF CROWLAND—THE BATTLE OF THE PARSONS—CROMWELL AND THE FENMEN	101
VII.—A PURITAN COMMANDER—HOW THE ESSEX MEN CAME IN—THE SIEGE OF KING'S LYNN	123
VIII.—THROUGH LINCOLNSHIRE TO MARSTON MOOR	140
IX.—QUARREL OF MANCHESTER AND CROMWELL—CROWLAND AND NEWPORT—SIR HUDIBRAS AND SIR ROGER	166
X.—CROMWELL AND THE NEW MODEL ARMY—RECRUITING FOR NASEBY—THE HOUR AND THE MAN	188
XI.—THE LAST RALLY OF THE KING—THE FIGHT AT HUNTINGDON—THE KING'S FLIGHT THROUGH THE FENS IN DISGUISE	210
XII.—THE ARMY, THE PARLIAMENT, AND THE KING	233
XIII.—THE SECOND CIVIL WAR — RISINGS ALL OVER EAST ANGLIA—FIGHTING AT NORWICH, BURY ST. EDMUNDS, STAMFORD, CAMBRIDGE, LINTON, AND ST. NEOTS—THE SIEGE OF COLCHESTER—THE EXECUTION OF THE KING	252

CHAPTER. PAGE
XIV.—TAXING THE ROYALISTS — THE FORTUNES OF COMPOUNDERS—SEQUESTRATORS AND THEIR WAYS . . 290
XV.—A RELIGIOUS REVOLT—THE PURITANS AND THE CLERGY—UNHAPPY RURAL ENGLAND 312
XVI.—CROMWELLIANA AND BIOGRAPHY—EVOLUTION OF THE IRONSIDES—CONCLUSION 333

APPENDICES.

I.—SOCIAL AND PUBLIC LIFE DURING THE CIVIL WAR . . 363
II.—PAYING AND FEEDING THE ARMY 373
III.—THE EASTERN ASSOCIATION COMMITTEES 382
IV.—DEPRIVED ROYALIST CLERGY IN CAMBRIDGESHIRE . . 390
V.—THE "FIRST CENTURY OF MALIGNANT PRIESTS" . . . 396

ILLUSTRATIONS.

I.—CROMWELL'S HOUSE AT ELY 12
II.—PART OF THE KING'S PALACE AT ROYSTON 35
III.—CROMWELL ARRESTING THE SHERIFF AT ST. ALBANS . . 86
IV.—RUINS OF CROWLAND ABBEY 108
V.—FACSIMILE TITLE-PAGE OF THE "SOULDIERS POCKET BIBLE" 127
VI.—PLAN OF THE SIEGE OF COLCHESTER 280
VII.—"NORBOROUGH HOUSE, THE SEAT OF THE CLAYPOOLES" . 337
VIII.—BRIDGET (IRETON) FLEETWOOD 338

EAST ANGLIA AND THE GREAT CIVIL WAR.

CHAPTER I.

INTRODUCTION — CROMWELL AND HIS NEIGHBOURS AT HUNTINGDON, ST. IVES, AND ELY.

BEHIND the pageant of history, in which fame has too often been restricted to placing its seal upon great issues which have ended in signal triumph or defeat, there have been fruitful causes and arduous pioneer work which have not always had their due. Marston Moor, Naseby, Dunbar, and Worcester, historic names which have cast a glamour over the turmoil of the Puritan revolution, are often but the convenient labels which get tacked on to the name of Oliver Cromwell as a means of remembering his place in history, with too little regard for the toilsome and thorny pathway, and the intensely human trials and difficulties, which the hero of the Commonwealth had to travel and to face before he reached those giddy heights which have caught the light of history. There remains, therefore, the opportunity of exploring the humbler but not less interesting field in which arose some of the peculiar difficulties and the remarkable successes of his work, and of tracing those fruitful streams which fed the irresistible torrent of Cromwell's genius.

In the Great Civil War between Charles I and his Parliament the Eastern Counties of England earned the distinction of presenting the one great historic unity, which enabled these counties to hold their own, and, whether for good or ill, to practically determine the fate of the rest of the kingdom in the struggle. Here the essential elements of the Puritan revolution—the revolt against abuse of human authority in religion and of Royal prerogative in the State—came into sharpest conflict. In these counties arose the one man whose acts were destined to colour all our subsequent history ; and here arose, too, the ever-victorious Ironsides, who with the 'Soldier's Pocket Bible' in their knapsacks, went forth with sturdy purpose and resistless valour, to roll back the tide of war from their own borders, and to carry the Parliamentary cause to victory at Marston Moor and Naseby. It would, therefore, be no undue straining of comparisons to assign an almost unique position in the Civil War to the counties and people of East Anglia—to that famous Eastern Counties' Association which, with its headquarters at Cambridge, became, under the controlling power of the one man Oliver Cromwell, the great Parliamentary recruiting-ground ground whose forces were destined to turn the scale in favour of the popular cause at more than one critical point in the War.

The issue between King and Parliament, as it presented itself in the first instance to the men of the Fens, was one upon which there was little room for mere chauvinism. These men of the Fenlands, while they were loyal to the principle of kingship, were prepared to judge the King, or rather his ministers, by principles of government ; and, as those principles were thought to be subversive of the true Protestant religion, in which and in the God of Heaven they did verily believe, it is not surprising to find that the bulk of the people in these Eastern Counties were emphatically against the King and the Bishops.

In East Anglia there were two dominant factors which seem to suggest a possible explanation for the prominence which the Eastern Counties assumed as the great recruiting-ground for Parliament, and the sturdy yeomen's service which its inhabitants gave to the cause for which Parliament took up arms. One of these factors was the comparatively limited number, within part of that region, of courtly or titled families likely to have attachments to the King's person and his Court; the other and more potent factor was the sharp contrast which the dominant Puritan faith of this region presented to the ecclesiastical tendency of the times in high places. Yet in no case in those momentous months for the counties of England, can it be said that the people, even with such a pronounced Puritanism as that which prevailed in East Anglia, ever thought of directing their protestations against the King as the personal head of the nation, but simply against the principles which those in high places were urging the King to adopt. This is a distinction which it is always necessary to bear clearly in mind in order to understand how it was that the voice of the people was so overwhelmingly against the King when the quarrel began, and yet that some of these same people were found fighting for the King when the quarrel had reached the stage of actual war.

But with this kind of secession from the logical effect of their protestations, of which the county of Hertford and other counties with numerous courtly families presented some notable examples, the Fenmen, and for the most part Norfolk, Suffolk, and Essex, were but little troubled after the first tug was over. With the exception of the part of the Fens bordering upon the sphere of the Earl of Newcastle's Army, these counties also felt less of the misery of civil war than fell upon the homes of the inhabitants in many quarters elsewhere. If, as I believe to be the case, this peculiar experience was due less to their geographical position than to the sturdy united purpose with which they kept their own borders clear of the immediate horrors of war, and contributed in a memorable degree to its prosecution in other fields, then some record, however imperfect, of their share in an eventful time should not be without interest. Here, if anywhere, was to be found in a pre-eminent degree that 'depository of the sacred fire of liberty' which history has justly credited to the old Puritan stock, and it would have been strange indeed if in the great struggle between King and Parliament this region had not played a conspicuous part.

With the old pamphleteers, and with some even of the more dignified historians of the time whose example has not been entirely lost upon modern writers, it was the fashion to paint the chief men among the Puritans and the Ironsides as men of mean origin, of little education, and a disregard for all the gentler courtesies of life—a set of men united only by one fanatical purpose of usurping all authority in religion and morals. There may have been such men attracted to the Parliamentary cause, as events unfolded ; but it is not necessary to follow these men and approve of everything that was done in the name of Parliament when, at a later period of the struggle, the Army became the dominant factor in the nation, to recognize that in that sturdy ' No !' which came thundering up from the counties of England, and from nowhere more sturdily than from the Eastern Counties, against the abuse of Royal prerogative when the struggle began, the men by whom the cause of Parliament was being first set in motion, were, for the most part, men who stood for all that was best in the character of the nation. Then, if not later, the Parliamentary cause was the popular cause—

> The people's prayer, the glad diviner's theme,
> The young men's vision and the old men's dream.

The leaders of the hard-handed men of the Fens will very well bear looking at for a moment as we find them in their daily duties when the times were calling them to exchange the homely occupation of husbandry for the sterner business of war.

Of chivalry such as was shown to the King in a losing cause, and devotion to old institutions without regard to their uses, it may be we shall find little among these sturdy Puritan folk of East Anglia ; but of the true chivalry of a band of men united for the assertion of great principles, we shall see a fine spirit of comradeship, in striking contrast with that morose and hypocritical view of life which historical caricature has too often fixed, rather indiscriminately, upon the Puritans. Indeed, one of the most interesting and remarkable things about the attitude of these Eastern Counties, out of which was to arise a sort of Pride's Purge of the Royal mismanagement of the nation's affairs, was the way in which a number of comparatively young men of character and position, united by ties of family life or neighbourhood, and animated by firm religious conviction, banded themselves together to resist the abuses which had spoilt for them the meaning of Church and State ; or, failing this, to make their home in a freer country beyond the seas, as so many earnest men had already done. A few of these individuals stand out with sufficient clearness, during the years before the War began, to be worthy of notice, and by public acts as well as position, Oliver Cromwell was already at the head of the group. For the purpose of fixing his local connection with persons and places in Huntingdonshire and Cambridgeshire, rather than as a matter of general history, it is necessary to state very briefly what that position was.

When Sir Henry Cromwell, of Hinchinbrook, whose splendid and sumptuous style of living had earned for him the name of the 'Golden Knight,' passed away in 1603, his son Oliver (not *the* Oliver, but his uncle) entertained King James at Hinchinbrook on the occasion of that magnificent royal progress of the King from Scotland to the English throne. This Oliver Cromwell, the King's host, was then knighted ; but in 1627 there was a change at Hinchinbrook, which Sir Oliver sold to the Montagues (in later times the Earls of Sandwich), and Hinchinbrook passed out of the Cromwell family. While the above was being enacted a much more interesting event was happening in the same family in a quieter way. Robert Cromwell, brother of this Sir Oliver, had married Elizabeth, the young widow of William Lynne, of Bassingbourn, Cambs. Elizabeth Lynne had lost her husband and one child within a year of her marriage.[1] Her maiden name was Steward, and she was a daughter of William Steward, farmer of the tithes at Ely. About the year 1591 Robert Cromwell and his wife settled down in the town of Huntingdon to farm his portion of the family estate left to

---

[1] William Lynne and their infant child, apparently by the wish of Mrs. Lynne, were buried in Ely Cathedral. This William Lynne came of a family of note, as the monumental brasses formerly in Bassingbourn Church testified—" Pray for the soule of Richard Lynne, Esq., and Alice his wife, wch Richard was vice chamberlayne to the excellent Princess Margaret (mother to the redoubted King Henry the Seventh), Countess of Richmond and Derby. Wch Richard deceased 3 Jan. 1509, 8 sonnes and 3 daughters."—COLE MSS. Brit. Mus.

him, and in a substantial house, between the market-place and the river Ouse. Whether Robert Cromwell brewed beer from the brook, or only made malt from the produce of his lands, is of little consequence; brewing of beer was not in those days so much of a trade as it is now. But in this house Oliver Cromwell was born on April 25, 1599, the fifth child of a family of ten.

The idea sometimes expressed attributing a mean origin to Oliver Cromwell loses its force when it is remembered that at this time nearly half the gentry of Huntingdonshire bore the name of Cromwell. Young Oliver, therefore, had a large number of influential relations in the county—Uncle Sir Oliver, of Ramsey; Uncle Henry, of Upwood, near Ramsey mere; Uncle Sir Richard, who had been member for Huntingdon in Queen Elizabeth's reign; and Uncle Sir Philip, of Biggin House; to say nothing of multiplied relationships of the degree of cousins, in which degree through his aunt Elizabeth he became related to Cousin Hampden of Ship-money fame.

Educated at the Huntingdon Grammar School under Dr. Beard, young Oliver came over to Cambridge in 1616 and entered at Sidney Sussex College. Here he remained only for a year, and then went up to London for a time, it is supposed to study law, returning, after his marriage to a daughter of Sir James Bourchier, an Essex magistrate, to live at Huntingdon the life of an ordinary country gentleman. In 1628 he was returned as a Member of Parliament for Huntingdon, and sat there amidst the stormy scenes when Speaker Finch was held down in the chair while the Remonstrance was being passed; and, when Parliament was dissolved, to be summoned no more for eleven years, he returned to Huntingdon, but lived there for only a short time.

In May, 1631, Oliver Cromwell sold the estates at Huntingdon and at Hartford close by, and left his old home and the place of his birth,[1] which he had represented in

---

[1] At Huntingdon the site of the house in the High Street in which Cromwell was born, is still identified by the house which stands upon it—"Cromwell House"—the residence until recent years of Captain Bernard, and now of Mrs. Bernard, his widow.

Parliament. Why he left the county town, in which the gentry of those times liked to have their town-house, as wealthy men do in London to-day, and selected the neighbouring town of St. Ives, and what he did there, have been left in a great deal of obscurity. Yet the solution is probably not far to seek.

At this time Cromwell had come under the influence of profound religious conviction, and nothing could be more natural than that he should turn to kindred spirits in seeking advice in his worldly affairs. At St. Ives the Slepe Hall estate had come by inheritance to Henry Lawrence, eldest son of Sir John Lawrence of St. Ives, who had taken his M.A. degree at the Puritan College of Emmanuel in Cambridge, and had recently married Amy, daughter of Sir Edward Peyton, of Isleham, Cambs, a Puritan like her father and a woman remarkable for her piety. To this friend and relative Cromwell seems to have turned, and the two sturdy Puritans, Cromwell being then thirty-two years of age and Lawrence thirty, who were destined to come together again so strangely in exalted stations, of which neither of them could have dreamed, took up the relationship of landlord and tenant by Cromwell's hiring part of the Slepe Hall estate.[1]

To these lands Cromwell, with his wife and five young children, came, and stocked them with the £1,800 realized from the sale of the Huntingdon estates. Here, in the character of grazing-land farmer, on the flat, moist meadows saturated by the Ouse and its overflowings, Cromwell made his home for five years—1631–1636. Here in the ancient cattle market of St. Ives, on the cobble-stone paving now called the Broadway, Oliver Cromwell mingled with the yeomen of the Fens and bought and sold cattle. In the old sheep market in the High Street, his ewes, tups, and wethers were known by the letters " O. C." marked in reddle on their backs ; letters which were so soon to convey a very different meaning to other folk than farmers and yeomen. Every Sunday, down the old Market Place from Slepe Hall one sees, through the medium of other eyes—Noble's, the old parish clerk's, and certain 'vague old persons' who remembered

[1] See *Gentleman's Magazine* for July, 1815, in which appears a lucid account of the Lawrences and their relation to St. Ives and to Cromwell.

him—Oliver Cromwell, 'wearing a piece of red flannel round his throat owing to inflammation from which he suffered,' passing along to the Parish Church, a fine building on the banks of the Ouse, still pretty much as Cromwell saw and worshipped in it, excepting the fine modern spire. Under the very wall of the churchyard, with tombstones built into it, flow the dark waters of the Ouse. Here Oliver Cromwell passed moodily along with his neighbours as the bell 'tolled in' for service, and looked out across the great stretch of waters at flood-time.[1] Here, 'with thoughts bounded by the Ouse river and thoughts that go beyond eternity,' Cromwell listened to Mr. Downhall, the minister, who was ejected when the troubles came over the land. In the daily affairs of his neighbours Cromwell took an active interest, and attended parish meetings, even for so small a business as the appointment of road surveyors, as the St. Ives parish books still testify.

In January, 1636, his uncle, Sir Thomas Steward, died at Ely and left Cromwell his estates there; the Slepe Hall lands were given up, and Oliver left St. Ives and went to live at Ely, though not without leaving behind him evidence of his attachment to Puritan institutions, in the letter addressed from St. Ives 'to my very loving friend, Mr. Storie, at the sign of the Dog, Royal Exchange, London,' and appealing for his continued support of the Weekly Lecture at St. Ives or Huntingdon.

The letter to Mr. Storie, the entries of Cromwell's name in the parish book, one of which has been cut out, and that dim little vision of a piece of red flannel round his neck as he walked to church on Sundays, are all that remain of local colour respecting Cromwell's life at St. Ives; though when Noble wrote his book on the *House of Cromwell*, he spoke of "a great number of swords which have the initials of Oliver upon them" being dispersed in the town, and that "the farmer who now rents the estate he occupied, marks his sheep with the identical marking-irons which Oliver

---

[1] Here at a later date another great man looked over the wall into the dark waters and gave us this little word-picture: "The Ouse flows here, fringed with gross, reedy herbage and bushes, and is of the blackness of Acheron, streaked with foul metallic glitterings and plays of colour."—CARLYLE, "Letters and Speeches of Cromwell," i, 67.

used, and which have 'O. C.' upon them." The lands which Cromwell farmed, seem to be identified with reasonable certainty as lying somewhere between the present new Cattle Market, the Railway Station, and the River Ouse; lands to which the old Slepe Hall would have a not unpleasant outlook. The house in which Cromwell lived had, in Noble's time, disappeared; and Mr. Atkins, an attorney, had built 'a handsome one' upon the site. It was this house of Mr. Atkins, the attorney, which Carlyle saw in use as a boarding-school; and this has now disappeared, and a new 'Slepe Hall' has been set up for the school, at some distance from the town, to further confuse the future historian perchance. The site of the Slepe Hall of Cromwell's time is now marked by modern houses standing behind the new Cattle Market, known as "Cromwell Terrace" and "Cromwell Place."

The only structural relic remaining in St. Ives directly associated with the name of Cromwell, is the rather notable ruin of what is known as Cromwell's Barn; standing on the right of the road leading from the High Street towards the river. One end, a side, and part of the other end of the massive walls of this once spacious 'barn' now form boundaries of a garden to a modern house.[1] Noble says Cromwell 'built' this barn, but under what ancient Agricultural Holdings Act any sane man with only £1,800 to stock his farm with, would have found it possible to erect such a very massive structure for a tenancy which could be determined as this was, I do not know. It was probably in existence long before Cromwell came to St. Ives; may very well have been used by him as a convenience for the land upon or near to which it was situated, and so obtained the name of Cromwell's Barn. The ruins have rather an ecclesiastical appearance, and it is sometimes called the Priory Barn.

Leaving St. Ives, Cromwell took up his abode in Ely, taking with him his wife and children and his widowed mother from Huntingdon. At Ely he succeeded to the office of

[1] Now occupied by Mr. Warren.

farmer of the tithes, vacant by the death of his uncle Sir Thomas Steward, and lived in the Glebe House set apart for the person who held the office of tithe-farmer.

During those quiet years at St. Ives and the first years of his residence at Ely, Cromwell was no idle spectator of the stirring events in the life of the nation, or of life in the Fens. The writ for Ship-money had come out while he was at St. Ives; and upon the very day he was writing that letter to Mr. Storie in support of the Puritan lecture, his cousin John Hampden was standing up at the head of his neighbours in the parish church of Great Kimble, in Buckinghamshire, and refusing to pay Ship-money. Prynne, Bastwick, and Burton had had their ears cut off in Palace Yard, and Jennie Geddes had hurled her stool at the Dean's head in Edinburgh about the Bishops. Then there came the excitement all over England about the Ship-money trial, which lasted three weeks, and made Mr. Hampden 'the most famous man in England.' Cromwell himself had continued his public activity in Ely, had become one of the trustees of Parson's Charity; and had gained notoriety over the great work of draining the Fens, not so much against its actual accomplishment as against injustice to his neighbours over the manner of doing it. The scheme was 'extremely unpopular,' and 'particularly amongst the commonalty, who had a custom of commoning and fishing in dry times'; and Cromwell at a great meeting at Huntingdon had so actively opposed it, that it was dropped for a time. His action gained him 'great accession of friends,' and procured for him the title of 'Lord of the Fens.'[1]

To this period of his residence in Ely belongs the most direct connecting link between Oliver Cromwell's life in the Fens and the present time which now exists. Taking it altogether, with its associations and its present suggestive condition, there is, perhaps, no more interesting house in England than the modest structure still known as Cromwell's house in Ely. Overshadowed almost by the Cathedral and the Bishop's Palace hard by, this plain, substantial house

[1] Noble, i, 187–8.

became the rooftree of the man whose indomitable spirit dared to assert, against all 'innovations' to the contrary, the principle that cathedrals and bishops are only of value in proportion as they help to build up the spiritual life of the people : 'they that build up spiritual temples, they are the men truly charitable, truly pious,' were the words with which Cromwell had taken farewell of St. Ives. In these two almost contiguous houses, the Bishop's Palace, in which Matthew Wren, Bishop of Ely, was concerning himself with the outward performances and ceremonials of public worship, and the tithe-farmer's house, where Oliver Cromwell concerned himself with the management of the tithes on week-days, and from which he walked along Palace Green to the Church or Cathedral on Sundays—in these two houses, considering the character of the two men who inhabited them and the causes for which they stood, there was an epitome of the Puritan revolution of the deepest significance, in view of what was so soon coming to pass.

The house in which Oliver Cromwell, his wife, his mother, and his children took up their abode in Ely, during several eventful years, was built at the west or north-west corner of St. Mary's Churchyard, with the great tithe-barn— 'the biggest barn but one in England'[1]—on one side and the churchyard on the other. It is still standing almost in every respect as when occupied by Cromwell, excepting for a piece of new brickwork which closes up the end wall where the great tithe barn has disappeared. It is a square, substantial two-story house, with reception rooms on either side of the modest entrance hall, and has the appearance of being likely to stand a long time yet. On the left as you enter is the commodious panelled reception room, in which Cromwell doubtless received his guests, while on the right is a room in which he probably transacted his business about the tithes. In the rear are the domestic offices, and on every hand are curious recesses and cupboards, let into

[1] The Great Tithe Barn at Ely, which was demolished by order of the Dean and Chapter in 1843, was 219 ft. 6 in. long by 39 ft. 5 in. wide, and with walls four feet thick, appears to have somewhat resembled the lesser structure at St. Ives. See Proceedings of the Cambridge Antiquarian Society.

CROMWELL'S HOUSE AT ELY. *(From a photo by Frith & Co., Reigate.)*

the massive walls, in which young Dick, Oliver, and Henry may have put fish hooks and other juvenile belongings. Opposite the entrance is the ancient spiral staircase, a curiosity in itself, up which Cromwell and his family ascended to bedrooms, for the most part remaining just as when he and his family slept in them. Upon the ground floor in the rear, with an outlook into the churchyard, is the old kitchen with its ancient floorbricks, gnarled, cracked, and worn by generations of footfalls, carrying you back to the old domestic scene in which Mrs. Cromwell and her maids bore the ordeal common in so many homes at that time, of taking up the daily round of duty and suspense while their lord and master went forth, with fiery speech and doughty sword, to rouse his neighbours and lead them to victory. In these old rooms the Cromwells had three more children born to them—Mary, afterwards Lady Fauconberg; Frances, whom Charles II was said to have had thoughts of marrying; and a son who died in infancy. The house is still maintained in tenantable repair, and is in private occupation. In the rooms in which Oliver Cromwell brooded over the private sorrows and heroic public necessities of his time, men and women in this highly civilized age resort with their smaller temporary anguish to which the dentist ministers. The homes of men play many parts![1]

It was during his residence at Ely that the letter was written to his cousin, Mrs. St. John, containing Cromwell's reference to his early life—" Oh I lived in and loved darkness and hated light; I was a chief, a chief of sinners"—which some of our historians have taken too literally, for their own credit as well as for that of Cromwell. Half an hour spent in the vestry of some little Calvinistic meeting-house, even in this nineteenth century, would have modified a great deal that has been written as to the supposed wickedness of the early life of Cromwell, and perhaps of Bunyan also, in so far as it

[1] Is it too much to hope that this house, still remaining in all the essential features which made it a home for a great Englishman, should be placed under some kind of public trust in the nation's keeping? At any rate, it is some little satisfaction to be able to present in these pages a picture of the house of which Carlyle hoped, "for Oliver's sake some painter will, perhaps, yet take a correct likeness."

rests upon their own confessions. Cromwell's self-abasement, in his letter to Mrs. St. John, was simply a phase of the Calvinism of the time. A narrow creed, a self-deceiving creed, it may perhaps be called, but its language of self-condemnation cannot, unless supported by independent evidence, bear the essentially vulgar construction that it indicates any exceptional depravity in secular life.

With these local reflections, we come to the point at which Oliver Cromwell was brought into intimate contact with other members of Cambridgeshire and Huntingdonshire families, besides his sympathetic young Puritan landlord of St. Ives—young men of like sympathies with himself and with the courage of their convictions. Many a yeoman's son from these Fenlands and elsewhere had already followed the men of the 'Mayflower'; and when Hampden's trial was decided against the champion of popular rights, Cromwell, with characteristic promptitude, decided with Hampden and others to 'leave his native country to enjoy liberty of conscience which was denied them in it.' But just as the parochial clergy were jealous of and resented the Puritan habit of going out of the parish to hear sermons elsewhere, so the King became jealous of this growing tendency of influential young men going out and founding settlements beyond the seas. In the month of April, 1638, only two years before the summoning of the famous Short Parliament, eight ships were lying in the Thames with passengers on board bound for New England. Charles I, little knowing what the act meant for himself and his throne, gave orders for staying of the ships and likewise for the 'putting on land of all passengers and provisions therein intended for the voyage.' In those ships were John Hampden and Oliver Cromwell, upon whose departure or detention was hanging one of the greatest 'if's' of history of ancient or modern times. Twelve months later two young men of influential families in Cambs and Hunts departed for New England. These were Samuel Desborough, of Eltisley, brother of the famous Major-General who married Cromwell's sister, and William Leete, son of John Leete, of Doddington. Leete was a clerk in the Bishop's Court at Cambridge, but being impressed with the 'oppressions and cruelties then practised on the conscientious and virtuous Puritans,' he examined their doctrines and became a Puritan himself. Joining with young Desborough and with a party of about forty under Mr. Whitfield, a minister, the two young men sailed for Newhaven, and, like Lawrence and Cromwell, will be met with again in exalted stations of life. Other intimate friends of Cromwell whom we shall meet again in more stirring scenes, were Valentine Walton or Wauton, of Great Staughton, near St. Neots,[1] already married to Cromwell's sister Margaret, and the Russells of Chippenham, near Newmarket. Among Cromwell's early neighbours at Huntingdon there were also young Edward Montague, of Hinchinbrook, and Viscount Mandeville, of Kimbolton, the future Earl of Manchester, ready to come out on the popular side; and Stephen Marshall, son of a glover at Godmanchester, who had, as a boy, gleaned over the Cromwell lands. Having graduated at the Puritan College of Emmanuel, Marshall will likewise be found in high places fighting for Parliament with unrivalled eloquence of speech, if not with the sword. It is time, however, that we turned from the 'searchings of heart' of these Puritan folk to their causes in the events which were happening around them.

When, at last, a Parliament was again to be called, some of Oliver Cromwell's friends conceived the idea of his standing for the town of Cambridge, of which he was not yet even a freeman. According to one authority,[2] Cromwell's friends recommended him so highly to the Mayor of Cambridge that the latter, though a Royalist, exercised his right of conferring the freedom of the borough of Cambridge upon Cromwell. He was sent for by the mayor, and

---

[1] It is an interesting coincidence that Sir Oliver Cromwell, of Ramsey, and George Walton, of Great Staughton, were the captains who marched at the head of the Huntingdonshire forces to Tilbury to repel the Spanish Armada, and that another Captain Oliver Cromwell and another Captain Walton, relatives of the former, should command the Huntingdonshire forces raised by Parliament. Some of the speeches of old Sir Henry Cromwell, the 'Golden Knight' of Hinchinbrook, rousing his neighbours in Huntingdonshire to fight for the defence of their religion, threatened by Spain, might also have been made by the more famous Oliver Cromwell, his grandson, fifty years later. See "Huntingdonshire and the Spanish Armada," by the Rev. W. M. Noble.

[2] Heath's "Flagellum."

there, on January 7, 1640, a few weeks before the opening of the Short Parliament, Oliver Cromwell appears visibly in the Town House at Cambridge, before the Court, 'arrayed in a scarlet coat, layed with a broad gold lace, and was sworn and saluted by the mayor.' According to custom, Cromwell had, it seems, 'caused a good quantity of wine to be brought into the Town House, with some confectionery stuffe, which was liberally filled out, and as liberally taken off, to the warming of most of their noddles.' It is further suggested, that while in this mood those in the secret design, hinted, at an opportune moment, that 'Mr. Cromwell would make a brave burgess,' and that, as a result, Mr. Cromwell was returned for the town of Cambridge.

All this may be substantially true as a record of what happened, and yet the reason assigned for it and the motive be utterly unnecessary and absurd, considering that Oliver Cromwell had already sat in Parliament for Huntingdon, and was well known throughout both counties. Cromwell could have had, even at this time, no need of any doubtful or designing recommendation of this kind. The point of importance is, that shortly after this, Oliver Cromwell became Member of Parliament for Cambridge, and had come fairly into the stream where great events were to centre in the years that were coming. In that famous Short Parliament, which sat only for three weeks, Cromwell's colleague in the representation of Cambridge was Mr. Thomas Meauties. In October of the same year, in the election for the more famous Long Parliament, the contest for the Borough of Cambridge is said to have been so close, that Oliver Cromwell was returned by only one vote; and with him was returned (in place of Thomas Meauties) John Lowry, a man of some note in the next ten years.

There are glimpses of Cromwell upon his first appearance in the Long Parliament in November, 1640, which are enough to show what kind of man the town of Cambridge had chosen. The first glimpse shows us Cromwell in his plain and ill-fitting suit addressing the House to such purpose as to astonish the courtly young Sir Philip Warwick, and lessen his reverence for the great Council's listening

so to what Oliver had to say. There is another even more interesting glimpse of Cromwell, in a story told by Clarendon which has a local bearing. It shows us Cromwell sitting as a member of a Committee of the House upon a question of an enclosure of waste land, enclosed without the consent of the tenants, and sold to the Earl of Manchester, of Kimbolton, believed to have been the Soke of Somersham, near St. Ives. The Fenmen appeared before the Committee, and 'Cromwell appeared much concerned to countenance the petitioners, who were numerous, together with their witnesses . . . . and seconded and enlarged upon what they said with great passion'; and when Lord Mandeville, on behalf of his father the Earl of Manchester, desired to be heard, and 'with great modesty related what had been done,' it is further alleged by Clarendon (who was presiding) that Cromwell replied to him so rudely and in such language that "every man would have thought, that as their natures and their manners were as opposite as possible, so their interest could never have been the same."
. This reference to 'their interest' means the side they were taking in the quarrel with the King, and it is a striking testimony to the strength of conviction of the justice of their cause, entertained by so many of the young men of the time, that this young Lord Mandeville is the same man whom we shall meet with Cromwell, leading the Fenmen to victory at Marston Moor. Hampden's prophetic remark upon Cromwell's speech at the opening of the Long Parliament is more significant still. Descending the stairs with Lord Digby, with Cromwell below them, Digby said: " Pray, Mr. Hampden, who is the sloven who spoke to-day? for I see he is on our side by his speaking warmly." "That sloven you see before you," Hampden replied, "hath no ornament in his speech; but if we should ever come to a breach with the King—which God forbid!—that sloven will be the greatest man in England."

CHAPTER II.

SHIP-MONEY RIOTS—STRANGE SCENES IN THE CHURCHES—
PETITIONS AND PROTESTATIONS.
(1640-41.)

THE causes of the Civil War are too well known to the most casual reader of general history to need particular mention here; but among the grievances of the people there was one which brought the official life of the counties—from the High Sheriff down to the petty constables—into such frequent and unpleasant conflict with the people in almost every parish, that an exception must be made with regard to it. I refer to the objectionable impost of Ship-money. By none of the people of England was Hampden's trial more keenly watched than by the inhabitants of the Eastern Counties, and though the law went against them, the tax was still regarded as an injustice. They might not be able to lawfully refuse to pay, but there was one thing that they could do—they could leave the initiative for its local enforcement severely alone; and this they did until the levying and collecting of the offensive tax came to almost a deadlock; and the Sheriff in many cases was left alone to do the work.

The precept or writ for Ship-money upon a county was addressed to the Sheriff of that county, and he in his turn had to call upon the chief constables of every hundred to apportion the amount; the chief constables had to call upon the petty constables and overseers and further apportion the sums fixed upon the hundreds into so much upon each parish, and it was then further assessed upon the inhabitants of such parish. The inevitable result was, that if the chief constables ever called the petty constables together—some did in a half-hearted kind of way, and some did not—it was only to find that the petty constable reported too often that if he called a meeting in the parish for the purpose of assessing the tax no one would attend it. This state of things placed the Sheriff in an awkward predicament: if, as in some cases, he did the work of apportioning, assessing, and collecting the tax by his own officers, he soon became the most unpopular man in the county; if he did not do so, he was liable to be sent for to the Star Chamber.

In Hertfordshire Thomas Coningsby, and in Cambridgeshire Thomas Pychard, were examples of the former, and in Huntingdonshire Sir William Armyne came perilously near the latter. In adjoining counties there were many other cases of resistance to the tax, which will show what was the temper of the people of these Eastern Counties during the first half of the memorable year of 1640.

On the 20th of February, 1640,[1] Thomas Pychard, Sheriff for Cambridgeshire, certified that "the assessment of the £3,500 ship-money charged on that county he cannot get in as commanded, by reason of the neglect of some of the chief constables and the refractoriness of others." In Huntingdonshire the state of things was even worse, for Sir William Armyne had certified "in obedience to your commands I have used all diligence in assessing and collecting ship-money for this county, but as yet have not received a single penny of it; so soon, however, as any shall come to my hands, I will not fail to pay it into the Treasurer of the Navy."

About five weeks after this, March 20, 1640, Sir William writes again to the Council these interesting particulars:—

"I received the writ and instructions for levying £2,000 ship-money on this county the 27th December last, and proceeded to distribute the charge upon every town and

---

[1] According to the old style of reckoning the year, which ended on March 24, this would have been 1639; but to save confusion I have thought it best to adopt the modern style of commencing the year on January 1, unless a date occurs in an actual quotation.

parish with all possible diligence, but cannot prevail with the inhabitants to make their particular assessments; though I have issued out sundry writs to that effect."

The same difficulty occurred in Bedfordshire, where Mr. Richard Child, the Sheriff, pleaded that he did try to do his best and made twenty-four distresses, but he could not get anybody to buy the goods seized. Essex, Suffolk, and Norfolk were no more forward in the business than their neighbours.

In Norfolk, Thomas Windham, the Sheriff, complained, in the month of April, he could get but little money in, and that he had himself made up for the defects of some of his neighbours. At last, by May 28, he was able to report the sum of £1,000 got in with 'inexpressible difficulty,' and by distresses at which there were few buyers. The Suffolk people were still more 'abounding in their remissness and obstinacy,' for Sir Simonds D'Ewes, the Sheriff, was obliged to report that upon April 21, the day upon which £8,000 was to be paid in for the whole county, he had expected to get £1,000; 'but now fears he shall not get in £200.' He asks what he is to do, and says that 'innumerable groans and sighs are the daily returns he receives instead of payment.'

Seven days after the Short Parliament was dismissed the Sheriff of Essex was sent for and examined for having collected very little Ship-money and not distrained upon the refusers[1]; and the Sheriff of Hunts was still making equally small progress.

Thomas Pychard, of Trumpington, Sheriff of Cambridgeshire, who, upon his own acknowledgment, was not a man of any great influence in the public affairs of the county, meeting with almost uniform refusals to pay, took his bailiffs to seize defaulters' cattle, with, in some cases, disastrous results to the bailiffs. At Babraham, one Giles Jocelyn was alleged

---

[1] In the trial of Archbishop Laud, one of the witnesses, Samuel Sherman, stated that he and the other two collectors were fetched up from Dedham and brought before the Council to answer their pretended offence for refusing to collect the tax. He was sent to the Fleet, where he lay three weeks, and in his absence his silver spoons were distrained for his own subsidy.—Lords' Journals.

to have used 'unlawful weapons' and prevented the levying of Ship-money; but it was at Melbourn, near Royston, and other places in that neighbourhood, that the most determined resistance was made. Here is the account in the Sheriff's certificate :—

> "The humble certificate of Thomas Pychard, Esqre, Sheriffe of the County of Cambridge, unto the Right Honourable the Lords of his Majesty's most honourable Privy Counsell,
>
> "Sheweth that in the execution of his Majesty's writ touching the business of shipmoney, the persons hereunder named, together with above 100 more of the inhabitants of Melbourne (whereof the collectors of Shipmoney for that town were present), upon Friday the twelfth of June instant, did grievously wound and beat five or six of the Sheriff's bayliffs and servants, they hardly escapinge with their lives, and they and others have since used many threatening speeches towards them, insomuch as they dare not go about that nor any other service for his Majesty."

The parties complained of were John Pettitt, Edmond Wood, collectors; John Neale, Benjamin Medcalfe, Leonard Evens, Edmond Jefferson, Roger Andrewes, Nathaniel Andrewes, John Thurgood, John Hitch, William Wood, all of Melbourne in com' cant'.[1]

The bailiffs sent by the Sheriff state in their depositions that they "were sent by Thomas Pychard, Esq, High Sheriff of the County of Cambridge, to certain towns[2] to gather up ship-money upon the 12th day of June last, and as they came homeward they called at Melborne, and demanded of the collectors, Edmond Wood and John Pettitt, the ship-money, who answered they had some of the poor men's money, but the rich men had not paid, nor could they get them to pay it. Whereupon the bailiffs demanded of the said collectors the rates for the ship-money, and they would see if they could make them to pay it, but the collectors refused to show them the rates . . . whereupon the said bailiffs . . . attached the bodies of the said collectors to have brought them before the High Sheriff, and instantly thereupon John

[1] State Papers, Charles I, vol. cccclvii, No. 55.
[2] Other places which resisted the tax were: East Hatley, Shingay, Litlington, Croyden, Westwick, Caxton, St. George Hatley, Croxton, Papworth Agnes, Knapwell, Boxworth, Gravely, Ockington, Longstanton, Rampton, Wisbech, Tidd St. Giles, Chatteris, March, Wimblington, Doddington.—Ibid.

Neale, Benjamin Medcalfe, Leonard Evens, Edmond Jefferson, Roger Andrews, Nathaniel Andrews, John Thurgood, John Hitch, brother of William Hitch, and William French, the elder, with the number of a hundred more men, women, and children, assembled together against the said bailiffs, who sought for the constables and desired their aid to keep the peace, which was denied, and ill words given, and an assault threatened, and then the said bailiffs and sheriff's men, fearing some hurt would be done, made a proclamation that all should depart only the collectors who were attached, and then showed them the writ of assistance, which notwithstanding, the whole multitude rescued the said collectors and fell upon the said bailiffs and sheriff's men with stones and staves, and hedge staves and forks, and beat them and wounded divers of them, and did drive them out of the highway, into a woman's yard, and into her house for their safeguard, and were forced for safeguard of their lives to get out of the town a back way, which notwithstanding, some thirty or forty able men and boys pursued them above a quarter of a mile, stoning them and driving the bailiffs into a ditch, where some of their horses stuck fast, and the said multitude gott some of the bailiff's horses and carried them away."

The Melbourn offenders were proceeded against, but a jury refused to find them guilty. Easy-going Sir William Armyne, Sheriff for Hunts, had despatched to the Council on June 24 one of those well-meaning letters telling how affairs were looking in his county :—

"I have employed my best endeavours to assess and collect the ship-money in Huntingdonshire ; but have met with so many difficulties and found such a general backwardness that I thought it my duty to acquaint you therewith, that further order may be taken as to you may seem meet. The Mayor of Huntingdon and the Bailiff of Godmanchester, I have called upon them divers times and acquainted their town clerk with his Majesty's pleasure, and hope they will speedily pay in the money. The chief constables for the rest of the county have received four-and-twenty warrants since January last under my hand for the assessing . . . . I myself have had divers meetings, with the chief constables,

Great Civil War. 23

petty constables, and others, who say they are unable to pay by reason of so many taxes lately imposed upon them."

This placid communication, with its four-and-twenty paper warnings from Sir William's armchair, ended by his asking if he shall 'send forth warrants to distrain their goods.' No wonder that this old document is to be found with this characteristic endorsement upon it—"The Sheriff is to be quickened to execute the writ at his peril, and the Lords marvel that he should write such a letter after so many directions from his Majesty and the Board"! Poor Sir William! But he was between two fires, and that of the Fenmen was so powerful, that the four-and-twenty warrants with which he relieved his official conscience, and the resolve of the Lords in Council that he be 'quickened,' do not seem to have had any very notable effect by the time the next return of Ship-money paid in was made.

The dissolution of that famous Short Parliament, which did at least show what was the common sentiment of the people of England, marks the beginning of the conflict between King and Parliament, in other ways besides the collection of Ship-money.

The ceremonial of public worship in the parish churches was reversing the simple habits to which old men and women were accustomed, in a direction which was especially repugnant to many, and 'put upon the churches the shape and face of Popery.' These things, in an age when any move in the direction of Popery roused bitter memories, made the coming struggle turn largely upon religious convictions. When, therefore, the King sought to impose this ecclesiastical system upon Scotland, to march against the Scottish Covenanters was regarded as fighting against the Gospel and in favour of the Pope, and some remarkable scenes among the soldiers required to march northward in the Summer of 1640 were witnessed. In Hertfordshire, Bedfordshire, and Essex, the men drafted for the service refused to march, and became mutinous; and the trouble spread into other counties.

The County of Cambridge had to impress and forward three hundred of these unwilling soldiers to repel the Scottish army, but unfortunately, just as they were being got together the Lord Lieutenant, the Earl of Suffolk, of Audley End, died, and the deputy-lieutenants were in a difficulty about warrants, etc. At last the three hundred men were got together at Cambridge, but seemed likely to be more trouble to the deputy-lieutenants than to the Scots! There at the Cambridge market in the month of June, they are creating no little stir about the service.

"Saturday last the three hundred pressed soldiers in Cambridgeshire fell into great disorder in Cambridge. They pressed the deputy-lieutenants for somewhat, which was granted them, and when they saw they got their desire so easily they pressed for somewhat else, which the deputy-lieutenants neither might nor could grant."[1] The soldiers then threatened the deputy-lieutenants, and 'fifty men with halberts' were called out to be their guards, but the three hundred pressed men set upon the fifty and soon disarmed them. Then some of the trained soldiers were called together with their arms, but these were also disarmed by the mutinous soldiers. By this time a new Lord Lieutenant had been appointed in Lord Maynard (who was also Lord Lieutenant for Essex), and he was sent down to Cambridge to examine into the disorder, with unpleasant results to himself.[2]

In Suffolk there was a similar state of things, and Sir Thomas Jermyn was ordered to go down and punish the like disorders. At Beccles the mutinous soldiers played high games, held a mock court of justice upon 'a man and a wench' for some laches, and 'many mad pranks they have played which are not fit to be written.' In Essex the pressed men were equally troublesome, and Lord Maynard begged that they might be allowed to march northward,

---

[1] Letter of June 23, 1640, in State Papers.
[2] There is, in the Carew Transcripts, in the Public Record Office, a petition from Lady Maynard in the year following, which refers to the injuries his Lordship received in this mutiny of 'the barbarous souldiers,' having 'kindled all the summer in his blood,' and been the cause of 'his violent fever and consequently of his soddaine death.' His Lordship appears to have made his last will and testament just before going to suppress the tumult, which implored the King 'in case he should be slaine in the mutiny of the souldiers in Cambs' for the favour of his son's wardship.

for 'they are obstinately resolved to die rather than go by sea.' The Norfolk men had a similar dread of a sea-voyage, and refused to stir that way. The following graphic account of the Essex and Cambridgeshire men's conduct is furnished by a letter from Lord Maynard, Lord Lieutenant, dated July 27 :—
"I am ashamed that I have to trouble you so often about the same thing, but the insolencies of the soldiers billetted in Essex are every day increased by new attempts, insomuch as they have now, within these few days, taken upon them to reform churches ; and even in the time of divine service to pull down the rails about the Communion Tables, and in Icklinton [Ickleton, near Royston], in Cambridgeshire, to force the minister to run over a river, and the minister at Panfield, near Braintree, to forsake his charge and family to save his life." The Earl of Warwick, writing on the same day, supplements this with another characteristic incident concerning Captain Rolleston's soldiers billeted about Braintree—

"The soldiers had been reasonably quiet of late until this last occasion, which was caused by a barrel of beer and fifty shillings in money sent them by Dr. Barkham, of Bocking, of whose kindness it seems they took too much, for I found them much disordered by drink that day, and they went to his church and pulled up the rails about the Communion Table and burnt them before their Captain's lodgings ; the like they did at another town near. The ringleaders I have sent to the house of correction at Chelmsford."

In the hundred of Broadwater in Hertfordshire,[1] after the impressed soldiers had been disbanded, five of them went to a gentleman's house where Captain Brockett was, and pretending the captain had detained their wages, threatened to have their money or his blood ; but the captain met them

---

[1] In Hertfordshire nearly a score of churches were entered and the rails round the communion table were pulled down by the soldiers. At King's Walden twenty-four soldiers entered the church on Sunday morning, and passing up the aisle took their seats in the chancel, and at the close of the service they ' before all the congregation tore down the rails and defaced the wainscot,' and then coolly invited themselves to dine with the churchwarden ! Sir John Jennings, member for St. Albans, was sent to the Fleet prison for being remiss in not punishing the offenders ; in fact, like the Melbourn jury and Ship-money, the jury in this case had declared that they found the churches had been entered, but the names and habitations of the rioters they knew not.

on their own ground and 'wounded one of them with his sword, whereof he died next day.'[1] In Suffolk there were disorderly scenes. At Ipswich the rails around the communion table in St. Lawrence Church were burned down with broom faggots.

Under such omens the 'Bishops' War,' as it was called, was not likely to succeed. The Scots crossed the border, took Newcastle, the King returned to York, and the post travelling by way of Huntingdon ruffled Dr. Rowe of Trinity Hall and other College Dons of Cambridge with the 'sad Northern news.' But to the common people it was good news, and the newsmongers in the street sang 'Gramercy, good Master Scot'! The summoning of the Long Parliament in November was the beginning of the period of petitions and protestations which now only stood between the country and civil war.

The attempted 'Bishops' War' had been sufficient to turn the current of men's thoughts from Ship-money and things civil to things ecclesiastical. The whole country was ringing with protestations, and in Puritan East Anglia the Bishop of Ely was considered, next to Archbishop Laud, the head and front of offence. So, as early as December 19, 1640, Parliament received information of 'a very high nature against Matthew Wren, lord Bishop of Elie, for setting up idolatry and superstition in divers places, and exercising and acting some things of that nature in his own person ; and because they hear the Bishop of Elie endeavours to make escape out of the Kingdom,' the House desired their Lordships of the Upper House to 'think of some course to put him in security.' This they proceeded to do effectually by requiring the Bishop to find bail for his appearance to answer the 'censure of Parliament' in the sum of £10,000, which the Bishop consented to and hoped to get friends to be bound for him, but the respite was a short one.

The intensity of feeling which the impending struggle called forth can only be understood by reference to the religious aspect of the quarrel. Where the squire, the

[1] "Hertfordshire during the Great Civil War."

maltster, and the yeoman assembled, in court house, tavern, or market-place, the maintenance of the reformed religion was always the crowning point contended for; while for the toiler in the Fen, on the lea, or in the village malting, the whole issue of the coming conflict was summed up in the rousing words 'No Popery!' The Gunpowder Plot was fresh in the recollection of all excepting the children, and the King's marriage to a Catholic increased the dread of a reversion to the old supremacy.

With the Hertfordshire petition against grievances, supported by Mr. Capel, their member and future Royalist hero, and by Sir Harbottle Grimstone, an Essex member who declared that "they begin to say in town that the Judges have overthrown the law and the Bishops the Gospel," the year 1640 left a strange heritage to 1641 and to the country, of grievances to be redressed and protestations to enforce. In May, 1641, the famous Protestation was sent down into the shires; to Cambridge in particular by Mr. Oliver Cromwell and Mr. Lowry, the town members, and upon being laid before the Corporation there was 'signed by nine of the Aldermen and most of the commonalty.'[1] Strafford, 'the one supremely able man the King had,' was sacrificed in the tumult; and the country folks who went up to see the execution 'rode back in triumph waving their hatts, and with all expressions of joy'; through every town they went crying, 'his head is off! his head is off!'[2] Already strange dividing influences were at work, and the religious side of the quarrel intruded into official life. Mr. Foxley, 'an antient man,' preaching before the Judge at the Hertford Assizes, is alleged to have declared that 'none could be saved but a Puritan.'[3]

At St. George's Church, Norwich, a Mr. Whale, curate, "upon going into the pulpit to preach took the hymn and service book, and stamped it under his feet, saying that he

---

[1] The Protestation signed was in these words: "I, A B, do, in the presence of Almighty God, promise, vow, and protest to maintain and defend, as far as lawfully I may, with my life, power, and estate, the true reformed Protestant religion expressed in the doctrines of the Church of England, against all Popery and Popish innovations within this realm," etc
[2] Warwick's "Memoirs," p. 164. [3] Baker MSS., xxxiv, 31.

came not there by any prelaticall popish imposition of hands; he was sent from God."

At Hingham, Norfolk, Mr. Violet, "in his prayer before the sermon, confessed that 'wee have offended Thee in wearing the surplisse, in signing with the crosse, and using the ring of marriage.'" The communion rails in Hingham Church were pulled down 'by some of ye zealots of that parish,' and "they report that they intend to rayle about the common horse pond with them, next the highway, commonly called the 'Parson's Pond.' The young ruffians (who did ye feat) were hired with half a barrel of bear."

Mr. James Willett, of Little Cheshall, Essex, said that "if there were no superstitions here [meaning the Church of England] then there were none at Rome"; and a curate at Witham, in the same county, was beaten in church for crossing a child in baptism.[1]

The other extreme was represented by a petition out of Huntingdonshire — a long controversial document about schismatics and sectaries, and disavowing other petitions against the Book of Common Prayer, complaining of the many conventicles, of the way in which 'at all public functions, as assizes, sessions, fairs, and markets,' they were 'earnestly labouring to draw the people to them'; by which 'it was feared they were aiming at some great change and mutation in the present state of the Church government.' If the Protestation meant anything, this was undoubtedly true, and even these Laudian petitioners of Huntingdonshire were sensible of the 'common grievances of the kingdom,' and acknowledged the efforts of Parliament for 'the suppression of Popery.'

In July, Dr. Holdsworth, Vice-Chancellor of the Cambridge University, was called to account for an oration containing some reflections upon the proceedings of Parliament, and was sent for to Parliament a second time for approving of the action of the Vicar of St. Ives (Cromwell's old minister), in refusing to give the communion to those who 'out of stubborness refused to come up to ye table.'

[1] Baker MSS.

By November the news of the massacre of the Protestants in Ireland had added fuel to the flame, and there is recorded that significant utterance of Oliver Cromwell, when, at the close of a memorable debate, lasting till two o'clock in the morning, the Grand Remonstrance passed by only nine votes, he whispered in the ear of Falkland that 'if the Remonstrance had been rejected, he would have sold all he had next morning, and never have seen England more, and he knew that there were many other honest men of the same resolution.' Clarendon's comment upon this, 'so near was the poor Kingdom at that time to its deliverance,' will always be variously interpreted.

But none of these protestations were directed against the King personally, who on his return from Scotland was received with flattering speeches. The Mayor of York embodied the joyfulness of the hour in fine poetical imagery, bringing in the tunefulness of the bells, the flowers of Spring (in November), and the citizens' wives and their little ones. Arriving at Stamford, His Majesty was met by the Mayor, Mr. Richard Langton, who, after describing himself as the King's 'abject lieutenant,' enlarged upon the loyalty of his fellow-citizens, and proudly declared that 'each would have bin glad to have entertained the place of speaker.' At Huntingdon the courtly strain swelled into greater volume, both municipal and academic, for the University of Cambridge sent over its members primed with eulogistic Latin verse; and the Mayor of Huntingdon, in his speech to the King, boasted that 'although Rome's hens should daily hatch of its preposterous eggs crocodilicall chickens, yet, under the shield of faith, by you our most Royal Sovereign defended, and by the King of Heaven as I stand, and your most medicable counsell, would we not be fearful to withstand them.'[1]

There are glimpses in old parochial accounts of money spent in bonfires at Cambridge; and King's College had a bonfire of its own, for which a dignified Latin entry of

---

[1] 'Five most noble speeches,' etc. Nicholas' Correspondence, Evelyn's Diary, iv, 134.

half a crown appears in the Bursar's accounts. But the courtly manifestations were not in all cases spontaneous, for even the churchwardens of St. Edward's, in Cambridge, acquit themselves of a perfunctory service in these terms: 'For ringing and a bonfire at the King's returne out of the north, we being commanded therto by the Justices, 1s. 5d.'[1]

As the King drew nearer to London, his politic behaviour towards his subjects became a matter of concern to Secretary Nicholas, who, writing to His Majesty of 'diverse principall gent. of Hertfordsh: who were desirous to tender their duty at Ware,' added this astute piece of advice: "I humbly conceave it would not be amisse for your Majestie in these times to accept grac'ously ye affec'ons of your subjects in that kinde, whereby you will have opportunity to show yourself grac'ous to your people as your Majestie passeth, and to speake a few good words to them, which will gaine ye aff'ons (especially of ye vulgar) more then anything that hath bene donne for them this Parliamt."[2]

In a second letter to His Majesty, before he had reached Ware, Sir Edward Nicholas urged the policy of stopping at Ware "that ye better sorte may there kisse your Royall hand, and ye rest be spoken to by your Majestie, it will give them very great contentmt . . . . and that county being soe neere a neighbour to London, it wilbe a good encouragemt and comfort to your well affected people here [in London] to understand that they have neighbours that have ye like dutifull affec'ons to your Majestie's person and governmt."

In a few short weeks the rejoicings over the King's return were forgotten, and interest again centred in the subject-matter of the Protestation. On December 30, the Bishop of Ely was arrested and sent to the Tower. The charges against him included the common one of ordering the communion table in churches to be removed into the chancel and set altarwise, and that when the people were enjoined by him to come up to the rails to receive the communion, and they, 'for fear of idolatry and superstition,' dare not come up, he

---

[1] "Church Bells of Cambridgeshire," by Canon Raven, p. 47.
[2] Nicholas' Correspondence in Evelyn's Diary.

excommunicated them, and they left England and travelled into Holland.[1]

Among other charges against Bishop Wren was this curious one. It had been the custom in the Diocese of Ely to adopt a different style of ringing the bells when there were to be prayers only, to that adopted when there was to be a sermon. The result was, that the Puritan folk listened for those bells which summoned them both to a sermon and to prayers, and not much to those which signalled prayers only. So the Bishop commanded that there should be no difference in the ringing of the bells for the two different kinds of service. He ordered prayers to be read in hood and surplice; and in one parish the clergyman not having any, the Bishop ordered that no prayers should be said in the church until the articles were provided, and as it took a fortnight to get them, the parishioners went without any service for two Sundays. Whitelock says that when the Bishop was committed to the Tower, he was 'by few pittied.'

The impeachment by the King of the Five Members and of Lord Kimbolton set all England aflame. The people of the shires went up in their thousands carrying petitions to Parliament against things amiss.

On Tuesday, January 11, an impressive cavalcade of horsemen crowded the great highways converging upon the Metropolis. The 4,000 Buckinghamshire men came up with the Protestation stuck in their hats,[2] and 'mightie multitudes' out of Essex, Hertfordshire, and other counties; and the

---

[1] "The Wren's Nest defiled, or Bishop Wren anatomized," etc., 1104, b. 53, Brit. Mus. Lib.

[2] "Nay, yet, to make the beautie and brightnesse of that foresaid Tewsday's sunshine of comfort yet more glorious to our eyes and hearts; that very same 11th Jan., I say, being Tewsday, came a numerous multitude of Buckinghamshire men on horsback, in very fair and orderly manner, with the Protestation in their hats and hands; and since which time, even immediately after, mightie multitudes out of Essex, divers thousands out of Hertfordshire, Berkshire, Surrey, and other counties of the Kingdom, in brief from all Shires and Counties of the whole Realm, came still one after another to London to exhibit their petitions to the Parliament in the causes aforesaid; from all parts swelling in the stream of affections and petitions, all having one desire, all I say as one man unanimously consenting in this one thing, namely, a serious and settled resolution to petition and pray a speedie refining and reforming of persons and things amisse among us."—Vicars, "God in the Mount."

Bedfordshire men, above two thousand in number, were seen riding through Finsbury Fields 'four in a rank with their protestations in their hats.'

In Hertfordshire a petition carried up by 4,000 knights, gentlemen, and freeholders eloquently expressed the burdens of all the rest. Of the House of Lords they asked that 'the voting of Popish Lords and Bishops' might be removed out of that house, and that 'evil councillors may be taken from about his Majesty.' To the House of Commons they were more emphatic—

"That this Church and Kingdom, being by the prelates, those multitudes of corrupt and scandalous ministers (their creatures) and Popish party . . . . evil ministers of state, and great swarms of projectors . . . . brought to a sad and almost desperate condition, and thereby the splendour of His Majesty's Crown and dignity dangerously weakened and eclipsed . . . . the petitioners take upon them the humble boldness to declare their readinesse and great engagements according to their Protestation to stand to, and defend, to the utmost peril of their lives and estates, the King's Majestie and High Court of Parliament, with all the power and privileges of the same . . . . against all Popish and other malignant opposers, who endeavour, either by evil counsell, secret plots, or open force, to hurt or prejudice the same, or to make divisions betweene his Majesty and the Parliament."

On January 25, Pym delivered these petitions at a conference of Lords and Commons, and in an eloquent speech told them that "their lordships might in these petitions hear the voice, or rather the cry, of all England; the groans and miserable complaints of all."

During January and February the stream of petitioners continued citywards, Essex, Colchester, King's Lynn, Cambridge town and county sending in their petitions. So numerous, says Rushworth, were the complaints and petitions touching grievances, that the whole House was divided and subdivided into above forty Committees to hear and examine them.

CHAPTER III.

THE KING DEPARTING FROM HIS PARLIAMENT—RIVAL
PROCLAMATIONS.

(1642.)

THE year 1642 opened with a remarkable instance of the way in which the people of East Anglia regarded the issue in the coming struggle. The Epiphany Quarter Sessions at Cambridge were made remarkable for a gathering such as the County had hardly ever witnessed upon any similar occasion; all present being animated with a resolute purpose to have the County put into a position of defence when, as now seemed inevitable, the quarrel commenced with pike and gun. The scene is so well described in the letter addressed to Lord North, the Lord Lieutenant of the County, that the required space may very well be given to it here—

"Letter to Dudley, Lord North, Lord Lieutenant of Cambridgeshire, read in the House of Lords, Feb. 25th, 1641-2.

" Right Honourable,—

" We have received a public request at our last general Quarter Sessions in open Court, from the better sort of the inhabitants of our country [county] that were there (and a greater Sessions for the appearance we never saw, beyond the assembly of any Assizes if we shall respect only the country people). Their earnest desire was, that we would move your lordship to make use of your authority to your Captains for a present muster; that the arms we have may be dressed and viewed, their defects supplied, and our soldiers often drilled and exercised as is frequently done in many countries [counties] about them. Another request they made at that time, which was, that their money in Mr. Crane's hand may be put into arms, which we also allowed unto, but would not conclude upon it before we had first acquainted your lordship with their motion. The imminent dangers we may expect from these miserable times, and the great care we hear every country [county] takes to prepare themselves for their own defence, invites us to do the same; and therefore, with our neighbours, humbly request your lordship to grant their desires, that there may be a present muster to make good their arms, and a frequent exercise of their soldiers, which will (as we conceive) encourage them to stand better to them when any occasion shall require.

"Thus humbly taking our leaves, we rest
Your lordship's humble
and faithful servants,
Jo. Cutts, Tho. Symons,
Dudley Pope, Tho. Duckett.[1]

On the other hand, some students of the Cambridge University sent up a petition to 'shoot back those arrows of suspicion newly cast upon us by seducers. To be seducers is an easy matter you'll say if sophistry with her fallacies may entitle us, but we have sucked better milk from the tears of our mother—our mother who never yet was more dejected, yet from the dust may ride upon the clouds and in her due time shine.'

About the same time Lady Sussex at Gorham Bury, near St. Albans, was despatching one of her characteristic letters to Sir Ralph Verney, member for Aylesbury—"These distracted times put us all in great disorders, but I hope we shall not be killed yet. Your Parliament flies high, but truly it is a happy thing, I think, they have so much courage to stand to maintain their rights." [2]

Through the County of Hertford, King Charles I, having sent the Queen, with the Crown jewels to pawn, to a place

[1] Lords' Journals, Feb. 25, 1641-2.
[2] Verney MSS., Hist. MSS., Com. Reps.

Great Civil War. 35

of safety in Holland, set out upon that eventful march away from his Parliament, and there commenced what Fairfax afterwards described as 'the first incident of the drama which soon afterwards filled the stage with the thunder of drums and trumpets.' On March 3, His Majesty, with the Prince of Wales and a train of noblemen, had reached the royal house of his father, King James I, at Royston, and here he lingered as if reluctant to take the fatal step of refusing Parliament its desires respecting the Militia. On the first day at Royston His Majesty yielded a point as to the impeachment of the Five Members and Lord Kimbolton, by issuing a declaration instructing his Attorney-General 'wholly to desist further proceeding against the persons accused.'[1] For four days the negotiations at Royston went on over the Militia, His Majesty returning 'most polite declarations,' but yielding nothing; and on the 7th he went on to Newmarket, leaving the young Prince at the old country house of his fathers.

From this scene in the old Palace at Royston, there is an interesting glimpse afforded of how the burden of the nation's affairs weighed upon the Royal temper, and how doubtful the outlook already appeared even to the young Prince, afterwards Charles II, now a boy of twelve years of age. Writing from Royston, two days after the King had gone on to Newmarket, to the 'Lady Marie,' his 'most Royal sister,' the young boy Prince expressed himself in this frank and sensible fashion upon the Royal outlook:—

Part of the old Palace at Royston, where Charles I refused to give up the Militia.

"My father is very disconsolate and troubled, partly for my Royal mother's and your absence, and partly for the disturbances of the kingdome. I could wish and daily pray that there might be a conjunct and perfect uniting between my father's Majesty and his Parliament; that there might be a perfect concordance with them in the subject of the

---

[1] Broadsheet in Trinity College Library, Cambridge.

removal of the grievances of the country and the ruining of our decayed joys. We are as much we may merrie, and more than we wood sad, in respect we cannot alter the present distempers of these turbulent times. My father's resolution is now for York, where he intends to reside to see the event or sequell of these bad, unpropitious beginnings, where you may direct your letter to
Your loving brother,
CAROLI PRINCEPS.
Royston, March 9, 1641-2."[1]

While the King was at Newmarket, moody and troubled with the tendency of 'these bad, unpropitious beginnings,' the young boy Prince Charles, accompanied by the Duke of Buckingham and other nobles, left Royston in his coach on Saturday, March 12, for Cambridge, there to meet the King and other noble lords from Newmarket, to renew the eventful journey Northward on the Monday. There, at Cambridge, on the Saturday, Sunday, and Monday morning, a characteristic scene was enacted. Remembering the gathering at the Quarter Sessions, it is not surprising that the county people were very little in evidence to show their loyalty to the young Prince, and that the townspeople were moved with pity for the unfortunate position of the King rather than with resolution to stand by His Majesty. But the University was more faithful to old traditions, and upon the arrival of the Prince turned out its 'young schollers and Baccs. of Arts' in brave array. Forming up in a line for the Prince to pass through, they "did stand in the street from Eman: Coll: gate to the west doore of St. Mary's in y^t formality, and as the Prince passed by them in his coach they said with a loude voice, 'vivat Princeps,' etc. The Vice chancellor met the Prince, welcomed him with an oration and the presentation of a pair of gloves, which the Prince did wear during the time of his stay."

The Prince visited King's College Chapel, where another speech and the presentation of a Bible took place,[2] and

[1] E. 140 (16), Brit. Mus. Lib.
[2] The Bursar's accounts of King's College show that £3 0s. 6d. was expended upon this present.

thence to the Regent House, where he received the degree of Master of Arts. At Trinity College he was received with more orations, and more gloves were presented and wine was drunk. After this the Prince witnessed at Trinity Hall, the performance of an 'English Comedy,'[1] with which he was 'very well pleased.'

After these ceremonies the Prince took coach for Newmarket to join the King. There the Parliamentary Commissioners, Pembroke and others, asked his Majesty once more 'whether the Militia might not be granted as was desired by Parliament, for a time,' to which his Majesty "swore by God, not for a single houre; you have askt that of me in this was never askt of a King, and with which I will not trust my wife and children." Having thus replied with the emphatic last word between the country and civil war, His Majesty left his tennis-courts at Newmarket to renew his journey Northwards. But the good will of a wealthy University may be of great value in these times, and so his Majesty, encouraged by the Prince's reception at the University, decided to pay a flying visit himself to Cambridge.

On Monday, March 14, both the King and the Prince, with the noble lords in their train, had reached Cambridge, and again the University made up for lack of enthusiasm from the town and county. As the King came into the town from Newmarket way, to make 'but a short stay in regard they had to go to Huntingdon that night,' there was a demonstration of the 'young schollers and Baccs, etc.,' who stood in the street "from Jesus Coll: to Trin: Coll: gate, and as his maj^{tie} and the Prince passed, said 'Vivat Rex! Vivat Princeps!'" They left their coach 'at the end of the rayles,' and came to King's gate, where the Vice-Chancellor and heads of Colleges met them and presented the King 'with a fair Bible.' From King's College they went to Trinity College Chapel and thence to St. John's, where they were entertained by Dr. Beale, the Master, with a 'travelling banquet,' of which His Majesty "eate a little

[1] Cowley's "The Guardian," afterwards known as "The Cutter of Coleman Street." In the Bursar's accounts of Trinity College for this year there is an item for 'Dr. Cooley's Comedy.' There is also an entry of £4 15s. 10d. for 'wine for ye King's entertainment.'

and gave the Prince a good store to put in his pocket, and then the noblemen and the rest of his followers made quick despatch of the remainder."[1] After a valedictory speech from the Public Orator the King and the Prince were conducted to their coach, and again 'The schollers shouted *Vivat Rex.*'[2]

The correspondent of an old contemporary newspaper adds to this that the University saluted the King "with such vehement acclamacions of 'Vivat Rex!' as I never heard ye like noise heer before upon any occasion. At his parting one tells me that he [the King] thus spake to ye Vice chan: 'Mr. Vice chanc: whatsoever becomes of me I will charge my sonn, upon my blessing, to respect ye University.'"

And so His Majesty, disconsolate and troubled about 'these bad, unpropitious beginnings,' leaves Cambridge for Huntingdon in a melancholy mood, flattered by the attentions of the University, yet weighed down and 'much discontented that neither the Sheriff nor any gentlemen of Cambridgeshire did meet him.' The fact was, that the gentlemen of Cambridgeshire had just then a demonstration of quite an opposite kind in hand; and Sir John Cotton, of Landwade, near Newmarket, knowing their temper, thought it best to keep out of the way. For Cambridgeshire the King's journey was received with a silence which meant much more than words; a silence only broken by 'the women and others in the town of Cambridge,' who followed the King's coach and 'humbly and earnestly entreated the King that he would return to his Parliament, or they should be undone.'

One little glimpse such as this of the women of Cambridge besieging the King's coach with their tears, enables us, better than acres of formal parchment history could do, to realize the infinite pity and sadness of it all, as the people witnessed the widening breach in the Constitution by the drifting apart of the King and Parliament. Here in the

---

[1] "For a banquet and wine for ye entertainment of His ma^tie and ye Prince, £6 8s. 0d. For or Coll. share of His maties and ye Prince's entertainment in ye University, £21 13s. 8d."—Bursar's accounts, St. John's College, Cambridge, 164⅜. King's College seems to have been more especially concerned with the reception of the Prince, for which the Bursar credits himself with this item: "Solut. pro expensis in receptione Principis, £32 10s. 8d."—Bursar's accounts, King's College, 1642.

[2] Baker MSS., vol. xxxiii, 235-6. Camb. Univ. Lib.

heart of Puritan East Anglia, whatever it might be among the people in the City, the struggle was not to be entered upon with a light heart, but as a serious business. The die was cast, however, and the coach with the King and his melancholy, and the boy Prince with his pockets full of cakes, rolled on towards Huntingdon, with this little consolation, that the Sheriff of Huntingdonshire, Richard Stone, of Stukeley, had ventured to Cambridge to meet His Majesty, and got knighted for his pains. For the temper of Huntingdonshire did not come out quite so emphatically for Parliament as did that of Cambridgeshire. As an instance of the apprehension of coming trouble, it is related that a fish, brought from the sea to Cambridge market, being cut up, a book was found in the bowels of the fish, which, 'being a new way of sending books to Cambridge, gave some amount of curiosity.' Upon looking into the contents of the book it was found to be "A Preparation to the Cross," a book written in the reign of Henry VIII; and its coming to Cambridge in this strange way 'alarmed good men,' and it was looked upon as an admonition to 'prepare for sufferings.'[1]

There is a letter in the "Squire Papers" which, whether authentic or not, may very well stand for Cromwell's activity at this juncture—

"Dear Friends,

"It is not improbable that the King may go through Huntingdon on his way to Stamford. Pray keep all steady and let no peace be broken. Beg of all to be silent; or it may mar our peaceable settling this sad business. Such as are in the County Array bid go; all of you protect, at cost of life, the King from harm, or foul usage by word or deed, as you love the cause.—From,
"Your faithful
"Oliver Cromwell."[2]

I have found no trace of any disturbance at Huntingdon. On the contrary, the King appears to have slept at Huntingdon that night; and before resuming his journey on the

[1] Baker's Hist. of St. John's College, Cambridge.
[2] App. to Carlyle's "Letters and Speeches of Cromwell."

following morning despatched a letter to Parliament about Ireland, and declaring against the validity of any Act or Ordinance that had not received the Royal Assent, and with it this letter to Lord Littleton, Keeper of the Great Seal :—

" Charles R.

" Right trusty and well beloved Counsellor, we greet you well. Our will and command is, that at the next sitting of the House of Peers (after your receipt of these) you deliver our message (sent enclosed) to be read at our said House, and afterwards communicated to our House of Commons. For which they shall be your warrant.

"Given at our Court at Huntingdon on this 15th of March, 1641 [2]." [1]

Clarendon says that when the message and letter from the King at Huntingdon reached the Houses of Parliament— " I have not known both Houses in more choler and rage than upon the receiving this message, which came early to them on Wednesday the sixteenth of March." He adds that the day before had been spent in preparing all things ready for the execution of the Ordinance of the Militia, and that "when the King's message from Huntingdon was read the next morning, and seemed to be against their votes of the day before, they concluded that it could not be sent from the King, but had been inserted in blanks left in the town for such purposes," until the messenger declared that he received it from the King's own hand. On the same subject, Whitelock says that upon the receipt of the King's message from Huntingdon, Parliament were "the more exasperated by the report from the Lords who were sent to him [the King] unto Royston ; that at the reading of that part of the message [from Parliament] concerning Mr. Jermyn, the King had said, ' it is false !' and when they read that of Captain Legg, the King said, 'that's a lie !'" [2]

The House sent back their reply to the King's message in these words :—

" Resolved, etc., that this House shall insist upon their former votes concerning the Militia ; and that those persons

[1] Lords' Journals.   [2] " Memorials," i, 165.

that advised his Majesty to absent himself from the Parliament are the enemies of the Peace of this Kingdom."

That emphatic last word having been said by King and Parliament, it may be of interest to see what was the temper of Cambridgeshire, Huntingdonshire, and other Eastern Counties in the conflict which was now inevitable. The very next day after those academic 'Vivats' and women's tears had moved the King, now to cheerfulness, now to melancholy, in Cambridge, the knights, esquires, and freeholders of the county were riding in, amidst other 'Vivats' doubtless, from all parts of the Fens, until an imposing array of horsemen was ready to set out for the Metropolis. At Cambridge they were joined by an organized party representing the town, and while the King rode on to Peterborough and Stamford, the great procession moved on with increasing numbers through the South of the county towards London. There, on Wednesday, March 16, they were crowding around the doors at Westminster for the opportunity of adding their voice to the great volume of popular opinion on the side of Parliament. As many as could squeeze into the House did so—into both Houses, in fact—and this is the petition which they presented :—

"To the Right Honourable the Lords in Parliament assembled. The humble petition of the Knights, Esquires, gentlemen, and commoners of the County of Cambridge and the Isle of Elie.

" Sheweth

"That the many pressures and heavy grievances which we for years past have groaned under, have of late, by your pious and noble endeavours, received comfortable relief in part, and your petitioners much cheered with the good hopes conceived of your lordships' further care and zeal for a perfect cure for the future, most graciously manifested to all by your lordships' late happy concurrence with the honourable House of Commons, who (to the great joy of us) have hereby hitherto gone on in a blessed progress towards a thorough reformation in Church and State ; the serious consideration whereof, and all that great blessing and benefit we receive thereby, your petitioners, in the duty of their gratitude, humbly present themselves, their lives, and their fortunes, in the defence of your noble persons.

"May it therefore please your lordships to accept this, though thus long delayed, as the resolved assurance of our fidelities to your lordships, proceeding in a happy concurrence, for the glory of God and the public good; which your petitioners in all humility conceive will not be a little advanced if your lordships please to speed a settling of God's worship according to His Word, the blessing of a religious ministry, removing of unwarranted orders and dignities, the steps unto popery, purging the Universities, banishing all popish clergy, excluding ill councillors, punishing delinquents, relieving our distressed brothers abroad and fortifying ourselves at home. Wherein we beseech your lordships to go on with as much zeal and speed as the pressing necessities of the times require.

"So shall we, as we are bound, pray for the increase of your lordships' happiness here, and in the fruition thereof hereafter."[1]

A similar petition was presented to the Commons, and the Houses 'did give them thanks.'

On March 25, the knights, gentlemen, and freeholders of Huntingdonshire followed the example of Cambridgeshire and drew up their petition, but instead of going up to deliver it in person entrusted it to one of the members for the county.

In this petition the knights, gentlemen, and freeholders of Hunts put in a special plea and justification of "the religious members of the House of Peers," their neighbour, "the Lord Kimbolton of our shire," who had been impeached with the Five Members, but of whom they added: "we are confident of his loyalty, and have so absolute an opinion of him that he is not guilty of the least of these articles wherein he is arraigned."

Similar petitions had, some few weeks before, been presented by the county of Essex, complaining of the effect of

[1] Lords' Journals.

the 'unparalleled breaches upon the liberties of Parliament,' upon the 'cloathing and farming, the two trades of our country [county], whereby multitudes of our people have lived,' and adding that the petitioners 'tremble to think what may follow thereupon.'

The Suffolk people also sent up their petitions deploring the innovations in the Church and 'multitudes of monopolies' and public grievances in the State; and also the decay of the clothing trade, 'upon which the livelihoods of many thousands do depend.' The Norfolk people in their petition, after urging the deposition of the Bishops and Popish lords, waxed eloquent over 'multiplicity of grievances which have disturbed our county,' and prayed that 'the clear spring of your sacred and unanimous resolutions may run like a pure fountain of justice, without either the hindrance or let of any.'[1]

In the words of Carlyle—"The question puts itself to every English soul, which of these will you obey? In every shire, in every parish, in court houses, ale houses, churches, markets, wherever men were gathered together, England, with sorrowful confusion in every fibre, is tearing itself into hostile halves, to carry on the voting by pike and bullet henceforth."

Throughout the shires of East Anglia the great issue was dividing men everywhere and cutting with 'sorrowful confusion' into the ties of family life, until 'they of the same household were found in hostile camps.'

In Cambridgeshire the two county members took opposite sides—Sir Dudley North for Parliament, and Mr. Thomas Chichely, of Wimpole Hall, for the King. In Huntingdonshire there were divisions going to the roots of family life. In three of the leading Huntingdonshire families there were strange searchings of heart over the conduct of younger members of old Royalist families, and speculation among the public upon which side the great houses of Kimbolton and Hinchinbrook would go. Kimbolton Castle had, in these stormy times, meant for the Huntingdonshire people an embodiment of

[1] E. 132 (20), Brit. Mus. Lib.

the Star Chamber, Ship-money, and the 'Bishops' War,' which the Earl of Manchester had supported with his influence and his money. But there was a strange pathos in the fact that the old Earl had, so to speak, one foot in the grave, and that his son Edward Montague, the young Viscount Mandeville and the future Earl, was, by the irony of events, to be the leader of the Puritan party in the House of Lords, and destined to reverse all the late traditions of his house in a few short months. At Hinchinbrook there was a similar conflict of natural ties and public duty. Here Sir Sidney Montague, brother of the old Earl over at Kimbolton, and member for Huntingdon, was standing out for the King, while his son Edward Montague we shall soon see in command of forces for Parliament.

With the former possessors of Hinchinbrook it was the same. Sir Oliver Cromwell, now of Ramsey, son of the 'Golden Knight,' and his son John, were on the side of the King, while of the families of his brothers, Robert of Huntingdon, and Sir Philip, of Biggin House, there were strange contrasts, this son for King, that for Parliament; with this curious result, that four Oliver Cromwells were taking sides in the fray—Sir Oliver of Ramsey for the King, *the* Oliver and his son Oliver, of Ely, and Sir Philip's son Oliver, of Biggin, for Parliament. This, briefly, was the state of things in the two great Huntingdonshire families of the Montagues and the Cromwells—the two branches of the Montagues at Kimbolton and Hinchinbrook, the Cromwells now somewhat scattered. Similar divisions in official and private life were taking place all through the Eastern Counties as elsewhere. Parliament sent down its members to see that the control of the Militia was secured, and Oliver Cromwell was among the most active of these.

When, at last, the Proclamation of Parliament for putting into execution the Ordinance for the Militia in the several counties had been practically settled, there was a strange conflict of authorities. Side by side almost with the Proclamation of Parliament there was that of the King— the one commanding the officials to act for putting the Militia in training, the other forbidding them; and so, says

Sir Dudley North, 'this war first began in paper by manifestoes and declarations.'[1] The dilemma was a most crucial one—on the one side, all the strength and promise of a great popular cause impelling forward; on the other, all the force and respect for old associations and oaths of allegiance holding back. The 'sorrowful confusion' was all the greater by reason of the old use of names and things being almost identical on both sides; for both sides were drifting into a war in which each was to fight for the defence of 'King and Parliament,' but with a difference wide enough to make war inevitable.

As early as May 10, Major-General Skippon had appeared in Finsbury Fields with the trained bands of London, consisting of above 8,000 soldiers, and the Members of Parliament were entertained by the City; "all men," says Clarendon, "presuming that the example of London with such ceremony and solemnity would be easily followed throughout the kingdom." The first notable instance of this, but with a strange conflict of rival proclamations, occurred in Lincolnshire. Lord Willoughby of Parham summoned the chief constables to a meeting at Lincoln to give an account of the arms, etc., in their respective hundreds. "They assembled with all alacrity, even beyond expectations, there being the fullest appearance of them that we have observed upon any occasion heretofore, so as out of about four score in this great county not above two or three of them were absent. Neither did the King's Proclamation (published on purpose, as we conceive, throughout the county, and which some had officiously fixed upon the gates of the inn where we met) . . . . as we are informed, any whit deter or hinder them."[2]

At one of the musters of the Militia which followed, at Caistor, Lincolnshire, Captain William Booth, a Royalist, armed with the King's proclamation forbidding their assembling, read it to such company as were assembled in a tavern, 'thereby endeavouring to dissuade many of the soldiers from

---

[1] Passages relating to the Long Parliament, Somers' Tracts, vi, 565.
[2] Letter from Committee at Lincoln in Lords' Journals.

shewing their arms.' He added sarcastic remarks upon the small muster at Lincoln, that 'there was a brave appearance at Lincoln of some fifteen or sixteen men.' For these words the Captain had to answer to Parliament. The King wrote to Lord Willoughby informing him that for mustering the trained bands of the County he would be called to account, and would be esteemed and proceeded against as 'a disturber of the peace of our kingdom,' to which his Lordship deprecated commands 'which must needs make him false to those that rely upon him.'

The temper of Essex is shown by the "Petition and Resolution of the captains of hundreds and other inhabitants of the County of Essex," in which, on June 8, they say :—

"Thus, with our hands upon our swords we stand ready at your command to perform our vows to God and oaths of fidelity to his Majesty in taking up arms against these false flatterers and traitors who abuse his Royal favour, intending under the glorious title of his name and standard to fight against the peace and honour of their Sovereign, against religion and the laws, and to make a prey and spoil of three flourishing kingdoms at once; and so spend our dearest blood in the defence of the lives and liberties of our countrymen; the laws which are the life of our liberty and peace, religion more precious than both; and the King and Parliament, in whose rights lieth bound up the life of all the rest."[1]

The dilemma did, however, weigh heavily upon the conscience of many, and Mr. Robert Smith, the High Sheriff for Essex, having received the King's proclamation forbidding the trained bands to muster or exercise, appealed to Parliament to know what he was to do; to which Parliament replied by declaring the King's writ to be illegal, and directed that "Mr. Smith and all other Sheriffs shall be protected in whatever they do in the service and by authority of Parliament."

In Cambridgeshire, on June 14, Roger Daniel, the University printer at Cambridge, was issuing copies of a

[1] Lords' Journals.

printed paper, headed, "By the King, a Proclamation," which forbade 'All levies of forces without his Majesty's expressed pleasure signified under his great seal, and all contributions or assistance to any such levies,' which proclamation 'all sheriffs, justices, mayors, bailiffs, and constables' were required to publish.[1] Parliament then sent down the members for the Cambridge University to see that its own proclamations were read in the Colleges, and to obtain certificates from the masters and heads of Colleges that they were duly read.

The propositions of Parliament for raising sinews of war, money and plate, to be advanced with the security of the public faith with 8 per cent. interest, gave a serious air of business to warlike preparations. Away over at Cratfield, in Suffolk, Mr. Eland, the vicar, entered in his accounts, the like of which was happening in all shires and villages of East Anglia, the cost of four men's dinners with their horses for going to Yoxford to pay in 'the money and plate lent to the parliament upon the propositions,' and for 'two nags and a mare lent the parliament upon the propositions.'[2]

The King at the same time came forward with an offer of 8 per cent. interest for loans advanced to himself, addressed to the University of Cambridge, from York, June 29, 1642. In this letter he complained that, notwithstanding his proclamations declaring that it had not been his intention to make war upon Parliament, 'horse is still levied and plate and money brought in against us.' He instanced his 'perpetual care and protection of such nurseries of learning,' as a ground for expecting their extraordinary assistance, and assured them that whatever was paid to the bearer, John Poley (proctor and Fellow of Pembroke Hall),[3] 'shall be received by us as a very acceptable service.'

There is good reason to believe that Mr. Poley took back a substantial sum to the King from the various Colleges, for, three weeks afterwards, Secretary Nicholas writes that

---

[1] Broadside in Trinity College Library, Cambridge.
[2] Cratfield Parish Papers, per Rev. Canon Raven.
[3] Cambridge Portfolio.

'the University of Oxford has voluntarily sent in £10,000 to the King, and that of Cambridge a fair proportion also.'

Meanwhile the efforts of Lord Willoughby to secure the Militia in Lincolnshire, had provoked a remarkable demonstration for the King. The Earl of Lindsay, Sir Edmund Heron (the High Sheriff), Sir Jervase Scroope, Sir Charles Dallison (the Recorder of Lincoln), and other Royalist gentry, were making a brave bid for the King to come amongst them. Like His Majesty, these gentlemen had been staggered by Sir John Hotham's shutting the gates of Hull against the King, and they now appealed to the fears of the country people, declaring that 'their county was likely to prove the seat of some dismal tragedy, the seat of a deplored War,' and they conceived the idea that to bring His Majesty to Lincoln would be 'a helpful means of preventing that misery.' The King accepted their invitation, and for the time being he came, he saw, he conquered! The people of Lincoln and of all the country-side assembled in their thousands. In their wild enthusiasm they lost, for the moment, all idea of the true proportion of things; and only saw in the King's coming amongst them an event which could be summed up as being 'to the glory of God, the honour of His Anointed, the credit of religion, and proof of our loyalty.' The 'joyful, unanimous, orderly confluence' of people assembled, 'yielded not much in number and nothing in weight' to the much-talked-of 60,000 who met the King at York. For four miles 'the way was a throng,' and the air resounded with their 'peals of shouts and vocal acclamations.' The great crowd shouted, "A King! A King! A King!" The gentry, 'not satisfied with sounds,' drew their swords; and the clergy, between 200 and 300 in number, 'echoed and redoubled their gratulatory salutations' with the more classic 'Vivat Rex!' The city of Lincoln, forgetting the excuse of the Plague, which had hindered obedience to the call of the Parliamentary Lord Lieutenant, and, 'pregnant with alike joyful conception,' came forth in brave array, with their Recorder, Mayor, and Corporation, and trained bands; 'in so much that many think Wednesday was the funeral of the new Militia.'[1]

Sir Charles Dallison, the Recorder, having persuaded himself that the people were living under the best possible government, in his flattering speech of welcome to the King, had the boldness to declare that 'the people of this nation have been most happily governed under your Majesty.' For his own part, he added the assurance, 'prostrating himself at his Majesty's feet,' he offered 'himself, estate and fortune,' to His Majesty, and made the same offer for the Mayor and Corporation of Lincoln. The King's reply to this speech was a frank admission of open war between himself and Parliament. The Militia Ordinance of Parliament he declared to be against the known laws, imposed upon them against his express consent, and in contempt of his regal authority; and that whoever presumed to execute or obey the same he should proceed against, as against those who actually levied war against him. He urged them not "to be frighted with apprehensions that this country [county] is like to be the seat of war; the seat of war will be only where persons rise in rebellion against me; that will not, I hope, be here."[2] Having assured them, 'upon the faith and honour of a Christian King,' of his intention to live and die in their defence, and to be 'as tender of the Protestant religion, the laws of the land, and the privilege of Parliament as of his own life and crown,' the King departed, and returned by way of Beverley.

The Royalist cause had gained some acclaim, and considerable promises of support; but behind all sentimental attachments, even Lincolnshire was haunted with the troublesome question of 'What was now to be done?' The King had come and gone; the 'new Militia' was not 'buried,' and in his own admission that there was going to be war, His Majesty was a better prophet than in his forecast of the seat of war, by which, of all the Eastern Counties, Lincolnshire was destined to suffer most.

[1] "A true relation of his Majesty's reception and Royal entertainment at Lincoln, etc.": Brit. Mus. Lib., E. 108 (27).
[2] Rushworth's Historical Collections for June 15, 1642.

In town and village men were bracing themselves for the conflict; private families looked forward with dread to the extreme pass to which things were tending, and began to think of retreats for themselves and possessions. From Gorhambury, near St. Albans, garrulous old Lady Sussex, the 'old men's wife,' who married four husbands, writes: "I hope in God we shall have no fighting. . . . . I am loth to eat in pewter yet, but truly I have put up my plate, and *say it is sold.*"

Out of the growing confusion and distressful omens, Mr. Cromwell, member for Cambridge, is discernible; as, impelled by hot zeal for the cause of Parliament, he is getting arms for his neighbours, of which the first authoritative evidence is afforded in this entry in the Commons' Journals: "Whereas Mr. Cromwell hath sent down arms into the County of Cambridge for the defence of that county; it is this day ordered that Sir Dudley North shall forthwith pay to Mr. Cromwell one hundred pounds which he hath received from Mr. Crane, late High Sheriff of the County of Cambridge, which said hundred pounds the said Mr. Crane had remaining in his hands for coat and conduct money."[1]

As soon as the townspeople of Cambridge had got hold of their muskets, it is alleged that some of the more forward actually began to fire into the windows of certain scholars, and the members of the University found it necessary to purchase arms for their own defence.[2] In fact, arms had been secretly coming into Cambridge as into other places: 'fifteen chests full of arms had been conveyed from London to Cambridge'[3]; but upon their arrival in Cambridge, the Mayor got wind of it and seized upon ten chests, which he

---

[1] In the Public Record Office, preserved among the State Papers, is an interesting memorandum certifying the paying over of this £100 from Mr. Crane the late High Sheriff to Sir Dudley North; the paying of it by the latter to Mr. Cromwell, and Cromwell's receipt for the same. Mr. Cromwell had, according to D'Ewes, moved for an order to allow the townsmen of Cambridge to raise two companies of Volunteers, and to appoint captains over them, and the House on the same date made order for moving the Lord Lieutenant to that end.
[2] "Querela Cantabrigiensis."
[3] Diurnal of Occurrences in Parliament.

was ordered by Parliament to 'keep for the peace and safeguard of the said town of Cambridge.' But the scholars of Trinity College had succeeded in getting the other chests into the College before the Mayor could prevent it. One of the chests of arms which came down to the University was addressed to Dr. Wiseman, of Trinity Hall, who paid for the same and for their carriage to the Bull Hotel,[1] but afterwards had them seized by Mr. Oliver Cromwell, 'pretending the authority of Parliament.'

The same kind of thing was going on in towns all over the Fens, and, what is more, the Militia and Volunteers were gathering on village greens and in the fields near towns in response to the rousing call of drum and trumpet.

On July 21, the Volunteers of Boston, Lincolnshire, and divers well-affected persons were 'training themselves in fields near the said town'; at Bury St. Edmunds the people were training in the use of arms under Robert Chaplin, also 'in the fields near the said town'; at King's Lynn they were training under Captain Slaney, and Parliament, foreseeing the strategic importance of the place, ordered special care to be taken of the town and of the powder magazine. Meanwhile, through the month of July, the conflict of proclamations continued by every means available — by carriers, by special messengers, and by the post. In the parish churches on Sunday, the unfortunate clergyman was between Scylla and Charybdis; from the Parliament he received a proclamation respecting the Militia, which he was commanded to read to his congregation; from the King he received a proclamation denouncing the proclamation of Parliament, and appealing to his allegiance not to obey the orders of Parliament; and a third proclamation he received from Parliament forbidding him at his peril to read that of the King. The result was, that before the parson had disposed of these rival proclamations, to his own satisfaction or that of his congregation, he had openly committed himself to one side or the other, and had to take the consequences.

---

[1] In the papers in the College Library there is preserved the bill of Dr. Wiseman's chest of arms, as printed in Cooper's " Annals of Cambridge."

In the Eastern Counties the Puritan element was generally strong enough to make the Parliamentary proclamation the safer one to handle; and where a clergyman had the courage to defy this element, some strange scenes occurred, of which the following are typical.

The Rev. Mr. George, Vicar of Cople, Beds, standing up before his congregation with copies of the three proclamations in his hand, spoke thus :—"Judge whether I am to obey God or man! By God's word I am commanded to obey the King. I find no such command for the Parliament"; and he 'threw away the two declarations of Parliament scornfully,' read the King's proclamation, and in the end was sent for to London, committed to prison, and fined £100 by Parliament. In the parish church of Hartist, in Suffolk, Mr. Gibb, the parson, was asking his parishioners 'to give attention to one of His Majesty's declarations,' whereupon 'one Master Coleman, a parishioner, openly replied that he might be ashamed of himself to read His Majesty's declaration, and therefore he would fetch the Parliament's declaration, which was a great deal better, to be published unto them.' Some wrangling in the church followed, and Mr. Gibb, the parson, used some words for which he was sent up to Parliament to answer. Daniel Chandler, of Oakington, in Cambridgeshire, before leaving his parishioners to go to the King, read in church a proclamation from Parliament, as far as 'Lords and Peers in Parliament'; but when he came to 'the House of Commons' he threw it away, saying, "What had he to do with the House of Commons?"

In Huntingdonshire Lewis Phillips, under-sheriff, and Henry Burnaby, bailiff of the hundred of Toseland, had to answer for publishing the King's proclamation, and Burnaby also for 'unseemly speeches' about Sir Samuel Luke, member for Bedford, and was afterwards indebted to the magnanimity of the old knight in supporting his plea for release. In the Eastern Counties, wherever the gentry sought to execute the King's commands, they were, says Rushworth, 'as oft as they attempted to show themselves,' crushed, and their endeavours defeated by the freeholders and yeomen. The Mayors of Hertford and St. Albans, for publishing the King's proclamation, were summoned to the bar of the House and committed to prison. Upon his return when liberated, the Mayor of Hertford had his personal expenses allowed by the Corporation, but at St. Albans they disallowed the expenses of their Mayor, even his coach hire down to St. Albans on his release.

When, in the Summer months of 1642, members had been sent down into the shires at Quarter Sessions or Assizes to advance the cause of Parliament, the Royalist justices and clergy would also assemble to advance the interests of the King, and some stirring scenes ensued of which the city of Ely was a witness. The Bishop had been released from his imprisonment in May and was again using his influence in the Isle for the King. There, while the magistrates were sitting in the Shire Hall at the Quarter Sessions or Assizes, a memorable gathering was crowding into the market-place. In the midst of a knot of Royalists was Dr. Hill, parson of Coveney and Manea, 'very earnest to have the Earl of Essex proclaimed a traitor in the marketstead in the face of the court.' In due course Mr. Hollman, the under-sheriff, Mr. Cutler, bailiff of the Liberty, the Bishop's crier, Mr. Andrews, a barrister, and an official retinue appeared upon the scene armed with the King's proclamation. The strident tones of the herald brought out Parliamentary Major Dodson and others from the Dolphin, and 'seeing the Bishop's crier, about to publish the proclamation,' Dodson asked him 'who set him at work?' He replied, 'What have you to do withall?' to which Dodson replied, 'Whoever read it would have his hand cut off'! 'Whereupon there was like to be a mutiny.' Dr. Hill rushed into the Shire Hall, and complained to the magistrates that 'he had been hindered from reading the King's proclamation.' Captain Humberstone March and another magistrate went down into the market-place to make peace, and, dissuading Dodson from further resistance, got him out of the way. In the meantime Dr. Hill had seized his opportunity, and 'did charge with halberts and had the proclamation read.' Dodson was dissuaded from resistance lest he should have 'articles brought against him' and get some damage, 'the Bishop and his friends being too powerful.'[1]

This reference to the power of the Bishop and his party was probably true, but in his next endeavour for the King the Bishop came in conflict with his powerful neighbour, Mr. Cromwell, the tithe farmer.

[1] Depositions in the case of Dr. Hill, parson of Coveney and Manea, Minutes of Committee for Scandalous Ministers, Add. MSS. Brit. Mus. Lib.

CHAPTER IV.

CROMWELL AND THE COLLEGE PLATE—RAISING THE KING'S STANDARD—TUMULTS IN EAST ANGLIA—THE BATTLE OF EDGEHILL.

(1642.)

IF the power of the Bishop was, for the moment, too much at Ely, the power of the University might be expected to be greater still at Cambridge; and it is significant that while the King saw the importance of obtaining contributions from the University, Cromwell was equally alive to the importance of preventing it, and securing this key to the Eastern Counties. Clarendon says that 'some eminent governors in the University gave the King notice that all the Colleges were very plentifully supplied with plate,' and that the King, 'in that melancholic season at Nottingham,' despatched two gentlemen to Oxford and Cambridge. These gentlemen were the bearers of a letter in which the King, on July 24, wrote to the Vice-Chancellor—
" Trusty and well-beloved, we greet you well. Whereas we have great reason to acknowledge the willing expressions of the affections of both our Universities in the late supply afforded to us in this time of necessity ; and particularly being informed of the further readiness of all or most of our Colleges in Cambridge to make offer of depositing their plate into our hands for the better security and safety thereof; we have .... thought good to will and require you to signify to that our University, that what College plate soever any of the Colleges in the same shall resolve to commit

into our custody . . . . we shall receive it as further testimony of their loyal affections to us ; and faithfully promise to restore it again to them to the utmost value when our propositions for the peace of this kingdom shall be hearkened unto . . . ."

But College plate was worth looking after for Parliament, as well as for the King ; and in the scramble for its possession there occurred in these old historic halls strange scenes of bustle and confusion, and outside them, exciting incidents of yeomen riding to and fro through the ripening cornfields of the Fens. To the King's appeal, the Colleges responded by voting and packing up their plate. On August 8, St. John's College agreed to send off its plate to the King : 2,065½ oz., 'packed in 2 fir boxes,' marked with the letters ' S. J. C.' At Trinity, soldiers were guarding the treasure, but they were equally in danger of other soldiers.[1]

Parliament authorized Mr. Cromwell, member for Cambridge, and Mr. Valentine Walton, member for Huntingdonshire, to go down and intercept the carrying off of the treasure. Mr. Cromwell got together some troops from the western parts of Cambridgeshire, and took up a post of observation at Lowler Hedges, between Cambridge and Huntingdon ; while his brother-in-law, Mr. Walton, tried with indifferent success to get men together for the like purpose, in and about Huntingdon. To get away the plate from the Colleges could only be done by eluding Cromwell at Lowler Hedges. The task was entrusted to Mr. Barnabus Oley, Vicar of Gransden and President of Clare Hall, who ' was acquainted with all the byeways through which they were to pass '; and so, 'passing through byepaths in the night, that very night in which Cromwell with his foot beset the common road,'[2] he had the honour of laying a part of the treasure at His Majesty's feet.

But the plate which Mr. Barnabus Oley got away with in the night-time represented only a part of the hurried packing up of College treasure intended for the King, and for those

---
[1] ' Bestowed on the souldiers and those that watched ye plate in ye New Court.' —Bursar's Accounts, Trinity College.
[2] Baker MSS., x, 368.

who deferred the work until next morning there would be the member for Cambridge to reckon with.

Cromwell's next move was to go straight to the point by marching his men, or some of them, boldly up to the Colleges in Cambridge, to stop the flow of treasure at the fountainhead. The whole of this incident of getting away the College plate was, in itself, a remarkable prelude to actual war. Though Cromwell and Walton were acting under orders of Parliament, it was a veritable Gordian knot; for even the Sheriffs of Hunts and Cambs, though ostensibly present, with the *posse comitatus*, to 'keep the peace,' were really there to facilitate the task of the Colleges—Sir Richard Stone, Sheriff of Hunts, by active assistance, and Sir John Cotton, Sheriff of Cambs, by a more passive attitude. What it was that induced Cromwell to leave his post in the cornfields and march his men up to King's College, is disclosed by the depositions of witnesses, taken at a later date, concerning Captain Docwra, of Fulbourn. The first is a certificate of the Cambridge Committee:—

"We humblie certify that Captain James Docwra his offence is this, that upon a letter from Sr John Cotton, Knight, for raising of the trayned band, whereof he was then Captaine, and bringing them to Cambridge, pretending to keepe the peace .... at such time as Lieutenant General Cromwell raised a force in the west side of Cambridgeshire to withstand the carrying away of the said plate."

John Linsey, of Cambridge, gent., sworn, said that "Capt. James Docwra did march into ye towne of Cambr. with his company for ye conveying away of ye plate .... to ye King. Notwithstanding an order that was shown him from ye House of Commons that he should desist from ye busines, he denied to yield obedience to ye said order and answered yt he had a warrant from ye King for what he did. Then .... ye said James Docwra did march away with his company into King's Colledg, where ye plate was loaden and readie to be conveyed to ye King, with his colours flieing and drums beating."

"Stephen ffortune of Cambr., gent., sworne. That James Docwra of ffulborne Esquire, and his sonn went into the

Towne out of the chappell yard, but newes comeing that Collonel Cromwell was at hand, then he with others did run wth a pistoll in his hand as for life and shut up ye gates [1] and sent out a drume with one Capt. Briscoe, who was accompanied wth ye said Capt. Docwra's sonn, he being then Ensigne to his father, and one or two more with them, and made proclamation whoer was for ye King should come to ye King's Colledg, there they should have armes and pay, but those yt were not for ye King should get them out of ye Towne. Whatsoer is above written I sweare to be true." [2]

In the county of Huntingdon a number of Royalist gentry had been trying to divert Cromwell's attention, while the party in charge of part of the treasure had eluded his vigilance. Some gentry of Huntingdonshire were placing difficulties in the way of Mr. Walton, their member. On August 8, John Merrill wrote from Huntingdon to Lord Mandeville, son of the Earl of Manchester :—

"Ordinances of Parliament are little regarded, good people openly reviled and threatened, the town of Huntingdon so disaffected to Capt. Walton, that when he sent out his warrants to raise two hundred of the train bands to resist the force that would have carried Cambridge plate into the North, some others did send out and employ their strength the other way, and very few of the train men would come at time. The Mayor and some other inhabitants had left the town. Mr. Henry Cromwell [Sir Oliver's son, of Ramsey] came with 50 men armed, and with horse and muskets, through Huntingdon on Saturday morning last, to help, as some think, to conduct the plate against Capt. Walton's Ordinance and force, the country nothing persuaded to accommodate the Parliament either with horse, arms, plate, or monies. . . . If your lordship yield not your present assistance you will assuredly find that nothing will be done. . . . I know no way at this present to fetch up the spirits of our freeholders, but either to appear in your

[1] At this time King's College buildings were to the north of the Chapel on the site of the University Library, the present entrance to which, opposite Great St. Mary's, was the old King's College gate here referred to, and consequently at a point where the excited crowd would assemble.

[2] State Papers, Interregnum, G., vol. lxxxviii, pp. 649–655.

person, or send someone among them whereby they may receive encouragement. Oh! the base and cowardly spirits of men that may prove the Parliament's desertion and their own destruction! The corrupt clergy and gentry are raging mad with us, especially against myself, which makes me think we are now come to ripeness and that the Lord hath decreed to afflict and scourge this nation for the manifold crying sins thereof."[1]

This affair of getting off the Cambridge plate had interested the whole country-side. In fact, a great crowd had gathered somewhere on the Huntingdon road leading out of Cambridge. Some of them could not refrain from taking sides; for afterwards, in the day of reckoning for 'compounders,' Richard Langley, of Hemingford Grey, Hunts, an old man seventy-six years of age, pleaded that his only delinquency consisted in 'being a spectator, with hundreds more, when the University plate of Cambridge was intended to be carried through the county.' Sir Capel Bedle, Sir Robert Osborne, Mr. Ringstead, and other private individuals were called to account over the incident.

In Cambridge, Mr. Cromwell was also turning his attention to securing the place itself for Parliament, and on August 15, there was carried up to Parliament this significant piece of intelligence: "Mr. Cromwell, in Cambridgeshire, has seized the magazine in the Castle at Cambridge, and hath hindered the carrying of the plate from that University; which, as some report, was to the value of £20,000 or thereabouts."[2] Parliament hastened to pass an Ordinance indemnifying Mr. Cromwell, Mr. Walton, and 'divers inhabitants and well affected persons in the counties of Huntingdon, Cambridge, and elsewhere' for their action as an acceptable service to the Commonwealth, for which they were to be 'protected and saved harmless by the authority and power of Parliament.'

[1] Duke of Manchester's Papers, 503.
[2] Commons' Journal, ii, 720. That Magdalene College was one of the Colleges which packed up its plate for the King and had it taken for Parliament, is clear from a later order of the House of Commons—"that the plate belonging to Maudlyn College in Cambridge . . . . shall be forthwith brought to London."

At a time when good horsemanship was universal and long, hard riding a necessity, the patrolling of the great highways, and attempts to get to the King at York before the storm of war burst upon the nation, were productive of some heroic adventures and memorable rides. In the hot Summer days of August, with the plague scattered here and there, and soldiers in ambush in the cornfields, belated followers of the King down the North Road to York were hard put to it. Of this class was Sir John Bramston, the Shipmoney Judge, of Skreenes, near Chelmsford. The King had summoned him to York, but he was old and infirm and 'can only travel in a coach,' and 'the dangers of the North Road were great.' As an alternative he sent off his two sons, John, a lawyer like his father—until 'the drums and trumpets blew his gown over his ears'—and Francis, on horseback to the King at York, to give an account 'how his case stood.' From Chelmsford to Cambridge, from Cambridge to Stamford, and from Stamford to York, they rode, completing the journey in three days 'on the same horses.' They presented their father's case to the King, who replied—"Why should your father ask leave? .... Your father is not soe old but he may endure the journey .... his presence is necessary for my service." After one day's rest they remounted their horses and rode back to Skreenes in three days more, but not without incident. At Stamford, John, the narrator, states that his brother Francis "grew faint with the length of the journey and the heat of the weather." Instead of finding a welcome at an inn at Stamford they encountered the watchman of the town, who directed them a way to avoid the town, the plague being there. "What to doe I could not tell; he could ride no farther. We alighted and layd him downe upon our coates and cloathes, and I made one of the men [their servants] ride to some mowers that I espied at a distance cutting barlie, to buy some drinke. The fellow caught up their botle and came right away, and the men came running after him. Wee gave him some of their drinke, which refreshed him somethinge. We satisfied the laborer, and sent to the next village, where we gotte something to eate, and soe rode on our journey. . . . . In our return on Sunday neer Huntingdon, betweene that and Cambridge, certain musketeers start out of the corne [some of Cromwell's men lying in wait for the College plate] and command us to stand; tellinge vs wee must be searched, and to that end wee must goe before Mr. Cromwell, and give account from whence wee came and whither we were going. I askt where Mr. Cromwell was? A soldier told vs he was 4 miles off. I said it was unreasonable to carrie us out of our way; if Mr. Cromwell had binn there I should have willingly giuen him all the satisfaction he could desire, and putting my hand into my pocket gaue one of them 12*d*., whoe sayd wee might pass. By this I saw plainly that it would not be possible for my father to gett to the Kinge with his coach, and he could goe in no other way."[1]

On August 17, Parliament committed the care of the town of Cambridge to Mr. Oliver Cromwell, the Mayor, and three Aldermen, with these emphatic instructions:—

"You are required and authorized to exercise and train the Train Bands and Volunteers in the town of Cambridge, and shall lead and conduct them against all forces that attempt to seize upon that town, or to disturb the peace of it; and you are authorized to fight with all such persons, to kill and slay them, and by all means to defend your town from all hostile attempts there. You are likewise authorized to disarm all Popish recusants, and all other dangerous and ill affected persons who have opposed the orders and proceedings of Parliament, or endeavour to oppose by the Commission of Array or otherwise."[2]

In similar fashion the city of Norwich was in the grip of Parliament. The constables were to lock the gates at nine o'clock at night and allow no one in or out until next morning; the Corporation sent up its old stock of gunpowder to London to be exchanged 'for some of the best sort,' and sent over to King's Lynn—which had got itself behind some brass cannon from London—for Mr. Christian,

[1] Autobiography of Sir John Bramston, Knt. (Camden Society), pp. 85-6.
[2] Lords' Journals.

the engineer, to advise about the defences of the City, for which his fee still figures in the old books.

The Cambridge University did not like the control set up around it, and petitioned Parliament, pleading that the sending of the plate from some of the Colleges to the King had been 'not at all to foment any war.' They complained that 'certain men' had commenced to sequestrate the libraries and goods of some of the masters, and begged that the actions of 'some few particular men, some of whom were obliged to the King as their royall founder, might not redound to the depriving of several colleges of all possibility to continue in the University.'[1]

With the actual raising of the King's standard at Nottingham on August 22, about six o'clock in the evening of a very stormy and tempestuous day, and with little other ceremony than the sound of drums and trumpets, all the pent-up excitement of the last few months broke forth. Along the hill-tops of the eastern arm of the Chilterns, the old beacon fires flashed the tidings over East Anglia—

> Till broad and fierce the star came forth on Ely's stately fane,
> And town and hamlet rose in arms o'er all the boundless plain.

On every hand the air was full of the incessant beating of drums, the drilling of Volunteers for Parliament being varied by attempts to execute the King's Commission of Array, with strange conflicts of authorities. In Huntingdonshire, Mr. Valentine Walton 'sent out his warrants to summon in some of the Trained Bands,' when Mr. Heyton, one of the Chief Constables, caused the chain to be chained up and would not suffer them to go, and said "he would not obey the Parliament, for he had received a warrant from the King."

The King sent out batches of proclamations in all directions with Commissions of Array addressed to well-known men in each county. The messenger who was carrying these documents into Norfolk was intercepted. Mr. Cromwell and others were directed to set strong watches,

---

[1] Papers relating to Trinity College, vol. iii, in the Muniment Room, Trinity College.

sufficiently armed day and night, upon the several bridges of Germanes, Maudlyn, Soame, Stow, Downham, and all other bridges and ferries between the town of Cambridge and King's Lynn, for the apprehending of all horses of service for the wars, arms, ammunition, or plate sent to His Majesty,[1] and also to prevent persons coming from the North into these counties for the purpose of executing the King's Commission of Array.

Sir John Hobart, of Blickling, 'with five cases of pistols, three carabines, and two little short pieces of brass,' hurried down from London into Norfolk with a pass from Parliament; and everywhere men were arming themselves, their houses, and their servants. The bailiffs of Great Yarmouth were empowered to 'cause the saide towne to be fortified,' their ordnance to be mounted, the town to be put into a posture of defence, and to do 'divers other things for keeping the town faithful to the Parliament.'[2]

While the King's standard was being raised at Nottingham, a characteristic scene was being witnessed at Colchester, where Sir John Lucas had been preparing to set out from his house there, with horse and arms towards the King. Unfortunately Sir John, like Bramston, had delayed his start a little too long, and found it necessary to keep his movements secret and set out in the night-time. Everything was in readiness at midnight on Sunday for a start at one or two o'clock on Monday morning. But one of Sir John's servants betrayed the secret to the captain of the Parliamentary Trained Bands. When Sir John and his followers were about to march from his house, at one or two o'clock in the morning, by the back gate, he found 'a strong guard sprung up from under the hedge,' a gun was fired as a signal to the town, where 'drums struck up, and the whole town was raised.' Four or five hundred Volunteers were soon on the spot, the beacons were fired, and horsemen were sent forth into all the country-side 'to call in the country against the Cavaliers in Sir John Lucas's house.' A rush was made for the house, which was speedily entered. Here the first man they encountered was

[1] Lords' Journals.
[2] Yarmouth Corporation Records, Hist. MSS., Rep. 9.

Mr. Newcomin, parson of Trinity Church, Colchester. It is alleged that they 'tore his clothes off his back, beat him with cudgels and halberts, and with infinite exclamation carried him in triumph through the chief streets of the town.' Having lodged parson Newcomin in the Common Gaol, the party returned to Sir John Lucas's house. Entering the ladies' chamber and meeting Lady Lucas, they 'set a sword to her breast and required her to tell where the arms and the Cavaliers were.' These arms were soon found and carried to the Town Hall; Sir John, his lady, his sister, and his mother were carried off to the Moot Hall. The house was plundered, the servants were made prisoners, and one of the oldest was tied to a tree, with a sword placed to his throat and lighted matches between his fingers, 'while one Joe Furly, a pragmatical boy, examined him concerning his master's intentions.' Wild rumours flew about the town of Cavaliers being concealed, and Sir John's house was then 'battered down,' the deer killed in his park; and it is alleged that St. Giles' Church was broken into and the Lucas family vault, and that with pistols, swords, and halberts they transfixed the coffins of the dead.[1] The Mayor interfered; Sir Thomas Barrington and Mr. Harbottle Grimston (Member and Recorder for Colchester respectively) were sent down to 'discountenance such plunder'; but at the same time they issued a proclamation declaring Sir John guilty of treason.[2] Major Thomas Wade gives some further particulars, stating that "the rude people are come to such a head, being a mixed company of town and country, that we know not how to quiet them. Believe we could not repress them if we had five trained bands, unless they were killed. We feel they will not stay here, for they say they will go to Lady Savage's at St. Osyth, and some other places about the town."[3]

The unruly mob made their way to St. Osyth, the residence of the Countess Rivers, who being a Catholic was not likely to find much favour. Aware of her danger, Lady Rivers and

[1] Mercurius Rusticus.
[2] Sir John was taken up to London, but afterwards released on bail of £40,000. Mr. Newcomin, the parson, was kept in the Fleet Prison for about a month, and then, 'being never called for,' was discharged.—Ibid.
[3] Hist. MSS., Com. Rep., x, App. vi, p. 147.

Great Civil War. 65

her family had escaped, and she was making her way to her house at Long Melford, Suffolk. St. Osyth was plundered, and some of the party pursued her Ladyship towards Long Melford. The fate of Lady Rivers caused some anxiety among the gentry on the Parliament side as well as amongst the Royalists, and Parliament issued a declaration that "no soldier should pillage any Papist's house without the command of his captain."[1]

The Earl of Warwick, of Leigh's Park, near Braintree, was away at sea ; but his steward, Arthur Wilson, a Great Yarmouth man, was sent off with some few men and a coach and six horses to fetch the Lady Rivers to Leigh's Park for safety, little dreaming how difficult would be the enterprise. Coming to Sudbury, the sight of a coach and six brought crowds of people about them before they could reach the market-place. The horses' heads were seized, the coach surrounded by a furious mob, and all hope of getting the next three miles to Melford in time to be of assistance to Lady Rivers was lost. The people declared it was Lady Rivers' coach, some declared Wilson was Lord Rivers himself, and he adds— "They swarm'd about mee, and were so kind as to lay hold of mee." He appealed to them to hear him speak, and then told them he was steward to the Earl of Warwick, "a lover of his countrie & now in the Parliament's employment," and said he had letters in his pocket if they would let the magistrates see them. At this time the 'tops of the trees and all the windows were thronged with people,' who took up the cry of the crowd, 'letters! letters!' The Mayor of Sudbury handled the letters, while the crowd of people manifested 'an ytching desire after the coach horses.' At last Mr. Mann, the Town Clerk, was able to recognize Wilson as the Earl of Warwick's steward, and he was rescued from the mob. Hearing of alarming rumours from Long Melford, he left his coach behind at Sudbury, and he and his party mounted the horses and rode out by a by-way towards Melford 'to listen after the Countess.' Upon reaching Sir Robert Crane's house near Melford, he found

[1] Husband's Collection, p. 590.

that Lady Rivers had 'in her owne person escaped to Bury.' Sir Robert Crane informed him that, although a Parliament man, he had himself been obliged "to keep a train band in his own house to secure himself from the fury of the rabble, who threatened him for being assistant to her ladyship's escape."[1]

At Melford the crowd set upon her Ladyship's house and pillaged it; dug up all likely places 'where money might be hidden,' drank the wine and beer and 'let it out to knee deep in the cellar.'[2]

From Long Melford the Countess made her escape to Bury St. Edmund's, where the townspeople refused to admit her, and 'the gates were shut against her for an hour or more.' At last she was allowed to lodge in the town for the night, and next morning 'with a strong guard' she was conveyed out of the town, and 'keeping herself as private as she could the Countess made her way to London and so escaped molestation.'[3] These Essex rioters also threatened to march to the Earl of Suffolk's house at Audley End, but prompt action was taken by the Essex magistrates to restore order.

Both in Essex and in Cambridgeshire the Militia Ordinance had been delayed by the absence of lord-lieutenants, and on Monday, August 29, Sir Dudley North and Sir John Cutts, of Childerley, were ordered to go down from London into Cambridgeshire for putting the Ordinance in execution. At this time Cromwell's hands were full of affairs concerning his neighbour, Bishop Wren of Ely, and college dons in Cambridge, from which the reader may see how bitter was the feeling against such as got the name of Papists. On the same Monday, August 29, there is, for instance, this glimpse of 'a troop of well affected horsemen,' meeting together near Cherryhinton, Cambridge, 'with the intent of searching Papists' houses.' Being disappointed at the small store of arms and ammunition they found, one of their number suddenly remembered that they had 'missed one of

[1] Wilson's Narrative in Peck's "Desiderata Curiosa," lib. ix, pp. 23-5.
[2] Diary of John Rous (Camd. Soc.).
[3] Mercurius Rusticus.

the greatest Papists in the whole kingdom,' Dr. Wren, Bishop of Ely, and declared that it was 'not improbable that the Papists had made his house their magazine, he being the chief author of these troubles in this kingdom.' So, furnishing themselves with powder and shot, they marched for the Bishop's Palace, at Downham, to 'search his treasury withall, promising to clip his wings[1] if they could catch him.' Their zeal was fanned by stories that the Bishop's steward had beaten a man's brains out for asking for his wages, and that the Bishop himself 'entertained the deboist Cavaliers'; that his power in the Island had been great and uncontrollable; and, on the other hand, encouraged by the fact that the Isle 'had a store of good horses and able men, though very rude in their discipline, for want of expert commanders.' This was the testimony of George Hubbard, of Downham.[2] When the troopers reached the Bishop's Palace at Downham, they found the Wren had flown; or, rather, that he was busy with a nest elsewhere—at the Cambridge Colleges—and so they had the run of the place. From the Palace they brought away 'a great trunk full of marvellous rich silver and guilt plate, and money, as some report on credible information, to the value of at least £1,000, together with a great piece of ordnance and ammunition, all of which were found in the said Wren's house.'[3]

While this was happening at Downham, the Bishop appears to have reached Cambridge, where an attempt was being made to execute the King's Commission of Array. Mr. Russell, of Shingay, Cambs, brother of the Earl of Bedford, and the Earl of Carlisle, were assisted in this enterprise 'by the said Bishop Wren and the other doctors'[4]; by the Masters of St. John's, Queen's, and Jesus Colleges, in fact. Their

---

[1] The origin of this phrase, put into the mouth of Cromwell by the writer of the "Squire Papers," respecting Royalists, there can be no doubt is to be found in the punning use made of Bishop Wren's name. See "The Wren's Nest Defiled," p. 31.
[2] "Joyful Newes from the Isle of Ely," E. 115 (9), Brit. Mus. Lib.
[3] Vicars' Parliamentary Chronicle.
[4] This account [E. 115 (14), King's Pamphlets], contrary to the accepted account of the Bishop's arrest at Downham, seems to suggest that he was arrested with the heads of Colleges at Cambridge.

arrest by Cromwell's prompt appearance upon the scene is thus described :—

"Down he [Cromwell] comes again in a terrible manner, with what force he could draw together, and surrounds divers Colleges, while we were at our devotions in our several chapels; taking away prisoners several doctors of divinity, heads of Colleges, viz., Dr. Beale, Master of St. John's College, Dr. Martin, Master of Queen's College, and Dr. Sterne, Master of Jesus College, and these he carries with him to London in triumph. . . . . They were led captive through Bartholomew Fair and so far as Temple Bar, and back through the City to prison in the Tower, on purpose that they might be houted at or stoned by the rabble rout."[1]

Other Royalist accounts speak of the heads of Colleges and a cartload of treasure being brought up 'guarded with 500 horse,' and that their captors 'made of them a show to entertain the people,' and that 'in the villages through which they passed, the people were called by some of their agents to come and abuse and revile them.'[2]

While Mr. Russell, of Shingay, was appearing with the King's Commission of Array in Cambridge, his brother, the Earl of Bedford, was marching from London with a Parliamentary troop against the Cavaliers under Sir John Watts, of Mardocks, near Ware. At Hoddesdon they were met by Sir Thomas Dacres, member for the County, who told them 'he feared they should have a battel betwixt that and Hartford . . . . withal encouraging them to proceed valiantly, intimating the justnesse of the cause and many noble encouragements.' Near Ware the troops prepared for the expected battle, charging with bullet and marching bravely forward in the darkness until they found themselves face to face with what appeared to be a hostile camp, but which was in reality the Parliamentary force guarding the town of Hertford, and here they were joyfully received by their friends. On Monday, August 29, they marched to Hadham Hall, the seat of Lord Capel, searched

[1] "Querela Cantabrigiensis."
[2] News from Cambridge in E. 115; also in Mercurius Rusticus.

the place, and found arms sufficient to arm about a thousand men, with ten horses, great saddles, pistols, and carbines.[1] Lady Capel 'used them with much respect, much lamenting the unfortunateness of her husband.'[2] At Sir Thomas Fanshaw's at Ware Park, where two gunsmiths had been employed for three months repairing armour, they found '2 pieces of ordnance, several barrels of powder, musket and pike.'

On that stirring August 29 there is a glimpse of a ship landing in a creek near Skegness bringing twelve heavily-laden trunks from Holland. This, and Sir William Ballingdon, with two officers and eight cavaliers, were seized, together with a 'canonical parson' and a servant of the Earl of Lindsey who had been free with their speech. The Cavaliers threatened revenge upon Boston, and King's Lynn sent over five pieces of ordnance and 1,000 Volunteers well armed. The cannon were placed in the passages into the town, and scouts sent out, but the Cavaliers thought better of it than to appear.

It was amidst such scenes as these that the great conflict began in which the King was drawing around him the sons of gentlemen, and Parliament had to make a beginning with a large proportion of undisciplined men, many of whom were those 'tapsters and decayed serving men' who sorely vexed the heart of Cromwell.

One of the most notable things about the great struggle upon which the King and Parliament were openly launched by the end of August, 1642, was the entire absence in the public mind of any idea that the rival forces were entering upon what might be a long campaign. On every hand the idea prevailed that one great battle would decide the quarrel. There was, therefore, a most intense feeling of eager anticipation and of fearful looking forward to the first shock of arms, the prospect of which weighed heavily upon the public mind. The Earl of Essex received his appointment as Lord General 'for King and Parliament' .in melancholy mood, and the members themselves were

[1] A Perfect Diurnal.   [2] Special Passages in E. 115.

reluctant to see him set off, as D'Ewes says, 'against his distressed sovereign, being now reduced to the greatest calamity of any person living,' his messages to the two Houses having been 'rejected with infinite scorn and contempt.'

But there was now no drawing back, and the opening days of September saw the first great army of the Parliament marching through Hertfordshire with the confidence of the City behind it, that 'it would make short work with the King and his supporters.' Along Watling Street, on the track of the soldiers of ancient Rome, the City troops marched, regiment after regiment, in their many-coloured coats—grey, green, blue, red, and even white—as was the custom on both sides, wearing only their orange sashes to distinguish them from the red-sashed Royalists. The sight of the Parliamentary colours bearing the brief but eloquent motto "God with us," and on the reverse "*Cave, adsum,*" aroused the enthusiasm of the people as the soldiers passed along. When the Earl of Essex followed with his brilliant staff, his features, grave and melancholy, expressed the sense of a terrible responsibility, while his impedimenta contained the family escutcheon, his coffin and his shroud ready for his funeral, should fate so ordain! The scene was an impressive one, yet not lacking in stimulus and hope, for when the Earl set out from London to St. Albans his march commenced "in a way of triumph . . . . waited on by Parliament, and millions of people lined the highways . . . . the multitude crying out 'Hosanna!'"[1] On every hand were to be seen the orange colours among the people, worn by women as well as men, "until," says the Royalist Saunderson, "every citizen's dame, to the draggle-tail of her kitchen, had got up that colour of the cause." How the tramp of armed men impressed the inhabitants is reflected in one of those characteristic epistles of Lady Sussex of Gorhambury, written when the soldiers were passing almost in sight of her Ladyship's windows:—

"We have a great store of sogers at Sentabornes came to-night. They say three score carts of ammunition and things for that use, and ten great pieces [artillery] drawn

[1] Warburton's Memoirs.

upon wheels, and the Inns of Court gentlemen to guard my Lord's person has come too, they say very fine and well horsed. . . . . They talk strange things of my Lord of Essex, that he will fetch the King to London dead or alive; this is high, methinks, for people to talk so. If these sogers be passed I hope we shall have no more to frighten us."

Everywhere drums were beating, trumpets sounding, and men were marching to their colours; parish constables were running to and fro with their warrants for bringing in the men, each with his month's pay.[1] From Fenland and from the Eastern Counties, troops of horse and companies of foot came pouring in to join the main body at Bedford and other centres. Oliver Cromwell is among them as captain of a troop of horse, and his boy, young Oliver, is there as a cornet. Cromwell's neighbours, too, are there—his brother-in-law, Walton, member for Huntingdonshire, and his boy, Valentine, who was to meet his fate at Marston Moor; the Desboroughs, too, and young Edward Montague, of Hinchinbrook, who, according to Noble, "when a little more than eighteen years old, by virtue of a commission, raised a thousand men in Cambridgeshire and the Isle of Ely."

At Northampton the Earl of Essex had got together an army of 20,000 men, and his speech to the soldiers shows that beneath his melancholy there was a fine, generous sympathy with the men. Addressing his army, 'assembled for the defence of His Majesty and the maintenance of the true Protestant religion,' he declared his intention to 'stand by the soldiers, that even the poorest soldier should have justice'; and he added: "Neither will I engage any of you unto danger; but I will, in my own person, run equal hazard with you, and either bring you off with honour, or (if God so decreed) fall with you, and willingly become a sacrifice for the preservation of my country." On the other hand, the King, now drawing across England, addressing his soldiers, declared to them: "You shall meet with no enemies but

[1] "On sight, bring to us one month's pay for your dragoons and foot; if any refuse to pay the tax, seize all his horse, arms, plate, etc."—Warrants of Sir Samuel Luke and others in Orlebar Papers, Hist. MSS., Com. Rep.

traitors, and most of them Brownists, anabaptists, and atheists, such as desire to destroy both Church and State. . . . . You cannot fight in a better quarrel, in which I promise to live and die with you."[1]

Complaints of the King's favouring Catholics, the arrival and capture, at Yarmouth, of the 'Queene's Shipp'[2] from Holland, with 140 officers and men and 300 barrels of powder, with the Queen's letters on board, and the King's description of the soldiers of Parliament, all helped to fire the resolution of those marching against His Majesty, at a time when, as Gardiner says, "to thousands of Englishmen Puritanism was the very Gospel itself; the voice of God speaking to a careless generation."

The first great shock of arms, to which everybody had looked forward to settle the quarrel, which took place at Edgehill, on Sunday, October 23, was one full of strangely pathetic incidents. Beginning with the old Norfolk Royalist, Sir Jacob Astley's historic prayer and command: "O Lord! Thou knowest how busy I must be this day. If I forget Thee, do not Thou forget me.—March on, boys!"—and varied by the King's despairing appeal to Lindsey: "Go, in the name of God, and I'll lay my bones by yours." The first conflict was but a mad rush at each other, without method, without organization; with plenty of valour, but little generalship. The result was a strange confusion of issues—half victory, half defeat on both sides; but this one great fact remained, that the Puritan soldiers of the Eastern Counties and of London had held their part of the field with Cromwell at the head of an unbroken troop of horse. For the rest, the King's Standard had been wrested from the hands of his Standard-bearer, Sir Edmund Verney, the 'stainless knight,' who was among the slain.[3] Sir Jervase Scroope, the old

[1] Somers' Tracts.
[2] In the Yarmouth Corporation Records is an Order of Parliament declaring the lawfulness of the action by the bailiffs in seizing this ship from Rotterdam, "driven by stress of weather into that [Yarmouth] port."
[3] A pathetic comment upon his own frank admission to his son, Sir Ralph Verney: "'I have eaten his [the King's] bread, and served him near thirty years, and will not do so base a thing as to forsake him, and choose rather to lose my life—which I am sure to do—to preserve and defend those things which are against my conscience . . . . for I have no reverence for Bishops for whom this quarrel subsists."

Lincolnshire Royalist, who had opposed Lord Willoughby over the Militia of his county, was found by his own son, lying on the battlefield, among the dead and wounded, stripped, and with seventeen wounds in his body. The exposure to the cold of a frosty night staunched the flow of blood from his wounds, and he was carefully tended, carried off the field and taken to Oxford, where, says Clarendon, he 'wonderfully recovered.' On the other hand, Parliament lost one troop of horse, which, at the first charge, went over to Prince Rupert; but failing to throw away their 'orange tawny scarfs,' seventeen of them got killed by mistake by their Royalist friends to whom they went over.

The most conflicting and sensational rumours of the result of the battle spread towards London, and into the Eastern Counties. One man 'proffered to pawn his life that the King was taken'; and another said that 'the Earl of Essex was slain; that it was a bloody battle, four thousand men slain on each side, and neither King nor Prince within three miles of the armies when they fought.[1] Others, says Clarendon, "who fled from the field, reported all for lost, and the King's Army so terrible that it could not be encountered. Some had seen the Earl of Essex slain, and heard his dying words, 'that everyone should shift for himself, for all resistance was to no purpose.'"

The King sent out his account of the battle, enjoining its publication in all churches and chapels. This gave many a Royalist clergyman the opportunity of saying a word for the King; as at Furneaux Pelham, in the north of Hertfordshire where Mr. Hancock, the vicar, who, having distinguished himself by walking up and down the churchyard in the night-time armed with his sword, when his communion rails were threatened, now came out boldly by declaring in his sermon that he was "overjoyed to thinke that God should put it into the heart of the King to fight the Lord's battel on the Lord's day to uphould the ould antient Catholic faith." Parliament, finding His Majesty's declaration to be 'full of scandals and invectives against the Parliament,' issued a lengthy proclamation of its own.

[1] Hist. MSS., Com. Rep., v, 161.

The fact that the great issue was not to be decided by the first shock of arms was not the only discovery made at Edgehill. It was also found at the very outset that the Parliamentary Army, even in the zealous Eastern Counties, needed men who could bring the discipline and habits of the trained soldier into every company. The attempt to remedy this caused a little soreness in the Puritan ranks, for when the necessity arose for bringing up reinforcements to meet the King at Brentford, Captain Farre, 'in the behalf of the county of Essex,' made a very free, plain speech to the Earl of Warwick on the policy of changing captains. "Our Essex soldiers," he said, "are all men of able estates, whose zealous affections to their King and country had thus led them forth to give a clear testimony of love and valour." The Earl commended him for his free, soldierly speech, but said : —" If your Essex soldiers be offended at the election of other captains let them consider that the present occasion doth require men bred in warre, and experienced in those affairs. In Holland they have hazarded their lives and spent some blood to gain a perfect knowledge in all warlike discipline. Yet I prefer them not as men of greater ability, much less loyalty, than the other captains. Yet, as they cannot both serve in the same places, let them not think it any dishonour in point of war to suffer the Commonwealth to be served by others as well as themselves."

'To prevent the King's Army coming to London' was the great object of Parliament when it was known that the two shattered armies were marching by two different routes towards the City. To this end the counties of Norfolk, Suffolk, Cambs, Hunts, Herts, and Beds were directed to raise 7,000 foot and 600 horse, and there was equal anxiety about the contributions. When Sir Dudley North and Sir John Cutts were sent down into Cambridgeshire for the advancement of this business, they called a meeting at Bottisham for the East of the County, and there is a glimpse of one, Mr. Munday, parson of Wilbraham, standing at the door of the inn where the Commissioners were sitting, and as the people came up with their offerings, doing his best to dissuade them, declaring ''t is treason to lend or give.' In

Norfolk, contributions came in handsomely for Parliament, £40,000 in the hands of Sir John Potts and others, for which the Committee for the Advance of Money offered to furnish a guard for its safe convoy up to the Guildhall.

With the renewal of hostilities so near as Brentford, and the turning out of all London with the marching of trained bands to the rendezvous at Turnham Green, the war began to be looked upon as a reality, and personal and domestic life was already feeling the stress in the counties near. Lady Sussex, writing from Gorhambury, expressed this in one of her ill-spelled missives, which is worth giving in its native dress :—

" My fear is most of prince ropperte [Rupert], for tho say he hath littill mercy when he comes. I am hear in as sade a condisyon as may bee. i have made up some of th dors and pilede them up so with wode that i belive my hose is able to keep out a good many now ; if wee escape plonderinge i shall account it a great marsy of god ; the are all about us hear in such grivus fears that if they see but a gentellman ridinge, they think it is to robe them." [1]

Two little incidents connecting the county of Huntingdon with Parliament marked the close of the first act of the great drama. The old Earl of Manchester had died and was buried at Kimbolton, while Rupert's artillery was thundering through the streets of Brentford, and his son Viscount Mandeville, the new Earl, had, in the House of Lords, with Pym in the House of Commons, to announce the new War Tax. The new Earl's relative, Sir Sidney Montague, of Hinchinbrook, member for Huntingdonshire, appeared in the House a few days afterwards, on December 3, and was offered, and refused to take, the Protestation 'to live and die with the Earl of Essex,' giving as a reason that 'he had a proclamation of the King's in his pocket, proclaiming them traitors who should take it.' [2] For this, Sir Sidney was straightway committed to the Tower and Huntingdonshire deprived of one of its members, though still claiming his son as one of the bravest of its soldiers.

[1] These interesting letters of Lady Sussex are preserved in the Verney MSS. at Clayden House : see " Memoirs of the Verney Family," by Lady Verney.
[2] Perfect Diurnal.

CHAPTER V.

A GREAT HISTORIC UNITY—THE EAST ANGLIAN COMPACT
—CROMWELL AND THE ROYALISTS—THE FORTIFICATION
OF CAMBRIDGE.

(1642-3.)

All the past of time reveals
A bridal dawn of thunder-peals
Whenever faith has wedded fact.

TENNYSON.

WHILE the King appealed to the virtue of a chivalrous devotion to his person as King for a common bond of association amongst his followers, Parliament sought for a bond of association in a new principle in the history and government of the English nation. It was a bond, not for the defence of this or that person's pre-eminence, as all the hostile background of feudal England had been, but for the principle of religion —religion without ' Popery '—in the government of a nation. It was a strange parting of the ways, and nowhere did the new principle find a more uniform and determined assent than in the Eastern Counties. To this principle and the need for it the neighbouring counties of Cambridge, Hertford, Bedford, and Buckingham, on December 19, set their hands in the following vigorous protestation :—

" It is notoriously known to all men how great the violence, oppressions, and plunderings of those wicked men, forrainers, Papists, malignants, and traytours, which call themselves the King's Army, have and doe daily exercise in this kingdom, and that commissions for raising of more forces are daily issued to Papists, whereby our religion is like to be altered to Popery and our just privileges overthrown. . . . . They therefore . . . . solemnly protest and covenant before God and one another that they will willingly and resolutely sacrifice their lives in this religious and just quarrel, and that they will never lay down their arms till this which is called the King's Army be dissolved . . . . unless they be commanded by both Houses to the contrary, which they hope they never shall." [1]

At first the Association principle of defensive action was taken up by resolution at market ordinaries, by which contiguous towns and districts, finding themselves threatened by a common danger, resolved to associate themselves together for the security of their homes and kindred. But the very uncertainty which brought such compacts into existence was fatal to their permanence, and they were shattered by the altered demands for meeting the first danger which had called them forth. In the association of counties the same fluctuating character was equally fatal to permanence in cases where the feeling was at all evenly divided, or where the associated counties became involved as the theatre of war.

In the history of the Civil War there was only one Association having within it the requisite elements of permanence—a favourable situation of the counties forming it, the character of the people dwelling within its borders, and the leaders, or rather the one man able to weld together its factors into an irresistible whole. That Association was the famous Eastern Counties Association, composed at first of the 'frontier' counties of Hertfordshire and Cambridgeshire, and the seaward counties of Norfolk, Suffolk, and Essex, to which were afterwards added Huntingdonshire and, as soon as the Fenmen got a sufficient grip of it, Lincolnshire.

Parliament commenced the organization by requiring all the deputy-lieutenants of Essex, Suffolk, Norfolk, Hertford, Cambridge, and the Isle of Ely, to summon together at

[1] Diurnal of Occurrences in Parliament.

convenient centres the freeholders and other inhabitants to a sort of wapentake, at which all arms and likely forces to be raised were to be surveyed and reported. The deputy-lieutenants were further enjoined to explain to the inhabitants at such meetings 'what present and imminent danger and necessity the whole kingdom is now reduced unto by the wicked advice, attempts, and conspiracies of papists and other persons now about His Majesty.' They were also authorized to fortify or destroy, in case of the fear of invasion by the King's Army, all bridges, etc., along the principal passages into the several counties. Out of this effort there arose at the end of 1642 the germ of that famous Eastern Association, the one great historic unity which was destined to keep its own borders free from the worst evils of civil war, and to furnish those stout sinews of war which carried the Parliamentary cause to victory on other fields. The Ordinance for the Association passed the Commons on December 10, 1642, and here is the resolution of the sturdy yeomen who adopted it and silenced the few Royalist gentry of East Anglia :—

"Whereas the Lords and Commons now assembled in Parliament have taken into their consideration that in these times, so full of division and danger as these are, an union of our hearts and forces is most conducive to the public good and safety of the whole kingdom, and have therefore ordained that the inhabitants of the counties of Essex, Suffolk, Norfolk, Cambridge, and Hertfordshire, together with the Isle of Ely and the county of the city of Norwich, should enter into an Association with one another for the maintenance and preservation of the peace of the said counties : therefore, in pursuance of the said order and the better to form a mutual confidence in one another, we whose names are hereunto subscribed do hereby promise, testify, and declare to maintain and defend, with our lives, powers, and estates, the peace of the said counties, and to aid and assist one another under the command and conduct of such person as now hath, or hereafter shall have, by the authority of both Houses of Parliament, the command in chief of all the forces of the said counties, according to the true intent and meaning of the said Order of the Association, whereunto we do most willingly give our assents, and neither for hope, fear, or other respect shall we relinquish this promise."[1]

But it was not enough that the counties through their deputy-lieutenants should pledge themselves; the bond of unity, to be effectual, must rest upon the common sentiment of the people. Parliament, having an immense regard for that fine phrase the 'well affected inhabitants,' set about influencing public opinion with some of the resources, and probably some of the wiles, of a modern general election. The printers were set to work, and 'Association' books were turned out by the thousand and sent down into the shires, to all market towns and to places where the hundreds centred. Meetings were summoned in moot halls, market houses, and churches, where, in eloquent speeches, members and others sent down for the purpose descanted upon the 'justnesse of the cause,' and roused the enthusiasm of the meeting until the Royalist who wanted to know more about the Association before he joined it, was silenced. The resolution of Association passed, and then came the 'collection.' 'Having associated yourselves, what will you do to make your association effectual?' The answer to that question was such a 'collection' as had never been made in East Anglia since the people rose to repel the Spanish Armada. The leading man present would offer to find 'a musket and a month's pay'; another man would follow with the offer of a musket, and a neighbour would step in and guarantee the pay. Smaller men would unite and furnish a man and pay between three or four of them. Others came forward with old pieces of armour, and then there was the widow's mite and the small contributions of a shilling and upwards; and so the collection of men, money, and arms accumulated from all quarters of the shires.

History has been silent about the small beginnings of this famous East Anglian compact, which meant so much for Parliament and for England in the days which were to follow; but there are a few welcome traces of here and

---

[1] Tanner MSS., cclxxxiv, f. 44; also printed in Rushworth.

there a footprint of the old Puritan folk wending their way to the trysting-places in the county of Suffolk. Some of the old documents containing them are here printed for the first time. They are taken from the Tanner MSS. in the Bodleian Library, Oxford. The first is an example of the letter and supplies of books sent down into each county, and is addressed to Norfolk Committee-men by Sir William Heveningham—

"Sir,

"I send you here foweir score Bookes of the Assotiation and Instrutions all Printed togeither, and also a Copie of a Letteir, and warrant written into Essex, which you may make vse of if you please, which Letteir and warrant is sent alreadey into Essex as I am Informed; and They call all the Contrey in to fiue places and goe all togeither, I meane Membeirs of the House and the Deputie Leiftenantes of the Contie of Essex; and all those that were assistants in the Propotitions, are also to assiste in euery of those Deuisions which are deuided in to fiue deuisions. They begine their worke the day afteir New Yere. Sir Thomas Woodhouse, Sir John Holland, Sir John Poottes [Potts], and Mr. Framingham Gaudey are to assiste the Deputie Leiftenantes and Commissioners for the propotitions att the Committe of the fiue Conties and I thinke reported to the House and approued of. My respects and seruice from

"Your assured louing frend
to serue you
W. Heueningham.

"To my Honored Frend
Sir John Hubbartt
and to the rest of the
Deputie Leiftenants
these
Norwich.

"These Bookes are to be sent only to all the citteys and Markett Townes if you will haue any more I pray Lett me receiue your furtheir Directions; but these I haue aduentured to try and send downe to you."[1]

[1] Tanner MSS., cxiv, f. 98.

Great Civil War. 81

From the other documents preserved in the Tanner MSS, we obtain interesting examples from three Suffolk parishes of what was being done with these letters and books all over East Anglia. From Lavenham, a village lying between Sudbury and Bury St. Edmund's, the most complete example is afforded. The first of the Lavenham documents sets forth the full resolution of Parliament just given, which, having been passed by the meeting, was attested by a long array of signatures and 'marks' of various kinds—altogether ninety names, leading off with Francis Copinger. But of more significance than this overwhelming response of the Lavenham folk to stand together, is the evidence of the volunteer spirit which animated individuals and families. Here is the record of those who needed no eloquent speeches to fire their zeal :—

"Lauenham
in Suffolke.

"Herein is Subscribed the names of those that Find Voluntarie Armes and who Serue in the Same. All which are all redy Sentt to Cambridge with a month's pay acorrding to the Ordenance of Both houses of Parlamentt for the defence of the Fiue Counties as Expressed in the Association

"they went vnder Captaine Richerson of Hadely.

FINDE.		SERUE.	SOLDIERS.
"Mr. Doctour Copinger, a Coslett		—×—	John Sare.
Mr. Henry Copinger, sen., and Richard Pecocke, a muskett ...		—×—	John Rooff.
Mr. Frances Copinger, a Coslett and muskett		—×—×—	John Huntt and Robert Warrin.
Mr. Isaacc Creme and Gilbertt Wells, a muskett	: m :	—×—	Edward King.
Mr. James Allington John Browne, 11s., a muskett... ...		—×—	George Beamon.
Mr. Thomas Browne, a muskett		—×—	Edmund Randall
Roger Kerington and Lionell Mills, a muskett ...		—×—	Daniell Eldered.

FINDE.	SERUE.	SOLDIERS.
Mr. John C. (?) and Richard Paine, a muskett	—×—	Thomas King.
Arthir Buttcher and Thomas Vnderwood, a coslett	—×—	William Simons.
John Hilton, Frances Pinchbeck Georg Hamond and Andrew Brownsmith, a coslett	—×—	John Moutten.
William Wiles and Nicholas Wells, a coslett	—×—	John Buttcher.
John Pinchbeck and John Boyden, a. m....	—×—	James Steuens.
William Plaistoe, William Boswell and Robert King, a m	—×—	Robert Reson.
Samuell Dansdie, Henry Rudland and John Lingwood, a m	—×—	William Huntt.
Isaac Lomeley, William Russell, and Thomas Kentt, a m	—×—	Thomas Skinner.
Edward Browne, Lionell mills jun. and natham Lambin, a m	—×—	William Settins.
Abraham Gurling Georg Frost and John Ankle, a m	—×—	Richard More.
Dauie Wilding Raphe Blise and John Gipson, a m	—×—	Robertt Deacon.
Richard Palmer Thomas Gutteredg Raphe Ferier and Peter Salter, a m	—×—	James Gladmell.
John Lomeley and Jossua Blower, a m :	—×—	Robertt Aston."[1]

Then, beside the above volunteering, the Lavenham folk put their hands, to the number of about forty, to the following document, as a result of the meetings :—

"Lavenham in Suffolk.

"Wee whose names are hereunder written doe hereby engage our selues to prouide Horses and Armes and to maintaine and Finde att our owne proper Costs and Charges and att all times to haue in a Readinesse for the seruice of

[1] Tanner MSS., cclxxxiv, f. 43.

this and those Other counties now Associated together by the Authority of Both Howses of Parliamentt : soe many men Compleately Armed and Furnished, and such Horses, geldings, naggs and mares as we have Seurally and Respectiuely Subscribed, to be Comanded, led and conducted in to any partes and places within the said Countyes by such person as now hath or hereafter shall haue Comand in cheiff of all the Forces of the said Counties

"vid. of Essex Suffolke, Norffolke Cambredgsheir and Herteforde Sheir together with the Isle of Ely and Cittie of Norwich :

"Henry Copinger, senior, Francis Copinger hath already sent at his owne charges one compleate Coslett and one muskett, and hath giuen ,them three poundes in mony fr one moneths paye." [1]

[Here follow the other signatures, many of which have already been mentioned in the Volunteer list.]

Lavenham was only one place. Four or five miles to the north-west of Lavenham and nearer Bury St. Edmund's is the village of Shimpling. The Shimpling document is even more interesting than those of Lavenham, as evidence of what a small place could do, and of the zeal which prompted the smaller folks to contribute. It belongs to a little later date than the others, but can best be introduced here.

"Shimplinge the eight Daie of March Anno Dom. 1642 [3]

These whose names by vs are heir under written haue giuen ther Consents to Joine in th asotiacion accordinge to th Booke of Directions and what Armes they will Finde as Followethe.

"John Weeles, clarke, will finde a muskete compleat: but no paie.

Widowe Coppinge will contribute 10s.

George Causon will Contribute 10s. for the paie of Mr. Welles musket.

[1] Tanner MSS., cclxxxiv, f. 41.

Thomas Gardner will finde a muskete Compleat and twenty shillings of money.

William Gallante, widowe Hammond, Thomas Coe and John Smythe, will Finde a muskete Compleate and twenty shillings of money.

Henry Garner, John Pawsey, Thomas Halstead, John Coe, Thomas Causon and Thomas Game will finde a muskete compleate and twenty shillings of money.

Rychard Pawsey will finde an ould head pece and a sword.

"They that did Joine befor the commicions was John Plampin, to finde a musket and 20s. Fraucis Johnson and John Johnson his sonn to find a muskete and 20s.

These are all that will find armes, the reste haue Consented to asotiate as followethe."[1]

Twenty-six names are attached, including 'widowe Game,' making the third widow in the lists. Shimpling was happy in its Parish Constables, whose names also appear, John Plampin finding a 'musket compleate.' The five 'trained men' whom Shimpling fitted out are deserving of mention— "Edmund Smythe, Geiles Hammond [the widow's son?] Roger Coe, James Corder, and George Johnson"—all honest Shimpling family names, who may, for aught anyone knows, have lived to figure in the muster roll of the Ironsides.

Alpheton, another parish in the same district, referred to in the same class of documents, passed a similar resolution to have 'in a readinesse for the seruice of this and those other counties now associated,' so many men 'compleately armed and furnished' and its promised quota of 'horses, geldings, naggs, and mares,' and added these interesting particulars :—

"The names of those that will finde armes and ioyne in the assotiation.

John Wine jun., Nicholas Hayward, John Lister and Richard Michell will finde a muskett. Volunteere Kidson.

Steuen Coe will contribute 1s.

John Wine sen. will contribute 10s.

Dauid Turner will contribute 10s.

[1] Tanner MSS., cclxxxiv, f. 45.

James Hibble will contribute 10s.
William Baldin will contribute 10s.
Josuah Comsbie, Roger Caman, Simon Game. Volunteere, a muskett, Watesam."

Twenty-six names are added as 'those that did onely consent to the assotiation.'[1]

In the foregoing transcripts the reader has typical examples of what was going on all over East Anglia. Multiply one of these parishes by four or five hundred for the one county of Suffolk, and again by four or five, for the Associated Counties, and one has some idea of what the common sentiment of East Anglia was doing for Parliament with this bond of association. Multiply in a similar way these contributions of a parish—its corslets, its muskets, trained men and volunteers, 'ould head peces,' swords and money—and one has an idea of how the sinews of war came in, and may imagine, too, the growing force of armed men marching in from the broad acres of Norfolk and Suffolk, from the far-away corners of Essex, from the stagnant Fens, and from the hills of Hertfordshire, to the rendezvous at Cambridge, when, as we shall see presently, that town was in danger of falling into the hands of the Royalists.

The year 1643 opened with these two other notable facts. The King had got himself established at Oxford, in a strange compound of University, city, camp, and Court, to which Royalist gentry were flocking in with all speed ; Parliament was concentrating its efforts upon securing the sister University town of Cambridge. These two centres, the one in touch with the Royalism of the Western Counties and the other with the Puritanism of the Eastern Counties, were destined to become permanently associated with the rival parties in the struggle. Yet the distinction of Oxford for King and Cambridge for Parliament was not quite true in the academic sense, for the University of Cambridge never took kindly to the presence of the Parliamentary soldiers, and at this date was showing a degree of interest the other way which made vigorous measures necessary for securing the town of Cambridge itself.

[1] Tanner MSS., cclxxxiv, f. 42.

CROMWELL ARRESTING THE SHERIFF AT ST. ALBANS. *(From a drawing by F. G. Kitton.)*

In those defensive measures, Oliver Cromwell, member for Cambridge, captain of a troop of horse, and shortly to be a colonel, was taking an energetic part, and yet finding time to ride in hot haste, now here, now there, wherever a firm hand was needed for nipping some Royalist movement in the bud. The first of these adventures took place in Hertfordshire, where, in St. Albans market-place on market-day, Mr. Thomas Coningsby, High Sheriff, had on January 14, 1643, surrounded himself with his *posse comitatus*, and, accompanied by Dr. Seaton, rector of Bushey, and other Royalists, was at the Market Cross about to read the King's proclamation, virtually aiming at getting the Trained Bands of the County out of the hands of Parliament, and to lay down their arms. Mr. Coningsby had succeeded in posting the proclamation 'upon several places in the market,' when 'Captaine Cromwell,' who was on the march with his troop of horse into Cambridgeshire, by direction of Parliament, 'to secure that towne and county, and to raise more forces there for that purpose,' had somehow got to hear of the High Sheriff's proceedings. Riding into St. Albans, his troops formed up around the excited market crowd. Six of the troopers were deputed to arrest the Sheriff, but Mr. Coningsby's supporters rallied around him in such force that the sadly ruffled person of the Sheriff was released from the grip of the troopers, 'whereupon the High Sheriffe went again to the Market-Crosse, where the said confused multitude proclaimed him their lawful High Sheriffe.' Calling for more of his troopers, Cromwell renewed the struggle, and 'some twenty more of the said troopers, being well horsed and armed,' followed the Sheriff and his friends as they retired into 'the inn yard where he abode.'

The struggle was renewed, the gates closed and 'barricadoed' against the multitude, and Mr. Coningsby and his Royalist friends[1] were secured and sent up to London to answer for their adventure.[2]

---

[1] One of them, named John Thomas, a saddler, two years afterwards petitioned the King at Oxford, on the strength of his share in the exploit, for the appointment of saddler to His Majesty, and obtained the post.—Carew Transcripts, P.R.O.

[2] Vicars' Parliamentary Chronicle, p. 256.

Elsewhere it was the same—here and there a Royalist official, rather than the common people, standing in the way of Parliament. Getting back to Huntingdon, Cromwell had to reprove a former fellow-magistrate, Mr. Barnard, who had been 'wary in his carriage'—'Be not too confident; subtlety may deceive you, integrity never will.' In Cambridgeshire there was a difficulty with the Sheriff. The old arrangement of one Sheriff for Cambridgeshire and Huntingdonshire had been renewed after a few years' interruption, and Sir Robert Coke was taken in custody by Parliament. Then his successor, Mr. Rose, with Mr. Playter and Sir Benjamin Ayloffe, Sheriffs for Suffolk and Essex respectively, were sent for to produce their commissions of Shrievalty. Meanwhile towns were getting fortified—King's Lynn, which had contributed liberally to Parliament, being allowed to spend £400 of its contributions upon its own fortifications, and Yarmouth, in a similar way, £1,000.

The chief event in the months of January and February for the Eastern Counties was the rallying of their forces to repel a threatened attack upon Cambridge, which, by common consent, was looked upon as a place which must be held for Parliament at all hazards, as the headquarters of the new Association movement. Lord Capel had returned to his county to find his store of arms carried off from Hadham Hall ; and, getting together a strong force of his neighbours and others, he was hanging around ready to fall upon Cambridge upon one side, while some of Rupert's forces were reported to be marching towards it on the other.

It was under these circumstances, and to avert a threatened disaster to the Parliamentary cause at the outset, that the Counties of East Anglia came out so bravely with the firstfruits of the Association principle. In every centre, in which those zealous offerings of 'compleat cosletts,' 'muskets,' swords, and 'ould head peces' had been so freely made, the trained men were hurrying in at the beat of drum, and falling into line ready to march under appointed commanders for the rendezvous at Cambridge for the expected attack upon that place, tidings of which were ringing all over the Eastern Counties. The Volunteers of Norwich and Yarmouth, before starting for Cambridge at the end of January, were stimulated by Mr. Bridge, 'preacher of God's word,' who, in a sermon before them upon the text "Be of good courage, and let us play the men for our people and for the cities of our God" (2 Sam. x, 12), urged upon his hearers that good courage was requisite 'for magistrates, for ministers, and for these gentlemen that have listed their names for this great service for God and their country.'[1] The threatened danger appealed to the people of London as well, as appears by this passage in the newspapers :—

" Letters are come from Stony Stratford which inform to this effect. That forces above 1,500 are come thither for new quarters, and it is conceived will possess themselves either of both the roads of St. Albans and Hatfield, and so keep all manner of provisions of cattell from us, or else go to Cambridge and possesse themselves of that, and so wholly spoil the association of those parts, who this week offered to bring 40,000 right men into the field, had they but Arms. . . . . The great feares that the Counties East from London are in caused them to send in many thousands to Cambridge, both horse and foote ; they accounting that place a Bulwarke to the rest ; these men come to Cambridge, are very couragious, and desire to goe and see their King, and destroy his and their enimies."[2]

In this temper, towards the end of February, they marched their Volunteers, without much regard to uniforms, and with such arms as could be had, from the remotest parishes in Essex, Suffolk, and Norfolk, all meeting at Cambridge, where, with other regiments from London, the classic atmosphere of the University was sadly ruffled with the roll of drums and the blare of trumpets, and the clamour and the clatter of a huge Volunteer Army variously estimated at from 15,000 to 30,000.

Two important facts emerge from the hurly-burly and the cramming of soldiers into the College Halls at Cambridge. Lord Capel, thinking it 'more policy to dispense with honour

[1] Pamphlets in St. John's Coll. Lib., Cambridge.
[2] Special Passages.

in that service than purchase it at so dear a rate,' retired from the unequal contest and marched Westward. Oliver Cromwell had become Colonel of a regiment, and a man of no mean authority in Cambridge and the neighbouring counties. A Royalist print states that "Mr. Cromwell, one of the burgesses of the town of Cambridge, calling himself a Colonel, summoned before him divers of the commonalty of the counties of Essex, Suffolk, Norfolk, Cambridge, and Hertford, and spreading the report amongst them that Prince Rupert and his forces was at hand, urged them to join together to repulse the common enemy, 'that united forces were more proper for these times than distracted mindes.'"[1]

When the great muster of horse and foot thus suddenly called together found themselves with no adequate purpose to serve, most of them were sent back to their homes, and it is said that 23,000 of those who were disbanded engaged to be ready to march to Cambridge again at three days' notice. A thousand men were retained at Cambridge as a garrison for that place, which was to be henceforth the seat of this new-found power of numbers in the Eastern Association and an uncongenial home for the University and its traditions.

Colonel Cromwell, now in possession of Cambridge 'for King and Parliament,' with '800 horse and foot raised in the Association,' had four pieces of ordnance sent down to him by Parliament, and in the opening days of March town and University were being turned almost inside out by operations for securing the place against attack in the future. For necessary works at the Castle, and at various points along the river, the fortification of Cambridge was made the subject of an appeal to all the surrounding villages in which Cromwell's strength lay. In all parish churches around Cambridge on Sunday, March 12, there was delivered by the constables to the churchwardens, and by them to the minister, an interesting document issued from the old Committee rooms of Cambridge, which shows how strangely the duties of the clergyman and the sympathies of his

[1] Mercurius Aulicus, March, 1643.

congregation in the village church on Sunday were mixed up with the reading of warrants, appeals, ordinances, and proclamations arising from the stress of war. How this appeal was presented and responded to, is known in, at least, one instance. At Fen Drayton, near St. Ives, Constable Norris delivered the warrant from Cambridge to the 'churchwardings,' and here it is :—

"Com. Cant. (Cambridgeshire to wit). *To all and every the Inhabitants of Fen Drayton in the Hundred of Papworth.*

"Whereas we have been enforced, by apparent grounds of approaching danger, to begin to fortify the town of Cambridge, for preventing the Enemy's inroad, and the better to maintain the peace of this County :

"Having in part seen your good affections to the Cause, and now standing in need of your further assistance to the perfecting of the said fortifications, which will cost at least Two Thousand Pounds, We are encouraged as well as necessitated to desire a Free will Offering of a Liberal Contribution from you, for the better enabling of us to attain to our desired ends—viz. the Preservation of our County—knowing that every honest and well affected man, considering the vast expenses we have already been at, and our willingness to do according to our ability, will be ready to contribute his best assistance to a work of so high a concernment and so good an end.

"We do therefore desire that what shall be by you freely given and collected, may with all convenient speed be sent to the Commissioners at Cambridge, to be employed to the use aforesaid. And so you shall further engage us to be

Yours ready to serve,

Oliver Cromwell	Robert Twells, maior
Thomas Martyn	Tho. Atkinson
Terrell Jocelyn	Saml Spalding
Tho. Duckett	Robt. Robson
Robt Castell	Edward Almond
Robt Clarke	Willm. Grayve

Edward Clenche
James Thompson

James Blackley
William Welbore
Thomas Buckley
Stephen Fortune
Nicholas West
Robert Ibbett
Rich. Pettit
Richard Timbs
George Felsteed
Tho. Bert
Willm Burton

Cambridge, this 8th March, 1642 [3].

"Note—what shall be by you gathred deliver it to Tho. Noris, this bearer."

This interesting document was further endorsed apparently by Mr. Norris in true Dogberry fashion :—

"Deliver this wrighting to the Church Wardings, who are to deliver the same unto the minister or curate, to be published in the Parish Church the next Sunday after the receipt thereof, and what shal be by you collected lett it be endorced on the backside heerof, together with a declaration what is given by every partickular person, and then delivered unto Thomas Norris the bearer heirof."[1]

Whether the minister at the close of the service improved the occasion is not known, but, fortunately, at Fen Drayton the record is complete, for the endorsement shows that 'fifteen persons' out of the congregation contributed between them the sum of £1 19s. 2d., which was duly paid over to William Welbore, one of those whose names are appended to the document.

The expense of fortifications was not the only care, for that 'month's pay' which the villages of East Anglia had sent with their men to Cambridge had got exhausted, and Captain Nelson, in charge of the Suffolk men, had no money left to pay for the billet of his soldiers, and Cromwell had to write to the deputy-lieutenants of Suffolk : " Truly he hath

[1] Bowtell MSS., ii, 123.

Great Civil War. 93

borrowed from me, else he could not have paid to discharge this town at his departure." Colonel Cromwell was eager to be off into Norfolk for pressing business there, and added this postscript to his letter: "I hope to serve you on my return; with your conjunction we shall quickly put an end to these businesses, the Lord assisting."

While the Cambridge proclamation was being read in the parish churches on Sunday, March 12, Cromwell was making a forced march into Norfolk, intelligence having come in that the 'King's good subjects in Norfolk and Suffolk . . . . had drawn themselves together into a body.'[1] Cromwell, at the head of 1,000 horse, marched away from Cambridge to Norwich, 'having notice of a great confederacy held amongst the malignants of a town called Lowestoft, being a place of great consequence.' After sending out parties to Royalist houses in the neighbourhood—'returning with old Mr. Castle, of Raveningham, and some arms of his, and of others'—Cromwell, hearing that Sir John Wentworth and Captain Allen had been captured at Yarmouth on coming over from Lowestoft to change dollars, and that the town of Lowestoft was fortifying itself, he, between five and six o'clock next morning, with five troops and eighty Norwich Volunteers, marched towards Lowestoft. Near Yarmouth he was met by the Volunteers of that town, 'who brought four or five pieces of ordnance'; and here is the record of what happened at Lowestoft:—

"The town had blocked themselves up, all except where they had placed their ordnance, which were three pieces; before which a chain was drawn to keep off the horse. The Colonel summoned the town and demanded if they would deliver up their strangers, the Town, and their Army?—promising them ther favour if so; if not, none. They yielded to deliver up their strangers, but not to the rest. Whereupon our Norwich dragoons crept under the chain before mentioned; and came within pistol-shot of their ordnance, proffering to fire upon their cannoneer, who fled; so they gained the two pieces of ordnance and broke the chain; and they and the

[1] Perfect Diurnal.

horse entered the Town without more resistance. When presently eighteen strangers yielded themselves, among whom were, of Suffolk men, Sir T. Barker, Sir John Pettus ; of Norfolk, Mr. Knyvett of Ashwellthorpe, Mr. Richard Catlyn's son . . . Mr. F. Cory. . . . Mr. Brooke, the sometime minister of Yarmouth, and some others escaped over the river. There was good store of pistols and other arms ; I hear above fifty cases of pistols. The Colonel stayed there Tuesday and Wednesday night."[1]

On Friday, March 17, Colonel Cromwell, with the prisoners, and Mr. Trott, of Beccles, reached Norwich, and on Saturday the prisoners were sent off to Cambridge. Vicars says that "had this business been delayed but one day longer it would have cost a good deal of hot blood ere the town could possibly have been taken, for there were listed to have met them . . . . as many more knights and gentlemen."[2] Parliament thanked Colonel Cromwell 'for this great service,' and authorized him to dispose of the prisoners at such places as he thought fit.

The secret of Cromwell's triumphs was thus early manifest in the effectiveness of his intelligence department, the promptness of his decisions, the rapidity of his movements, and the power with which he struck home. No sooner had the Lowestoft prisoners been sent off in charge of a troop of horse to Cambridge than Cromwell, after one night's rest and a few hours for attending service at Norwich, set out on Sunday night for King's Lynn, 'because the malevolents in that town began to raise combustions there, and to declare themselves against Parliament.'[3] Riding hard all night, Cromwell and his troopers entered the town on Monday morning ; and here, as at St. Albans and at Lowestoft, promptly 'did a good service in freeing them from the danger of their Malignants by disarming them and securing the town, and

---

[1] Letter from John Cory to Sir John Potts, of Mannington, printed by Carlyle, "Letters and Speeches," i, 109.
[2] "God in the Mount," ii, 265. See the reference in the "Squire Papers" that intelligence of the affair was brought to Cambridge 'by the man that sold fish.'
[3] Certain Informations.

also seized upon a small barque with arms coming from Dunkirk.'[1]

By Wednesday, March 22, Cromwell had marched back to Cambridge, having since Sunday week ridden from Cambridge to Norwich, from Norwich to Yarmouth and Lowestoft, from Lowestoft back to Norwich, and thence to King's Lynn and back to Cambridge, besides crushing Royalist risings, and brought in Royalist gentry prisoners from various parts of the two counties.[2] Finding on his return to Cambridge some of the Essex men from Colchester ready to disband and go home for want of pay, Cromwell despatched a letter to the Mayor of Colchester, urging upon them that 'one month's pay may prove all your trouble. I speak to wise men—God direct you.'

For the necessary works at the Castle at Cambridge, houses were pulled down; and at the river bridges it was a part of the "University's Complaint" that the soldiers "have seized and taken away materials of our intended buildings of the worth of three or four hundred pounds in timber . . . . conferred towards re-edifying of an ancient college [Clare Hall], and have pulled down, demolished, and defaced five or six fair bridges of stone and timber [St. John's,[3] Trin., King's, Garret Hostel, and Queen's] and have spoiled a goodly walk with a new gate pertaining to one of our colleges [King's Coll.] upon pretence of keeping out the Cavaliers." The works at the Castle included 'rampants with three irregular bastions, and, as measured in 1802, had a height of 16 yards and a diameter of 70 feet; the whole of the earth works had acquired great solidity by means of a strong course of retentive gault and firm white clay.' On the south the entrenchment was strengthened by the great hill, and on the north was a part of the old Castle

---

[1] Perfect Diurnal.
[2] In these efforts to free the Association of its chief Royalists, Mr. Walgrave, Sheriff of Suffolk, Mr. Gosllin, Mayor of Norwich, and others were secured; and in some of the demonstrations one of the cannon in the Norwich Market Place burst and killed and wounded seventeen persons.—Bowtell MSS., ii, 126; Blomfield's "Norfolk."
[3] "H. paid to P—— H—— and others for helping about the Bridge when it was taken down by violence of the souldiers, and laying up the timber."—Bursar's Accounts, St. John's Coll., 1643.

trench, and brick buildings were erected as barracks for the soldiers.[1]

The troubles of the University did not end with the imprisonment of their dons; for since that event Dr. Holdsworth, the Vice-Chancellor, for setting Roger Daniel, the University printer, to work printing the King's Proclamations, hadbeen sent up to the Tower; and the writers of the "University's Complaint," a Cambridge book, though published at Oxford,[2] take up the tale of what was happening upon Cromwell's return from Norwich and King's Lynn. They quote the protection orders of the House of Lords, "that no person shall presume to offer any outrage or violence to the colleges or other buildings of the University,"; the similar order of the Earl of Essex, and then complain that these protections were 'blasted in the bud' by the warrant of Lord Grey of Wark, commander of the Association forces, authorizing entry into the houses of malignants, or of those that refused to contribute, and to seize upon horses, arms, etc. Of their experiences during the progress of the fortifications, they give these particulars, for which the impartial reader will make some small allowance for the source.

"Instead of carrying us all to London goals (thanks to our multitude and not to their mercy), they found a device to convey a prison to us, and under colour of fortification confined us only in a larger enclosure, not suffering any scholars to pass out of the town, unless some townsman of this tribe would promise for him that he was a *confider*, as they called it. And with this entrenchment for almost two years together (we are forced with unspeakable grief of mind to think), what profanations, violence, outrages, and wrongs our Chapels, Colleges, and persons have suffered by the unparalleled fury of rude soldiers. . . . ."

The narrative proceeds to recount what happened on March 23, and on Good Friday. "The whole Senate (the

---

[1] Bowtell MSS., ii, 126 to 129, where a plan of the works is given.
[2] "Querela Cantabrigiensis, or a Remonstrance by way of apologie for the banished members of the late flourishing University of Cambridge, by some of the said Sufferers: Oxioniæ Anno Dom. 1646."

representative body of it), being solemnly assembled in the Regent House, were there violently environed with great bands of armed soldiers, who wanted nothing but a word to despatch us because we would not vote in a matter as they would have us, though that matter did not any what concern them or their cause more than the conferring of a degree upon such a man as the whole University in their conscience judged unworthy of it. Then sundry members of the Senate were forthwith seized and imprisoned by the Committee in no better lodgings than the common Court of Guard."

It is further stated that "as Dr. Power, the Lady Margaret Public Preacher, was making his way across the Market Place he was pursued by a confused number of soldiers shouting 'A Pope! A Pope!' and vowing high vengeance if he offered to go into the pulpit, whereupon the church was straitway filled with great multitudes; and when some . . . . told them it was a University exercise and to be by Statute performed in Latin, they replied they knew no reason why all sermons should not be performed in English that all might be edified, threatening withal to tear the hoods and habits which graduates then wore according to the University Statute."

Complaint was made to Lord Grey of Wark, the Commander of the Parliamentary forces, but it is alleged that "no course was taken to prevent these growing mischiefs, and so the divine appointed by statute to preach *ad clerum* was enforced to return *re infecta*, and glad to escape so."

"And that religion might fare no better than learning in the University Church . . . . our Common Prayer Book was torn before our faces, notwithstanding our protection from the House of Peers for the free use of it; some now great one[1] encouraging them in it, and openly rebuking the University clerk who complained of it before his soldiers."[2]

Another Royalist account[3] says that "Lord Grey of Wark and Master Cromwell did . . . . deal very earnestly

[1] Cromwell is indicated in the margin.
[2] "Querela Cantabrigiensis."
[3] Mercurius Aulicus.

with the heads of Colleges to lend £6,000 for the public use, and that the motion not being hearkened unto they kept them all in custody till midnight." The writer adds that when Cromwell found them to stick to their resolution he said to a friend : " They would have been content with £1,000 or less . . . . that the people might have thought that one of the two Universities had been on their side."

As the work of defence proceeded, the scheme was enlarged so as to embrace the bridges across the Ouse in Huntingdonshire, and to raise the cost from £2,000 to £5,000. The Grand Committee for the Association sitting at Cambridge, with Cromwell foremost among them, drew up a second proclamation, and sent it out to be read in the churches on April 7. It differed in some respects from that issued a month earlier. In this later appeal it was urged that the fortification of Cambridge was 'of great concernment for a place of retreat and rendezvous in any pressing danger.' Further provision was to be made for securing the bridges across the Ouse at Huntingdon, St. Ives, Offord Mills, and some others. Upon these grounds they appealed for a liberal contribution, and the appeal was again signed by Oliver Cromwell, the Mayor of Cambridge, and others. The postscript in this case contained similar directions to the parish constable, churchwardens, and minister, as in the Fen Drayton document, with this significant addition : " To return unto us the names of all them that are rated to the poor that refuse or do not give towards so good a work."[1] The signatories include Association Committeemen not on the other—T. Barnardiston, Matthew Peckover, Maurice Barrow, Ad. Washington, Jo. Raven, and other Association men.

All this indicated the growing importance attached to Cambridge as the headquarters of the Association, and the Association Committee had their hands so full that a Sub-Committee had to be appointed to deal with affairs of

[1] Stowe MSS., 807, ff. 204-5, Brit. Mus. Lib. When the Assessment order for contributions towards the fortification of Cambridge was delivered at Norwich, "they gathered from house to house, the well affected (as they termed them) giving freely, and the rest out of fear."—Blomfield, "History of Norfolk."

lesser moment, consisting chiefly of Cambridge men. Stringent orders were issued against soldiers dealing with or pawning their accoutrements, against tippling in taverns, inns, and alehouses, or in Courts of Guard. The Grand Committee sat at the Bear next Sidney Street, and the Sub-Committee in a room 'next the Grand Committee Chamber.'[1] As for civilians, no one was allowed to go above the Great Bridge after eight o'clock in the evening or before five o'clock in the morning, and boatmen could not convey anyone by river without a ticket from the Commissioners, and without such a ticket no one could pass through a Court of Guard.

But outside the town of Cambridge stirring events were drawing Cromwell away. The Queen, returning from Holland with money from pawning the Crown jewels, had reached York, though she had on landing at Bridlington to take refuge in a ditch from the fire of the Parliamentary ships; and that association of the Catholic influence of the Queen with the 'Papists Army' under Newcastle, had begun in earnest against which the Puritans of East Anglia were destined to come into sharp conflict. Viscount Camden, another of the Cavendishes, with his headquarters at Stamford, was alarming all the Fens, and events were pointing to the great work of Cromwell in that quarter. To Sir John Burgoyne, of Potton, Beds, Cromwell wrote from Huntingdon, on April 10, this stirring appeal respecting the 'Camdeners':—" These Plunderers draw near. I think it will do well if you can afford us any assistance of Dragooners, to help in this great Exigence. We have here about six or seven Troops of Horse; such, I hope, as will fight. It's happy to resist such beginnings betimes." [2]

Alarms were coming in from all sides, of an advance of Royalists eastward towards the Associated Counties, now from Huntingdonshire, now in Hertfordshire, where 'every hose they say bought armies and gons to defend them.' The Associated Counties again rose as one man, and marched

---
[1] Printed papers in Bowtell Collection, ii, 129.
[2] Carlyle, Letters and Speeches, i, 113.

in thousands to Cambridge, the town of Sudbury distinguishing itself by sending two pieces of ordnance. Earl Grey of Wark marched away from Cambridge across Hertfordshire at the head of 4,000 foot and 1,500 horse, and joined the Earl of Essex before Reading in time to secure that stronghold before the King, with Prince Rupert fresh from the taking of Birmingham, arrived to bring it relief. To Cromwell was left the task of dealing with the 'Camdeners,' who were striking terror into the people of South Lincolnshire, 'fetching in horses and provisions for fifteen miles round.' The forces marching against them from Cambridge, 'who will make them runne in all likelihood,' and the regiment of 'stout Norfolk blades' marching by way of Wisbech and Crowland, the reader will have an opportunity of following in the next chapter.

CHAPTER VI.

THE FIRST SIEGE OF CROWLAND—THE BATTLE OF THE
PARSONS—CROMWELL AND THE FENMEN.

(1643.)

The farmers gave them ball for ball
From behind each fence and farmyard wall.
LONGFELLOW.

A ROUND Crowland, or Croyland, the quaint little citadel of the Northern Fens, the tide of the Fenmen's valour broke again and again upon the fringe of the army of 'white coats' under the Earl of Newcastle and the Royalists of Lincolnshire. Standing in the heart of 'the deepest fennes and water stagnating off muddy lands,' a Venice in miniature with its waterways and pile-driven causeways, yet full of inhabitants, and the ruins of the Abbey dominating all the rest, Crowland was in these troublous times a sad little idyll in grey, a citadel in the silent marshes. Its situation in the midst of the waters justified the proverb that 'all the carts that go to Crowland are shod with silver,' and the comparison by Fuller between Venice and Crowland—"that being cited in the sea, this in a morass and fenny ground, so that a horse can hardly come to it."

Here, again and again, the Cavaliers out of Lincolnshire gathered in defiant strength, drawing around the spot the noisy current of the war, as by boats and other marshland contrivances the siege was pressed up the crooked waterways and along causeways, up to within gunshot of the embrasured outline of the fortified Abbey itself. Clumsy drake and saker pounded away at the old venerable pile, beautiful still in its ruins, and anon, troopers fought their way over the quaint triangular bridge which still spans the site of the legendary pool of mingled waters; wild fowl rose in swarms for miles around, stirring with restless, vagrant wings the 'moist dark vapours' which brooded over the Fens. Again and again the old Abbey walls echoed the cannonade until the echoes must have stirred in their graves those venerable monks whom Turketul found here in the dark ages, and others, too, with uneasy memories of that dire vision of the evil spirits of the Fens which so sorely beset St. Guthlach [1] when he first penetrated this solitary fastness.

Out of the shadowy background of Crowland tradition, an event of intensely human and dramatic interest was shaping itself in the month of April, 1643, which probably had few parallels in the Civil War. It came about in this way. The parsons of Crowland and Spalding, like many others, took opposite sides in the strife; Mr. Styles, the parson of Crowland, being as pronounced a Royalist as Mr. Ram, of Spalding, was a Puritan. In a moment of extreme zeal, in January, 1643, Mr. Ram, seeing his neighbours of Crowland actually cutting off approaches and throwing up earthworks around their stout little citadel in the waters, ventured to remonstrate with them in a letter dated Spalding, January 31, 164$\frac{2}{3}$. In this letter Mr. Ram entreated the Croylanders to accept the advice of a friend, who, "though but a stander by, perhaps sees more than you that play the game." Further he appealed to their reason.

"Do you think that to take up arms, to make bulwarks and fortifications without commissions, to disobey all warrants and commands, are not very high contempt? Can you imagine that the Parliament or Committee of Lincoln will endure such affronts, or can you hope to defend yourselves against such forces as may easily and speedily be raised against you?

---

[1] See Dugdale's "History of the Fens" and Heathcote's "Reminiscences of Fen and Mere."

Surely your numbers and your preparations are not so great but that a small power may prevail against you! Neither is your town so inaccessible but that it may be approached many wayes: a piece of ordnance will soon command and batter down your houses, at two or three miles distance; besides, it is possible in a very short time to famish your town by cutting off all supplies of corn and other provisions. . . . . If others came to your aid Croyland is not able to receive a considerable number of men. . . . . Good neighbours! think seriously upon these things, and do not desperately ruin yourselves and your posterity, but hearken timely to the counsel of peace. . . . . Assure yourselves that if the forces at Lynn, Cambridge, Northampton, Nottingham, Lincoln, Boston, and Spalding be able to reduce to the Parliament's obedience . . . . you will not long escape them: my counsel therefore is that you will play the parts of wise men; lay down your arms and submit yourselves."

But sturdy little Crowland, confident in its strength, turned a deaf ear to Mr. Ram's counsel, while Mr. Styles, their parson, master of his little island, became more determined for the King and sought the first opportunity of repaying the parson of Spalding for his interference. The fortifications were pushed on, and parson Styles was joined by Captain Welby and by Captain Cromwell, one of the numerous cousins of Oliver, and either of Ramsey or Biggin, Hunts. Under these leaders a body of 'Croylanders' sallied out to the neighbouring town of Spalding, which was comparatively undefended; and they turned the tables upon Mr. Ram to some purpose! The story of the little drama is graphically described by Vicars and to some extent in the old news-letters, but these are second-hand compared with the narrative of Mr. Ram and his fellow prisoners, whose plain, unvarnished account of a singular episode in the war is as follows:—

"Upon Saturday, 25th March, being Lady Day, early in the morning Captaine Tho. Stiles, and Capt. Cromwell, Mr. Wil. Styles, minister of Croyland, with about 80 or 90 men, came to the town of Spalding, which at that time was utterly unfurnished with men and arms, whereof they had intelligence the evening before by some of our malignant and treacherous neighbours; near break of day they beset the house of Mr. Ram, minister of the town, where they took J. Harrington, Esq., and the said Mr. Ram, and in a violent and uncivil manner carried them away to Croyland, at the entering whereof all the people of the town [of Croyland] generally were gathered together to see the triumph over the prisoners; which put us in mind of Sampson's entertainment when he was taken by the Philistines. Some others of our town they took the same time, but released all save Edwd Horne, one of Capt Escort's sergeants; so we three were left together under strong guard, and about ten days after Mr. Wil. Slater of Spalding, a man 66 years of age, was taken by some of their scouts and made prisoner with us. Our usage for dyet and lodging was indifferent good all the time of our imprisonment, which was five weeks, but some insolencies we were forced now and then to endure. Capt. Styles one day quarrelled with us for praying together, and forbade us doing so, saying we should pray every man for himself; threatening to take away the Bible from us . . . . and by no means would permit us to have pen, ink, or paper, though Mr. Ram did earnestly sue to him for them, and protested that he would write nothing but what they should see or hear if they pleased.

"After we had been there near three weeks, on Thursday, 13 April, some companies of our friends advanced towards our relief, whereupon about eight o'clock that night we were carried down to the bulwark on the north side of the town, where we continued amongst the rude soldiers and townsmen till after midnight. But by reason that our forces fell not on that night we were carried into an alehouse, where we continued till daylight. . . . . When our companies approached nearer to the town, then we were brought forth again, and another prisoner, Daniel Pegg, of Deeping, added to us, and carried to that part of the town where the first onset was given, being all of us fast pinioned and made to stand in an open place where the cannon began to play, while we were all five of us set upon the top of the breastwork

.... where we stood by the space of three hours, our friends shooting fiercely at us for a great part of that time before they knew us. Capt. Harrington [with the attacking party from Spalding] took one of his soldier's muskets, charging with pistol powder, and himself made three shots at his own father ; he and all the rest of the soldiers from that side supposing we had been Croylanders that stood there to brave them. Their works were very strong, and well lined with musketeers who were backed with store of hassock knives, long scyethes, and such like fennish weapons, and, besides, without their works was a great water, broad and deep, which encompassed all that side of the town.

"The minister of the town, Mr. Stiles, was very active all the time of the fight on the west side of the town, where he commanded in chief, running from place to place, and if fearful oaths be the character of a good soldier he may well pass muster, which made us not so much marvel at the abominable swearing which we continually heard from every mouth ; yea, even when the bullets flew the thickest. But as the fury of the assault began to abate in those parts, so did it increase on the north side, whither presently Mr. Ram and Sergeant Horne were posted, and there set upon the bulwark, for our friends on that side to play upon, who plied us with great and small shot for a great while together, supposing Mr. Ram had been the vapouring parson of the town. Many of our dear and worthy friends [the Spalding friends who came to their relief] have told us since how many times they shot at us with their own hands, and how heartily they desired to despatch us, but the Lord of Hosts, that remembereth the hairs of our heads, so guided the bullets that of the multitude that flew about our ears .... not one of them had power to touch us, blessed be the name of our God !

"After we had continued three hours more upon the north work our forces began to retreat, and then we were taken down [from the bulwarks] and guarded to our lodgings. .... Upon this great victory, as the Croylanders vaunted, one Mr. Jackson, a minister in the town, drew the people into the Church, where he read certain collects by way of thankfulness for their good success,[1] and most part of the night following was spent in drinking, revelling, and rayling upon the Parliament and Roundheads . . . . insomuch that there was scarce a sober man to be found amongst them. The last Sabbath that we were prisoners he [Mr. Jackson] preached, and in his sermon did mightily encourage the people to play the men . . . . saying that the cause was God's . . . . that all good people of the land prayed for them . . . . that 'these holy stones pray for you, these holy books pray for you . . . . the holy vestments pray for you, that holy table prays for you,' etc."

Just when the prospects of Mr. Ram and his friends were the darkest, relief was at hand from forces under Colonel Cromwell, who had marched from Huntingdon to Peterborough with a regiment of horse, and with him was his son young Oliver, already a captain of a company though only twenty years of age; while Colonel Hobart had marched across from Wisbech way with a regiment of foot—'stout Norfolk blades.' On appearing before Crowland a drummer was sent in by Captain Dodson, but was detained, and the spirit in which the reinforcements continued the siege is shown in a letter which Colonel Sir Miles Hobart somehow got into the hands of Mr. Ram :—

"It is one of our principal ends to relieve you, and by God's assistance we will doe it or die, but Ile make your Captain speak your language and deliver you whom he so basely surprised, and if he forthwith doe it not ile spare neither man, woman, nor child ; the unworthy detection [sic] of Captain Dodson's drummer, contrary to the laws of arms, deserves no mercy, but if you well refer yourselves to me Ile doe that which befits a Christian and a gentleman ; otherwise there is nothing to be expected but the total ruin of town and people."

---

[1] Or, as Vicars has it—"Now this the wicked Croylanders took as a victory, and one Jackson, a Balaam's priest in the town, a right son of Belial, brought the Croylanders to Church and read certain collects (out of his idol service book) by way of thanksgiving for their good success, as they impiously called it."
—"Jehovah-Jireh, God in the Mount."

But the task of reducing the little stronghold was not an easy one, and it was rendered the more difficult by the heavy rains which were adding to the natural protection of deep waters around the place. How the attempt fared will be gathered from the continued narrative of Mr. Ram and his friends.

"We heard no more of our [Spalding] friends coming to relieve us till Tuesday the 25th of April, and then the town was assaulted on three sides by part of the regiments of those noble gentlemen Col. Sir Miles Hobart, Col. Sir Anthony Irby, and Col. Cromwell. When the forces advanced somewhat near the town Master Ram was again called for, and brought out of his lodgings and carried with all speed to the north bulwark, and there being very straitly pinioned, but was laid within the work upon the wet ground, where he lay for the space of five hours, often entreating that he might be set upon the bulwark by reason of the extreme numbness of his limbs . . . . but they would not suffer him. That Tuesday proved a very wet and windy day, and so continued till Thursday morning, that most of our companies were forced to quit their moorish rotten quarters and to retreat. . . . . On Thursday in the afternoon all the companies were drawn down upon the three approaches or banks, by which the town only is accessible by land, who so plied the Croylanders upon every quarter that their hearts began to fail, divers of them stealing away into the coverts and moorish ground on the East of the town, which they called Poron,[1] so famous for fish and fowl ; and many more that night followed their fellows. On Friday morning those that remained set the best face they could upon a bad business, and seemed as if they would fight it out to a man, but before daylight they moved for a treaty, which being granted they sent their unreasonable propositions, which being torn asunder and scorned, our men advanced and entered the town without opposition ; some of the chief actors got away, yet some

---

[1] The Great Porsand, which drains the North Level, in the region of Morris Fen.

The Ruins of Crowland Abbey.

were taken in the town [1]—Capt Styles and Master Jackson minister of Fleet. Of Croyland, only one was slain and one hurt. Of our men were killed five and some 18 or 20 wounded, whereof some are since dead, their wounds being incurable by reason of their poisoned bullets. .... Thus it pleased the Lord to deliver us out of our imprisonment, and miraculously to preserve those that were appointed to die." [2]

This account is signed by Mr. John Harrington, Mr. Ram, Mr. Slater, and Mr. Horne, the four imprisoned Spalding men whose capture and release led to this little siege of Troy in the heart of the Fens. The Royalists captured in Crowland were 'clapped in prison at Colchester, Ipswich, and other places.' Colonel Edward King, of Ashby, High Sheriff of Lincolnshire, appears to have been in command of the relieving force from Spalding. It happened that Mr. Styles, the parson of Crowland, was amongst those who escaped. The parson of Spalding and his fellow prisoners, after all their hard usage, found their way back to their neighbours at Spalding. Mr. Ram, the Puritan minister of Spalding, appears to have remained undisturbed afterwards.[3]

The headquarters of the Parliamentary forces which came to the siege of Crowland were at Peterborough, only a few miles away. While at Peterborough the soldiers laid rough hands upon the Cathedral,[4] and Cromwell himself paid visits to his native county to some purpose. According to a contemporary account Cromwell's soldiers made their first breach upon the great west window of the Cathedral,

---

[1] When the garrison was taken, either at this or one of its sieges, it is said "one of the town soldiers, affrighted, got up to the top of the church, above the wood wherewith it was covered, and walked along till he came to a place where wanted a board; there, whether casually stepping down (or being admonished by the soldiers calling upon him to come down) he hung a long time by the arms, till at last being a weary he fell into the Church, which is of a great height; but yet was not so dashed to pieces by the fall, but that he lived a day or two."—Gunton, " Hist. Peterborough," p. 92.

[2] Divers Remarkable Passages, etc., King's Pamphlets, Brit. Mus. Lib., E. 104 (34).

[3] Under the Act for appointing Parish Registrars in 1653, Mr. Ram was appointed for Spalding, Cowbit, and Weston; and the certificate of his appointment was signed by Mr. John Harrington, the 'religious gent' who suffered with him on the bulwarks of Crowland, and who had then become a justice of the peace. Mr. Ram was buried amongst his own people in 1656. (Extract from Spalding Parish Register, per Dr. Perry, of Spalding.)

[4] See Mercurius Rusticus.

and spoilt its 'variety of ecclesiastical history.' It is said that a few days after the despoiling of the Cathedral "a finger of divine vengeance touched Cromwell. . . . . For, being at that time quartered in the house of Mr. Cervington, commonly called the Vineyard, at the east end of the Cathedral, out of the court of which dwelling there was a passage into the churchyard, ascending by three or four stone steps, Cromwell, as others did, riding up those steps his horse fell under him, and rising suddenly under the lintels of the door, dashed his head against the lintels, so that he fell to the ground as dead, was so carried into the house, and it was about a fortnight ere he could be recovered ; those who were eye-witnesses affirmed that the blow raised splinters in his scalp near a finger's length."[1]

While engaged in this business of 'eating up the fat clergy of Peterborough,' as a news-letter described it, Colonel Cromwell paid visits to various parts of his native county and to his former neighbours. The glimpses we get show him in the exercise of a Spartan discipline towards his future Ironsides, and a rigid distinction between private inclination and public duty.

"Colonel Cromwell is for the present at Huntingdon with some fine troops, to which are added some countrymen of Huntingdonshire and other Counties ; the Enemy fled, as is conceived to Newarke, upon the noyse of him. The Colonel exercises strict discipline, for when two troopers would have escapt, he sent for them back, caused them to be whipt at the Market Place in Huntingdon, and, being before dismounted and disarmed, he turned them off as Renegadoes. The motion of my Lord Grayes is of like eminence, for when at Cambridge the troope of one Captain Riches would not advance upon command, he caused them all to be environed, and commanded them to dismount, otherwise they should be shot, which they did, and then being disarmed they were discharged as refractories, and other more right to the cause mounted in their roomes. . . . . As for Cromwell he hath 2,000 brave men, well

---

[1] Gunton's "Peterborough," p. 92.

disciplined: no man swears but he pays his twelve pence ; if he be drunk he is set in the stocks, or worse, if one calls the other 'Roundhead' he is cashiered ; insomuch that the countries where they come leap for joy of them, and come in and join with them. How happy were it if all the forces were thus disciplined."[1]

A serious reflection upon Cromwell's humanity while in Huntingdonshire, if it were supported by any less partizan authority than the ultra-Royalist print in which it appeared, was the following :—

"It was this day advertised by letters out of Huntingdonshire that Colonel Cromwell hath committed many barbarous outrages in several parts of that county, robbing and spoiling all men of what sort soever whom he was pleased to style malignants ; and in particular, that having made great havoc among the orthodox clergy of those parts, he came at last to the house of one Master Wilson, an ancient and painful minister, whom he handled in so rough and rude a manner that a son of his, being then in the house (who also was in holy orders), was forced according to his natural duty to make intercession for his father, and amongst other motives which he laid before him told Cromwell that the wheel might turn, and he might stand in need of that mercy which now was in his power to show. At which Cromwell became so furious and impatient that he told him he would spoil his preaching, and presently caused him to be hanged up and bored his tongue through with an hot iron."[2] I have found no confirmation of this improbable story in other Royalist prints of the time.

Of more personal interest than the foregoing was Cromwell's visit to Sir Oliver Cromwell, his Royalist uncle at Ramsey, as described by Sir Philip Warwick, who visited the old knight some time afterwards. Sir Oliver told him that when his nephew Oliver visited him with a good strong party of horse he asked him his blessing, and that the few hours he was there " he would not keep on his hatt in his presence ;

[1] Special Passages, April and May, 1643.
[2] Mercurius Aulicus, May 7, 1643.

but at the same time he not only disarmed but plundered him, for he took away all his plate."[1]

With his 2,000 well-disciplined, brave men, the beginning of the famous Ironsides, Cromwell, on May 12, was 'marching against Newark'; or rather for the general rendezvous at Grantham, for which the 'stout Norfolk blades' who came to the relief of Crowland had been lying 'conveniently at Spalding.' On May 13, in the evening, occurred that skirmish before Grantham, so graphically described by Cromwell himself:—

"It was late in the evening when we drew out; they came and faced us within two miles of the town. So soon as we had the alarm we drew out our forces, consisting of about twelve troops—whereof some of them so poor and broken, that you shall seldom see worse; with this handful it pleased God to cast the scale. . . . . After many shots on both sides we came on with our troops a pretty round trot, they standing firm to receive us; and our men charging fiercely upon them by God's providence they were immediately routed and ran all away, and we had the execution of them two or three miles. I believe some of our soldiers did kill two or three men apiece in the pursuit."[2]

"The whole fortune of the Civil War," says Gardiner, "was in that nameless skirmish" in which "a body of Puritan horsemen had driven twice their number before them as chaff before the wind."

While Cromwell was leading his Puritan horsemen in that first victorious charge, efforts were being made to maintain the supremacy of Parliament in his native county, in the Isle of Ely, and at King's Lynn. In the latter town the Mayor was struggling with desperate odds against the overwhelming influence of Royalist neighbours by inviting the deputy-lieutenants "one day in a weeke to dinner at the towne charge."[3]

The Royalist gentry who were troubling the town were Sir Hamon le Strange and his sons, of Hunstanton Hall,

[1] Warwick's Memoirs, pp. 251-2.
[2] Carlyle, Letters and Speeches, i, 118-9.
[3] Lynn Corporation Records.

Sir Charles Mordaunt, Lord Allington, Sir Robert de Gray, and others, whom Parliament authorized the Mayor and Justices to search for and apprehend and convey them to Parliament, or to the Castle at Wisbech. In the Isle of Ely, where the future Ironsides, Captains Fleetwood, Whalley, and Desborough, had been empowered to seize malignants' horses and arms, etc., there was a little adventure in the city of Ely on a Sunday which is thus described by the Association Committee sitting at Cambridge, writing to the deputy-lieutenants of Essex : " On last Sabbath they sent a troop of the Lord General's horse and two companies of foot of their own volunteers, with four of their own commissioners, to Ely, whither they put down some disturbances." The vigorous measures of Cromwell before marching into Lincolnshire, and the needs of the county, resulted, a few days later, on May 26, in the County of· Huntingdon being added to the Eastern Association. Henceforth the great task for the Association and its forces was to secure the County of Lincoln by sweeping the Camdeners from the Fens, crushing the whitecoats under Newcastle, and co-operating with Fairfax in the north.

Cromwell, still in Lincolnshire, was bent upon the great work of securing that county, now fighting, now writing urgent appeals for money—one of them to far-away Essex, to send more men to check the Marquis of Newcastle and his six thousand foot and sixty troops of horse, and money. " Lay not too much upon the back of a poor gentleman who desires, without much noise, to lay down his life and bleed the last drop to serve the cause and you." Cromwell's appeal to Essex was supported by the Association Committee at Cambridge, on the ground that three Companies had been taken away from Cambridge, that Cromwell wanted Sir John Palgrave's regiment from Wisbech, but more especially because the Queen was on her march with 1,200 horse and 3,000 foot, and if reinforcements were not sent the Cambridge garrison might mutiny and disband, and 'ten brave pieces of ordnance, almost mounted for service, besides a good fort . . . . be a prey to the enemy.[1]

[1] Barrington MSS.

This was at the end of May and the beginning of June, when the Parliament's outlook began to be depressing, for a temporary advantage of Fairfax at Wakefield was followed by the tidings of Chalgrove Field. Here 'the Roundheads fought as they had never fought before,' but against superior numbers. On June 18, the great warrior patriot, John Hampden, is riding off the field 'with his head bowed low over his horse's neck,' and bearing in his shoulder the wound which England will feel to-morrow. After six days' suffering at Thame he breathed out his patriotic soul in the prayer—"Save my bleeding country . . . . let the King see his error. O Lord, save my country!" The shock of that event vibrates in ever-widening circles, far into the Eastern Association, where men speak with bated breath on the one side and ill-concealed triumph on the other. In the parsonage house at Cheveley, near Newmarket, for instance, Robert Levett, the Royalist parson, greets John Raby, of Newmarket, as he enters the room, with a knowing accent in the usual query of the times, "What news?" to which Mr. Raby replies, "We hear there is a lord or great commander slain," and Parson Levett rejoins, "He is a Roundhead; 'tis well he is slain, thereby he hath escaped a hanging."[1] Into Essex the tidings spread with increasing interest, for Anthony Nicoll writes to Sir Thomas Barrington, of the Essex Committee:—"Poor Hampden is dead, and I profess to you I have scarce strength to pronounce that word. Never kingdom received a greater loss in one subject; never man a truer and faithfuller friend!"[2] Hampden himself, in one of the last letters he ever wrote, had written to Sir Thomas, appealing through him for the support of the Essex people:—"The power of Essex is great, a place of most life of religion in the land; and your power in the country is great, too. The difficulties of this war need the utmost of both." Truly a great leader had fallen in this famous cousin of Cromwell, to whom even Clarendon gives this handsome testimony:—"When this Parliament began the eyes of all men were fixed upon

[1] Minutes of the Committee for Scandalous Ministers.
[2] Barrington MSS.

him, as their Patriæ Pater, and the pilot that must steer the vessel through the tempest and rocks which threatened it ; and I am persuaded his power and interest at that time was greater to do good or hurt than any man's in the kingdom, or than any man of his rank hath had in any time, for his reputation for honesty was universal."

The depressing effect of Hampden's death was increased by other circumstances. The Earl of Essex, Lord General for Parliament, wanted to resign, and Sir Thomas Fairfax, shut up in Bradford, had to cut his way out, and after a weary march, wounded and sore, reached Hull, his own wife being left a prisoner with the army of Newcastle, and his own child being left behind dying, as was believed, by the wayside, though afterwards recovered. The Marquis of Newcastle now had nothing but Hull and Cromwell's flying squadrons between him and his design upon the Eastern Association; the Queen was marching from Newark, Sir William Waller had been beaten in the West, and the Earl of Essex was hanging along the borders of Bedfordshire, with Prince Rupert threatening, and his own resolution wavering, until Londoners raised the taunting query whether he was afraid to fight the Queen as well as the King! In despair Parliament sent Commissioners to the Scots for aid, and it seemed for the moment as if everything was hanging upon what could be done in the Fens by the small handful under Cromwell.

By the middle of July the town of Cambridge was able to report, "our town and Castle are now very strongly fortified, being encompassed with breastworks and bulwarks,"[1] and all passes through the Fens were being watched and strengthened. From Ely, demi-culverin were being dragged across the Fens to Wisbech to fortify the Horseshoe Pass; and at the Hermitage Pass, near Earith, where the Ouse enters Cambridgeshire, Tyrrell Jocelyn, a member of the Hunts Committee, surrounded by alarms, bravely held out hopes of being able to keep the post 'for a week.' Thus far Huntingdonshire had had enough to do to defend itself,

[1] Bowtell MSS., ii, 135.

without contributing much to the Association, and Parliament, recognizing that the county 'now become the frontier of the Associated Counties,' was enforced to make extraordinary provision of horse and foot to safeguard itself, 'against the incursions of the plundering enemy,' allowed the county to collect its weekly assessments, and, for the time being, apply the same to the defence of the county.

It was on July 18, that intelligence came to Huntingdon and Cambridge of the hot work upon which Cromwell was entering around Stamford, with the 'Ca'ndishers,' or Camdeners, under the Hon. Charles Cavendish, Viscount Camden. The Huntingdonshire scouts came riding in hot haste to the Committee at Huntingdon acquainting them that 'this night at two o'clock they received intelligence from Peterborough that the King's forces, 400 in number, appeared before that town.' It is to this incident that the stirring letter, attributed to Henry Cromwell, son of Colonel Cromwell, in the "Squire Papers" refers. , Colonel Cromwell was on the borders of Northamptonshire ready to fall back upon Stamford ; Colonel Palgrave's regiment was lying about Whittlesea, ready to defend Peterborough.

"To Captain Berry at his Quarters, Whittlesea. These, in all haste. 18th July, 1643.

"There is great news just come in by one of our men who has been home on leave. The Ca'ndishers are coming on hot. Some say 80 troops, others 50 troops. Be it as it may we must go on. Vermuyden has sent his son on to say we had better push on three troops as scouts, as far as Stamford ; and hold Peterborough at all costs, as it is the Key to the Fen, which if lost much ill may ensue. Our news says Ca'ndish has sworn to sweep the Fens clear of us. How he handles his broom we will see when we meet; he may find else than dirt to try his hand on, I think ! Last night came in letters from the Lord General, also money, and ammunition a good store.

"Our men being ready we shall ride in and join your troop at dawn. Therefore send out scouts to see, also good intelligencers on foot had better be sent after ; they are best, I find, on all occasions. Hold the Town secure ; none go in or out on pain of law of arms and war.—Sharman is come in from Thrapston ; there was a troop of the King's men driving, but got cut down to a man—not far from Kettering by the Bedford Horse, and no quarter given, I hear.

"Sir, this is all the news I have. My Father desires me to say pray be careful ! Sir, I rest
Your humble Servant,
Henry Cromwell."[1]

The Cavaliers, 'from Bever [Belvoir] Castle and Newark,' were driven from Peterborough by Colonel Palgrave, and retired to Stamford, 'whither they called in the country and began to fortify apace; but it pleased God to send Colonel Cromwell to them from Northampton side, or Rockingham, with six or seven troops and some foot.'

Of the proceedings before Burghley House, the Committee at Huntingdon, writing to the Essex Committee on July 19, with a pardonable pride in their distinguished neighbour, say :—

" Our scout now returned from Stamford tells us that this morning early noble Colonel Cromwell, Col. Hobart, with Col. Palgrave, set down before Burleigh House by Stamford (wherein was 2 colonels, 6 captains, with about 200 horse and 300 foot). At the first setting down Cromwell sent a trumpet to summon the Cavaliers with offer of free quarter, to leave only the place and their arms. Thereto the Cavaliers returned they would neither give nor take quarter, but would fight it out to the last man. Whereupon the Colonel caused the ordnance to play upon the House, but a few hours proved no good would be done that way. Whereupon our Colonels caused their musketeers in three squadrons to draw up to the House ; that in a little time the Cavaliers sounded a parley. Whereupon the Colonel sent to the ——— not to kill a man more upon pain of death. In this manner the house, all the commanders and soldiers, were taken with all arms and whatever else, and

---

[1] Carlyle's "Letters and Speeches of Cromwell," i. Unless Noble and otherrs are wrong about the respective ages of Cromwell's children, this letter, with its ather stilted language, from a beardless youth of fifteen, tells rather against the authenticity of the Squire Papers.

not above 6 men slain on both sides. And while this was doing the Colonel sent out Captains Dodson, Wauton, and Disbrow, to meet with 400 of the enemy, and had notice were going to assist the Cavaliers. Captain Dodson being first in with them was wounded and beaten from his horse, but rescued by Captain Wauton, and then together falling upon the rabble slew above 50 of them and wholly dispersed and routed the rest."[1]

There is, I am told, a tradition at Stamford that when Cromwell was about this stirring business of the storming of Burghley House, he stayed with a Miss Wingfield, a relative of his, and on her entreaty did not destroy the house. It is also related, as an instance of Cromwell's gallantry to Royalist ladies, that in connection with the taking of Burghley House, he presented a painting of himself, by Walker, to the widowed Countess of Exeter, which is still preserved at Burghley.[2]

The majority of the prisoners taken at Burghley were sent to Cambridge, where during this Summer the University had lamented "how our scholars daily grow desolate . . . . how in our colleges our numbers grow thin and our revenues short . . . . how, frighted by the neighbouring noise of war, our students either fled their gowns, or abandoned their studies, how our degrees lie disesteemed."[3] But if they neglected their studies, the scholars, at any rate, interested themselves in the Royalist prisoners, and added to the troubles of the Committeemen, as the following letters will show :—

"Cambridge Committee to Sir Roger North and the rest of the Committee of the Associated Counties :—
"Noble Gent,
"Colonel Cromwell having sent about 200 Cavaliers into Cambridge, taken at Burghley House, we thought fit to send them to London to be disposed of by your approbation and wisdom, either by land or sea, because it is not unknown to you that the town of Cambridge is malignant

[1] Barrington MSS.
[2] Fenland Notes and Queries.
[3] Petition of University, Lords' Journals, vol. vi, pp. 80-1

enough, and we fear the sickness has much dispersed about the Spittle House end, and our garrison weak, so as to continue them here would be both a danger and charge to the town and consequently to the whole Association.
"Cambridge the 27th of July, 1643."

The Committee for the Associated Counties also wrote to the Speaker in a similar strain, and complaining of the commanders among the prisoners holding correspondence with the scholars, and growing 'bold and insolent.'

They sent up 224 prisoners to London, and among them the Sheriff of Rutland, and also Captain Welby, of Gedney, one of the leaders in the night surprise and capture of the parson of Spalding. Welby was committed to the King's Bench, and, in 1649, was pleading that he had been in the King's Bench six years, 'in great want.' In that year he was allowed to compound, and pay a fine of £100.

From Stamford Cromwell and his forces marched towards Gainsborough, and near that place he met the handsome young General, Lord Cavendish, at the head of an advanced part of Newcastle's army. A sharp engagement ensued, of which Cromwell, having got back to Huntingdon, on July 31, gave these graphic particulars to the Suffolk Committee :—

"When we all recovered the top of the hill we saw a great body of the enemy's horse facing us, at about a musket shot or less distance, and a good Reserve of a full regiment of horse behind it. We endeavoured to put our men into as good order as we could. The enemy in the meantime advanced towards us, to take us at disadvantage, but in such order as we were, we charged their great body, I having the right wing. We came up horse to horse, where we disputed it with our swords and pistols a pretty time, all keeping close order, so that one could not break the other. At last they, a little shrinking, our men perceiving it, pressed in upon them, and immediately routed this whole body, some flying on one side and others on the other of the enemy's Reserve; and our men pursuing them had chase and execution about five or six miles.

"I perceiving this body, which was the Reserve, standing

still unbroken, kept back my Major, Walley, from the chase; and with my own troops, and the other of my regiment, in all being three troops, we got into a body. In this Reserve stood General Cavendish, who one while faced me, another while faced four of the Lincoln troops, which was all of ours that stood upon the place, the next being engaged in the chase. At last General Cavendish charged the Lincolners, and routed them. Immediately I fell on his rear with my three troops; which did so astonish him that he gave over the chase, and would fain have delivered himself from me. But I, pressing on, forced them down a hill, having good execution of them; and, below the hill, drove the General with some of his soldiers into a quagmire, where my Captain-lieutenant slew him with a thrust under his short ribs. The rest of the body was wholly routed, not one man staying upon the place."[1]

But this event only brought the victorious troopers in sight of the main army under Newcastle, lying regiment behind regiment, in formidable array. There was nothing for it but to retire; Gainsborough could not be held, and the task of freeing Lincolnshire of the Cavaliers seemed as far off as ever. Lord Willoughby was obliged to give up Lincoln, and, having got into Boston, wrote to Cromwell at Huntingdon these despairing words :—

"Since the business of Gainsborough the hearts of our men have been so deaded that we have lost most of them by running away. . . . . So that now I am at Boston, where we are very poor in strength, so that without some speedy supply, I fear we shall not hold this long neither. . . . . If you will endeavour to stop my Lord of Newcastle, you must presently draw them [the forces] to him and fight him. For without we be masters of the field we shall be pulled out by the ears one after another." He urges Cromwell to hasten the foot to Boston, "for if the enemy get that Town, which is now very weak for defence for want of men, I believe they will not be long out of Norfolk and Suffolk."

---

[1] Carlyle, Letters and Speeches, i, 124.

From Huntingdon Cromwell, on the receipt of the above, immediately sent off to the Committee at Cambridge the following rousing epistle :—

"Huntingdon, August 6th, 1643.

"Gentlemen,

"You see by this enclosed how sadly your affairs stand. It's no longer Disputing, but out instantly all you can! Raise all your Bands [Trained Bands], send them to Huntingdon; get up what volunteers you can; hasten your Horses.

"Send these Letters to Norfolk, Suffolk, and Essex without delay. I beseech you spare not, but be expeditious and industrious! Almost all our Foot have quitted Stamford: there is nothing to interrupt an Enemy but our Horse, that is considerable. You must act lively; do it without distraction. Neglect no means. I am

Your faithful servant,

Oliver Cromwell."[1]

Cromwell, in his letter to Essex, whence the men had refused to march to Cambridge, 'some because it is harvest and some desiring more pay,' wrote "hast, hast, post hast!" as follows :—

"You see by this enclosed the necessitye of goinge out of our old pace. You sent indeed your part of the 2000 foote, but when they came they as soon returned. Is this the way to save a Kingdom? Where is the doctereine of some of your countye concerninge the traynd bands and other forces not goinge out of the Association, I wish your force may bee ready to meete with the enemie when hee is in the Association. Hast what you can; not your part only of 2000 foote but I hope 3000 foote att least. Lord Newcastle will advance into your bowells. Better joyne when others will joyne and joyne with you then stay till all be lost; hasten to our helpe. The enemie in all probability wil be in our bowells else in ten dayes; his armie is powerfull. See your men come and some of your gentlemen and ministers come along with them that so they may be

[1] Baker MSS., xxxiv, 429.

delivered over to those shall command them, otherwise they will returne at pleasure. If we have them att our armie wee can keepe them. From your faithful servant."[1]

Two days later Cromwell was at Peterborough sending all available Foot to Spalding, and again appealing to the Committee at Cambridge to send on more Horse to Huntingdon and to him—"gentlemen, make them able to live and subsist that are willing to spend their blood for you!"

With the powerful army under Newcastle still unbroken, with King's Lynn ready to declare for the King, with the fall of Bristol and Parliamentary reverses in the West, with caricatures of the inactive Earl of Essex and his pipe and his glass, chalked on the walls in London; and women wearing white ribbon pelting the soldiers and clamouring for peace at the door of Parliament, it seemed as if there were nothing left to sustain the popular cause but the Puritan pulpits and Cromwell's cavalry charges. Almost the only thing in which Parliament could take comfort was in thanking Colonel Cromwell for his 'faithful endeavours to God and the Kingdom'; and, unless this small leaven of valour in the Fens could be spread over a wider area, there seemed little hope of greater success in the future.

[1] Barrington MSS.

CHAPTER VII.

A PURITAN COMMANDER—HOW THE ESSEX MEN CAME
IN—THE SIEGE OF KING'S LYNN.

(1643.)

" When thou goest out with the host against thine enemies, keepe thee then from all wickednesse. . . . . Be valiant and fight the Lord's battells."—*The Souldiers Pocket Bible.*

THE 10th of August, 1643, marked a new departure in the prosecution of the War for Parliament, which now began to turn its attention to the one part of its forces whose valour had known no defeat, and to the lesson which Cromwell's successes were teaching. It was not to this date that we must look for any actual enrolment of the Ironsides. They had been emerging from the 'sorrowful confusion' of the times with every step in Cromwell's method of rejecting 'the tapsters and decayed serving men' in favour of men having a conscience in their work. But it was the first broad recognition of the valour of a few men who were the salt of what now seemed everywhere else to be a losing cause. It was, therefore, a time for heroic measures, and the act of the Earl of Manchester in stepping down from the dignified position of Speaker of the House of Lords into the thick of the campaign at such a critical juncture was one of those personal sacrifices which give a crowning touch to the heroic principle whereever it is struggling for dear life, as it was just then in the Fens. A Puritan of the Puritans, and yet a nobleman of great territorial influence, when the Earl of Manchester took up his commission [1] as commander of the Association forces it gave something of an éclat to the measures which were to follow.

To make the new arrangement more significant, Cromwell, one of the four Colonels under the Earl, was given the command of the Horse in the counties of Huntingdon, Cambridge, and the Isle of Ely; and, with Manchester at last coming down amongst his own people, there was a degree of confidence and resolution which promised to bear fruit in the impending crisis. But commanders were of little use without men, and Parliament added ordinance to ordinance until the levies upon the Associated Counties called for 10,000 men to defend 'the true Protestant Religion,' against 'idolatry,' Papists, and 'other dangerous persons.'

For the better ordering and disposition of men and money coming in from the Eastern Counties, there was a fresh appointment of Committeemen to sit upon the Grand Council for the Association at Cambridge. Most of the members appointed had done similar duty before; but the appointment of trusty men in place of the wavering made a new departure. The rules and instructions laid down for their guidance also bring into clearer view the functions of this Grand Council of War than is done by any previous order. Seven of the Council were to form a quorum, providing there was one present from each of the Associated Counties. The delegates came up to Cambridge by turns, two from each county, for a period of fourteen days' duty, receiving 35s. per week for the service. If more than the two appointed from each county were present they had power to vote, though it was not their turn; and Members of Parliament for the Associated Counties had a seat on the Committee *ex officio*. The instructions provided that the Grand Committee were to assemble at Cambridge, and, 'in these times of imminent danger, to use all diligence to promote the service they were entrusted withall.' They were further enjoined :—

[1] The old Parchment granting the Earl his 'commission as Major-General of the Association Forces' is still preserved in the Manchester Papers in the Record Office.

"That they have a special care of all the frontiers, that the Isle of Ely be supplied with fitting forces to resist all sudden surprizes and invasions, and shall from time to time send out scouts to discover in what manner any enemy approacheth near to the frontiers. That the said Committee shall order and dispose of all the Associated Forces . . . . and, if more forces are wanted, to give notice to the deputy-lieutenants, and that every County may see their forces paid, and that a Register be kept of all the proceedings of the Committee."[1]

They had also to see that no stranger entered Cambridge or the Isle of Ely without a certificate of good affection from four of the deputy-lieutenants of the County whence they came. They had also to see that the Committees of individual counties did their work in sequestering estates of 'malignants.' They commenced their duties under special difficulties, owing to the demand for labour in the harvest field; but the approach of Newcastle's army, with all the hurly-burly of actual war in the Fens, was a more pressing evil than the delay of harvest work.

On August 14, the Earl of Manchester sat as Speaker in the House of Lords, and then, having obtained leave to take Mr. Ashe, a member of the Westminster Assembly of Divines, with him as his chaplain, he departed for Cambridge to take up his duties as Commander of the Association Army, leaving to Lord Grey of Wark, the former commander, to take up his place as Speaker in the House of Lords.

The new Association Committee lost no time in getting to work, and their first act was to welcome the new Commander of their forces by this resolution: "That the Earl of Manchester shall have as great entertainment as Major-General of this Brigade of the Associated Counties as any Major-General hath that is at this present in the service of Parliament."

While Parliament, with the assistance of the counties of the Association, was organizing the material power and resources of the Eastern Counties, there was another kind of

[1] Lords' Journals, vi, 176-7.

weapon being prepared in some obscure alley in the city of London, which was destined to have an immortal share in the valour of the Ironsides. The efficient service of sword, musket, and pike in the sinewy arms of the Fenmen meant a great deal if their region was to be kept clear of the " Papists " under Newcastle, but no Puritan armour would be complete which took no account of the "sword of the Spirit," for those select men under Cromwell who were to know no fear but the fear of God. The tradition that every man in Cromwell's Ironsides was provided with a pocket Bible, which has come down to us as an accompaniment of Puritan valour, is now a matter of definite history. Mr. George Livermore, of Cambridgeport, Massachusetts, was, it appears, the first to discover the fact that the Bible, which every man in Cromwell's army 'carried in his knapsack, and daily read and sang praises to God,' was not the whole Bible, but "the Souldiers Pocket Bible," consisting of appropriate quotations from the Scriptures, 'printed in pocket form, which was generally buttoned between the coat and the waistcoat next the heart.'

Exactly one week before Parliament introduced the great movement for the organization of the Eastern Counties, this famous "Souldiers Pocket Bible" was issued in readiness for serving out to every man in the legions who were going forth under Manchester and Cromwell. The " Souldiers Pocket Bible " was edited by Edmund Calamy, a noted Puritan, minister of St. Mary, Aldermanbury. A facsimile of the title-page is given on the opposite page.

There are only two copies of this famous little book now known to be in existence. One of these is preserved in the British Museum and the other is in the United States of America. The former bears the endorsement by Thomason, the collector of the King's Pamphlets, next the printed year 1643, of "Aug. 3rd," apparently as the date of publication, which brings us actually to within seven days of the great scheme for placing the East Anglian forces under the new Puritan Commander and the special appointment of the grand council at Cambridge. The book is a small octavo of sixteen pages, including the title-page. All the texts are

THE
SOULDIERS
Pocket Bible :

Containing the most (if not all) those places contained in holy Scripture, which doe shew the qualifications of his inner man, that is a fit Souldier to fight the Lords Battels, both before he fight, in the fight, and after the fight;

Which Scriptures are reduced to severall heads, and fitly applyed to the Souldiers severall occasions, and so may supply the want of the whole Bible; which a Souldier cannot conveniently carry about him:

And may bee also usefull for any Christian to meditate upon, now in this miserable time of Warre.

Imprimatur, *Edm. Calamy:*

*Jos.*18. This Book of the Law shall not depart out of thy mouth, but thou shalt meditate therein day and night, that thou maist observe to doe according to all that is written therein, for then thou shalt make thy way prosperous, and have good successe.

Printed at *London* by *G.B.* and *R.W.* for
Aug: 3 G.C. 1643.

selected, with the exception of two, from the Old Testament, and are such as refer generally to battle and victory, and intended to nerve the soldiers for the strife. The texts are arranged in groups, with appropriate headings by the Editor, such as — " The Souldier must not doe wickedly," " The Souldier must pray before he goe to fight," " The Souldier must be valiant for God's cause," etc., etc.

Of this famous little book a modern soldier has said :—

" In my humble opinion the soldier who carries this Bible in his pack possesses what is of far higher value to him than the proverbial marshal's baton, for if he carries its teaching in his head and lets it rule his heart and conduct he will certainly be happy and most probably eminently successful." [1]

If this can be said of it from the modern point of view, it is not difficult to realize how powerfully the terse, pointed commands, prophesies, and promises in the book, influenced those men of stern Puritan mould who were being raised in these harvest months of 1643 for the great effort to thrust back the tide of hostile forces which were steadily flowing into the Association under the Catholic Queen's favourite commander, the Marquis of Newcastle.

By the side of this equipment of Scripture text and pike and gun, Parliament sent down into the counties of the Association some of the most doughty champions among the Westminster Assembly of Divines, to 'stir up the people to rise for their defence.' In trumpet tones these famous Puritan preachers fanned the enthusiasm of East Anglians to enrol themselves under the banner of Parliament. That the " Souldiers Pocket Bible " and the discourses of the orators from the Westminster Assembly of Divines were charged to the full with the battlecries of the Old Testament, with but little of the spirit of the New, does not, I think, warrant the suggestion that this supreme effort to rouse the Eastern Counties against a 'Popish Army' was a mere seventeenth-century proclamation of the Gospel of hate. At any rate, the

---

[1] Lord Wolseley in the Preface to the Facsimile of the book published by Mr. Elliot Stock.

"Souldiers Pocket Bible" was a special compilation for a special purpose.

"A souldier must not doe wickedly; doe violence to no man; nether accuse any falsely, and be content with your wages; lean not to thine own wisdom; a souldier must crie unto God in the very instant of the battell; fear ye not them which kill the body; when thou shalt go forth to war against thine enemies and shall see horses and chariots moe than thou, be not afraid of them, for the Lord thy God is with thee."

These were the commands and marching orders, and these the principles of conduct, which were to hold so sternly and influence so mightily the men of East Anglia in that wider organization of their forces which now seemed imperatively necessary if the Cavaliers were to be kept any longer out of their borders. With this Soldiers' Pocket Bible in their knapsacks the rude yeomen of the Fens went forth in the spirit of the old Maccabæan epic, responding to 'the pleasing dreadful call,' and believing verily that it was 'the cause of Heaven, a noble cause,' in which 'justice with courage is a thousand men.'

How the position of affairs moved the people is shown by the voluntary efforts of those who were exempt from assessments, the young men and maidens whose zeal had been acknowledged by Cromwell a week before this memorable 10th of August. They had evidently conceived the idea of raising a company of foot of their own, but Cromwell, knowing the need for cavalry, suggested raising a troop instead.

"Huntingdon, 2nd August, 1643.

"Sir,

"I understand by these Gentlemen the good affections of your young men and maids; for which God is to be praised. I approve of the business: only I desire to advise you that your 'foot company' may be turned into a troop of horse; which indeed will, by God's blessing, far more advantage the Cause than two or three companies of foot; especially if your men be honest, godly men, which by all means I desire. I thank

God for stirring up the youth to cast in their mite, which I desire may be employed to the best advantage; therefore, my advice is that you would employ your Twelve-score Pounds to buy pistols and saddles, and I will provide four-score horses; for £400 more will not raise a troop of horse. As for the muskets that are bought, I think, the country [county] will take them of you. Pray raise honest, godly men, and I will have them of my regiment. As for your Officers I leave it as God shall or hath directed to choose; and rest,

"Your loving friend,
Oliver Cromwell."[1]

About the same time the City of Norwich afforded a somewhat similar instance of the raising of a 'Maidens' Troop,' thus referred to by Wallington: "The virgins of Norwich, hearing of the Cavaliers' violent outrages committed upon their sex wheresoever they get the victory, are so sensible of their reputations that they have readily contributed so much money as hath raised a goodly troop of horse for their defence, which is called 'the Maidens' Troop.'"[2]

The motive for extraordinary exertions was ever present in this month of August, on the 11th of which the Committee of Cambridge was urging "the approach of the northern forces so near threatening to all that ought to be dear unto us" as a reason for a full meeting of the deputy-lieutenants of the Association at Bury St. Edmunds, to resolve upon means "to stop, if not repel, so formidable, yet Popish enemy." Ships laden with Danes were reported off the Norfolk and Suffolk coast, and Parliament raised its demand for levies from the Associated Counties to 20,000 men, 'with gunners, trumpeters, and chirurgeons.'

By August 16, the Earl of Manchester had got to Cambridge, and was receiving a presentation of fish from the Corporation. He was in command of 4,000 foot and 1,500 horse, already come in from the Association. Towards the latter end of August the Huntingdonshire Committee were in terror about a report of Cromwell and his forces being required to march

[1] Carlyle, Letters and Speeches, i, 127-8.
[2] Historical Notices, ii, 171.

westwards, and urged the Earl of Manchester to "have a care of many thousands of souls that if the forces be gone are likely to perish by the 30 troops of horse that the Earl of Newcastle hath in Lincolnshire." Cromwell was about Peterborough and Boston, and the Earl of Manchester was at Norwich, and the Associated Counties had "already completed an army of about 8000 horse and foot, and so soon as their harvest is once over (which for the present much retardeth their proceedings), the Earl of Manchester will doubtless have a very brave and considerable army as any in the kingdom, to be a terror to the northern Popish army if they march southward."[1] Out of Norwich they are limbering up their old demi-culverin and fauconets—a brass demi-culverin weighing 4,800 lbs., one of iron weighing 3,400 lbs., and fauconets of lesser weights—and hauling them across to King's Lynn,[2] where Sir Hamon le Strange has got the upper hand of Mayor and Corporation, and himself installed governor, with Lady Alice keeping him company, promising to advance thousands of pounds, and that twenty others shall raise as much more. Captain Poe, skirmishing around with some Essex troops, wrote home that, "if relief from the sea can be prevented, they cannot hold out more than five days, altho' they have 40 pieces of ordnance, and can get more from their ships. He is informed that the enemy in Lynn have 1200 muskets, and 500 barrels of gunpowder."[3]

The way in which some of the Essex men came in for this service at the siege of Lynn and in Lincolnshire preserves something of the distinction, even in the Association forces, between the men after Cromwell's own heart deserving the name of Ironsides and the miscellaneous levies pressed into the service in a great emergency. The result of the extraordinary demand for men in harvest-time is well illustrated by the response made by the county of Essex. A Puritan county, it had sent out men of a fine stamp as volunteers, but when it came to pressing men, on such a large scale, for

[1] Perfect Diurnal.
[2] Blomfield's " Hist. Norfolk."
[3] Letter in Barrington MSS.

service at the farthest corner of the Association, with the influence of the Lucas family of Colchester still operative, and Sir Charles fighting with Newcastle for the King in Lincolnshire, Essex recruiting and the Essex men sent in were of an indifferent character. The particulars which follow are to be found chiefly in the Reports of the Historical MSS. Commission—Report No. 7—dealing with the MSS. now in the possession of the Lowndes family at Barrington Hall, Essex.

The Essex men were coming in in driblets and in a ragged and tattered condition, which led to some interesting correspondence between the Association Committee at Cambridge and the Essex Committee.

"Cambridge, Aug. 31.—The Association Committee to Sir Thomas Barrington and the rest of the deputy-lieutenants of Essex :—Some companies of foot are sent hither from you, but in so naked a posture that to employ them were to murder them. Their demands are arms, coats, clothes, and shoes, wherein how far you are engaged to them by promise, or how far by the common use and custom, we do not certainly know ; but things of necessity, as weapons, arms, drums, and colours, must be had, and that at the charge of your county. If not sent at once there will be a mutiny. The magazine at Cambridge affords them not . . . . The future rendezvous of all Essex foot is to be at Chesterton (a small mile wide of Cambridge), with direction to send to the writers [the Association Committee at Cambridge] for further order to march."

Another letter adds—"We have provided red coats for such as we have sent away of yours ; we shall trust to you to furnish the rest and to send them with arms, drums and colours, and other accutrements."

A few days later Sir William Harlackenden writes to Sir Thomas Barrington from Cambridge :—"There is great stir among the soldiers for coats and shoes and money. Sir W. Rowe has persuaded me to let them have coats and some shoes, and he has bespoken 200 coats, which will cost 12s. each. I never saw worse tattered soldiers for the General. Many foot captains are so poor they are forced to have money. The treasury is very low : be pleased to send a supply, and so every week. I was yesterday with Col. Cromwell at Ely, at dinner, to let him know Lord Manchester's pleasure by word of mouth, that Essex forces shall come up, horse and foot, towards Lincolnshire. Col. Cromwell told me yesterday he sent away all his forces towards Lincoln, and his self would march this day. For his scouts brought word of 8000 of the Earl of Newcastle's forces appeared. I pray God it be not true."

Edward Berkhead, writing to Cambridge from the "Dragoon's Den," at Romford, of the desperate efforts he had made to get the Essex men off, frankly says, "if fair-play will not force the malignants, foul will," and he adds that he has "crowded through all difficulties to send away the forces." Writing to Sir Thomas Barrington, he declared that "It took a saddler ten days to mend the old saddles. The country brought in such trash that two-thirds were unfit for service. . . . . I never saw such indisposition in men to the service in my life. . . . . I think we must have another troop to force these out, but I hope this day to send them packing."

Sir Thomas Nightingale to Mr. Middleton at his house at Stansted writes that "he has received warrant that this small town shall find three nags with muskets and able riders. . . . . Besides, we are to find men well affected to the Parliament, but where we shall find them God in Heaven knows; for we do not. As for the men . . . . if my life lay on it I know not where to get one, much less the town three. So this piece of a town must find four, and Clavering, which is three times as great a parish, find but four." [1]

The Earl of Manchester, having 'gotten within musket shot of the town of Lynn,' wrote concerning the Essex forces

---

[1] There are glimpses in the MSS. at Barrington Hall of three poor constables in Essex who complain "that altho' they have impressed men the men will not obey the warrants, the constables being poor men ; they ask for authority to charge persons better than themselves to assist them." But the constable, as the visible authority of Parliament within the parish, must be taught that the warrant of Parliament must be supreme, and so the pathetic little document is endorsed—' The constables fined at £10 a piece.' Yet the constables had real obstacles to contend with, as in the father of one Christopher Jellson in the same county, "who did resist us [the constables], and said he 'should not com exsept th depty leaftennants came and fetcht him themselves.'"

which had reached him :—" I have here divers men sent out of Essex, and as many of them I believe are run away as are come ; and those whom you have sent have no arms, clothes, nor colours, nor drums. I earnestly entreat you to send arms and other provisions with those men you send, or else I pray send no more. . . . . Hasten hither all the force you can with money and arms, for otherwise they are by far more dreadful to me than any enemy."

Harlackenden sits down again with his pen and writes home to his neighbours in Essex, winding up with this eloquent appeal :—" Your labours I doubt not shall be rewarded from Heaven, your names clothed with honour on earth, and your posterity receive eternal mercy. . . . . There are 200 coats ready for the soldiers. The poor soldiers long for them, and the time of year calls for them."

At the same time Cromwell was urging his select method in a letter to Suffolk :—" I beseech you be careful what Captains of Horse you choose . . . . a few honest men are better than numbers. . . . . If you choose godly, honest men to be Captains of Horse, honest men will follow them, and they will be careful to mount such. . . . . I had rather have a plain russet-coated Captain that knows what he fights for, and loves what he knows, than that which you call 'a gentleman' and is nothing else. I honour a gentleman that is so indeed."

Meanwhile affairs in King's Lynn had come to a head, and the Earl of Manchester, with 3,000 horse and 1,500 foot, 'blocked up the passages to the town by land, and the Earl of Warwick did the like by sea.' The members for the town, Mr. Toll and Mr. Percival, were imprisoned, or confined to their own houses with soldiers guarding them. A Royalist newspaper[1] commended the inhabitants of the town of Lynn, who "like honest subjects and true Englishmen have kept his lordship out of their town, telling him flatly they kept the town for his Majesty, and by the help of God would so keep it against whomsoever, which they are able to do being so strongly fortified that Kimbolton may as soon raise

[1] Mercurius Aulicus.

his good father from the dead as force his entrance into Lynn." The same writer in the next issue adds the assurance that "his lordship has as much hope of Heaven's gates as to enter into Lynn."

With the Earl of Manchester, Colonel Cromwell and Sir Miles Hobart had 'gone to sit down before it,' Captain Poe having previously taken possession of all the bridges between Downham and Lynn. "It was much disputed whether it were not better to proceed by blocking up rather than to take it by force, the town being of that strength that no ordinary power could take it had they that which was fit for defence;' but it was at last resolved to take it by force, and for that purpose it was thought good to seize the town of Old Lynn, which is in Marshland, which by a party of my Lord's force was securely taken and ordnance planted, which kept the town in continual alarm and did so terrify the people with their shot and granadoes that they durst hardly abide in any of their houses that were towards that side; the shot flying daily into the houses in the Tuesday market-place and other places. The town was approached in several other places, two of which were on the side next to the moat, the one by the Causey [? causeway] that leads to the south, the other to the East Gate."[1] An alarming incident in these operations is thus recorded:—

"On Sunday the 3rd of September in the afternoon, and in the middle of the sermon, came a shot of 18 lbs. weight in at the window over the west door of St. Margaret's Church and took the middle pillar a great part off and broke it in many hundred pieces, dispersing them in all directions all over the church. One piece of the stone fell into a seat at the lower end of the church, where five men set, split the board before them, on which they laid their books; but no harm was done to them. The preacher, a reverend divine named Mr. Hinson, left his sermon and came out of the church, and all the people departed in a most confused manner; some leaving their hatts, some their books, and some their scarves; but, praised be God, no further hurt was done to any person."[2]

---
[1] A Brief and True Relation, E. 67 (28).
[2] Richard's "History of Lynn," vol. iii, pp. 758-9.

The news-letter already quoted continues :—"We resolved upon storming the town on Saturday morning, and to that purpose had called in many boats, with which we intended to take it by water, and many cartloads of ladders, which we intended for the land side. . . . . During this hot service we lost four men. . . . . One lieutenant had his arm shot off. . . . . It was with a cannon shot through the porthole; so skilful were they that they would shoot three times into one porthole. In this violent playing with cannon and small shot we believe above 80 lost their lives on both sides."[1]

Another account says that "Colonel Cromwell hath battered them sorely from Old Lynn, the shooting of whose ordnance hath slain divers men, women, and children, and that the lamentable shrieks and cries of women and children are heard a great way out of the town, and yet the townsmen are so cruel and hard-hearted to them that they will not suffer them to depart the town; that the Army's forces have cut off their fresh water, and that the townsmen have felled all the trees about this town to bereave the Earl's Army of approach and shelter; that the Lynn ships are in league with Newcastle."[2] On the same date *Mercurius Civicus* writes of Colonel Cromwell having "battered down part of the market place, and some houses in New Lynn."

Finding that the storming of the place was to take place on the Saturday morning, and that the Earl had advised them to send the women and children out of the town, a treaty was accepted. The town demanded that it should be left with its own government as hitherto; that the fortifications should be demolished, and that 'malignancy' should be pardoned. The Earl replied by reminding them that they had received the disaffected, disarmed and imprisoned the well-affected, including members of the House of Commons, and had used money and arms collected for Parliament to defend the town against the Parliament. "Yet, to prevent effusion of blood, if they will deliver the town by Saturday nine in the morning, they shall have privilege and freedom;

[1] E. 67 (28).
[2] Certain Informations, Sept. 7.

as for freedom from Ordinances of Parliament, they must expect no such thing."

While the conditions of surrender were being debated from seven at night till eight the next night, 'a dinner time only excepted,' the town, 'or rather the unruly soldiers,' shot at the besieging forces, 'contrary to accord, and fell to work upon their works.' One account says that "some of the townsmen issued out and begun to cut the banks to let out the water, whereof seven were slain by the besiegers and set up naked against the gate near the town, whom the Lynners may see, but dare not come out to bury them."[1] The result of the twenty-four hours' debate was carried to the Mayor, when there were some 'explainary exceptions' and debating as to throwing open the gates. During this parleying the Parliamentary Horse and Foot were drawn out in imposing array into the meadows, and 'put into such posture as might be most terrible to the enemy, making a large front when God knows what depth they stood!' Then, 'with beating drums and sounding trumpets, as if we had been presently to march into the town,' Colonel Russell, who had the van, with Colonel Walton in the rear, marched on foot to the East Gate, when he was informed that the season of the night would not permit the opening of the Great Gate, and they 'must therefore be content to march one by one at the wicket.'

As the conquerors were about to enter, the Commissioner came back to the wicket and told them that "there was a rude multitude . . . . that swore none should enter there, and if any did they would be the death of them . . . ." There was a parley of nearly two hours, "some saying articles must be performed, others that they would not condescend nor obey, nor should the Mayor and Commissioners' acts bind them, crying 'shoote! shoote!' and one cannoneer they turned out because he would not give fire upon us. At last one of them cried 'give fire!' which being in the dead of night made some of the countrymen and others on horseback [spectators riding by the side of the foot soldiers] to fall off

[1] Certain Informations.

their horses, and some into the ditch, so terrible was the word 'give fire!'"

At last they were allowed to enter, and in their passage through the town to the Tuesday market-place "not one man appeared, only the women who for the General cried 'God bless us!' whether for fear or love you may guess." Next morning the Earl of Manchester marched from his headquarters, 'with his life-guard, a brave troop' and 'did repair to the sermon, where one of his chaplains [Mr. Ashe] preached to give God thanks for his happy and peaceable entry.' The Earl, says the account I have quoted, "made his headquarters at the house of Alderman Toll, the member of the House of Commons, who was so roughly dealt with in the time of the siege that he was constrained to make an escape out of a window into the arm of the sea, his house being guarded in all parts by musketiers. . . . . Colonel Walton hath for the present the government of the town: thus we see how Providence orders; he that was lately locked up three days and three nights at Oxford in a poor chamber without food, is now governor of as great and strong a town as Oxford." [1]

The conditions for the surrender of the town were agreed to between the following Commissioners: for the Earl of Manchester—Sir John Palgrave, Colonel Russell, Colonel Walton, Mr. Philip Calthrop, Mr. John Pickering, Mr. Gregory Gawsell, Mr. John Spilman, and Mr. William Good; for the town—Sir Hamon le Strange, Sir Richard Hovell, Mr. Clench, Mr. Dereham, Mr. Pallet (Recorder), Mr. Hudson (Mayor), Mr. Leek, and Mr. Kirby, who were to remain as hostages until the conditions were performed.[2]

Cromwell's share in the siege of Lynn was confined to the earlier stages, and before it ended he marched away with his Horse for pressing service in Lincolnshire. It is apparently to this period that the tradition belongs which is recorded in Watson's "History of Wisbech," published in 1827:—"At Needham Hall, the residence of Mr. William Dow,

---

[1] "A Brief and True Relation of the Siege and Surrendering of King's Lyn, etc.": King's Pamphlet, Brit. Mus., E. 67 (28).
[2] Rushworth, v, 283.

at Elm, three miles distant from Wisbech, is preserved an ancient table of oak (entirely of one solid piece) which is rendered remarkable by the circumstances of Oliver Cromwell having reposed on it one night; and there is now living in the parish of Elm a person far advanced in years who well remembers his grandfather saying that, when he was a boy, he saw Oliver Cromwell and his troops pass by the avenue leading to this hall; and that the person then inhabiting the mansion offered to Cromwell his best bed, which he declined, observing that perhaps the next day he should have to sleep in the open field, therefore, in preference, he chose to pass the night on this very table. Such of his officers as could be accommodated were supplied with beds, and the rest of his troops took shelter in the outbuildings and premises. The term the old man used was that this occurred during the time Cromwell was 'ransacking the Fens,' and that he made a building called the Nine-Chimney House, at Emneth, the adjoining village to Elm, his headquarters, which spot is now in the occupation of Mr. John Graham Dow, whose house stands near the site of the old building."

Cromwell had at this time almost completed his regiment of 1,000 horse, which he raised 'in and about Cambridge' (Bowtell MSS.), and what use he made of them will be seen presently.

CHAPTER VIII.

THROUGH LINCOLNSHIRE TO MARSTON MOOR.

(1643-4.)

THE capture of King's Lynn removed a thorn from the Parliament's side, but there still remained the formidable task of driving back Newcastle's legions out of Lincolnshire, completing the strategy upon which Cromwell was bent, of uniting with Fairfax in Hull, and thus bar further advance of the Cavaliers from that quarter. The letters of the Queen to Newcastle show clearly that the King desired him to lead his army southward through the Associated Counties, and that he was only restrained by the fact that Hull and Fairfax could not be left unheeded.[1] In support of this Fairfax himself says that "his [Newcastle's] orders (which I have seen) were to go into Essex and block up London on that side."[2] This, again, is confirmed by a curious story told by one of Sir Samuel Luke's scouts, who, taken prisoner in Windsor Forest, was carried off to Oxford. Here he heard that the King's commission had been given to go into Essex with 8,000 foot, ten troops of horse, and 1,200 dragoons, with Sir John and Sir Charles Lucas as generals of Horse. He also heard that " 10,000 hands in Essex were ready to stand with them when they marched"; that they had men come every week out of Essex informing them how every man

[1] Firth's Lives of the Duke and Duchess of Newcastle.
[2] Short Memorials.

stood affected, one of whom came in the guise of a pedlar and brought horse-hair and tobacco on his back.[1] That the Marquis of Newcastle was expected, by the people in the Fens, to perform his part of the design, is clear from this certificate of Captain Dodson, of Wisbech :—

"To whom this may concern : The information of Richard Rose, given to me at Wisbech immediately after the siege of Lynn at my coming from thence to my only quarters at Wisbech as followeth :—

" Mr. Wilson and Mr. Lee being in discourse near Rose's shop, there came to them John Riches [or Richards], an apothecary, who, seeing Captain Dodson coming into the town, said : ' Look, yonder comes that rogue Dodson. I could find it [in] my heart to knock his brains out; he will never be killed else'; and Mr. Lee did reply wishing him to be patient awhile: 'there was one a coming, a doctor, who would let them all bleed in good, and he would do it to the purpose. . . . . He meant Newcastle, who would be here and let them bleed in the right vein.' Upon the advance of the Enemy I did secure the person of this John Riches and some ill-affected persons in Wisbech Church, until the danger of fight was passed, which God blessed with the victory, whereupon I released the said John Riches, and he confessed he said the aforesaid words. . . . . Thus far I can say in this business and no further. Witness my hand, March 12th, 1643 [4].

"William Dodson."[2]

This gossip of the Wisbech shopkeepers helps us to realize how the expected march of Newcastle's forces impressed the Fenmen. While the business of Lynn had been in hand, the Lord-General, the Earl of Essex, had made his notable march, at the head of 15,000 men, to the relief of Gloucester. Returning towards London, with the King's army hanging on his rear, he had to fight the Battle of Newbury on September 20, with doubtful success. In this engagement

[1] Barrington MSS.
[2] Minutes of Committee for Scandalous Ministers, in the case of Thomas Lee, rector of Newton, near Wisbech, Add. MSS. Brit. Mus. 15,672.

the great Lord Falkland fell, with the cry of "peace! peace!" on his lips. The removal within three months of two men like Hampden on the side of Parliament and Falkland on the side of the King was indeed a great national loss. But while Falkland's pathetic cry of peace died on the wind, Hampden's fall had left behind a heritage like that of Harper's Ferry and the consciousness among his followers that "his soul goes marching on."

On September 11, Cromwell, just after leaving his home at Ely, with the Earl of Manchester still before Lynn, had written to Oliver St. John respecting his troops and his difficulties :—

"I am now ready for my march towards the Enemy; who hath entrenched himself over against Hull. . . . . Many of my Lord of Manchester's Troops are come to me; very bad and mutinous . . . . *they* paid to a week almost; *mine* noways provided for to support them, except by the poor Sequestrations of the county of Huntingdon. My troops increase. I have a lovely company; you would respect them did you know them. They are no Anabaptists; they are honest sober Christians; they expect to be used as men! . . . . I desire not to seek myself . . . . I tell you the business of Ireland and England hath had of me, in money, between eleven and twelve hundred pounds. . . . . You have had my money: I hope in God I desire to venture my skin. So do mine. Lay weight upon their patience, but break it not! Think of that which may be a real help. I believe £5000 is due. If you lay aside the thought of me and my letter, I expect no help . . . . all will be lost if God help not! Remember who tells you."

By September 26, two notable events had happened. Cromwell had joined Fairfax in Hull, and was assisting in getting his twenty-one troops of horse across the Humber into Lincolnshire, where they could be of service. Parliament had taken the solemn League and Covenant—220 of them— and the Scotch condition of assistance being complied with, they were raising another expedition to march into England. Cromwell and Sir Thomas Fairfax, after a perilous march across Lincolnshire, began that companionship in arms which was to alter the face of the war.[1] In this march they were hard beset by the forces of Newcastle; but in the end Cromwell was able to write to the Suffolk Committee on September 28 :—" If God had not been merciful [the enemy] had ruined us before we had known of it. . . . . But we got to horse, and retreated in good order, with the safety of all our Horse of the Association. . . . . And for this we are exceedingly bound to the goodness of God, who brought our troops off with so little loss." A junction of the forces of the Earl of Manchester from Lynn with Cromwell and Fairfax's Horse, and the force under Lord Willoughby of Parham, now made up a very considerable army in readiness for the conflict which was inevitable.

But the condition of the Foot under the Earl of Manchester was far from satisfactory. The Essex men were still a cause of trouble, and those about King's Lynn and Boston were in a sorry plight. On October 2, Harlackenden, their treasurer, had got as far as Lynn to see for himself what their condition was, and he writes thus :—

"The Captains here are in great want of money. Colonel Cromwell tells me he wept when he came to Boston and found no moneys for him from Essex and other counties; he says he regards money as little as any man, but for his troops if they have not money speedily they are in an undone condition. He says he wonders how I will be able to see the troops of horse and dragoons and have no money for them."

In another letter he mentions the need of coats for the men, 2,100 in number, and that they must be 'of green cloth lined with red.'

At last the county of Lincoln had been formally joined to the six other associated counties (September 20), but the question of making the union a reality depended upon the two armies now drawing near to each other along the river

---

[1] Harlackenden, the Essex treasurer, says that the messenger that brought the news of Fairfax getting his Horse out of Hull and joining with Cromwell, "received it at the hand of Lady Fairfax in a favour, the motto 'rather dye than truth deny.'"—Barrington MSS.

Witham between Boston and Horncastle. The Earl of Manchester, Willoughby, and Cromwell met with Fairfax at Horncastle, a few miles off, and the forces were soon face to face with the Cavaliers under Sir John Henderson in the battle of Winceby, near Horncastle, which is thus described by Vicars :—

"All that night [Tuesday, October 10] we were drawing our horse to the appointed rendezvous, and next morning being Wednesday, my Lord Manchester gave order that the whole force, both of Horse and Foot, should be drawn up to Bolingbroke Hill. . . . . The Enemy also drew . . . . their whole body of Horse and Dragooners into the field, being 74 colours of Horse and 21 colours of Dragoons, in all 95 colours. We had not many more than half so many colours of Horse and Dragooners; but I believe we had as many men. . . . . The Enemy's word was 'Cavendish,' and ours was 'Religion.'[1] . . . . So soon as our men had knowledge of the Enemy's coming they were very full of joy and resolution. . . . . Our men went on in several bodies singing Psalms. . . . . Colonel Cromwell fell with brave resolution upon the Enemy, immediately after Dragooners had given him the first volley, yet they were so nimble as that within half pistol shot they gave him another. His horse was killed under him at the first charge and fell down upon him; and, as he rose up, he was knocked down again . . . . but afterwards he recovered a poor horse in a soldier's hands, and bravely mounted himself again. Truly, this first charge was so home-given and performed with so much admirable courage and resolution by our troops that the Enemy stood not another . . . . and thus, in less than half an hour's fighting, they were all quite routed."[2]

About 600 were slain, and 'many drowned in the chase; 114 were found in the water and mires next day; also about 7 or 800 taken prisoners.'[3]

On the same day the forces in Hull had sallied out. There was a tough fight over the trenches, men and arms were lost

[1] Rushworth says the words were "Newcastle" and "Peace and Truth."
[2] "God's Ark overtopping the World's Waves," p. 45.
[3] "The Scottish Dove," Oct. 3-20.

by Newcastle, including the twin cannon "Gog and Magog," also known as the "Queen's Pocket pistols"; and Newcastle marched away in the night-time and abandoned the siege.

Meanwhile the state of things at the headquarters at Cambridge was disheartening enough. The garrison had been depleted for the service in Lincolnshire, the delegates from the various counties were neglecting to attend the Association Committee, and, to crown all, Prince Rupert's horse were riding into Bedfordshire and threatening Cambridge itself. Captain Jordan, governor of the Castle, declared that fifty barrels of powder were required, for the store 'would not last above three hours' fighting.' The ditch about the Castle was going on slowly, and without it the place would be of 'little value,' but with it 'impregnable.' With the Oxford forces within a few miles, plundering at their pleasure, and the number of malignant scholars and others in Cambridge, Captain Jordan declared 'as a soldier' that if the enemy made a breach in there, all the Associated Counties and London itself would be endangered.[1]

The Cavalier forces had captured and begun to fortify Newport Pagnell, had carried off two of the Bedfordshire Committee from their meeting-place at Ampthill, and captured the town of Bedford. Sir John Norris had sent out his warrants for the Trained Bands to come in to defend Bedford, but 'as not above 18 men' came in he was obliged to give up the town. Sir John was taken prisoner, but made his escape, which was accompanied by this curious incident. Marching towards Hitchin with some of his force, a rumour spread into the town that the Cavaliers were coming, 'which put them all in alarm as far as Hartford, but they were only Sir John's troops bringing him home.'[2] Rumours spread into the Associated Counties that the King had captured Huntingdon.

In Cambridge the Royalists grew bold, and the Association Committee's members remaining sent despairing appeals to their respective counties for help. Sir William Rowe, the only member from Essex in attendance, prepared himself for the worst, and on October 18 wrote these heroic appeals :—

[1] Portland MSS.   [2] Parliament Scout, October 20, 1643.

"This morning we hear from Sir John Norwedge, by our scouts, that the Enemy entered Bedford betwixt three and four yesterday afternoon, and by night at Potton, within twelve miles of this place; so that your forces must march night and day to get into the town to relieve it. As you love religion, the laws, your country, the Church of God, and your true friend, W. Rowe. P.S.—We have certain intelligence that the design is for this place. And that there is no probability of their intent for Huntingdon, tho' the gentlemen and Committee there have given them a fair invitement by leaving it and quitting their guards; so that I think it is needless to send this message thither."

Later in the day, as the fears in Cambridge increased with the tidings coming in, Sir William sends off this eloquent dispatch to Sir Thomas Barrington :—

"If you would do a seasonable service to the State [not to speak of your friend, who is a lone and naked man here], let what help you can be instantly sent in hither. Alarums come thick and very near us, and a show would now do that which will not be redeemed but at an infinite charge. And how much the loss of this place may shake the country we love so well, and the whole Association, I appeal to you, and so throw myself and all into the arms of my Lord and Saviour; intending to live and die His servant.

"P.S.—Sending to the Officer of the Castle for some drakes to flanker our works along the river, I received this answer; that he would send none, that I had fooled him long enough, and bid the gentlemen take heed I did not fool them at the last. Judge upon these disobedient terms how I should serve you, or add any security to this place. Yet to leave it I am loath. Hoping you will not forget me."[1]

Before any help could arrive the Royalists in Cambridge were getting the upper hand; and when an attempt was made to make up a troop of horse in the town, they 'so cunningly plotted the business' that it was prevented by guarding the stable doors. Thereupon ensued a hurly-burly between townsmen on this side and on that. " Some of them

[1] Barrington MSS., Hist. MSS. Com. Rep , vii.

having got arms fell upon the prison, pulled it down, and let loose all the delinquent prisoners, and then fell upon the houses of the townsmen, crying, 'We are for the King, and for him we will fight and none other!' But at last the townsmen on the Parliament side prevailed, having killed some and wounded others."[1]

To meet the advance of the Cavaliers the Earl of Essex crossed over from Windsor to St. Albans, called out the Hertfordshire Trained Bands; the whole county rose with 'wondrous great alacrity,' and between three and four thousand met at Hitchin. They marched to Bedford, recaptured that town, drove out the Cavaliers from Newport Pagnell, and caused them to 'run away in a panic fear towards Oxford.'[2] From the Associated Counties the alarm was effectual in bringing into Cambridge a great muster of many thousands of the Trained Bands. But the service was only a temporary one, and two or three weeks later when the Earl of Manchester came back from Lincolnshire to Cambridge he dismissed 6,000 of them to their homes, leaving 500 or 600 in the garrison. Winter set in early,[3] and by the end of October, Captain Rich, describing the fortunes of the Essex men serving in Lincolnshire, wrote to Sir Thomas Barrington :—

"The winter is already come, and our lying in the field hath lost us more men than have been taken away either by the sword or bullet, notwithstanding which we are ready to persist, and unwilling to wait any opportunity of doing God honour and our country service." He adds that all the money he had he gave to the soldiers but thirty odd pounds for his own necessities in case of being sick or the like distress, and that was stolen off his horse when they lay in the field before Lincoln, and at the time of writing he had only 2s., and his troop without money, even for shoeing their horses and repairing saddles, etc. He begs that the common soldiers may be constantly paid, 'though the officers go without money at all.'[4]

[1] The Parliament Scout. [2] The True Informer, Perfect Diurnal, etc.
[3] "Nov. 6th, a hideous storm. Then snowy and untoward weather."—Evelyn's Diary. [4] Barrington MSS.

The Earl of Essex remained at St. Albans for his winter quarters with a vast army to feed ; more or less in a mutinous state for want of pay. In December 400 of the soldiers gathered together and threatened to pillage the town, and were only pacified by the presence of the sympathetic commander for whom they had thrown up their hats with an 'Eh for old Robin!' after Brentford fight. The Earl pleads hard for the men with the Committee of Safety—" My humble desire is that if there be no pay like to come by the latter end of this week, that I may know, I not being able to stay amongst them to hear the crying necessity of the hungry soldiers."

During the month of December the Earl of Manchester remained at Cambridge[1] with part of his army away in the snow about Gainsborough, 600 of his Foot sent into Newport Pagnell Garrison, and the rest 'at this present do guard St. Needs and Huntingdon and this town of Cambridge.' A glimpse of the landing of 800 Danes on the Lincolnshire coast, attacked and about fifty of them killed by the Train Bands, and the sending down of expert commanders to oppose them,[2] was the closing incident of a hostile kind for 1643. The Countess of Manchester was in Cambridge with the Earl, and a Christmas present of the value of £4 4s. from the Corporation to her Ladyship, was a reminder that amidst all the unnatural strife that golden thread which the season of peace and good-will has ever run through the home life of Christian England was not entirely broken when this lamentable year of 1643 came to its close.

Through the depressing months of the closing year, with soldiers billetted in the Colleges,[3] the University had been

[1] Matthew Peckover, alderman of Norwich, wrote from Cambridge on 16th November, 1643, to the Mayor of Norwich : " After my service presented these are to give you notice that the Earle of Manchester cam upon fryday night to Cambridge, and intends to quarter all this wynter at ye Mr [Master's] lodgings in Trynity Colledge."—MSS. Collections relating to Norwich, Add. MSS. 22,619, f. 137, Brit. Mus. Lib.
[2] A True Information, etc., E. 83 (8).
[3] The billetting of soldiers appears to have been general in the Colleges, of which the Audit Books of Jesus College contain entries. There are also entries in the Parish Registers of the burial of soldiers at this time, as at St. Edward's 9, at Little St. Mary's 5, at St. Benedict's 5, at All Saints' 2, and 5 at St. Clement's, besides " many others deposited in the Castle yard."—Bowtell MSS., ii, 136.

chafing against its fetters. Petitions went up to Parliament to be freed from sequestration; and one contemporary writer actually suggested, as a remedy for the distractions which kept the students away from Cambridge, that a place of study 'in a collegiate way' should be established in London. Trinity College petitioned the House of Lords urging that by reason of their estates being scattered in distant and remote counties they had been "bereaved of their rents," and in some cases sequestrators had distrained upon their Michaelmas rent and driven away their cattle, "albeit some of the said tenants had before that paid the same unto us."[1]

The Earl of Manchester supported these petitions by a friendly letter addressed to the Speaker in the Lords:—

"By virtue of the Ordinance of Sequestration, the Sequestrators for the town of Cambridge have sequestered all the lands and profits belonging to those Colleges which did convey their plate to the King. This is likely to breed a great distraction in the University, by reason that the Fellows and Scholars of those Colleges must be driven to very great extremities, having no other livelihood or subsistence. I shall not take the boldness to offer anything of my own sense to your Lordships, for I doubt not your Lordships, in your wisdoms, will think it better to endeavour the reforming of the University, rather than to hazzard the dissolving of it."[2]

Parliament at last issued orders protecting the University and Colleges from the sequestration of property held by them as corporate bodies, but set the Earl of Manchester the task of making them orthodox.

Colonel Cromwell, in the lull which a snowy Winter imposed, spent some time with his wife and family at Ely, and in his position as Governor of the Isle, turned his attention to the ceremonial still retained in the Cathedral services, though the Bishop was away in the Tower. Having a force of soldiers ready to obey his behests, he, on January 10,

---

[1] The College accounts for these years, which I have seen, afford evidence of considerable arrears of rents, and also of conflicts between the claims of the sequestrators and the College as to rents.
[2] Lords' Journals, v, 327.

gave expression to his views of the choir-service still kept up at the Cathedral, in the following characteristic letter addressed to Mr. Hitch, one of the Canons :—

"Ely,
"10th January, 1643.

"Mr. Hitch,

"Lest the Soldiers should in any tumultuary or disorderly way attempt the reformation of the Cathedral Church, I require you to forbear altogether your Choir-service, so unedifying and offensive—and this as you shall answer it, if any disorder should arise thereupon.

"I advise you to catechise, and read and expound the Scripture to the people; not doubting but the Parliament, with the advice of the Assembly of Divines, will direct you further. I desire your sermons, too, where usually they have been, but more frequent.

Your loving friend,
Oliver Cromwell." [1]

But Mr. Hitch did not feel inclined to give up, at the bidding of his powerful neighbour, his choir-service in favour of the joint product of Parliament and the Westminster Assembly of Divines; and so the visit of the soldiers, plainly hinted at by Cromwell, took place.

The effect of the visit, as recorded by Walker, shows the commanding influence which Cromwell was able, as citizen and soldier, to bring to bear upon his neighbours. "Notwithstanding this letter, Mr. Hitch continued to officiate as before. Upon which Cromwell, with a party of soldiers, attended by the rabble, came into the church in time of divine service, with his hat on, and, directing himself to Mr. Hitch, said: 'I am a man under authority, and am commanded to dismiss this assembly'; upon which Mr. Hitch made a pause; but Cromwell and the rabble, passing up towards the communion table, Mr. Hitch proceeded with the service: at which Cromwell returned, and, laying his hand upon his sword in a passion, bade Mr. Hitch to 'leave off

---

[1] Carlyle, Letters and Speeches, i, 145.

his fooling and come down,' and so drove out the whole congregation."[1]

The passing of the strictly disciplined troops of Manchester and Cromwell into Lincolnshire had brought out by contrast the more lax conduct of the forces there under Lord Willoughby of Parham, whom Cromwell accused of dereliction of duty and of encouraging the bringing in of young women as camp-followers. Sir Christopher Wray, a Lincolnshire Committeeman, defended Lord Willoughby, and three of Wray's sons inflicted a good cudgelling on one of Manchester's officers, and Willoughby himself actually challenged the Earl to fight a duel. Colonel Boynton and Colonel Pickering carried a message to the Bar of the House of Lords, who acted the part of peacemakers between the parties, and, enjoining them not to prosecute their differences any further, released Lord Willoughby from temporary custody.[2]

On January 31, a "remonstrance" was sent from Newark to the King on the condition of Lincolnshire. "All that county (excepting the little garrison of Belvoir) is now in possession of the Rebels, where they hold Lincoln, Gainsborough, Brigg, Tatshall, and Bolingbrook Castles, and that seditious town of Boston, as garrisons well fortified; and are able to draw together out of these garrisons above 5,000 armed foot, besides twenty troops of horse. . . . . And we cannot but expect that the whole confluence of Manchester and Cromwell's forces, and what can be raised from the Associated Counties, will be poured down more upon us if not otherwise diverted by other forces from your Majesty."

Meanwhile the Scots had crossed the border, 'up to their knees in snow.' The Solemn League and Covenant was being taken in the parish churches of East Anglia by the parishioners—standing up in the church uncovered, 'lifting up their right hands bare,' and then signing the same—and

---

[1] "Sufferings of the Clergy," part ii, p. 23. See the letter in the "Squire Papers" in which Cromwell, on a backwardness of some in the 'reforming' business, is represented as saying: "I heed God's House as much as any man; but vanities and trumpery give no honour to God, nor idols serve Him, neither do painted windows make man more pious. Let them do as Parliament bid them, or else go home."

[2] Lords' Journals, vi, 415.

in place of the old Committee of Safety a Committee was formed for both kingdoms, with powers and a responsibility to Parliament akin to the modern Cabinet. The King had summoned his Parliament at Oxford, and many members of Lords and Commons at Westminster had joined it, some to remain and others to come back repentant. Royalist families were leaving their ancestral homes and crowding into Oxford, living in mean apartments, and brightening up their straitened situation with splendid acts of devotion and romantic vicissitudes. Cromwell had taken the Covenant on February 5, and at the beginning of March was again in the saddle marching across Buckinghamshire, capturing Royalist houses, including Hilsden House, and many prisoners, some of whom were sent to Cambridge. Concerning the reception of these troops at Cambridge, the old Royalist "Querela" furnishes these indications :—

"When the King's prisoners, taken at Hilsden House, were brought, famished and naked, in triumph by Cambridge to London, some of our scholars were knocked down in the streets only for offering them a cup of small beer to sustain nature, and the drink thrown into the kennel, rather than the famished and parched throats of the wicked, as they termed them, should usurp one drop of the creature ; and it is much to be feared they would have starved them in prison there if a valiant chambermaid (Mistress Cumber's maid) had not relieved them by force, trampled under her feet, in the kennel, their great persecutor, a lubberly Scotch major."[1]

By the 10th of March Cromwell, 'having driven the Cavaliers into Banbury Castle,' and brought the sound of his trumpets within hearing of Oxford itself,[2] was back again at Cambridge, defending Lieutenant-Colonel Packer against complaints of his Major-General Crawford. "Sir, the State, in choosing men to serve it, takes no notice of their opinions ; if they be willing faithfully to serve it, that satisfies." In

---

[1] "Querela Cantabrigiensis."
[2] "One of Cromwell's trumpeters blew so hard that he put old Duppa into a fit of the cholick," is the irreverent remark of one of the Parliamentary newspapers ; the allusion being to Bishop Duppa of Chichester, who had retired into Oxford, and was ' very much with the King till his execution.'

these and similars words, Cromwell thus early showed his tolerance of views already objectionable to those with leanings to Presbyterianism—the Earl of Manchester and his Major-General Crawford among the number.

When, by the month of March, the movement of troops became practicable there was issued from Cambridge a stimulating pamphlet, " A Catalogue of remarkable mercies conferred upon the Associated Counties."[1] This was appointed to be read in the churches within the Associated Counties as a thanksgiving and means of stimulating the zeal of the inhabitants. This 'Catalogue' includes the 'quenching of the fire at Lowestoft'; 'the reducing of Croyland, which was a place strong by situation, and which had a professed Papist Governor'; the taking of Burghley House; the taking of Lynn, the victory at Winceby, and the taking of Lincoln and Gainsborough. For all these ' mercies' the thanks of the people were called for, "not for vain ostentation, nor that any honour should be given to any person, but that by commemorating these particulars your hearts may be enlarged and quickened in sincerity, to give God the glory due alone to Him " ; and " when we again go out we desire your prayers to the Lord, professing our trust to be in His name, and our rejoicing in hope that we shall have His presence to go along with us."

A few days before this the Hertfordshire people had petitioned Parliament against 'the intolerable burden of free quarter' of the Earl of Essex's huge army, seventeen weeks in their midst without pay ; and there were signs of tiring of the burdens. Peace overtures were brought forward, but like other attempts nothing came of them, and the Spring opened with the prospect of renewed hostilities on a larger and more decisive scale than had hitherto been possible. The Eastern Counties men, united with Fairfax, and with Leslie marching southward with the Scots, were now first in the public mind. The Earl of Manchester's army was reported to be 15,000 strong. " Neither is his Army so formidable in number as exact in discipline ; and that they

[1] E. 39 (13), Brit. Mus. Lib.

might be all of one mind in religion as of resolution in the field, with a severe eye he hath looked into the manners of those who are his officers, and cashiered those whom he found to be in any way irregular in their lives or disaffected to the cause. This brave Army is our violets and primroses, the first fruits of the spring, which the Parliament sends forth this year for the growth of our religion and the re-implanting of this kingdom in the garden of peace and truth."[1]

Before these preparations for the great crisis in the War had been completed, Cromwell had sustained a bitter loss in the death of young Oliver, who had served with him for eighteen months. The exact circumstances of his death are not known; but there is very good reason to believe that he died of small-pox, and probably while on those marches into Buckinghamshire which resulted in the taking of Hilsden House. "Col Cromwell has gone . . . . from Buckinghamshire to Stony Stratford and Brickhill, and begins to increase in power. He hath lost his eldest son, who is dead of the small-pox in Newport, a civill young gentleman and the joy of his father."[2] The other reference to the same event is in the "Squire Papers"—"Meeting Cromwell again after some absence, just on the edge of Marston Battle, I thought he looked sad and wearied, for he had had a sad loss; young Oliver got killed to death not long before I heard; it was near Knaresborough and 30 more got killed." Considering the ease with which direct intelligence could be obtained in London from Newport Pagnell, and that the reference in the "Squire Papers" is three or four months later than the news-letter, and only hearsay at that, I think the first account quoted is to be preferred.

One of the first effects of the method of Manchester and Cromwell in securing the survival of the fittest to fight in the Association Army, and of the successes already achieved by Cromwell, was to arouse a spirit of jealousy in other quarters. The Earl of Essex, although nominally the commander of all the forces for Parliament, saw his army drifting into a second place. The Parliamentary cause in the West

[1] Weekly Account.   [2] The Parliamentary Scout.

was in such a bad way that the Earl declared: "Last week there was but a step between us and death, and (what is worse) slavery." Sir William Waller's victory at Cheriton at the end of March bridged over that one step. Essex, though complaining, was not selfish, but declared that, although the Earl of Manchester was allowed an army of 14,000 while his own army was reduced in numbers, yet if it were the pleasure of Parliament he would again venture his life for the cause. Parliament was obliged to pay considerable regard to accomplished facts; and although the Lords favoured the idea of a superior command for Essex, which should include the Association Army, the Commons were able to urge that the Association Army was not raised by a general tax, but by a particular charge on the Association. But the Gordian knot was cut by the sword, for Manchester was already in action in Lincolnshire, and as some continued authority was necessary the Lords gave way. The great rendezvous of the armies under Essex and Manchester, fixed for April 19, at Aylesbury, did not take place, but Essex marched westwards alone to disaster and defeat at Lostwithiel, and the Association Army under Manchester and Cromwell was on the high road to fame at Marston Moor.

On April 11, Fairfax defeated the Royalists at Selby, taking 3,000 prisoners, and the Marquis of Newcastle[1] drew off from facing the Scots into York; the Scots followed him, and on the 20th effected a junction with the Fairfaxes. On the other hand, Royalists had swarmed into Lincolnshire again from Newark, to Lincoln, Sleaford, and even as far as Crowland.

On the 3rd of May, the Earl of Manchester sat down before Lincoln in a pouring rain, while Cromwell, with 2,000 horse, held a relieving force in check. 'At the signal of the great ordnance going off, the guns began to play upon the town of Lincoln,' at three o'clock in the morning, and frightened the people out of their beds. The Fenmen jumped into the works, set up their scaling ladders, "whereupon," says Rushworth, "the defenders left off firing, threw down

[1] Newcastle had been made a Marquis in the previous year.

mighty stones from over their works, which did the assailants more prejudice than their shot; yet at last, up they got, and slew about fifty in the works, and the rest cried for quarter, which was given them." The Governor, Sir Francis Fane, and a large number of other prisoners and arms, were taken, and "all the pillage of the upper town, which was taken by storm, was given to the soldiers."

A few days later the Earl of Manchester marched towards York, and Cromwell's Horse joined with those of Fairfax and the Scotch; "so that," writes a chronicler of the time, "they now have a brave body of Horse, 8,000 complete; they would be joyful to wait upon P. Rupert to York, and will endeavour to find him out. But it is thought the Prince . . . . will decline to meet. . . . . He loves not to meet a Fairfax nor a Cromwell, nor any of those men that have so much religion and valour in them."[1] The City of York, which had been already blocked up on two sides, was, by the arrival of the Earl of Manchester's Foot, surrounded on all sides, and its Governor, Sir Thomas Glemham, of Glemham, Suffolk, found himself shut in by his own neighbours, the 'Norfolk men.'[2]

With the Earl of Essex away in the West, and the Association Army before York, held there by the expected march of Rupert to its relief, the King found the Associated Counties and London practically undefended. Had His Majesty been blessed with good generalship instead of divided counsels, the last fortnight of June, 1644, would certainly have been the most critical period of the War for the Associated Counties, and the story of Marston Moor itself might have been very different. At the head of a powerful army, variously estimated at from 10,000 to 12,000, including 4,000 horse and fourteen pieces of artillery, the King, 'being in good condition to fight,' resolved 'no longer to live upon his own quarters, but to visit the enemy's country.' There were three courses open to His Majesty, each of which was debated at a council of war held on June 22—to march into the North, and join with Prince Rupert in relieving

[1] Mercurius Britannicus in "Cromwelliana."
[2] Slingsby's Diary, pp. 107-8.

York; to march into the Associated Counties, and draw off the Association Army under Manchester before York; or to march on London. Without committing himself definitely to any one of these courses, the King commenced an aimless march with his army across Buckinghamshire into Bedfordshire, feeding his army rather than fighting, and getting into a position which alarmed both the City and the Associated Counties, each fearing that it was the object of attack.

The Committee for both kingdoms in London wrote endless letters to various County Committees, towns, and garrisons—to Cambridge advising them to 'look to themselves,' assuring them for their encouragement that Sir William Waller had orders to march after the King; to King's Lynn urging Colonel Walton, the governor, to take measures for its defence; and to Ireton, Cromwell's deputy in the governorship of the Isle of Ely, urging him to look to and strengthen the passes through the Fens, to prevent the 'enriching and recruiting of the enemy in these counties which have been hitherto unplundered.'[1] To the Committee for the Associated Counties at Cambridge, the Committee wrote requiring them to summon 3,000 men out of Suffolk and adjoining parts to secure the town of Cambridge.

Meanwhile the King's army was marching either for the City or the Associated Counties; and nearing Newport Pagnell, Sir Samuel Luke 'let fly two or three of his great pieces, which set them packing.' They were soon overrunning South Beds and North Herts, with both Cambridge and London lying at their mercy. A party of the Cavaliers created a great sensation by riding into Dunstable, entering the Priory Church during service, 'cutting and slashing the people in Church and firing a case of pistols at the minister in the pulpit.' The Hertfordshire Committee wrote despairing letters for the recall of their forces serving out of the county to defend their borders; but there was no time for this, and the yeomen around Hitchin rose in their thousands with such weapons as they could find. To Major-General Brown was entrusted the command of such forces as could

[1] Committees' Letter-book in State Papers.

be got together — the red, white, and blue regiments of London and the Herts and Essex Trained Bands. On June 24, he had got to Barnet in a sorry plight, with only part of the red and white regiments come in; the blue regiment refusing to march without a month's pay![1]

The first contact of the Royal Army with the unarmed yeomen about Hitchin scattered them; most of them ran away at the first alarm. Major-General Brown wrote in despair:—"I cannot imagine what we shall do to secure ourselves, having no horse. . . . . Your pleasure I shall humbly await, and your orders obey, though to our utter ruin." Finding that the plot for securing the Isle of Ely was known, the King became greatly dispirited, and declined for the present advancing further towards the Association, but turned and played 'his great guns against the town of Aylesbury,' as the Hertfordshire scouts reported. These altered tactics weakened the zeal of County Committees, and Major-General Brown was obliged, after riding to and fro between Hitchin and St. Albans, to send out his own warrants in express term. By the 28th he had got together at Dunstable 4,000 foot, 1,000 from the City regiments and 3,000 from Herts and Essex, which marched to Berkhamsted to meet a convoy of 500 horse. At his headquarters at St. Albans, Brown heard of the King's defeating Sir William Waller at Cropredy Bridge, and at once commenced a forced march to join him on the borders of Northamptonshire. The junction was a source of weakness rather than strength, for those who had not already deserted Brown on the march, became so mutinous and 'uncommandable' that Waller confessed that such men were "only fit for the gallows here and hell hereafter."

The danger of attack from outside had thus passed away without drawing away or weakening the powerful Association Army under Manchester and Cromwell, now shaping themselves for the great battle of Marston Moor. Prince Rupert was marching thither out of Lancashire at the head of an army 20,000 strong, to the relief of Newcastle and his 6,000

[1] Perfect Diurnal.

men shut up in York. The Parliamentary commanders raised the siege, and drew out to meet the Prince on Marston Moor. Rupert avoided the challenge by crossing the Ouse ; but, having accomplished his object of relieving Newcastle, on Monday, July 1, he drew out his army to meet the Parliamentary forces. On Tuesday evening, July 2, the two great armies came into conflict, and the result was the battle of Marston Moor, in which for three hours, on a sultry Summer's night, from seven to ten o'clock, were combined an awful carnage and an impressive spectacle unmatched by any event in the Civil War ; or perhaps in the military annals of England.

The two armies were drawn up facing each other on the Moor, with only a ditch between them. There was desultory firing from two to five o'clock in the afternoon, and then all seemed over for that day, but it was only 'the lull before the bursting of the storm.' During the pause a prisoner released by Prince Rupert came into his comrades, in the left wing. He was called before Cromwell, and stated how eagerly the Prince had asked whether Cromwell was in this wing, and whether they would fight, " because if they would they should have their belly full," to which Cromwell replied, " and, please God, so shall he ! "

Cromwell, on seeing a battery placed over against him, ordered two guns forward ; this caused the men in the ditch to fire some shots, which brought on the main battle. By one of these shots Cromwell was wounded in the neck slightly, but to prevent alarm called out cheerfully to his men—'a miss is as good as a mile.' Cromwell's Horse on the left wing then charged the right wing of the Royalists, and the Eastern Counties Foot under Crawford went at the double and kept by the side of Cromwell's Horse as far as they could. The field-word given was for Parliament ' God with us,' and the word given by Rupert was ' For God and the King.' Watson, Cromwell's scoutmaster, gives this glowing account of the share of the Association forces :—
" The signal being given, we marched on to the charge, in which you might have seen the bravest sight in the whole world ; such disciplined armies marching to a charge came

down the hill in the bravest order and in the greatest resolution that ever was seen; I mean the left wing of our horse, led on by Lieutenant-General Cromwell, which was to charge their right wing, led by Rupert, in which were all their gallant men, they being resolved that if they could scatter Cromwell, all was their own. All the Earl of Manchester's foot, being three brigades, began the charge with their bodies against the Marquis of Newcastle's foot and Prince Rupert's bravest foot. In a moment we were past the ditch upon the Moor on equal ground with the enemy, our men going on a running march. . . . . Lieutenant-General Cromwell's own division had a handful of it; for they were charged by Rupert's bravest men both in front and flanks. They stood at the sword point a pretty while hacking one another. But at last it pleased God he brake through them, and scattered them before him like dust. At the same instant the rest of our horse of that wing had wholly broken all Rupert's horse on the right wing, and was in the chase of them beyond their left wing. Our foot of the right hand, being only the Earl of Manchester's foot, went on by our side, dispersing the enemy's foot almost as fast as they charged them, still going on by our side, cutting them down, that we carried the whole field before us."

The Marquis of Newcastle's regiment of white coats 'were almost entirely cut off, for they scorned to fly and were slain in rank and file, and the rest of that part of their army which escaped killing or being taken prisoners fled in confusion towards York.' In this pursuit the victorious Ironsides had got in the rear of the main battle and could not see what had happened. Returning from the pursuit, they were astonished to find that while Cromwell had swept the left wing of the Royalists from the field, Rupert had routed the Parliamentary right wing, who gave out as they fled that 'all was lost.' Among the stragglers met with was Fairfax himself, with blood streaming from his face and riding a wounded horse. He had got mixed up in the Royalist forces, was mistaken for the moment for a Royalist officer, and so escaped and was able to rejoin Cromwell. Then followed one of the most remarkable incidents in the history of the War. Cromwell's Horse and the Earl of Manchester's Foot, with the Scots under Leslie, gathered the stragglers from the broken centre and right wing to their own victorious phalanx, and advanced in good order to a second charge. Rupert, later than Cromwell in discovering what had happened in the part of the field each had left behind, returned to face Cromwell a second time; 'both sides being not a little surprized to see they must fight it over again.' The Royalists marched down the cornfields with great resolution, 'the face of the battle being exactly counterchanged.' The carnage was awful, but the better generalship prevailed; by ten o'clock the Parliamentary forces had cleared the field, recovered the ordnance and transport waggons taken by Rupert in his first success, taken the Prince's own artillery, and pursued the fugitive Royalists with great slaughter within a mile of York.

In order to form an elementary conception of the great battles of the Civil War, it is necessary to remember that these old Ironsides and Cavaliers were engaged, not in shooting each other from a distance, but for the most part at close quarters, literally hacking one another in pieces. This element in the fight enables one the better to realize something of the awfulness of the spectacle of that clash of arms during three hours of a sultry Summer's night on the Yorkshire moors, when the heavens above and the earth beneath were shaking with the artillery of God and of men.

"Just as both armies were joined in battle, and began a first encounter or assault of each other, it pleased the Lord that a sudden and mighty great storm of rain and hail and terrible claps of thunder were heard and seen from the clouds, as if heaven had resolved to second the assault with a fierce alarm from above."[1]

"Still darker and gloomier fell the evening, and closer and murkier was the air, as the thunder of the skies was more and more frequently echoed by the artillery where Cromwell was among the far left among the guns. At length the whole

---

[1] Vicars.

dark masses on either side seemed to catch fire from that flame, and bright and loud the artillery flashed and the musketry sparkled along those formidable ranks."[1]

In the lurid chiaroscuro of lightnings flashing from the heavy skies and of cannon belching fire along the hills, the images of Fairfax and Cromwell, riding now here, now there, through the blinding glare, loom large and Homeric in outline. But war is war in all times, and out of the awful carnage there comes, for us who are interested in the Eastmen's valour, one personal incident of a peculiarly human interest, when it is found that Cromwell's neighbour's son, in fact, his own sister's son, the promising young Captain Walton, of St. Neots, is *hors de combat*, with a leg shattered by a cannon-ball. It was upon this incident that Cromwell wrote the characteristic letter of sympathy to his brother-in-law of St. Neots, and colleague in Parliament and in arms:—

"To my loving Brother, Colonel Valentine Walton : These Leaguer before York, 5th July, 1644.

" Dear Sir,

" It's our duty to sympathise in all mercies; and to praise the Lord together in chastisements or trials, that so we may sorrow together.

" Truly England and the Church of God hath had a great favour from the Lord, in this great victory given unto us, such as the like never was since this War began. It had all the evidences of an absolute victory, obtained by the Lord's blessing upon the Godly Party principally. We never charged but we routed the enemy. The left wing, which I commanded, being our own horse, saving a few Scots in our rear, beat all the Prince's horse. God made them as stubble to our swords. We charged their regiments of foot with our horse, and routed all we charged. The particulars I cannot relate now; but I believe, of Twenty-thousand the Prince hath not Four-thousand left. Give glory, all the glory, to God.

[1] Warburton, ii, 457.

"Sir, God hath taken away your eldest son by a cannon-shot. It brake his leg. We were necessitate to have it cut off, whereof he died.

"Sir, you know my own trials this way,[1] but the Lord supported me with this, that the Lord took him into the happiness we all pant for and live for. There is your precious child full of glory, never to know sin or sorrow any more. He was a gallant young man, exceedingly gracious. God give you His comfort. Before his death he was so full of comfort that to Frank Russell and myself he could not express it, 'it was so great above his pain.' This he said to us. Indeed, it was admirable. A little after he said one thing lay upon his spirit. I asked him what that was? He told me it was that God had not suffered him to be any more the executioner of his enemies. At his fall, his horse being killed with the bullet, and, as I am informed, three horses more, I am told he bid them open to the right and left that he might see the rogues run. Truly he was exceedingly beloved in the Army of all that knew him. But few knew him; for he was a precious young man, fit for God. You have cause to bless the Lord. He is a glorious Saint in Heaven; wherein you ought exceedingly to rejoice. Let this drink up your sorrow; seeing these are not feigned words to comfort you, but the thing is so real and undoubted a truth. You may do all things by the strength of Christ. Seek that, and you shall easily bear your trial. Let this public mercy to the Church of God make you to forget your private sorrow. The Lord be your strength. So prays

"Your truly faithful and loving brother,
Oliver Cromwell."[2]

As to the number of the slain, 'the countrymen (who were commanded to bury the corpses) gave out that they interred 4,150 bodies.' About 100 Royalist colours, 'enough to make surplices for all the Cathedrals in England,' were taken, most of which the soldiers tore in pieces, 'delighted to wear the

---

[1] The trial was the loss of his own son Oliver: see ante, p. 154.
[2] Carlyle, Letters and Speeches, L, 152-3.

shreds in their hats.' Of his defeat Prince Rupert was reported to have said : "I am sure my men fought well, and know no reason of our rout but this, because the Devil did help his servants." As for the Marquis of Newcastle, he and his whitecoats, who had vowed to dye their coats in the blood of their enemies, will trouble the Fenmen no more with that old nightmare of a "Papists' Army"; for, the very next morning after the battle, the Marquis, with most of his valiant whitecoats left dead on the field, resolved to leave the country, took leave of Prince Rupert, and, conducted by a troop of horse and dragoons to Scarborough, set sail for and arrived at Hamburg four days later, and 'returned to England no more till the miraculous restoration of King Charles the Second.'

The Earl of Manchester sent off after the battle a brief dispatch, in which he says that "Prince Rupert saved himself by ye goodness of his horse; we took all his ordnance, his ammunition, and baggage. We took about 6,000 armes, and yet I believe there are some thousands left in the woods. . . . We began our fight on Tuesday in ye evening, and it was very hot for two hours."[1]

To the fame already obtained and the valour displayed by the men from East Anglia, the Royalist writer Heath pays this tribute :—" The Earl of Manchester's Horse were on the left wing of their Army. These were raised out of the Associated Counties . . . . commonly called the Eastern Association, and both for arms, men, and horses the completest regiments in England; they were more absolutely at the command of Colonel Cromwell, Lieut.-General to Manchester, an indefatigable soldier and of good courage and conduct."[2]

While the clash of arms was ringing on Marston Moor, the Constables of East Anglia were pushing on the recruiting; and when the news of victory came to hand, the Committee for both Kingdoms wrote in flattering terms to each county in the Association, thanking them for the service rendered

[1] Hist. MSS., Com. Rep., No. 7.
[2] "Chronicles of the late Intestine War," etc.

by their soldiers, "which hath been a special means under God of bringing our affairs into that prosperous condition in which they now are."

Two things of interest had come out of the great conflict at Marston Moor, and the lessons of the war during these Summer months of 1644. One was that Cromwell had gained, from Prince Rupert himself, that name of Ironsides which was also to be applied with equal fitness to the valiant men who had fought under him. The other was that the issue of the war must now be left more to the trained soldiers, and less to county trained bands, concerned mainly with the defence of particular areas.

CHAPTER IX.

QUARREL OF MANCHESTER AND CROMWELL—CROWLAND
AND NEWPORT—SIR HUDIBRAS AND SIR ROGER.

(1644.)

IT has been pointed out by more than one writer that the splendid success achieved by the Parliamentary forces at Marston Moor, induced in the minds of Manchester and other aristocratic commanders a misgiving whether it would not be possible to 'beat the King too well'; whether, after all, they could face the logical issue, so long as the King remained obdurate, upon which the struggle of the Civil War had launched them. At more than one time during the Civil War the old feeling and the old hope which had eagerly looked to some decisive action to put an end to the unnatural conflict, made themselves felt among the people. When the tension created by some great emergency had become relaxed, it was hard to get the counties to rise to the occasion for a further sustained effort beyond their borders, and especially if the men were wanted for harvest work. It was hard to make the counties accept the situation that war was to be so long a permanent factor in their midst; and they were ever looking for relief to the next great event.

The army of the Earl of Manchester, after the fatigues of Marston Moor, had become a prey to internal jealousies. Wearied and in want of pay and recruiting, when the army began to move slowly from Yorkshire towards Lincoln, it was alleged that Manchester refused to summon Royalist houses on the march. In passing Welbeck Abbey, Cromwell says the Earl 'was very backward and could hardly be persuaded to march for Welbeck.' But was there not, at least in this case, an excuse of chivalry? The Earl knew that in the chambers of Welbeck were 'the daughters and the rest of the children and family' of his old enemy, the Marquis of Newcastle, now fled beyond the sea. But Welbeck was summoned, and no sooner summoned than it surrendered. The Earl allowed the soldiers even the liberty to march away with their arms; but they, to the number of 350, preferred to lay down their arms and asked for tickets to go to their own homes, which the Earl granted, and then engaged himself for the protection and maintenance at Welbeck of Newcastle's children.

At Lincoln nearly a month was occupied, from August 6 to September 4, in negotiating about sending a part of the army into Cheshire against Rupert. On September 5 the army, having left 3,000 foot for the siege of Newark, reached Bourne. From Sleaford, Cromwell wrote to his brother-in-law, Colonel Valentine Walton, expressing a longing to get away to remedy the sad condition of the army in the West—"truly had we wings we would fly thither." "We have some amongst us much slow in action—if we could all intend our own ends less, and our ease too, our business in this Kingdom would go on wheels for expedition. But because some of us are enemies to rapine and other wickednesses we are said to be 'factious,' to 'seek to maintain our opinion in religion by force'— which we detest and abhor. I profess I could never satisfy myself of the justness of this war, but from the Authority of Parliament to maintain itself in its rights; and in this cause I hope to approve myself an honest man and single-hearted."

Proceeding slowly towards Peterborough and Huntingdon, the Earl of Manchester was being urged into opposite courses by the Derby House Committee in London, to hasten his march into the West to the assistance of the Earl of Essex and Sir William Waller; and, by his strong attachment to constitutional methods, not to take an army raised and paid by the Association away from that part of the country which it was especially intended to protect. His chief officers, including Cromwell, were impatient and clamorous over the delay, with increasing divisions on religious systems— the Earl and his Major-General Crawford for Presbyterianism, and Cromwell and other officers for Independency.

Just as the harvest of the Fens was being finished, there was a remarkable gathering of the Association Army and its officers around that old cradle of the Ironsides about Huntingdon, where the heroes of Marston Moor had arrived in unhappy mood after slow marches and many halts. While at Huntingdon, on September 8, the Earl received the intelligence of the defeat of the Earl of Essex at Lostwithiel, in Cornwall.[1] Some of his officers, it is alleged, showed signs of rejoicing at the news; and if, on the one hand, the event seemed to confirm the arguments for a more rapid advance and the folly of delay, there was something to be said for the Earl's attitude from the point of view of the Associated Counties. Upon the receipt of the news the Earl wrote the following letter :—

"For the Committee of both Kingdoms. My Lords and Gentlemen.

"I received this morning your Lo^{ps} lettre, together with a copy of my Lord Generall's lettre, which gives a very sad account of his present condition, of the which I have a very deepe sense. The Lord's arme is not shortned, though wee be much weakned. I trust he will give us a happy recovery. I shall, with all the speed I can, march in observance of your former orders. I cannot expect to have any recreutes, being I am to march soe sudden from these partes, which will be a great disappointing to me, considering the weaknes of these forces. I shall from tyme to tyme acquaint your Lo^{ps} with my marches. Concerning those differences which

[1] Of the Earl of Essex's unfortunate march from St. Albans into the West, a brief diary was found in the pocket of a soldier after the defeat at Lostwithiel, which briefly runs thus : "From St. Albans to Beaconsfield, from B. to Henly, from H. to," etc. ; "from Bodmin to Lostwithiel, and thence, like rogues, to ye divell."—Harl. MSS., 934, f. 64.

your Lo^{ps} take notice to be amongst some of this army, I hope your Lo^{ps} shall finde that I shall take such care as, by the blessing of God, nothing of the publique service shall be retarded.

"My Lords and Gentlemen, I am
your Lo^{ps} most humble servant,
Manchester.
"Huntingdon, Sep. 8, 1644."[1]

The *personnel* of the body of officers gave a peculiar interest to this halt of the Association Army at Huntingdon. The Earl was close to Kimbolton, Cromwell was at his birthplace, Edward Montague was at home at Hinchinbrook, Desborough was within a few miles of his birthplace at Eltisley, Pickering was near his relatives, if not his own home, at Whaddon; to say nothing of Frank Russell, of Chippenham, and of Ireton, future relations of Cromwell. It was a remarkable meeting-place, instinct with the pulses we associate with "auld lang syne" and touched with degrees of sadness. For the Earl there was the silent rebuke of the old Royalist Earl, scarce two years in his grave at Kimbolton. Young Edward Montague had seen his father go over to the King; Cromwell had lost his own son Oliver—a loss which on his deathbed still 'went to his heart'; and eye-witnesses were going over to Great Staughton, near St. Neots, to tell the tale to Margaret Cromwell (now Mrs. Walton) how nobly her boy, young Walton, had died amid the smoke of battle at Marston Moor. Cromwell had written that touching brotherly letter to Colonel Walton; and the two men who, as member for Cambridge and member for Huntingdon, had dared to face the ordeal of seizing the magazine and Castle at Cambridge before any blow had been struck, were sharing a common sorrow. These were sacred but stirring memories to the men who now found themselves hampered by a commander unwilling to move forward, yet impelled to vindicate the cause for which they had taken up arms and made great sacrifices.

[1] "Manchester's Quarrel with Cromwell," by Professor Masson, p. 25.

When, some time afterwards, affairs drifted into open quarrel between Manchester and Cromwell, and the charges formed the subject of examinations, the depositions of this group of stout fighting-men of the Association Army were taken; and so far as they related to the scene at Huntingdon may be here given as recorded in the State Papers.

Cromwell in his first examination stated that, while at Huntingdon, " Lieutenant-General Hammond with examinant [Cromwell] came to the Earl to desire his lordship that he would hasten his march in obedience to the commands he had received; he replied that 'he would hang him or them that should advise him to march with his own army into the West,' or words to that effect."

Colonel Pickering in his examination said that when the Earl came to Huntingdon the next day "he received intelligence of the great blow the Parliamentary Army had received in the West . . . . the Earl expressed his unwillingness to march more than ever." He had often heard the Earl protest that "he never liked this War, and was against it from the beginning, saying 'it was easy to begin a war, but no man knew when it would end, and that this was not the way to advance religion.'"

Quarter-Master General Ireton in his deposition said, that the Earl at Huntingdon "spoke with much contempt and indignation against the commands received at Huntingdon to march to Abingdon."

That the Earl had grown apathetic in the War, appears from other sources. There was, for instance, a certain 'Letter written out of Bedfordshire unto the Earl of Manchester and intercepted by one of his Majesty's scouts,' in which the writer urges their sad conditions, which are 'no romances,' but 'sad truths, as in good faith if they wake you not now from your lethargic dream, I think you must sleep till the last trumpet.'[1] On the other hand, the Earl had his difficulties to contend with. His victorious army had been reduced to 6,000 and was sadly in need of reinforcement; and of the plight in which the backwardness

---

[1] Brit. Mus. Lib., 669, f. 8 (13).

of County Committees left them he writes :—" The Treasurers, which are two gentlemen of good credit, doe assure mee that within these few days there was yet unpaid £30,000 of the former 3 moneths assessments; and of these last 4 moneths which is almost illapsed, there is nothing yet brought in. . . . . I must confesse, and I doe acknowledge it as a blessing from God, that both officers and soldiers have never yet refused any marching or duty for want of pay, and I hope they never will."

The Horse was indeed in a sorry plight, and upon reaching Hitchin Ireton wrote to the Earl, then in London, " having at several rendezvous taken special notice of the condition of the horse, I find, my Lord, that it is very miserable. Of divers troops the officers soberly and calmly profess that, having lent their own and borrowed all they could find in their troops to supply them that have wanted for mere necessaries (as shoeing horses, etc.), they had at the present many horses marching back for want of money to shoe them."[1]

Besides these purely military matters, however, there were, as usual, matters of religious scruple at issue, and the Independents were already beginning to assert themselves in a manner likely to create divisions. Cromwell spent some of the time while the army was hanging about Huntingdon by riding up to Westminster and having a hand in shaping the proceedings of the House of Commons, and getting in at the right moment a plea for 'tender consciences' and toleration.

Meanwhile the King's army had begun to move eastward again, and with Essex beaten it was necessary for Manchester and Sir William Waller to join their forces; and so at last the Earl of Manchester got on his way with his army across Hertfordshire. After the halt of many days around St. Albans and Watford, the half-hearted Earl and his impatient colleagues at last got as far as Reading and into the neighbourhood of stirring events once more. The attitude of the

---

[1] Manchester Papers, 545, Public Record Office; see also 543, the Letter from Mr. Crewe to the Earl.

Earl was being supported by the Associated Counties themselves, as the further examination of the officers, to be referred to presently, will show. Norfolk was especially backward in sending its forces away to the West, and the Committee of the Association sitting at Trinity College, Cambridge, made this urgent appeal :—" The extreame push of affaires that the Associated Countyes are now put to by the emptying there fource into the West doe ernestly styr us up . . . . in your diligence the safety of your county resteth . . . . we see very playnely that matters will be brought very soon to such an adventure as to be prepared for the worst . . . . and this we do give you to take into your consideration as we have importuned other countyes to the like."[1]

The Lincolnshire people also heard with dismay of the Earl's directions to march to the West, and their sorrow 'was not to be expressed' when it was understood he was to depart. Some crying, "what will become of us within this half-an-hour after my Lord's forces are gone ; the King's forces will come cursing and swearing, setting their pistols to our breasts, extorting money at their pleasure and plundering of others. What ! will my lord leave us now and not first destroy our enemies? All our love and respect to my lord's army will now be requited upon us ; there are so many among us that observe our smiles, which our enemies will turn into tears by blows and other cruelties ; what shall we do? Better set fire to all we have and be gone than suffer what we are like to do. These, with many more of like nature, took great impression upon the Army in so much that tears fell plenty on both sides."[2]

A fortnight afterwards Norfolk sent up a petition to Parliament : " Whereas we have binn at greate charge to range and mayntayne the armye now under the command of the Earle of Manchester, which by God's blessing hath hetherto kept out the enimy from amungst us, etc., doe humbly desire that the sayd army may be imployed neere the confines of our Association."[3]

[1] L'Estrange Papers.
[2] Wallington, Historical Notices, ii, 233-4.
[3] L'Estrange Papers.

Great Civil War. 173

The Committee of both Kingdoms wrote thus, with Essex's defeat fresh in their minds, to the Committee of the Association at Cambridge, and to the Committee of Norfolk :—

"You now see the sad effects of delay in executing the ordinance of 12th of July for raising requisite forces. If the directions and orders of Parliament and of this Committee had been expeditiously put in execution we had been nearer the end of our troubles than we are. We supposed your Foot had been with the Earl of Manchester long since. The Earl, who is now on the march, will by this slackness want a considerable part of the Army that was to have marched with him. We desire you to cause your contingent to march with all expedition."

The situation was a critical one from the Parliamentary point of view. The King had ordered Prince Rupert to join him in his march, and having gained a victory over Manchester's army of the Association as he had done over that of the Earl of Essex, the Royalist plan of campaign was to march against the Eastern Association and 'winter in Norfolk.'

At Reading the Earl of Manchester was repeatedly reminded by letters from the Counties of the Association of their concern at the distance of their forces and the doings of the Newarkers on the Lincolnshire side of the Fens. Even Suffolk wrote to the Earl "some reasons why they conceive the distance of their force might be a sad consequence to them."

The conflict with the King around Donnington Castle and the Second Battle of Newbury are matters of general history ; but in order to follow the fortunes of the Fenmen and those of the Associated Counties, it is necessary to quote further from the interesting depositions of the officers whose names have already been mentioned, especially as they disclose the Earl's defence. In these it was alleged that the Earl declared—" My Army was raised by the Association and was for the guard of the Association. It cannot be commanded by a Parliament without their consents "; and he often expressed "an exceeding inclination to return with his Army into the Association, seeing that

Cambridge must be our winter quarters."[1] The Earl himself wrote to the Derby House Committee thus:—"Your lordships very well know the obligacions I have to these countyes who have as farre as in them lay put this trust upon mee. I receive from them dayly letters expressing their great trouble that their forces are drawne soe farre from them"; and he reminds them that by ordinance these forces are not to be commanded any whether but with the consent of the Committees of the Association."[2]

Sir Arthur Haselrigg in his examination stated that the Earl declared that "if we beat the King 99 times, yet he is King still and so will his posterity be after him; but if the King beat us once we shall be all hanged and our posterity be made slaves."

Cromwell in his second examination, after giving a similar version, says he replied, "if this principle were true it condemned all our former fighting as foolish, and was an argument against fighting for the future, and a ground for making peace how dishonourable soever."

Major John Desborough said:—"I heard Mr. Gossell[3] at Newbury say to many of the soldiers who asked him for money that he had none for them till they should come into the Association, and when we can get thither 'you shall have all new coats and shoes besides money enough, but not a penny till then'; and he heard the Earl say about five days after Donnington was relieved that if the Committee of the [Eastern] Association did but write to him to come back to them he would march with his Army the next day, though the Parliament hanged him for so doing."

Colonel Pickering, in his further examination, says that the Earl said: "It is a pity we should leave those Counties who have paid us and parted with their money so willingly to us all this while and now by our absence be exposed to the incursions of an enemy."

Colonel Edward Montague, relative of the Earl, said that

---
[1] Scout-Master Watson's Examination.
[2] "Cromwell and Manchester's Quarrel."
[3] Mr. Gawsell, one of the Treasurers of the Association.

he heard the latter say "he was against this War in the beginning of it, and that if those who began it had to do it again they would be twice advised," or to that effect.

On the other hand, it was alleged against Cromwell in the narrative of "the Earl of Manchester's Campaign," written by his Major-General Crawford, the Scotch Presbyterian, that he (Cromwell) encouraged the Army to disobey Crawford's orders, that he favoured Independents as against others, and fomented mischief in the Army "all the way betweene Lincolne and Huntingdon," and that advantages over the Enemy were lost through Cromwell's inaction at Newbury. There are similar accusations in the anonymous statement by an opponent of Cromwell, which contains the following items of personal interest :—

"Colonel Cromwell, perceiving what might be done in the Ile by a small party, at my coming to him at Cambridge he told me he would make the Ile of Ely the strongest place in the world, and that he would out with all the wretches and ungodly men, and he would place in it godly and precious peopell, and he would make it a place for God to dwell in. . . . .[1] Yett at this day the Ile is . . . . become a meere A'msterdam, for in the chefest churches on the Sabbath day the souldiers have gonn up into the pulpitts both in the forenoone and the afternone and preached to the whole parish, and our ministers have satt in their seatt in the church, and durst not attempt to preach, it being a common thinge to preach in private houses night and day, they having gott whole famalyes as Independents into that Ile from London. . . . . At the springe, I being at Camebridge, ... I walking over the market hill there with Collonell Cromwell, I speak to him thus : 'Sir, if you would march up to Newarke with but 1500 of your horse you would spoyle Prince Rupert's market.' He said again, ' there is Sir John Meldrum and the rest would take the town for all the Prince.' I sayd to him againe, 'it ware as cheape

---

[1] Compare Walker, who says: "It is a plentefull and strong fastnesse, able to feed 40,000 men besides the ordinary inhabitants. . . . . Here (when all other helps fail) the Godly mean to take Sanctuary ; this shall be their last retreat from whence they will draw the whole Kingdome to parley upon articles of treaty and enforce their peace from them at last."—" History of Independency," p. 147.

for our horse to march as to ly still in the stables'; whereupon he was angry and bid me holld my tounge, I spoke I knew not what; yett he had then gallant horse, and I have heard him say that he had more horse in his troope that was at Edg hill then the Earle of Essex had in his whole armie." The writer adds that when the news of the rout of the Earl of Essex in the West reached the army at Huntingdon, "many of the Independents appeared soe joyful as though it had been a victory new gained to themselves."[1]

There is other evidence of a seriously divided feeling amongst the troops themselves, for a few weeks after that dilatory march Westwards, there is this little glimpse of an incident before Newport Pagnell. Sir Samuel Luke writes to the Herts Committee:—"I must confess it one of ye greatest mercyes that I have received of late that the towne was preserved when his Majesty's forces were last before it; for at that very time 2 of ye E. of Manchester's companies drew up one against another, and much hurt was done, and had I not interfered myself amongst them I do not know what ill consequences might not have followed."[2]

The essential point in the Manchester and Cromwell quarrel lay in the difference of point of view from which the two men regarded the ultimate purpose of the War. Manchester, like many others, never got beyond the idea that the War was an armed protestation; Cromwell regarded it as a means of compelling a settlement of the nation's affairs;—the one saw no finality in the further use of the sword, the other saw none without it. Cromwell's idea that the Earl's apathy sprang from a fear lest they should beat the King too well, and that he was yielding to reasons which would have been fatal to taking up arms at all, therefore went to the root of the matter. Where it was not just to Manchester was, that it did not sufficiently recognize the force of obligation which the Earl felt was pressing upon him in regard to the Association Army, by the conditions under which the War had been hitherto

---

[1] "Manchester's Quarrel with Cromwell," pp. 73-6.
[2] Luke's Letter-book in Stowe MSS.

carried on. The fact was, that a point had been reached at which fighting by County Committees must give place to broader and more effective methods of warfare, and Cromwell saw this and the Earl did not. Out of these differences was to arise the famous New Model Army, to be referred to presently.

With these glimpses of the difficulties of commanding an army to suit so many parties, we may return to the region of the Fens and the Eastern Counties, and see how affairs stood with the counties the Earl had been so reluctant to leave.

One effect of the absence of the Association forces in the West was to bring once more the Cavaliers from Newark quarter swarming up into the Fens during October. In September there had come a 'terrible allarum' of an attack upon Sir Robert Carr's fortified house at Sleaford, in which the Parliamentary force was outnumbered and obliged to retire to Lincoln. On Saturday, October 5, another alarm came to Huntingdon of five or six hundred Cavaliers having taken and taxed the town of Stamford, and about the same time they seized their favourite stronghold of Crowland once more, and another party marched towards Peterborough.

The seizure of Crowland aroused all the Fens, but the garrisons of Lynn and Boston were in this peculiar position, that each had 1,000 men besides officers seventeen weeks in arrear with their pay, and all warrants for raising money had to be signed by the Earl of Manchester and two of the Committee sitting at Cambridge; and to get over the difficulty Parliament empowered any two members of the Committee to sign warrants in the absence of the Earl. For Crowland itself immediate action was necessary, and on October 7, the Committee for both Kingdoms ordered 300 men to be sent from the Cambridge garrison to hold 'Horsey Bridge pass'; to call in the Trained Bands, troops out of Suffolk to join Fleetwood and Fairfax, and to send forces from Lincoln way to oppose the enemy, who had 'surprized Crowland' and got together 2,000 forces. Again the local and national ideas of the War came in conflict: the Cambridge Committee were uneasy about the Earl of Manchester's absence in the West, and the Committee for both Kingdoms assured them that their own safety was to be found in 'a happy ending of the war,' to which his Lordship's service in the West was likely to contribute.

The Counties responded to the fresh call upon them by sending their Trained Bands trooping through the Fens to Crowland; and by October 12, with Fleetwood's regiment and other horse, there were '4,000 at least' before Crowland. There in the heavy pouring rain the 4,000 did their best to get at the small band of 250 Cavaliers, with 25 horse, within the little citadel upon the waters, but the prospect was not hopeful even with such a force. "By the accession of Sir Thomas Fairfax and Colonel Rossiter, with the Trained Bands of Cambs and Hunts before Crowland, we were in a fair way to have regained it, did not the weather prevent us." So wrote Sir Samuel Luke, and on October 17 he was writing again that on the previous day he heard the weather had forced them to raise the siege, send back the Trained Bands to their own counties, while the Horse drew off to Stamford and Lincoln. The Trained Bands were not apparently dismissed to their homes, but drawn off for a time to convenient centres. Cambridge, for instance, was full of them, of which the old "Querela" writes :— "And when their ragged regiments, which had been louzing before Crowland nigh a fortnight, were commanded to Cambridge, forthwith the Colleges are appointed their kennels; and four score were turned loose into one of the least halls [Pembroke] in the University, and charged by their officers to shift for themselves, who without more ado broke open the Fellows and Scholars Chambers and took their beds from under them."[1]

But if the Cavaliers could not be ousted from Crowland 'by a soddaine storming' as had been hoped, it was possible to guard the approaches and prevent relief coming to them. This kind of service was being performed around Peterborough by Captain Middleton and some Parliamentary Horse from Huntingdon under conditions which might have taken the

[1] "Querela Cantabrigiensis."

heart out of less hardy men. Yet on October 24, the Captain wrote cheerfully:—"We are yet masters of the field, and are blocking up ye den of theeves, ye Croylanders. . . . . Captain Redman, my bedfellow under a hedge, desireth his humble service may be presented to your honour."[1] Fleetwood wrote about the same time that "ye unhappy losse of Crowland hath much endangered these parts, but I hope we have so blocked it up as to prevent that misery which would otherwise follow." Sir Henry Mildmay, writing from Cambridge, informed Sir Samuel Luke that "we have some men upon all ye banks of Crowland, not intended offensive, only to prevent ye adjacent parts from being plundered."

By Monday, October 29, the rains had abated, and the waters subsided, allowing a closer investment of Crowland. At the same time the Royalists from Newark, Belvoir, and other garrisons marched by way of Grantham, with 1,200 horse and 200 foot, intending the relief of Crowland. But the Association forces under Colonel Hacker went out to meet them, and, coming up with them at Denton, fell upon them with a 'mighty shout' after the manner of the Ironsides. " As soon as we came in view of the enemy our soldiers did abound that they shouted as if the skies would have fallen, and would scarce stay to be drawn up, so eager were they to fall on. Their courage seemed to daunt the enemy; for they fled, about 600 horse taken and 400 prisoners."[2] But the end of the siege was not yet, and, on November 6, the Commons passed an ordinance, which throws an interesting light upon the amphibious plans found necessary by the besieging party.

"An ordinance to prevent the excursions to Crowland garrison, lately taken by the King's forces.

"Whereas the late surprisal of the garrison of Crowland in the county of Lincolne by forces raised in opposition to the King and Parliament is very prejudicial and of ill consequence to the several counties associated under the command of the Earl of Manchester, as also to

---

[1] Luke's Letter-books.
[2] Hacker to Luke, Stowe MSS., Brit. Mus. Lib.

a great part of the county of Northampton next adjoining to the same, and by reason of the unseasonable weather the approaches to the said garrison are become so unaccessible, that though forces were drawn down to reduce the same, it cannot now possibly be done without much charge and difficulty, and whereas the best means to prevent these inroads, plunderings and other outrages of the said garrison, and also to hinder the same from provisions of corn and other supplies, is advised to be by erecting and furnishing of three several forts or sconces, the charge whereof will amount to near about £600, one near the place called Brother House in the county of Lincoln, another upon Dowesdale Banck in the said county, and the third upon Barrow Banck in the county of Northampton, each of which is to be manned with 50 men or thereabout, and to have attending to the same one boat of defence. . . . . It was therefore ordered that the forts be built and equipped and full power was given to rate and tax the county for the purpose, and that six score horse be sent by the Association for securing the county and blocking up of the said garrison of Crowland."[1]

The siege was continued during November, and, on the 19th, news reached the Association Committee sitting at Trinity College, Cambridge, 'by a letter taken in ye collar of a messenger's doublet,' of a design to relieve the besieged within fourteen days. There had, in fact, been another encounter with the Cavaliers in Lincolnshire on the previous day, who would have relieved Crowland, but the success of the Parliamentary forces inspired one, Jo. Archer, to write from Grantham :—" Had you stayed two hours longer you might have seen our soldiers return with increase of honour. . . . . They took many prisoners . . . . and arms. The malignant Queanes of Grantham spake it (that Col. Rainborow might heare it) 'they were as handsome men as any in ye towne before them.'"

Inside the little fortress of Crowland the defending force were beginning to 'suffer extremities for want of bread.'

[1] Lords' Journals.

The besieging force had the great advantage in this respect of a plentiful supply of fish and fowl in the surrounding waters, as appears by this testimony:—"It would vex your understanding unto wonder and unbelief to consider what shoals of fish, what flocks of fowl, have been accustomed to frequent and delight in that fenny place. . . . . It is a good sign that our boats, who are floating there to keep relief from coming into Crowland, do want for no varieties which the elements either of air or water can afford them."[1]

At last the unequal contest ended, in the first week in December, and the beleaguered garrison, finding the besiegers about to storm the place, surrendered on conditions. The Horse, being twenty-five, were allowed to march with their swords and pistols; and the Foot, being 250, had to leave their arms behind and march away to Newark. The Huntingdonshire people rejoiced in being "freed of our ill neighbours"; but Crowland had been lost and won so often that the London "diurnals" added cautiously:—"Crowland has been twice lost to us. I hope it shall not the third time; rather abolish that old abbot's seate, which would be a kind of Dunkirk by land and by water if the enemy had continued in it."[2]

The fall of Crowland checked other Royalist expeditions into the Fens, including a band of eighteen officers from Newark, who had marched as far as St. Ives for the purpose of falling upon some treasure,' £3,000, coming to Cambridge,' and of whom eleven were carried off prisoners to Cambridge, the rest escaping.

Just as Crowland was the point of contact of the Association forces and the Royalists from Newark, so Newport Pagnell, the strategic outpost and bulwark of the Association, was the point of contact with the King's forces from Oxford. The Governor of Newport Pagnell was Sir Samuel Luke, member for Bedford, and the original of Butler's "Hudibras." Through his hands, as Scout-master-General, had passed a great deal of information from scouts, messengers, and

---

[1] The London Post, December 10, 1644.
[2] The Kingdom's Weekly Intelligencer.

spies sent out 'to feel ye pulse of ye Cavaliers'; and his letters throw an interesting light upon the relation of Newport to the Association. The letters to and from Sir Samuel Luke for this period are preserved in the Stowe MSS. 190, and his Scout Reports, etc., in the Egerton MSS. 785-7, both in the British Museum Library. The letters include two from Oliver Cromwell, of little interest, not in Carlyle's list. If Sir Samuel Luke's letters are to be read literally it is wonderful that the garrison was ever kept together at all. In them we see that the bluff old knight had a characteristic way of saying what at the moment needed to be said; that he did not hesitate to give them point by cracking a joke or quoting a proverb; and that he generally put some point into his postscripts.

The view the Eastern Counties took of this stubborn outpost in their defences is reflected in their letters to Luke. Thus, the Association Committee write from Trinity College, Cambridge: "We are not ignorant how much it concerns us to have that garrison maintayned, but yourself cannot but take notice of the heavy payments that have fallen upon us." As to individual counties, the Cambs Committee wrote:—"We are not a little troubled by ye pressing occasion for money lying upon our counties; will do our best." The Huntingdonshire Committee wrote:—"The garrison of Newport being partly withdrawn and fighting elsewhere, they consider they ought not to pay the amount proportioned to them when the garrison was complete." The Herts Committee wrote from St. Albans:—"If Manchester cannot give you reinforcements, and a large body of the enemy approach, we will send you a company or two of foot. We have already vented so much money and men that we know not how to answer future ordinances." Essex acknowledged the importance of the garrison, but thought they had done their share, for maintaining the forces at Abingdon cost them £10,000 at least.[1]

But Sir Samuel Luke continued his eloquent appeals, highly coloured with hints at the danger to the Association

---

[1] These were the men who caused such trouble to Browne and Waller.

if he were not supported, and declared that he had "none but raw men, and neither victual, ammunition, nor anything else to hold out four days, and all the complaints and petitions I have poured out would neither procure me money to buy nor order to take up anything." He winds up with a reference to the King's desire to 'winter in Norfolk,' and, writing to the Herts Committee, declared that "his Majesty hath promised to lead his army into quarters yet untouched, where they can get plenty of plunder, to wit, the Eastern Association." In another letter he declares that if arrears are not paid he will resign his charge, as the troops are ready to mutiny. Three days later, on November 28, the old knight wrote to Sir Oliver Luke:—"I am not very well yet. Ye very sitting in ye church one sermon tyme, makes me ill two or 3 days after."[1] He was further worried about his scouts, and from a letter to his deputy, Samuel Bedford, it appears he had to rebuke the latter for employing the son of the Town Clerk of Stamford, a Royalist, as a scout. On December 29, some precise directions given for a surprise party show that even Sir Hudibras was obliged under stress of war to adopt the tactics of the Cavaliers.

"I would have you very careful to apprehend the Earl of Lindsey or the Earl of Peterboro, if you can meet with them, and be sure to see them safely brought hither. Whatever men you see, be they but serving men, bring them hither, and be as careful as you can that no man deceive you in woman's habit. Make sure of the stables, and presse the servants to as much discovery as you can . . . . . if you can light of any fat Beasts and can drive them along with you with safety, do so, whosesoever they are. The Lady Love's house is not far out of your way, who married Commissary Willmott. . . . . Whatever venyson you meet with or find in the lodge make the keeper bring it along with you. You shall not fail to have 40 horse to-morrow at Buckingham by 4 o'clock in the morning."

The astute diplomacy of the old knight was reflected

---

[1] A wag has endorsed the letter "Hudibras at sermon!" but there was nothing strange in this. Even Butler does not suggest that he was not a consistent Puritan.

in his subordinates. On December 14, Captain Pinkney, a paid canvasser employed to whip up the contributions from the Associated Counties for the Newport Pagnell garrison, was artfully insinuating to the Cambridge Committee that "the enemy doth bend towards the Association," and that "in their way, and not far from them, is the garrison of Newport Pagnell, which is ye bulwark of the Association; ready every day to be deserted of ye soldiers for want of wherewith to subsist—the worthy governor having done his utmost to prevent it, cannot longer perform without speedy supply, of which if ye enemy should have knowledge (as they seldome want intelligencers), and should in its weakness surprise, then would not the bordering counties be subject to their barbarous insolence"?

In the month of December the town of King's Lynn became once more the scene of a Royalist adventure, and of a curious little comedy which added another short chapter to the already romantic career of Roger Le Strange, of Hunstanton Hall, whose father Sir Hamon had surrendered the town of Lynn to the Earl of Manchester after the siege. Favoured by the recent seizure of Crowland, and the invitation of Norfolk friends, it is said, Roger conceived the idea of the recapture of Lynn. This scheme he laid before the King at Oxford, and made it appear so plausible that the King handed Roger, on November 28, the following commission :—

"Charles R.

"We having received from our trusty and well-beloved Roger Le Strange declaration of the good affection of divers of our well-affected subjects of our counties of Norfolk and Suffolk, particularly of our town of Lynne, as also some overtures concerning the reducing of our said town of Linne, we have thought fit hereby to return our Royal thanks unto our said well-affected subjects, and particularly to give our said trusty and well-beloved Roger Le Strange this encouragement to proceed in our service principally in the work of reducing the said town of Linne :

"First that, in case that attempt shall be gone through

withall, the said Roger Le Strange shall have the government of that place.

"Secondly, that what engagement shall be made unto the inhabitants of the said place, or any other person capable of contributing effectually to that service, by way of reward, either any employment in His Majesty's Navy or forts, or in money not exceeding the sum of £5,000, the service being performed shall be punctually made good unto them.

"Thirdly, that they shall in this work receive what assistance may be given them from any of our nearest garrisons.

"And lastly, that whenever our said town shall be reduced unto our obedience we shall forthwith send thither such a considerable force as shall be sufficient to relieve and preserve them; we being at the present even without this; fully resolved to send a considerable power, to encourage our faithful subjects in those parts, and to regain our rights and interests there.

"Given at our court at Oxford this 28 November, 1644, By his Majesty's command,

"George Digby."[1]

Armed with this document, which Mr. Micawber himself might have written, and elated with the prospect of the honours to be showered upon him, Roger made his way towards his old home. Had he been a more practical-minded man he might have felt some concern about the means of carrying out his design, but as a romantic dreamer, the piece of paper in his pocket was all-powerful. Making his way to Mr. Paston's house at Appleton Hall, 'within six miles of Lynne, which he made choice of in regard of the solitariness of the place,' he sent a note to an old sea captain in Lynn named Thomas Leman, requesting him to meet him at Appleton Hall. Captain Leman kept the appointment, and Le Strange acquainted him with the business, and, showing him his commission, said, 'in case the work succeeded it should be worth to him a thousand pounds.' Promising

[1] Lords' Journals.

to 'bring another with him next day to assist in the design,' the captain went back to Lynn, and told Colonel Walton, the Parliamentary Governor of Lynn, of the little plot. Colonel Walton advised him to keep his appointment and take a corporal of his with him. Returning to Appleton Hall with a corporal of the name of Hagger, dressed up as an old seaman, the captain had another interview with Le Strange, who questioned Hagger, the corporal, as to who he was, to which Hagger replied that "he was a poor man, living in Fishers End, in Lynn, and kept an alehouse, and was £40 the worse for the Roundheads." This was eminently satisfactory to Roger, who 'fetched out the King's commission from a hole under the canopy of his bed, read it to them, and put it in his pocket again'; and, having exchanged promises of secrecy with Hagger, offered the latter £100 and a cannonier's place if the design succeeded. Hagger played his part by proposing the manner in which the town of Lynn should be surprised, and suggested that Mr. Le Strange should provide 200 men; but in reply to this practical view of things, Mr. Le Strange 'acknowledged he knew not where to get the men.'

When the interview had gone thus far, a comical incident was happening in the courtyard below, where half a dozen other 'poor old seamen' had managed to gain admission on the plea of begging alms. 'The gentlewoman of the house ran up to Mr. Le Strange, and told him there were six or seven poor soldiers come from Lynn abegging, and he sent them down 12d. and wished them to be gone.' But Lieutenant Stubbings and his five soldiers, who were the six poor old seamen come from Lynn, to 'assist in the design,' rushed upstairs, and Corporal Hagger, the other old seaman, seized Mr. Le Strange, who, however, managed to pass the King's commission to Captain Leman, thinking he, at any rate, was to be trusted !

One other amusing turn in the comedy remains to be told. Lieutenant Stubbings knew his own man Hagger, but did not know the old sea captain Leman; and, demanding 'what he did there consulting against the State,' searched him; and, finding the King's commission upon him, carried him off in custody with Le Strange to Lynn. Here they were brought before the Governor, Colonel Walton, and Leman was at once discharged, 'having acted by order of the Governor.'[1]

Le Strange, in his defence at his trial, stated that he went from Newark to Oxford, "being a listed soldier in Major Cartwright's troop in the garrison of Newark, and that he was always of the King's party, and so declared himself, and conceived that Leman and Hagger were likewise of the same party." He was charged with having "come from the enemy within the quarters of the Parliament as a spy, and had plotted, contrived, and endeavoured the betraying of the town of Lynne, in the power of the Parliament, to the enemy"; he was found guilty, and 'sentence of execution was ordered accordingly.' But Roger escaped with his life, and was destined to turn up again in later risings for the King.

[1] Particulars of this incident may be found in Rushworth and also in the Lords' Journals. The two accounts supplement each other. The Lords' Journals account makes Captain Leman go to Appleton Hall twice, once alone and once with Hagger, but Rushworth treats it as one interview.

CHAPTER X.

CROMWELL AND THE NEW MODEL ARMY—RECRUITING FOR NASEBY—THE HOUR AND THE MAN.

(1644-45.)

We wanted one that felt all Chief
From roots o' hair to sole o' stockin',
Square-sot with thousan'-ton belief
In him an' us, ef earth went rockin'!
    J. R. LOWELL: *The Biglow Papers.*

"IT is now a time to speak, or for ever hold the tongue. The important occasion now is no less than to save a nation out of a bleeding, nay, almost dying, condition. . . . . I do conceive that if the Army be not put into another method and the War more rigorously prosecuted, the people can bear the War no longer, and will force you to a dishonourable peace."

In these memorable words Cromwell, on December 9, 1644, spoke in the House of Commons, and in his characteristic fashion with Gordian knots, ended the unfortunate quarrel which was dragging down the Parliamentary cause. Admitting that he might himself have been guilty of oversights, which 'can rarely be avoided in military affairs,' Cromwell, with the instinctive perception of the important thing to do at the moment, asked the House to waive 'strict inquiry into the causes, and apply themselves to the remedy which is most necessary.' He appealed to the patriotism of both Houses not to scruple to deny themselves and their own private interests for the public good, 'nor account it a dishonour done to them whatever Parliament shall resolve upon in this weighty matter.'

From the Earl of Essex and the Earl of Manchester downwards, including Cromwell himself, the Self-denying Ordinance foreshadowed in this speech meant the giving up of military commands and betaking themselves to their duties in Parliament. Cromwell could have scarcely expected at that stage, from a House in which Presbyterianism was in the majority, that any exception would be made in his favour alone. But his immediate duty was clear, and that was ever the guiding star of Cromwell's public life. The Self-denying Ordinance was passed the same day, depriving members of both Houses of any office in command, military or civil, during the continuance of the War. The Lords stood out for a time, but eventually the Ordinance with the scheme for remodelling the Army became law, and henceforth the War was to be the affair of professional soldiers. In the end the necessity for Cromwell's presence in the Army was grudgingly acknowledged by Parliament, and he gained all that he could have desired.

The attempt at a treaty with the King at Uxbridge failed, and the year 1645 opened with the prospect of renewed war and of a severe test for the new order of things which the New Model was to bring. If Presbyterianism were the stronger in Parliament and the Church, Independency was destined to prevail in the Army, and the parting of the ways begun at Huntingdon was only the commencement of wider issues, in which the quondam neighbours of Kimbolton and Huntingdon were to go different ways—the Earl as Presbyterian speaker, back to the House of Lords, and Cromwell as the head of the growing power of the Army.

The point of practical importance both for Cromwell and the Army, which remained to be proved, was whether the Self-denying Ordinance and the New Model would work smoothly, whether the soldiers would serve faithfully under new commanders. Upon this point Cromwell had spoken freely in the House for his own men. "I am not of the mind that the calling of the members to sit in Parliament will break or scatter our Armies. I can speak this for my own soldiers, that they look not upon me but upon you, and for you they will fight and live and die in your cause ; . . . . they do not idolize me, but look upon the cause they fight for; you may lay upon them what commands you please, they will obey your commands in that cause they fight for."

Manchester, as we have seen, looked upon the Association forces as territorial regiments in name and purpose, and sought to maintain an *esprit de corps* by drafting men from each county to keep up the regiment of that county—'I find this way to give the best satisfaction to the counties and made the soldiers more united amongst themselves.'[1] Cromwell took the broad national view, not merely of what was good for the Association and its integrity, but what was good for the country and most likely to make the War effectual. As for unity among the men, he sought this in unity of purpose and spirit rather than in unity of local interest, admirable as far as it went; but it was none the less true that the *esprit de corps* of the old order seemed likely to rebel against the changes involved in the new. In fact, those serving under Cromwell were among the first to protest against the expected loss of their leader. On January 12, Sir Samuel Luke, then in London, received this letter from his deputy, R. Cockayne, at Newport Pagnell :—

"I hard that there was a great mutinie at Camb[r] by Col. Cromwell's Regiment, who was to be put under another Col. & w[h] was a Scotchman; but they have resolved not to lay down their arms until, as they say, they have vindicated Col. Cromwell."[2]

The condition of the soldiers under arms at this time was not very favourable for imposing new and unpopular conditions. Sir Samuel Luke, governor of Newport Pagnell, was harassed for means of quartering the soldiers, but had still an eye for the humorous side of things. The men were already as thick in their quarters that they had 'to lie 2 or 3 in a bedd.' But this was not the worst of it, for

---

[1] Letter to Derby House Committee.
[2] Luke's Letter-book, Stowe MSS.

they had got into such straits for clothing that two of the soldiers had but one pair of breeches between them, and one of these had to remain in bed while the other wore the breeches and went on garrison duty![1]

In Hertfordshire there was disorderly conduct amongst the soldiers. Twelve of them werebrought up at St. Albans and two of them sentenced to death.[2]

To the men of the Eastern Counties the new modelling of the Army was a matter of great concern. The principle of a national standing army, separating the bearing of arms from the functions of civil life, was one which threatened the very existence of the Association on its original lines. These men of the Eastern Counties had banded themselves together in solemn 'protest and covenant before God and one another that they will willingly and resolutely sacrifice their lives in this religious and just quarrel.' They had placed themselves under a commander of great territorial influence and position; for eighteen months they had held together the most powerful counties in England for Parliament. On the military side they had swept the King's forces from their borders, and placed on the battlefield at Marston Moor 'the completest regiments in England.' They had vanquished and driven beyond the seas their dreaded enemy, the Marquis of Newcastle, and with him had departed, like their own marshland mists before the sun, that old nightmare of a 'Papist Army,' which had hung for so long over these Puritan Counties of East Anglia. They had earned for themselves special privileges and a distinct territorial army in which they took a natural pride. This was their strength, but it was also their weakness, as tending to set up a provincial view of the War. During these Winter months, with the apathy of their commander and the habit of the soldiers of looking for pay and clothing only when they got back to their native counties, the

---

[1] "The wants of the soldiery are such that they are not fitting to be put to paper, only I shall beg your Excellency's pardon if I acquaint you with one particular. There were 2 in my Company that had but one payre of Britches betweene them, soe that when one was up the other must upon necessity be in his bed."—Luke's Letter-book, f. 236, Stowe MSS., Brit. Mus.

[2] "Hertfordshire during the Great Civil War," p. 57.

Association had come perilously near the selfish position of fighting chiefly for its own little kingdom.

Though the system of warfare by County Committees had almost broken down where least expected, yet the Eastern Counties still clung to the Association principle, and at least one of their captains was at this time refusing to march with his Horse, having 'promised he would not stir out of ye county'[1] which had raised them. What the counties did not yet see was, that the man who had been mainly instrumental in bringing their Army into the foremost place, the man who put men of religion and conscience into his troops, was evolving for them a force which could not remain a purely defensive weapon. It was the strength of Cromwell, that, though a county man himself, he took a broad national view, while some of his neighbours were looking too much to themselves, and could see that this select weapon, welded together by the Association principle, had other work to do if the great cause of the people's liberties was to finally triumph.

On January 30, the Counties of the Association took into serious consideration, at a great Conference at Bury St. Edmunds, this question of the effect of the New Model upon the continued existence of the Association. The Conference was attended by the Deputy-Lieutenants and Committeemen 'selected and deputed from the Committees of the several Associated Counties of Norfolk, Suffolk, Essex, Hertford, Cambridge, Huntingdon, and Lincolnshire,' touching the relation of the Army of the Associated Counties to Parliament, and the danger that the inhabitants and the Association would suffer if the proposed New Model for the Army were adopted. There were present :—

Out of Norfolk—Sir John Palgrave, Sir Edward Ashby, Mr. Sotherton, Mr. Jeremy, Mr. Wood, Mr. John Spelman, Mr. Tobias Fryer (or Frere); and of the city of Norwich, Mr. Greenwood.

Out of Suffolk—Mr. Barrow (High Sheriff), Sir William Spring, Sir John Wentworth, Mr. Henry North, the elder,

---

[1] Luke's Letter-book, Egerton MSS., 787, f. 60.

Mr. Francis Bacon, Mr. Tirrell, Mr. Thomas Bacon, Mr. Lucas, Mr. Champlin, Mr. Gibbs, Mr. Brampton-Gurdon, jun., and Mr. Nathaniel Bacon.

Out of Essex—Colonel Sir Henry Mildmay, Mr. Raymond, Mr. Eldred, and Mr. Sorrell.

Out of Hertfordshire—Colonel Alban Coxe and Mr. Daughs.

Out of Cambs—Mr. Clench, Mr. Thompson, and Mr. Parker.

Out of Hunts—Mr. William Drury.

Out of Lincolnshire—Sir William Brownlow, Sir Thomas Trollop, and Mr. Montague Cholmley.

The choice of a chairman fell upon one of the Suffolk delegates, who reminded them that the occasion of their coming together was that the Association was in danger of disturbance; and, in order to place the debate upon a right footing, he read out the original " Foundation of the Association "—the declaration of Parliament, the resolution banding themselves together as an Association, and the resolutions of the Counties to aid and assist one another. It was then laid down that they must still have 'a body of an Army by the joining together of the Counties, that that Army must be under one head and must serve for the mutual defence of the Associated Counties'—in short, that the Association must not be given up. The Conference then fell to debating 'whether the New Model would impair the Association in this mutual succor of the Counties,' to which one of the Hertfordshire gentlemen ventured to remark that it might not do so "inasmuch as it would be for the safety of the kingdom." In other words, that the safety of the greater included that of the less. The Conference, however, agreed that the Association 'would be impaired in its succor of the individual Counties by the New Model'; and as to how far the Association itself would be impaired by the incorporation of its Army into the New Model Army, the Conference agreed that 'the ends and purposes thereof would be abrogated.'

Upon the discussion of the point whether they should endeavour to preserve the Association, 'the affirmation passed current until it came to the Hertfordshire gent,' who insisted upon a contrary view 'that it might be beneficial for the kingdom and for the counties.' The Conference was now getting on dangerous ground, and it was necessary to resort to the old formula of a protestation, disclaiming any wish to go 'contrary to the way of Parliament.' With this reservation a vote was passed to endeavour to preserve the Association. Thus far, 'the Conference proceeded in the forenoon.' Assembling again in the afternoon, the chairman brought in the draft of a letter which, 'being first read throughout, all keeping silence, was read the second time, every period thereof being debated aparte.' Mr. Sotherton, of Norfolk, 'brought in the instructions,' the discussion of which and the appointment of gentlemen to carry the letter and instructions to London, kept the five-and-thirty gentlemen together well into the night. The Conference was then dismissed 'by a Suffolk gent'; and "soe the meeting," says the old record, "which began with devotion and continued in unity, and finished in love, ended worthy of an Association, unhappy only in this that it was cut off by midnight." [1]

In the letter which was carried up to London it was submitted that "the sad apprehension had by the people of these counties of the alteration of the Army now in agitation in Parliament, as that which will take away from them not only the head and body of their strength, ... but also deprive them of means of future subsistence and confidence, and so render their promise of Association ineffectual which God Almighty hath hitherto graciously honoured by witness of his concurrence with success of victory to the Army and general peace for the most part even to their borders, to the wonderment of all observers and envy of the Enemy"; and they therefore asked "not to be left naked to the secret malignants at home nor to the watchful enraged enemy abroad," and pointed out how difficult it would be to raise recruits, especially under unknown captains and commanders. Nevertheless, they promised that "none of these discouragements or any

[1] Papers of the Duke of Manchester, No. 565. These and other important papers at Kimbolton have been handed over, by the late Duke of Manchester, to the Public Record Office.

private regard shall withdraw our zeal from the service of your honours the Parliament and the Kingdom." They ask that for the encouragement of the soldiers each county may have power to pay their own men, and that "our brothers the Scots may be speeded down to Newark to besiege that place, which hath been a sore to the Association from the beginning of these Wars."

This document was signed by thirty-five of the deputy-lieutenants and committeemen, chiefly from Norfolk, Suffolk, and Essex, the three counties having, by their comparatively isolated position, behind the frontier counties of Cambs, Hunts, and Herts, the strongest interest in the old system of raising local forces for the primary service of defending their own homes.

Meanwhile, Parliament had ordained that 'for new modelling it,' the army should consist of 6,600 horse, to be distributed into eleven regiments; 1,000 dragooners, to be distributed into ten companies; and 14,400 foot to be distributed into twelve regiments, each regiment of foot to consist of 1,200, to be under the command in chief of Sir Thomas Fairfax.

The crowning point was reached in this dignified scene in the House of Commons on February 19—

"Sir Thomas Fairfax was called in, and had a chair set for him, and the Sergeant stood by with his mace; and Mr. Speaker, by command of the House, acquainted him: 'That the Parliament of England hath commanded up your service hither from the northern parts; they have heard of your valour, and have had experience thereof, for their safety, and have now thought fit to put upon you the greatest trust and confidence, for the security of the Kingdom, this House, religion, and liberty, as was ever put into the hands of a subject. They have resolved to put a trust upon you, the command of a very great army, which they do not intend to employ you in for a matter of discouragement, but will take care such provisions be made to enable you to go on in this great business; that your thoughts shall be solely on action: and they are confident of your fidelity, care, and diligence in this cause of God, and the Kingdom, that lie at stake. And for the faithful services you have done for the public, I am commanded by the House to return their hearty thanks; and, under God, hope you may be a means to preserve this Kingdom; and if you have any propositions to make now, or hereafter, concerning the Army, the House will take them into speedy consideration.'"[1]

Amidst universal drilling for the New Model Army, and the pressing of young recruits, two things of general historical interest had been happening. Archbishop Laud, who, with the Bishop of Ely, had been regarded as the head and front of those " Popish innovations" against which the Puritanism of East Anglia had risen in revolt, had, in January, 1645, passed beyond the strife, from the hands of the executioner; while a young Puritan, who was to gain immortal fame of another kind, had entered the arena. Into the garrison of Newport Pagnell, with its chronic empty stomachs and two men in one pair of breeches, had come with the Bedfordshire recruits, a raw youth from Elstow, who was destined to shed an undying lustre upon English literature and the Christian life.

John Bunyan had reached the age of sixteen, the limit for compulsory service, and was about this time prest into the Army. He served, it is now proved beyond a doubt, on the side of Parliament in the garrison of Newport Pagnell.[2] Here he entered about the time when some forty of the soldiers were petitioning 'for ten weeks' pay, at least,' and asking with characteristic bluntness ' that they may not be put off this time with ye cocking of ye pistoll, or stearne threatening as formerly.'[3]

Sir "Hudibras" himself wrote: "The cryes and lamentations of the soldiers here are so great through misery and want that my pen is not able to express them." Yet all through these spring months of 1645, a year in which the air was 'so infectious that dogs, cats, mice, and

[1] Commons' Journal.
[2] Since writing upon this point in my "Hertfordshire during the Great Civil War," in which reference was made to the impossibility of such Royalist recruiting in Beds at the beginning of 1645 as could have brought young Bunyan into the Royalist ranks, the question has been definitely settled by Mr. Atkinson's discovery at the Record Office of the Muster Rolls of the Newport Pagnell garrison, in which Bunyan's name appears.
[3] Luke's Letter-book, Egerton MSS., 877, f. 49.

rats died,' and birds dropped dead in their flight, recruiting went on vigorously by ordinances of Parliament and by innumerable letters from the Committee for both Kingdoms to the County Committees. Now the Governor of Lynn was ordered to send as many men as he could spare to secure the passes around Wisbech ; now the fears of Suffolk, some of whose old soldiers had run home and created a disturbance, were reassured by the order to bring Manchester's regiments of foot to Huntingdon to protect the passes into the Association, and the arrival of Captain Axtell and another officer to deal with the runaways; and, again, the Committee had under consideration a petition from Colonel Dodson, Governor of Crowland, for its pay and maintenance, and were ordering 600 foot and 120 dragoons £300 a week for the defence of the Isle of Ely, and £400 for fortifications of 'Croyland Church.'

In this way recruiting and the New Modelling went on, while Cromwell and others were in the West ready to lay down their commissions under the Self-denying Ordinance. The Earl of Manchester had resigned his commission, and on April 22, Cromwell had actually arrived at Windsor to kiss the General's (Fairfax's) hands, and take leave of him ; but there came to London rumours of a movement of the King and his artillery from Oxford to Rupert at Worcester. The Committee for both Kingdoms recognized that the man to attack the convoy was Cromwell, and when he rose next morning to take his departure from Fairfax, he was confronted with the Committee's order, 'ere he was come forth of his chamber.' Joyfully he marched away at the head of his old regiment, now Fairfax's, and fell upon the enemy near Oxford, 'part of the King's horse and part of the Queen's regiment,' routed them, and 'had the chase of them for three or four miles,' taking 200 prisoners, 400 horse, the Queen's own colours, and pursued the rest into Bletchington House, which he captured.

At the beginning of May, the Committee for both Kingdoms, as a central intelligence department, was receiving and sending out reports of the King's movements, and whenever these indicated a junction of the King and Princes, warnings were sent to the Associated Counties. The Committee were distressed to learn that the Castle in Cambridge "is not provided with one day's victuals if an enemy should approach," and they backed it up with this Cromwellian sentiment :—"We conceive you might as well have no fortifications as no victuals. We recommend you to look to it that an enemy may not have it for the looking on."

Committeemen accustomed to fall back upon their own homes did not always see things from a military point of view, and in this respect their garrisons sometimes presented a marked contrast with the enormous stores of provisions found within some of the Royalist strongholds. What the Eastern Counties Committees could, and generally did do, was to have their Trained Bands in readiness to march to Cambridge, or to the borders of their shires, to repel a threatened incursion; and this they were required to do in May. One of the King's captains came to the Committee at Cambridge, protested 'to live and die with them,' but sought to betray the Isle of Ely to the King. The design was discovered and prevented, but it set Parliament debating over means for the defence of the Isle, and voting 1,000 foot, a troop of horse, and of dragoons, and £1,000 for this purpose.

At last the Cambridge Castle was getting within a stout fringe of fortifications—£300 voted for perfecting the works, £200 for victualling, and £200 for arrears for officers and soldiers. A similar vote of £300 was made for the garrison of King's Lynn; and County Committees were strengthened by the addition of men likely to put a little reality and earnestness into the business of preparing for the crisis.

Notwithstanding Self-denying Ordinances, Cromwell could not be spared from the Fen country, whose people he knew so well, and Parliament ordered him to take charge of the Isle of Ely. To the Grand Committee at Cambridge they wrote : "We hope his coming will be a good use for putting things there into a secure posture."

Cromwell was the last man to need the commonplace reminders of the Committee for both Kingdoms, and his first act was to require money and ammunition to be sent.[1] On May 29, with Naseby but little more than a fortnight ahead, there came a response in twenty barrels of powder, bullet, and match, £2,000 in money, and two sakers and four drakes—names for artillery, which may sound strangely to modern ears. The Committee for both Kingdoms appealed to the Associated Counties to bring in their forces to the rendezvous, encouraging them with the Hibernian assurance that Lieutenant-General Cromwell "will be in the Isle before this comes to you."[2] "I cannot but relate how sensible he was, and how he grieved to see the too much neglect of so important a place; which he did express fully before the Committees at Cambridge. He did give order for contriving better and more serviceable fortifications."

At the end of May there came a rumour to Cambridge that the King was at Peterborough; the six pieces of artillery had got into position in the Isle of Ely, and Cromwell was directing operations by summoning a meeting of 'inhabitants of these parts' at his old home of St. Ives 'for the prevention of the King's forces from invading the Association'[3] Vermuyden, by a forced march with his regiment from Grantham, came to join Cromwell, taking up a position around Peterborough with instructions to keep a sharp eye upon the movements of the King's forces, who were in reality then storming Leicester, and sending off 140 cart-loads of plunder to Newark. It was fortunate for the Associated Counties and for Parliament that Cromwell was once more appearing in person amongst the Fenmen. On June 4, he had ridden over from St. Ives to Huntingdon, whence he wrote to Fairfax concerning his work in the Isle:—"Since my coming into these parts I have been busied to secure that part of the Isle of Ely where I conceived most danger to be. Truly I found it in a very ill posture: and it is yet weak; without works, ammunition or men considerable,—and of money least; and then, I hope,

[1] Exchange Intelligencer, Brit. Mus., E. 288 (3).
[2] The Letter-books of the Committee for both Kingdoms are preserved in the State Papers, the excellent Calendars to which afford a ready means of tracing the letters quoted.
[3] Mercurius Civicus, May 29 to June 6.

you will easily conceive of the defence: and God has preserved us all this while to a miracle. The party under Vermuyden awaits the King's Army and is about Deeping, has a command to join with Sir John Gell if he commands him. So, 'too,' the Nottingham Horse. I shall be bold to present you with intelligence as it comes to me."[1] On the same day the Committee for both Kingdoms wrote to the Committee at Cambridge warning them against disaffected persons who had invited the enemy with a promise to deliver up the town to them. Cromwell rode over from Huntingdon to investigate, and was present in the old Committee-room there and signed the following document, drawn up by the Association Committee there on June 6, and sent off to the deputy-lieutenants of Suffolk[2]:—

"Cambridge, 6th June, 1645.
"Gentlemen,
"The cloud of the Enemy's Army hanging still upon the borders, and drawing towards Harborough, make some supposals that they aim at the Association. In regard whereof, we have information that the Army about Oxford was not yesterday advanced, albeit it was ordered so to do, we thought meet to give you intelligence thereof, and therewith earnestly to propound to your consideration, that you will have in readiness what Horse and Foot may be had, that so a proportion may be drawn forth for this service, such as may be expedient.

"And because we conceive that the exigence may require Horse and Dragoons, we desire that all your Horse and Dragoons may hasten to Newmarket; where they will receive orders for farther advance, according as the motion of the Enemy and of our Army shall require. And to allow both the several Troops of Dragoons and Horse one week's pay,

[1] Carlyle, Letters and Speeches, i, 170.
[2] "There were 53 of our men surprised in their quarters and carried prisoners into Oxford, and as they went to prison the cruel enemy did cut and hacked and wounded our men most cruelly; and these 53 men Sir Thomas Fairfax hath exchanged and sent up to London in carts, and some of them are in hospital and are very honest and religious men, that are Suffolk men (some came from Sudbury)."—Wallington, ii, 261.

to be laid down by the owner, which shall be repaid out of the public money out of the County ; the pay of each trooper being 14 shillings per week, and of a Dragoon 10/6 per week.

"Your servants,

H. Mildmay	W. Spring
W. Heveningham	Maurice Barrow
Ti. Midlton (sic)	Nathaniel Bacon
P.S. The place of Rendezvous for	Francis Russell
the Horse and Dragoons to be	Oliver·Cromwell
at Newmarket ; and for the Foot	Hum. Walcot
Bury. Since the writing hereof,	Isaak Puller
we received intelligence that the	Ed . . . (illegible)

Enemy's Body with 60 carriages was upon his march towards the Association, 3 miles on this side Harborough, last night at 4 of the clock."[1]

Of this letter Carlyle says : " The original—a hasty, blotted paper, with the signatures in two unequal columns [as imitated here], and with the postscript crammed hurriedly to the corner, and written from another inkbottle, as is still apparent— represents to us an agitated scene in the old Committee rooms at Cambridge that Friday."

This letter was backed up by one from the Committee in London, who asked the Committeemen of Suffolk not to look so much upon what they had to pay, with these alarms lying heavy upon them, as to consider what they might lose if the enemy prevailed 'to the plunder and spoil of all.' Suffolk, like the other counties, everywhere in such a ferment of agitation and suspense, responded by sending forth Colonel Brampton Gurdon, member for Sudbury, with his regiment of Suffolk horse, not only for the safety of the county but for the rendezvous for Naseby.[2]

Once more the town and neighbourhood of Cambridge witnessed the mustering of the forces of East Anglia to meet the demand for sending 3,000 foot and 1,000 horse

---

[1] Carlyle, Letters and Speeches, i, 172.
[2] " Recd. 16 days pay as Collonnell to Nasbe at 39s."—Entry in Gurdon Papers at Repton Hall.

to such place as Cromwell should appoint, and so great was the zeal that the Committee in London for once left it to the counties to fix their own proportion; for there was now no jealousy excepting for the honour of doing most, and the supply of men seemed likely to far exceed the demand. Cromwell himself was in no fixed quarters for many hours, but was riding all over the Fens, now looking to the passes and fortified places, now pushing forward the recruiting. Never since the summer of 1642, with its rival proclamations and the 'clipping the wings' of 'malignant' Bishops, Sheriffs, and Mayors, had the effect of Cromwell's indomitable energy and incessant riding to and fro been more marked, amongst his own people, than in this one supreme effort to rouse and weld together the forces and powers of the Associated Counties for the last great struggle with the King around Harborough.

There is every reason to believe that the evasion of the Self-denying Ordinance involved in keeping Cromwell in the field was not only popular in the Army, but throughout the Eastern Counties, if we may judge from the response made to the trumpet-calls of Cromwell. 'It was no sooner noised that Lieutenant-Colonel Cromwell was to be sent into the Isle of Ely, but the courage of the Association began to be high with hope and the City to be full of joy. You will find this commander within these few days to have a gallant army to join him about Cambridge.'[1] All over the Eastern Counties, the villages and towns sent in their men 'with incredible speed and alacrity. . . . . Three score men out of one poore petty village in Cambridgeshire in which to see it, none would have thought that there had been fifty fighting men in it.' Four brothers out of one family marched away from an east coast village to fight with Cromwell in the impending battle.[2] Hopes ran high with the assurance that 'our armies have shown themselves extraordinary swift in their motions to their rendezvous to

[1] A Diary, E. 288 (5).
[2] "There is a tradition in my family that four brothers Flaxman, from East Ruston, a village near Great Yarmouth, joined Cromwell's forces and fought under him at Naseby."—Letter to the author from Mr. Arthur J. Flaxman, New Court, Temple, London.

pursue the King's Army to some purpose, and to make the Royal pipe to play a new song.'[1]

At last the blind chess-board policy of the Committee for both Kingdoms, in seeking to checkmate every Royalist move, or hold or take some garrison, instead of preparing for a decisive battle, was improved upon by Fairfax marching, on June 5, from before Oxford, and coming into line with the other forces. Cromwell was still about Huntingdon and Cambridge, where "great numbers of the Associated Counties do daily join themselves with him. . . . . Some of them are but raw soldiers, yet a little exercise will make them expert; indeed, we have seldom cause to find fault with our new raised soldiers, especially out of that Association. A good cause and a good heart are two good prognostics of success." "Col. Cromwell increases more and more. . . . . Ely is reasonable strong, Peterborough hath divers troops and companies of dragoons who will be able to make that good." So wrote the garrulous old newspapers in those exciting days on the eve of Naseby fight.

It was quite clear on all hands that Cromwell's presence was indispensable, and yet he was only riding to and fro as a volunteer worker. "At such a moment the name of the man whose courage and conduct had scattered the army of Rupert and Newcastle at Marston Moor could not fail to be on every lip."[2] "To speak truth," wrote one of the old newspapers, "at this instance it were to be wished he were in the Army, for it is conceived by some the King will fight, and fighting he [Cromwell] might put more courage into his friends."

Fairfax and his officers brought matters to a climax by addressing a letter to the House of Commons urging the necessity of a Commander-in-Chief for the Horse, and "withal desiring that the valliant Cromwell might be the man."[3] In this letter they spoke of Cromwell in these terms: " The general esteem and affection which he hath, both of the officers and soldiers of this Army, his own

---
[1] Exchange Intelligencer, Brit. Mus. Lib., E. 388.
[2] Gardiner, ii, 200.
[3] Newspapers in " Cromwelliana."

personal worth and ability for the employment; his great care, diligence, courage, and faithfulness in the service you have already employed him, with the constant presence and blessing of God that have accompanied him, make us look upon it as a duty we owe to you and the public to make it our earnest and humble suit . . . . to appoint him unto this employment, which shall be received by us with that thankfulness and acknowledgment of your favour which may best express how sensible we are of so great an obligation," etc.[1]

The Commons promptly assented to the proposal, and this was as promptly accepted by Fairfax, who without waiting for the consent of the Lords, acquainted Cromwell of the decision of the Commons in these terms:—"You cannot expect but that I make use of so good an advantage as I apprehend this to be to the public good. Therefore I desire you to make speedy repair to this Army." He adds that "the enemy are as we hear, more horse than foot, and make their horse their confidence. Ours shall be in God. I pray make all possible haste towards your affectionate friend to serve you.—Tho. Fairfax."

Meanwhile, on June 10, the King's Councillors were meeting at Oxford, and warmly supporting a direct march upon the Associated Counties, and approached both the King and Rupert urging this policy. The King and the Prince, strong in everything but in united counsels, neither accepted this nor the alternative of a march against the Scots in Yorkshire, but drifted between the two with indifferent results hereafter. Fairfax had by this time got as far as Newport Pagnell, commanding "the bravest bodies of men, horse, and arms, so far as ye common soldiers, as ere I saw in my life . . . . the number is 8,000 Foot and 5,000 or 6,000 Horse." So wrote Sir Samuel Luke; and when Fairfax came into the garrison of Newport, the bluff old Governor excused himself from 'feasting' the General on the ground of his quarters lacking accommodation, and seems to have limited his hospitality to showing him round the

[1] Newspapers in "Cromwelliana."

works of the garrison, giving him 'a peale of ordinance' and providing him and his followers with wine.[1]

Among the hills around Market Harborough, where Fairfax's and the King's armies were drawing nearer and nearer together, and throughout the towns and villages of East Anglia, an immense amount of interest was taken in the question of whether Cromwell with his 1,000 horse and 3,000 foot would arrive in time for the impending battle. In the City men were discussing the question with equal interest, and the newspapers were expressing the hope that "he will come in time enough for a reserve, if not for the main battle." The Royalist Army gathering around Harborough were also interested in the question, and on Wednesday evening, June 11, a letter was sent off stating that the King's Army were much impressed by the news that " Ironsides." was coming to join with the Parliament's Army. On the same night Cromwell was getting together his forces 'about Bedford, Hitchin, and Royston; and are expected to come to him [Fairfax] this [Thursday] night.'[2]

Cromwell's place was in the van and not in the reserve; and, with the soldier's instinct for the time for decisive action, he, with part of the history of England hanging upon the issue, left behind the bulk of his newly raised men, advanced rapidly at the head of 600 horse, and at daybreak on June 13 came in sight of Fairfax's army, with this result :—" On Friday morning came Lieutenant General Cromwell to the Army as they were drawing to march after the King's Army towards Leicester. The Horse, at the appearing of the Lieutenant General, gave a mighty shout for joy of his coming to them."[3]

Fairfax had just returned from a midnight ride to an outpost, where, forgetting the password, he was detained by one of his own sentries; a Council of Officers was held which soon broke up, and "orders, were for drums to beat and trumpets to sound 'to horse!' and all their army to draw to a rendezvous." The evidence of activity spread

[1] Luke's Letter-book, Egerton MSS., 786.
[2] Mercurius Civicus, June 12.
[3] A more Exact and Perfect Relation, E. 288 (28).

to the Royalist camp, where it was instinctively known that "Ironsides" had come. The King was summoned from the chase and his army hurriedly drawn up in a strong position on Borough Hill, the Parliamentary Army being at Kisslingbury. The Parliamentary Army outnumbered that of the King in the proportion of 13,600 to 8,000, and were eager to revenge the 'plundering' of the Cavaliers.[1]

"Amongst the fierce Puritans of the Parliamentary horse there was stern joy at the arrival of the long-wished-for time when through their arms the cause of God was to be put to the test of battle,"[2] and the veterans of Marston Moor gave courage to the New Modellers from the Associated Counties, who had never yet been in battle. With the word "God is our strength" on the Parliament side and "Queen Mary" on that of the King, the two armies charged, one down the hill into the "valley of death" in Broad Moor, and the other up the hill, until the crash came. Then the Marston Moor tactics were repeated. Rupert broke through and routed the Parliamentary left wing, and Cromwell broke through and routed the Royalist left wing. Again Cromwell restrained his horse in the pursuit, and returned to the battle; Rupert again went too far to recover lost ground.[3] But the story is familiar: How Fairfax, with his helmet shot off, rode to and fro bareheaded beneath the hot June sun with bullets flying about him; how Skippon, the veteran soldier, dangerously wounded, declared that he would not stir from the field so long as a man would stand; how the King's carriage was captured, and his cabinet with the compromising letters—all these are familiar parts of the tragic story of Naseby field, which we

[1] "We cannot choose but fight with extraordinary courage, for every foot soldier that we have taken has 20s. or 30s. a man in his pockets; there was a sergeant taken that had £20 in his pocket, which will make men fight if they intend to fight. . . . . The soldiers that are taken are very full of money and plunder."—Luke's Letter-book, Egerton MSS., 786.
[2] Gardiner, ii, 211.
[3] Commenting upon the Parliamentary forces rallying again after a repulse, Clarendon says: "That difference was observed all along in the discipline of the King's troops, and of those which marched under the command of Fairfax and Cromwell . . . . that though the King's troops prevailed in the charge, and routed those they charged, they seldom rallied themselves again in order . . . . whereas the other troops if they prevailed, or though they were beaten and routed, presently rallied again and stood in good order till they received new orders."

may leave to their places in the history of England, and follow Cromwell and his Ironsides, who more especially belong to East Anglia as well as to England.

In the gloaming of this memorable Summer's day, on his return from the hot pursuit of the Cavaliers towards Leicester, the sturdy old Ironsides sat down on the field at Harborough, with the smell of powder in the air, and the havoc of war all around; and taking up the pen for the sword wrote on a sheet with two leaves—now faded and held together with paste in the repositories at the British Museum, in the following terms:—

"Harborough, 14 June, 1645.
"Sir,
"Being commanded by you to this service, I think myself bound to acquaint you with the good hand of God towards you and us.

"We marched yesterday after the King, who went before us from Daventry to Harborough, and quartered about six miles from him. This day we marched towards him. He drew out to meet us; both Armies engaged. We, after three hours fight very doubtful, at last routed his Army; killed and took about 5,000—very many officers, but of what quality we yet know not. We took also about 200 carriages, all he had; and all his guns, being 12 in number. . . . . We pursued the Enemy from three miles short of Harborough to nine beyond, even to the sight of Leicester, whither the King fled.

"Sir, this is none other but the hand of God; and to Him alone belongs the glory, wherein none are to share with Him. The General served you with all faithfulness and honour; and the best commendation I can give him is, that I daresay he attributes all to God, and would rather perish than assume to himself. Which is an honest and a thriving way: and yet as much for bravery may be given to him, in this action as to a man. Honest men served you faithfully in this action. Sir, they are trusty; I beseech you, in the name of God, not to discourage them. I wish this action may beget thankfulness and humility in all that are concerned in it. He that ventures his life for the liberty of his country, I wish he trust God for the liberty of his conscience, and you for the liberty he fights for. In this he rests, who is

"Your most humble servant,
Oliver Cromwell."

History has very properly taken note of that 'mighty shout' which welcomed 'Old Ironsides' and his 600 horse on the field of Naseby and of their doughty deeds, but has done less than justice to the large body of men in reserve which Cromwell left behind in that hurried march—a second line of defence, had the issue of Naseby failed, which had mustered all along the borders of the Eastern Counties. Take a single instance of what these Eastern Counties were doing to roll back the tide of war which threatened their borders. The county of Essex, although the most remote from the danger, was sending three regiments, marching for Cambridge by way of Saffron Walden. The Committee for both Kingdoms, finding that the army of Fairfax and Cromwell had got between the King's army and the Association, advised the Association Committee at Cambridge that these Essex regiments, excepting the horse, might be sent back to their homes. But the Committee at Cambridge knew better than send men home at such a crisis, which would just then have been as unpopular as it would have been foolish; and the regiments were kept at Cambridge, and the Committee in London shortly afterwards commended the Cambridge Committee in flattering terms for their prudence!

Taking the 3,400 which Cromwell himself had left behind in his forced march, the regiments which other counties of the Association as well as Essex were sending in, and those in the garrisons, there must have been a reserve of 15,000 men under arms along the borders of the Associated Counties in readiness to defend them from the contemplated attack had the issue of Naseby been unfavourable to the Parliamentary arms. Such a reserve could not have replaced the defeated army of Fairfax and Cromwell, but it was an eloquent answer to the resolution of the King's Council at Oxford, and as eloquent a testimony to 'the spirit and resources of East Anglia. The Association Committee at Cambridge had also shown a grip of the situation, set aside the convenience of its civil life, and out-generalled the fussy Committee in London, by keeping well in hand a sufficient military force to show a bold front for the Associated Counties whatever might befall.

The Association system of uniting for the defence of home, as well as fighting for a great principle in the field, was put upon its trial for the last time in its fluctuating history, and it came out of the ordeal, both at the headquarters at Cambridge and in the field at Naseby, with lasting honour which will never fade from the memory of East Anglia; and, whatever view may be held of the rival policies, with an *éclat* which will live in the history of England as the chief determining factor in the greatest conflict of ancient or modern times.

CHAPTER XI.

THE LAST RALLY OF THE KING — THE FIGHT AT HUNTINGDON—THE KING'S FLIGHT THROUGH THE FENS IN DISGUISE.

(1645-6.)

FOR the Eastern Counties, as for England, the victory at Naseby was the greatest event in the War, by reason of its nearness to their borders. In that event these counties had a vital interest; for that event they had made extraordinary exertions, and when the tidings of victory came there were thanksgivings and rejoicings in all the towns and villages of East Anglia. Cambridge spent money on wine, and voted money for the soldiers in garrison 'on Thanksgiving day in June.'[1]

Parliament voted Cromwell the pay of a Lieutenant-General of Horse from the commencement of the New Model Army, and another three months' exemption from the Self-denying Ordinance, an exemption which practically became permanent. The King was still fairly strong in numbers, and with the expected assistance of an army from France and Ireland, the papers concerning which, found in his cabinet at Naseby, had aroused indignation in the country, he was hoping to retrieve his fortunes. The West of England was almost the only English soil, with the exception of Newark, Oxford, and other garrisons, now

[1] Corporation Accounts, printed in Cooper's "Annals of Cambridge."

held for the King, and thither Fairfax and Cromwell marched against Lord Goring.

When the great crisis at Naseby had passed, recruiting in the Associated Counties raised the old feeling of repugnance to marching away into the west. An ordinance was passed for punishing runaways with death. Watch was directed to be kept at places through which the recruits passed on their way to the rendezvous at Reading, and, as example, the deputy-lieutenants were directed to deal with offenders in the several market towns, 'in some public place, and there openly, and not in private, examine and determine such offences, and upon proof to proceed to condemnation and execution of the offenders.'[1] The Constables having a disagreeable duty to perform, often took men of least use in the parish, and sometimes were ordered to take 'idle serving and such other able persons as live dissolutely or idly without employment.'[2] It was not from such men that the Ironsides sprang.

Parliament had by this time a sufficient grip even of the Cambridge University for wine to be drunk in College halls to celebrate the victory of Fairfax and Cromwell over Goring.[3] But the end of the conflict in the Fens was not yet. On the edge of harvest Lincolnshire was alarmed by the growing strength of the Newark garrison, and the Counties were urged to renewed efforts to get 'that thorn taken out of your sides.'

These fears were soon verified, for at the beginning of August the Cavaliers from Newark marched up to their old friends in Stamford; and while attempting to gather taxes and 'plundering the country,' Captain Allan rode out with about 100 of the Parliamentary Horse, fell upon them and routed them, taking 51 prisoners and fourscore horse and arms, and "besides five slain upon the place," says the narrative, "divers crept into the woods. They also rescued

[1] Lords' Journals.
[2] Warrant to the Constable of East Barsham, Norfolk, Le Strange Papers.
[3] "For six quarts of clarett wine in the Hall at dinner upon the day of thanksgiving for the rowting of Lord Goring's forces at Langport."—Bursar's Accounts, St. John's College, July 22, 1645.

the Alderman of Stamford with fifteen considerable countrymen whom the enemy had taken prisoners."[1]

Two or three weeks later the Cavaliers came again, taxed the town of Stamford, from which they obtained £200, and for the non-payment of the full sum demanded they again carried off the unfortunate Alderman 'and some others of the best affected persons there.' Colonel Dodson, governor of Crowland garrison, was directed to retaliate by taking 'the like course with some of their party . . . . that there may be means for the recovery of these prisoners.' This had the desired effect, but a few weeks later down came the Cavaliers upon the town, carried off the Alderman and his friends again, and this time he was detained for three months, when Colonel Dodson was again ordered to take into custody the same persons he had attached before, in order to procure the exchange and liberty of the Alderman and his friends.

These daring adventures of the Cavaliers brought down Parliamentary ordinances for securing Crowland and the Isle of Ely—500 foot, 100 dragoons, and £250 weekly for the Isle under the command of Colonel Russell as Governor, and 100 foot, 20 dragoons, and £50 a week for Crowland under Colonel Dodson as Governor.[2] King's Lynn was also getting uneasy about its defences; for the garrison having had no pay for a long time, 'a quarrel between them and the townsmen' was expected daily.[3]

While those famous captains of Ironsides, who had left their homes on the banks of the Ouse and the Cam— Oliver Cromwell, Edward Montague, John Desborough, Henry Cromwell, son of Sir Philip of Biggin — while this interesting group was engaged in operations in the west, leading up to the storming of Bristol, at which Henry Cromwell was dangerously wounded, and Montague and Desborough performed prodigies of valour, their neighbours about Huntingdon were for a time in the grip of the King's army. His Majesty, 'hugely revived,' since his overthrow

[1] Letter in Commons' Journals.
[2] Lords' Journals.
[3] Portland MSS.

at Naseby, by the propositions of his friends 'to raise a well-disciplined army . . . . and to lead their [his enemies] such a dance as to make them lose all the summer in following us,' was, in these sultry days of harvest, drawing round again towards the Associated Counties, with no considerable force to oppose him.

The Association Committee wrote, on August 15, from Trinity College, Cambridge, a despairing letter to the Speaker of the extremity of the soldiers in the garrison there, and the lamentable cries continually made by the poorer inhabitants of the town, for monies due to them for quartering the soldiers, and they add :—

"A castle there is, very considerable in Strength, allarms come both of the Enemy's strength, not farre from us, but what acompt is likely to be given or can be expected of a place where the Soldier is not inabled for Service, but discontented with Apprehensions of neglect, and being among a People prepared by Poverty for any mischiefe, wee humbly leave to your Honorable House to consider. Sir, the Officers and Soldiers are forty Weeks' pay in Arreares, above £3,000 is due for Quarter to the Towne for the soldiers of the Earle of Manchester's Army, and the Castle. Wee beseeche you, Sir, acquaint your Honourable Howse with it, and our humble Desires, that they please to order some reasonable Pay, for the Officers and Soldiers, to relieve their necessitys, and that they please to order out of what monies they think fitt, for the present Payment of the Quarters, all which is of much concernment to the Safety and Quiet of this place."[1]

Three days later the King, in his journey southwards, wrote from Doncaster to Secretary Nicholas, in the best of spirits, giving an account of his condition, "which considering what it was at the beginning of this monthe is now (thank God) miraculously good." The gentlemen of those parts were joining with him and hoped that the recruiting would make up 'a lusty stocke for the next year's Army.' But with Poyntz behind him in Yorkshire, the King's policy was to

[1] Printed in Cooper's "Annals of Cambridge," and by Neal ("Hist. of Puritans").

keep moving, and so he advanced to Newark, Belvoir, and towards Stamford, causing much concern about the Boston garrison, the fortifications of which were so large and irregular as to require a large force to defend them, and it was resolved to employ 'some skilful engineer' to bring them into a more regular state.

With no force to oppose his march, the King could easily hold his own in the field, while among the civil population the presence of His Majesty for the first time since the War began aroused the enthusiasm of the Royalists, and, for the time being, quieted the weaker Parliamentarians; with the result that the Cavaliers simply over-ran South Lincolnshire and Huntingdonshire. Near Stamford a force from Burghley House and Leicester fell upon the King's rear, and took 80 horse, colours, and prisoners, an act which could have been easily avenged had the King been in a mood to retrace his steps, for his army, according to Symonds, included 2,200 horse.

Entering Stamford suddenly on Saturday, August 23, the King made his quarters at the George Hotel,[1] and his soldiers made free of the town.

On Sunday morning, August 24, the King and his army resumed their march for Huntingdon about the same time that a force of 400 horse, raised in Essex and Suffolk, were marching from Huntingdon under Lieutenant-Colonel Le Hunt, Major Gibbs, and Captain Poe. Near Stilton the two forces met; a skirmish ensued with the advanced guards, in which the Cavaliers 'killed divers' of the Parliamentary force, and took Major Gibb prisoner.[2] In the face of superior numbers the Parliamentary Horse retired to Huntingdon, where the King's forces accordingly expected some little resistance, 'for it was made a kind of garrison, with some traverses and light works about it.[3]

With the Huntingdon people all atremble with excitement, about two o'clock on Sunday afternoon the King's army

[1] The George Hotel still exists in St. Martin's, Stamford, bearing on its front, carved in stone, the arms of Lord Treasurer Burghley, by whom it was built or re-edified.
[2] Symonds says the Major and 100 were taken.
[3] Slingsby's Diary.

drew in sight of the town and of the light earthworks behind which a small force of Parliamentary Foot, under Captain Bennett, had taken up a position with but little hope of anything but a temporary resistance. The King's forces drew up at the Bridge,[1] a short resistance was made in which Captain Bennett stuck bravely to his post, where 'he and his lieutenant and many of his men were slain,' and the King and his army entered the town. The actual resistance is thus described by Symonds:—"They a little disputed Huntingdon, but wee entered notwithstanding a large ditch encompassed it, lately scowered and cast up, and a breaste work and gate in the roade. Theese rebells ran away to Cambridge: all of them back and breast, headpiece, brace of pistolls; officers more. Every troop consisted of 100."[2]

At the King's entry, in a kind of triumph, those in the town who were for the King lost their heads with enthusiasm, and those who were for Parliament lost their hearts; and His Majesty passed along through the streets amidst a reception in striking contrast with the resistance at the Bridge, the Mayor of the town and the Bailiffs of Godmanchester leading the acclaim, and getting much complimentary bowing from His Majesty in return. The King made his quarters at the George Hotel—of which old inn, only a portion, a picturesque bit of staircase and balcony in the stableyard, now remains—while his soldiers repeated the Stamford tactics at the expense of the townspeople.

The news of the King's taking possession of Huntingdon spread to Cambridge, and threw the Associated Counties into the greatest alarm. To the Committee for both Kingdoms in London the news spread and letters were despatched, haste, post haste, to Fairfax in the west, and to the Associated Counties—now urging Norfolk to furnish provisions and forces for Lynn; to Suffolk and Essex to

---

[1] The skirmish probably extended across Godmanchester Common, which lies to the south of the Bridge. The Bridge itself, a fine structure dating from Edward I's reign, is still in almost its original state, and was described by the late Sir Gilbert Scott as certainly one of the finest in England.—Note to the author from the Ven. Archdeacon Vesey.

[2] Marchings of the Royal Army, etc., Harl. MSS., 944; also in Symonds' Diary, Camd. Soc.

get their horse and foot together to a rendezvous, spicing their letter with the item, "the King with 4,000 Horse hath taken Huntingdon"; and promising that the City Militia would march out as far as Barnet.

On Monday morning, August 25, the King sat down at his inn for reflection, and for the writing of dispatches concerning his affairs. On the Sunday evening news had reached him at Huntingdon of the success of his cause in the North, which had made Montrose 'master of all Scotland'; but this did not blind him to the fact that his position in England was deplorable enough. To his Secretary Nicholas he despatched this letter:—

"Huntingtoune, 25 Aug. 1645.

"Nicholas, I haue this morning receaued yours of the 13: Aug: with fower printed Oxford Papers concerning my published letters, & am glad to fynde that you there make so faire (indeed just as concerning my religion kingdome and frends) an interpretation of them, & particularly that you haue so great a confidence in my constansy to my just cause: and now me thinkes I wer too blame if I did not justifie the trewth of your opinions concerning me, by my own declaration wch is this, that let my condition be neuer so low, my successes neuer so ill, I resolue (by God's grace) neuer to yealed up this Church to the Gouernment of Papists; nor to injure my successors, by lessening the Crowen of that ecclesiasticall & military power wch my predecessors left me, nor forsake my frends, much lesse to lett them suffer when I doe not, for theire faithfulnesse to me, resoluing soone to liue as miserable as the violent rage of successfull, insulting Rebells can make me (wch I esteme far worse than death) rather then not to be exactly constant to these grounds, from wch whosoeur, upon whatsoeur occasion shall persuade me to receade in the least title, I shall esteame him ether a foole or a knaue; but you will aske me, *Quorsum hoc*? Yes, for without this warning the tender personall affection of some might giue me troblesome aduyce, & yet not blameable considering the present condition of my affaires, not knowing this

my resolution, wch I command you to publishe to all whom their quality or judgement makes fitt for such discourses, & so I rest,
"Your most asseured frend,
Charles R.
"You may say confidently & giue me for author that the peace of Irland is concluded, not yet knowing the particular conditions."[1]

Turning to his immediate necessities, His Majesty issued an order bearing his sign manual directed to Colonel Henry Cromwell—'kinsmen of ye other'—High Sheriff of Hunts, requiring him to issue warrants requiring all the inhabitants of Huntingdon, "between the ages of sixteen and three score to appear at the . . . . Huntingdon tomorrow morning, being the 26th present, by 10 of the clock, and to bring with them all the arms they have, where they shall understand our further pleasure. This they and every of them are to perform upon their allegiance, and as they will answere the same at theire perills. Given at our Court at Huntingdon this 25th of August, 1645."[2]

While these documents were being drawn up at the "George" in Huntingdon, His Majesty's forces were riding all over the surrounding country to the terror and ruin of the inhabitants; and it may be convenient here to let the old chronicles speak for themselves, with such allowance as may be necessary for their authors.

"It was particularly advertised that His Majesty, the Lord's Day before, entered the town of Huntingdon, and with much complimental bowing saluting of his good friends, as he passed through the streets, and was entertained with expressions of joy and acclamation as had not been heard there. The Mayor of Huntingdon and two bailiffs of Godmanchester and their brethren, as a further acknowledgement of their delight to see him, taxed the said town 5s., 10s.,

---

[1] The letter is endorsed by Nicholas—"The King to me from Huntingdon, containing his resoluc'on neuer to quit ye Church gouernement, his friends, or diminishe the Crowne of that military or eccl'all power wch was left him by his p^edecessors."—Nicholas Correspondence, in Evelyn's Diary, vol. iv, pp. 159-60.
[2] Add. MSS. B.M., 34,465, f. 110.

and 15s. a man (mean·men) and others at far higher rates, and presented His Majesty therewith in lump, which mayor, bailiffs and 43 others of his brethren (most royalists) for their loving expressions were carried away prisoners with the Army ; and many others of the town and other places known friends of them, carried away and forced to ransom themselves by money.

"Presently after the king came in, proclamation was made that, on pain of death, no soldier should plunder, and that full satisfaction should be made to any who complained of such grievances. No sooner was it made but they fell to plundering, carrying out of divers shops & houses 3 or 4 loads of goods and ware apiece. Amongst many Mr. Fulwood, apothecary, and the two king's woollen drapers can witness its truth, not leaving them one bit of household stuff in their houses, or wares in their shops. Every house was billited, though never so poor, some 20 or 30 in a house, who were by special order to provide both horse meat and man's meat, and 12s. a day to each soldier to spend, which was duly paid them, though they were forced to borrow it. In many quarters the soldiers fetched in sheep of other mens and the landlord paid them four or five shillings apiece for them, to dress them for their use, or else swore they would spit their children. Many houses were plundered to nothing, so that tables, stools, bedsteads and other combustible things lie broken in every room, after the bedding linen, pewter, and portable things are carried out. Very many people are left not worth one penny.

"At their parting they drove away both Huntingdon & Godmanchester herds of kine about 6 or 7 hundred and made them pay a mark a piece for them before they had them again. They left scarce a horse in either town nor in any other they marched through, so that the country knew not how to get in their corn yet out. The injuries on some particular men are many, and their cruelties inflicted upon some by tying lighted matches between their fingers and burning them are too many. They knocked off the irons of all the felons and other prisoners in Huntingdon jail, which were many, and condemned men in law for gross robberies and murders, who have all taken up arms for His Majesty.

"The King, to please the country, after many thousand pounds worth of goods sent away without any check, and many men undone, caused lots to be cast between four who had pilleged a poor glover (one Gumber) of about five shillings, and one to be hanged therefore, and at his departure gave the town and county thanks for their kind entertainment of him. One providence is observable that divers of the best affected to the Parliament have escaped with the least loss, and many of the King's best friends have suffered most in their persons and estates. Many of the Huntingdonshire malignants are convinced of their errors in supposing the King's Army saints, but find them more like devils. Some of our London malignants are changed in judgment being at Huntingdon and eye witnesses of what was performed."[1]

Another correspondent, writing apparently of the King's progress through Lincolnshire into Huntingdonshire, says:—
"It hath pleased God to cast us into a very sad condition, the King's army coming through our country hath seized upon all the men they could find and have taken away my master. They have at least a thousand of our countrymen prisoners with them and at least 3000 horses out of our county and Huntingdonshire. My master hath paid them down three score pounds on his own table before they carried away his person, no man knows where, nor what hardship he endures which is a great grief to us. The King hath enriched himself more than at least tenfold; 2000 resolved men would have beat him utterly, his men are so drunken and so earnest for plundering."[2]

The indiscriminate plunderings of Huntingdon and neighbouring towns is frankly admitted by Royalists. Slingsby says: "Here ye solgiers got some plunder, and among other things a long scrole of ye names of such as had taken ye Covenant with some letters, one whereof was given to ye King to read, which I saw, attaining the great

[1] Wallington's Historical Notices, vol. ii, pp. 266-70.
[2] Ibid.

dislike the men had to see how much ye people were adicted to adolize ye King, with many quotations and texts of Scripture."[1]

The Cavaliers during that Monday 'faced the town and University of Cambridge, and the fright of his [the King's] coming had driven the most factious out of the Colleges in the town.' As to Colonel Henry Cromwell of Ramsey, and his warrants, when the King was getting ready to leave Huntingdon on Tuesday morning for Woburn, there appeared at Godmanchester a body of the countrymen to the number of 400, to whom the King gave thanks and told them that he should not need them at that time.[2]

During that Sunday evening and all day on Monday drums were beating and trumpets were blowing all over East Anglia, and before Monday evening men were leaving the harvest fields and marching to the rendezvous once more at Cambridge. In Essex the rumour went that Cambridge itself had fallen into the King's hands, and so they thought it of no use to send their men; but made up for it as soon as the truth reached them. Of the use made of available forces, Mr. Lowry, member for Cambridge, wrote to Parliament in the morning that the King was leaving Huntingdon for St. Neots and Woburn. "I have been drawing all our forces these three nights into the fields . . . . which, I believe, standing upon our guard, both in town and field, hath hindered the King of his design [upon Cambridge]. The King marched from Huntingdon yesterday unto St. Eoates [St. Neots]. . . . We have sent six troops of our horse in pursuit of the King this morning."[3] He adds a postscript that the troops had retreated, finding the enemy with a strong party, "which hath put us into new fears, yet are however resolved to stand to it for the safeguard of the town."

[1] It is interesting to note that amidst all this hurly-burly at Huntingdon, the diarist Richard Symonds, an Essex man, whose antiquarian pursuits amidst the clash of arms form one of the curiosities of the Civil War, had got his sword into its scabbard, and with pencil and notebook in hand, was strolling round the churches. At Huntingdon, as at Stamford, he found that there were four parish churches, and his notes and miniature sketches may still be seen in the British Museum Library.—Harl. MSS., 944.
[2] Slingsby's Diary.   [3] Portland MSS.

Parliament, upon receipt of Mr. Lowry's letter, ordered Colonel Rossiter with his regiment of horse which had followed the King out of Lincolnshire and was now at Stilton, to march in pursuit of the King.

The alarms had brought a remarkable congestion of troops into Cambridge, and distant Essex, as well as Norfolk and Suffolk, came out handsomely, as appears by letter from the Earl of Warwick. "Upon this alarm of the enemy's coming to Huntingdon, I drew up all the forces of Essex, being 6000 Foot and 900 Horse, as also 4000 Foot and 500 Horse came out of Suffolk for the guard of Cambridge and the Isle of Ely." As soon as it was found that the King was marching away, most of this large body of men were dismissed to their homes, excepting 1,100 horse kept in the Fens to keep in the 'Newarkers' in the absence of Colonel Rossiter, who afterwards returned into Lincolnshire.

Among those who were carried off by the King's party were William Clerk and Trice Herne of Godmanchester. They had neglected to pay the fee farm rents to His Majesty; had paid them apparently to the Parliamentary sequestrators instead. So when His Majesty came that way he claimed his own, and in default carried off the two farmers prisoners to Oxford, their neighbours promising to relieve them; but they remained in Oxford for fourteen weeks, when they petitioned the King, setting forth that not only had their townsmen not kept their promise, but that the Huntingdon Committee "being earnestly solicited for your petitioners enlargement, they declare that your petitioners shall rott in prison here in Oxford before they will consent to any proposition for their relief and release, and threatened the messenger that if he came again they would lay him by the heeles. Soe that now your petitioners are in a most miserable condition, being destitute of all means of subsistence and present livelihood in regard they are farre remote from friends and acquaintances, besides their own wife and children at home ready to perish by reason of your petitioners long absence."[1]

[1] Carew Transcripts, Public Record Office.

An interesting sidelight upon the terror which the approach of the King's army occasioned at Cambridge is afforded by the narrative of a University student named Matthew Robinson, whose adventures were characteristic of the times. At the beginning of June he had started from Hull to make his way to Cambridge. Crossing Lincolnshire, he was pursued, and had a narrow escape from the Newark Cavaliers. He made his way to Spalding, and thence to the garrison of Crowland. Here he was kindly received by the Governor (Colonel Dodson), but was put into mean quarters, in which the gnats and the 'hummers' swarmed, so that he left 'thousands of them upon his bed.' Next morning he quitted Crowland for Peterborough, and travelling thence to Huntingdon reached Cambridge on June 9, and was entered at St. John's College. The news of the King's arrival and the fighting at Huntingdon alarmed all Cambridge and the University, towards which the King was believed to be marching. In the flight which ensued, members of Colleges could be seen 'two and three on a horse,' and others 'footed it' to places of greater safety with friends. Among them young Robinson and a companion took to flight again through the marshes, where even Crowland with its gnats and 'hummers' would have been a welcome refuge. But there had gone forth a summons for all 'the country' to come in for the defence of Cambridge, and the fugitive academicians met the 'rude rabble,' who, taunting them with their cowardice, made some of them turn back. Young Robinson saw his companion beaten, and he himself was taken back to Cambridge. Making the best of it, he offered his services to the Governor of the Castle, who armed him with sword, firelock, and bandoliers. Here he did night duty, and 'in the morning stole into the College with his gown, none knowing his new adventure,' until the King's forces had disappeared. Young Robinson lived to be a Fellow of St. John's.[1]

The bustling incident which had brought from 10,000 to

[1] "Life of Matthew Robinson, written by himself"; see "Cambridge in the Seventeenth Century," by Professor Mayor, p. 18 et seq.

12,000 men into Cambridge from Suffolk and Essex was a serious demand upon those counties while it lasted. The Suffolk Committee complained to Parliament that they had had to pledge their own individual credit for £5,000 before this, and now by this last alarm it was doubled.

While this little byplay was being enacted in the Fens the great tragedy of the war was moving on in the West, where Cromwell, Montague, Desborough, Pickering, and the rest of the Ironsides were engaged in storming Royalist strongholds. Bristol was stormed and taken in September, and Prince Rupert marched out under the necessity of asking for the loan of a thousand muskets to assist in escorting and protecting him in his march across country to Oxford. Winchester fell at the beginning of October, and then at last stubborn old Basing House, near Basingstoke, the fortified Royalist stronghold, with a circumvallation of 'above a mile in compass,' the house itself, 'fit to make an Emperor's Court,' and furnished with provisions 'for some years, rather than months'; it was a great prize for the Parliamentary soldiers. Other garrisons fell, one after another, until at the end of the year 1645 the King was beaten at all points in the field, whatever might be his prospects with diplomacy and the Church. A few garrisons still held out, including sturdy old Newark, to which the King returned once more. Here, too, Prince Rupert repaired to justify himself to the King over the loss of Bristol; the ill-feeling between uncle and nephew was patched up; and the King, amidst divided counsels, was drifting into the perplexing condition of not knowing from day to day with which party in the State and the Church it would be safest to throw in his lot for the future.

Newark still held out, calling for a levy of 4,500 foot out of the Associated Counties in the month of November for besieging the place. The Huntingdonshire people, learning that the King intended to keep his winter quarters at Newark, were anxious about the constant danger to their county, and set to work making impassable 'all the fords upon the Ouse from Earith to Emsburie [? Eynesbury], and made drawbridges at St. Ives, Huntingdon, and St. Neots.'

December 7 was, by order of Parliament, kept throughout the Eastern Counties as 'a day of Public Thanksgiving unto God for his singular mercies in preserving the said Counties so graciously from the fury and violence of the Enemy.'[1]

When, in the month of April, 1646, His Majesty was placed in the dilemma at Oxford of almost equal risk of being taken prisoner by the Parliamentary forces whether he stayed or fled, and was sorely beset as to his future movements—whether he should go to London and make peace with the Independents or fly to the Scotch army at Newark and accept Presbyterianism—there began, perhaps, one of the most romantic adventures of a strangely adventurous time. Twice the King had passed through Cambs and Hunts during the opening months of the strife, and again after his defeat at Naseby. But of all the eventful marches of the King the strangest was that which was to bring him again into the region of the Fens, a fugitive in disguise.

Starting out of Oxford at three o'clock in the morning on April 27, 1646, to escape from the tightening grip of the armies under Fairfax, Whalley, and Fleetwood, His Majesty, having cut off his hair and beard and assumed the disguise of a servant to his sole companions, John Ashburnham, Groom to his Bedchamber, and Michael Hudson, his " plain dealing chaplain," commenced one of the most humiliating journeys that any king ever had to undertake. Performing the menial office of carrying the cloak bag of his two companions, His Majesty took the risk of facing the decree which had gone forth from Parliament—that "in case the King shall, contrary to the advice of the Houses of Parliament already given to him, come, or attempt to come, within the lines of communication, that then the Committee of the Militia of London shall have power, and are hereby enjoined to . . . . apprehend and secure such as shall come with him, and to secure his person."

Finding no friend to welcome him as he drew near to London, His Majesty, after a three hours' rest, turned into Hertfordshire by way of Harrow-on-the-Hill.

[1] Lords' Journals.

"About two of the clock we took a guide towards Barnet, resolving to cross the roads into Essex. But after we were past Harrow-on-the-Hill, I told the King, if he were not known much in St. Albans Road it was much the nearer way to go through St. Albans and thence towards Royston, which he approved of. And so we passed through St. Albans, where one old man with an halberd asked us whence we came. I told him from the Parliament, and threw him sixpence, and so passed. After we had rid a mile a gentleman well horsed came galloping after us very fast, which put us in some doubt that we had been discovered in St. Albans. But, they two turning aside, I turned my horse to meet him, and saluting him found him very drunk, and so to avoid his company turned up another way till he was passed; and after went to Westhampstead, where we lodged that night."[1]

At whose house the disguised King slept at Wheathampstead at the end of the weary journey is not very clear. The probability is that it was at Lamer Park, the seat of Sir John Garrard, of which I have written further detail elsewhere.[2] In the examination of Michael Hudson, he adds that the "firste nighte when they wente from Oxford and lay at Withamstede the King helde out well . . . . that the King lay in a grande chamber and Mr. Ashburnham and I lay together."[3]

"Next morning took horse at day-break and went towards Baldocke, and, as we rid upon the way, it was resolved that I should go directlie away towards Southwell, and the King and Mr. Ashburnham towards Norfolk, and stay at the White Swan at Downham till I came back to them."[4]

At Graveley, between Stevenage and Baldock, Dr. Hudson left the King and Mr. Ashburnham to pursue their journey into the Fens, while he went to the French Ambassador at Southwell. After passing through Royston the King and Mr. Ashburnham "took up their residence on Tuesday night at a small village within seven miles of Newmarket, and at

---

[1] Examination of Michael Hudson: Peck's "Desiderata Curiosa," lib. ix, p. 21.
[2] "Hertfordshire during the Civil War," p. 62.
[3] MSS. at Welbeck Abbey.
[4] Peck, "Desiderata Curiosa," lib. ix, p. 21.

a common inn (I should rather suppose an alehouse) there. Qr. whether at Botsham?"[1]

The next stage of their journey was by way of Brandon to Downham, in Norfolk, where they lodged at the Swan. While the King and Ashburnham were at Downham, Hudson was with the French Ambassador at Southwell. On Friday, May 1, he returned to the King and Ashburnham with the proposals from the Scots ; and while the three were hesitating whether to proceed further by sea or by land "the Newes Books," or news-letters, actually arrived in Norfolk, giving accounts of the King's flight from Oxford in the habit of a servant. In order to escape discovery, it therefore became necessary for His Majesty to change his character. So they got him a black cassock, and the King 'bought a new hat proper at Downham,' and it was decided that he should assume the guise of a clergyman. Then, going to have his hair trimmed into a little better shape, the King had 'like to be discovered by a barber who said their hayres were cut with a knife,' and that 'the barber who last trimmed him was much to blame for it.' Altogether it was a sorry May-day for the Royal fugitive.

On Saturday morning, May 2, they left Downham and went to the adjoining village of Crimplesham, a mile distant, where in a little alehouse the King changed his garb into that of a clergyman. Dr. Hudson rode back to Downham to see if he could find a vessel to carry them by sea northwards, but he could find none. Having met a Mr. Ralph Skipworth, a Royalist, Hudson exchanged horses with Skipworth, who gave him 'a gray horseman's coat for the doctor, as he called the King,' and directed him the way through the Fens. The party then resumed their journey to Southrie Ferry, and thence to Ely, Erith, Stukely (Hunts), and to the village of Coppingford, near Stilton, where they arrived at ten o'clock on Saturday night, and stayed there

[1] MS. narrative in possession of General Cherry-Garrard at Lamer Park, Herts.
The daily record of the King's journeyings—"Iter Carolinum, being a succinct relation of the necessitated marches, retreats, and sufferings of his Majesty Charles the First from the 10th of January, 1641, until the time of his death, 1648"—stops short at this interesting journey of the King, and gives no clue to the places at which he stayed.

for the night and on Sunday. One of the most interesting glimpses of how the King and his two companions fared in this romantic journey, is afforded by the following local reference to this Sunday spent in concealment at Coppingford, which occurs in Hudson's confessions.[1]

"We lay at Copingforde in Huntingdonshire, one Sunday 3 May. Wente not to church, but I reade prayers to the King, and at six at nighte we wente to Stamforde. . . . . . I writte from Copingforde to Mr. Skipworth for a horse, and he sente me one which was broughte to me at Stamforde. . . . . At Copingforde the King and me with my hoste and hostis and two children, were by the fire in the hall; there was noe other chimney in the house."[2]

At Coppingford they were joined by John Brown, a Royalist publican of St. Ives, Hunts, who had already served them at Oxford, and who went on before them to Stamford to arrange for their quarters there. Travelling in the twilight and the darkness on that Sunday evening, the King and his companions reached Stamford at a late hour. Here they stayed for the night, and all the next day, either at Mr. Cave's house, a Royalist, well known to the King, or at the house of Mr. Wolph, a Royalist, formerly an Alderman of Stamford; for there are two references, each different, which can perhaps only be reconciled by assuming that the King did go to Mr. Cave's house but found reason to shift his quarters to Mr. Wolph's.

In the further confessions of Michael Hudson, shortly after the King's journey had brought him with the Scots to Newcastle, Hudson says that the King "was at noe gentleman's house but Mr. Cave's in Stamforde in all his journey. Mr. Cave knew the King and Mr. Ashburnham. He hath been a prisoner most times (?)."[3]

---

[1] Portland MSS., Hist. MSS. Com. Rep., 13, App., pt. i, vol. i, passim.
[2] See the confused attempt, as to dates, in Peckard's "Memoirs of Nicholas Ferrar" (p. 277), to show that the King visited Little Gidding. He may have called there the same night, and have been thence directed by Mr. John Ferrar to Coppingford, close by, for better concealment than a Royalist family and a public place like Little Gidding would afford; but there was no actual stay at the famous 'Nunnery' which had welcomed the King and irritated the Puritans in other days.
[3] Portland MSS.

On the other hand, Stukeley gives a very particular account of the King's arrival and stay at the house of Mr. Wolph, at Barnhill, in Stamford, where Mr. Wolph had been a large farmer. He states that the King and his companions entered by the gate through the wall of the town, and by this means avoided the bridge and the town; that here the King "lay in the chamber over the Hall, then the best chamber, and his most faithful guard Dr. Hudson lay in a little chamber next it with a stucco floor." Hudson's statement about Mr. Cave's house was not known to Stukeley, for it was lying buried away in a cupboard at Welbeck Abbey in the undeciphered portion of the Nalson Collection at the time Stukeley wrote.[1] Still, the narrative of Stukeley rests upon solid ground, for he was at a later time the purchaser of, and lived in, Alderman Wolph's house in Stamford, and received a personal narrative of the King's visit from Mr. Wolph's grandson, " who told him that his father was introduced into the King's presence, and that he had frequently heard his father relate this." The recently discovered statement of Hudson is consistent with the theory that the King may have visited Mr. Cave's but found it safer to go to Mr. Wolph's.[2]

At any rate, at Stamford they stayed for that night, and all day on Monday until eleven o'clock at night, when, travelling again in the darkness to Southwell, they came to the Scots army before Newark on Tuesday morning, May 5, after a strange pilgrimage of nine days, ever at the risk of being discovered. The King stated that he had passed through seven of the Parliament's garrisons and guards . . . . and was known in several places, 'but by such as he called honest men,' and that at one place he was desired to haste away because a warrant was gone forth to apprehend them.

When the news-letters brought into Norfolk the intelligence of the King's escape, there was great activity among the Parliament men, but the King had the start

[1] Hist. MSS. Com. Rep., 13, App., pt. i, vol. i, Preface.
[2] For Stukeley's account see " The Family Memoirs of the Rev. William Stukeley, M.D.," vol. iii, App., pp. 456–7.
Mr. Wolph's house is now owned and occupied by J. E. Atter, Esq., Town Clerk of Stamford.

of them, and had left Downham before Colonel Valentine Walton, Governor of King's Lynn, and Mr. Miles Corbett of Yarmouth, now Recorder of Lynn, had got any definite clue. They, however, set to work vigorously examining witnesses. They summoned into Lynn the constables of the surrounding parishes to give in the results of their hue and cry after the fugitive King, and to bring in witnesses from Royalist houses in the neighbourhood.[1] The following certificate of their labours was afterwards sent up to Parliament :—

"Miles Corbet and Valentine Walton to William Lenthall, Esq., touching the adventures of K. Charles I and Dr. Hudson in Norfolk.

"To the Honorable William Lenthall, Esq., Speaker of the House of Commons. Haste, Haste, post haste.

"Sir,

"Since our coming to Lynn we have done what service we were able. We have taken some examinations, and it doth appear to us that Mr. Hudson, the person that came from Oxford with the King, was at Downham, in Norfolk, with two other gentlemen, upon Thursday the last of April. We cannot yet learn where they were Friday night, but Saturday morning, May 2, they came to a blind alehouse at Crimplesham, about eight miles from Lynn; from thence Mr. Hudson did ride on Saturday to Downham again, and there two soldiers met with him, and had private speech with him. Hudson was then in a scarlet coat. There he met with Mr. Ralph Skipwith of his former acquaintance, and with him he did exchange his horse, and Skipwith and the said Hudson did ride to Southrie Ferrie, a private way to go towards Ely, and went by the way to Crimplesham, and there were the other two, one in a parson's habit, which by all description was the King. Hudson procured the said

[1] There is a tradition at Hunstanton Hall that the place was searched for the King, and the following entry in Sir Hamon le Strange's household accounts is worth reproducing: "June 1646, to Markant and Constable for their charges at Linn when Mr. Miles Corbett did send for my sonnes and them to examine if Kinge Charles had been at our house . . . . . 6s. 2d."—Household Accounts at Hunstanton Hall, per Hamon le Strange, Esq.

Skipwith to get a gray coat for the Dr. (as he called the King), which he did, and there the King put off his black coat and long cassock, and put on Mr. Skipwith his gray coat. The King bought a new hat at Downham, and on Saturday went into the Isle of Ely. Wherever they came, they were very private, and always writing. Hudson tore some papers when they went out of the house. Hudson did enquire for a ship to go to the north or Newcastle, but could get none. We hear at the same time there were 6 soldiers and officers, as is thought, at Oxborough, at another blind alehouse.

"Mr. Skipwith hath offered himself freely to us, and made a free discovery to us. We have committed him to the Mayor of this town, and have taken his examination, which is very long ; only thought it fit to give you this short account hereof. We find this town and the parts (neighbouring) ready enough to obey your commands."[1]

John Brown,[2] an innkeeper of St. Ives, was one of the witnesses examined. Brown had been in Oxford during the Winter, and on Saturday, May 2, came from Melton to Coppingford. He states that he went on before the King and Mr. Hudson on Sunday evening to Stamford, and lodged at the 'Falcon,'[3] but that the King lodged at a gentleman's house whose name he knew not. He went with the King, carried his linen, and made his bed, and went with His Majesty to Newcastle.

There is another incident connecting Brown with the service of the King, and also the friendship of Mr. Cave, of Stamford, with the King. In the next year (May, 1647) Brown was again at Stamford, charged with the task of getting to the King at Holmby a letter in cipher from Ashburnham, who was then at The Hague. Mrs. Mary Cave, daughter of Mr. Cave, of Stamford, undertook the delicate

---

[1] Peck's "Desiderata Curiosa," lib. ix, p. 8.
[2] This John Brown was servant to Ashburnham, and states that he had entered his service November 24, 1642, and had been "solely employed in the receipt and payment of such moneys as came to my master's hands for his Majesty's use."— Ashburnham's Narrative, Appendix, p. 37.
[3] Now the 'Red Lion' in the High Street.

task. By the good offices of a friend living at Holmby, she obtained the interest of the landlady where Captain Abbott, one of the King's guards, lodged, and upon the plea of seeking the honour of kissing the King's hand she thus obtained the assistance of the Captain himself. Unfortunately for her sex, the landlady could not keep the secret, but told her husband of the real object; her husband told Captain Abbott, he told the Commissioners, and the Commissioners arranged for the reception of Mrs. Mary Cave. On the day appointed, she arrived at the King's quarters at Holmby, was ushered into a room, and waited for the honour of seeing the King! Instead of this some ladies came into the room, and commenced to search Mrs. Cave, who, however, contrived, while standing back to the wall, to slip the letter behind the hangings. The expected letter could not be found upon her, and she was taken before the Commissioners and examined. She frankly admitted that Brown came to her house at Stamford, "a fortnight or three weeks since," with a petition from Mr. Ashburnham which he desired her to deliver to His Majesty, but not that she consented to do so, or that she had come to Holmby for that purpose.[1] A few days afterwards the letter was accidentally discovered behind the hangings, and according to the *Perfect Diurnal* of the same date, which says it was a letter from the Queen to the King, 'Lady Cave was committed to the care of the Mayor of Northampton.'

There are other passing references to the straits the King was put to in order to maintain the secrecy of his journey to the Scots army before Newark. Lord Bellasize, who was commanded by the King to give up Newark, says that he knew of the King's intention to come to Newark before he came, and of his coming to Southwell. "A letter of the King's purpos to goe thither came in a man's belly. He swallowed it in a billet and voided it twice."[2]

Concerning the King's stay in disguise at Downham, Stukeley gives the following in his diary under date 1746:—

---

[1] Ashburnham's Narrative, vol. ii, pp. 167, 171, 172.
[2] Portland MSS.

"The Rev. Mr. Shipley, of Downham, visited me. He says the 'White Swan' Inn remains there, and they have a perfect memory of King Charles I. lying there in 1646: there is some of the King's handwriting on a quarry of glass remaining in a window; and a walk by the town side called the 'King's Walk,' from his walk from there whilst waiting for Dr. Hudson's return from Southwell, where he went to make a bargain for the King's coming to the Scots."[1]

[1] Stukeley Memoirs, iii, 30.

CHAPTER XII.

THE ARMY, THE PARLIAMENT, AND THE KING.

(1647.)

THE year 1647 did not commence hopefully. The War had spent itself, garrisons had been 'slighted,' the Scots had been 'paid out' and crossed the border, but the solution for which peaceable men daily prayed was a long way off. The great unpaid army under Fairfax was in no mood to disband until it got its pay; and as it drew nearer to the City of London and did not hesitate to organize machinery of its own for making its voice heard, the fears of many that there might be even war between the Parliament and the Army which it had created were not quite groundless. The Army was not needed at home, might be dangerous to keep up, and Parliament suggested the plan of sending 12,000 of them to Ireland, and the rest to be disbanded.

On March 11, the Justices of the Peace and Deputy-Lieutenants of Essex, in a petition to Parliament, represented " how inconvenient it will be for so great an army to lay out their quarters so near the Parliament . . . . which makes us fear there is some design for an awing influence upon the proceedings of Parliament." They beg, now that God hath delivered them out of the hands of their enemies, that they may not be "eaten up, enslaved, and destroyed by an army raised for our defence, and that the army may be sent to Ireland for the recovery of that Kingdom."[1]

[1] Lords' Journals.

But the Army clamoured for its pay—"horse and dragooners, forty-three weeks in arrear with their pay; foot and train, eighteen weeks in arrear." In all, £331,000 was due to the Army. Parliament's promise to pay by monthly instalments, or by so much cash down, and the rest in debentures, found little acceptance; and with the headquarters of the Army as near as Saffron Walden, and the various regiments quartered in various parts of the Eastern Counties on the main roads to London, the outlook, between Presbyterians in the City and Parliament, and Independents in the Army, was ominous.

On March 12, Fairfax visited Cambridge, and besides being 'highly caressed,' and having a 'Latin oration made to him by a Fellow of Trinity College who had been a souldier in his regiment,' he was presented with 'a rich Bible,' and with 'a sumptuous banquet.' He was made a Master of Arts, and the Town also 'entertained him with a stately banquet.'[1]

On Sunday, March 21, the Parliamentary Commissioners, who had been sent down to Saffron Walden to induce the Army to volunteer for service in Ireland, met a conference of forty-three officers in Saffron Walden Church, over which Fairfax presided. The officers, before promising anything, required definite answers to certain questions—what regiments were to remain at home, who were to command those who went, and what security for pay and indemnity for acts done in the war was to be given. A second conference was held next day, Monday, March 22, but, instead of volunteering for Ireland, the Army set about a petition to Parliament. The Commissioners took offence, Parliament was shocked by this boldness, and even Cromwell did not approve of dictating to Parliament, whose commands for disbanding he had pledged the Army to obey. Colonel Wogan's narrative in the Clarke Papers gives this account of the Conference :—

"Our General commanded that all our officers should meete in the greate church at Saffron Walden to hear what the Commissioners had to say unto us. The general with

---

[1] "Item, for six pottles of wine for ye banquet to Sir Tho. Fairfax, £00. 13. 04. Item, to Mr. Bryan for a banquet for Sir Thomas Fairfax, £09. 06. 00."— Cambridge Borough Accounts, 1647. Printed in Cooper's "Annals of Cambridge."

the Commissioners came into the church, which was almost full. The general [Fairfax] made a shorte speech, told us how Parliament and the Kingdom were obliged to us for our faythful services, and desired they that would goe for Ireland to give in their names. . . . . Then Cromwell stoode up and made a long grave speech in behalf of Parliament, first to give the Army thanks for their never-to-be-forgotten services . . . . that he would gladly trayle a picke in that war of Ireland, and therefore desired us to consider what a holy war that was, and that it was a noble thing for us all that were young men to engage for that Kingdom."

At this point Captain Reynolds, Chairman of the Agitators, stood up for the grievances of the soldiers, upon which the same authority says that "Cromwell took on like a madman, and declared openly in the church that all those that had a hand in that remonstrance were enemies of the Parliament." The author of this partizan account, in fact a hostile witness, suggests that Cromwell's anger was only 'pretended fury,' but the more reasonable assumption is that Cromwell thought it better to accept the terms than run the risk of a new war.

On April 15 new Commissioners, Sir William Waller and others, were sent down to Saffron Walden to renew the efforts to induce the Army to volunteer for Ireland. Fairfax frankly and honourably declined the suggestion to put any pressure upon the soldiers; if it were a question of volunteering it was a case for 'free discussion.' In the afternoon the Commissioners met a conference in Saffron Walden Church of 200 officers, only to meet with the same pertinent questions as before. When the question of officers was being discussed some one in the church blurted out why could not they be allowed to go under their old commanders, and instantly the cry rang round the church, "All! all! Fairfax and Cromwell and we all go!" The meeting broke up with only a few volunteering for Ireland.

Some of the Essex clergy tried to get up petitions in their parishes in favour of the Army being disbanded, but as a set-off John Lilburne, "free born John," a prisoner in the Tower, who was in sympathy with the fiery spirits in the Army, found means of communicating with them, and there appeared an anonymous pamphlet attributed to Lilburne—" A new found Stratagem, framed in the old forge of mechiavalism, and put upon the inhabitants of the county of Essex." The writer urged that no relief was to be expected from Presbyterianism, and as they must have an army they might have a worse, and asked: "Whose poultry hath this army destroyed? Whose goods have they spoiled, or whose sheep or calves have they stolen?"

With the distrust of Parliament which was arising, there were rumours of a movement in the Army towards restoring the King; that the Army had sent a petition to the King, asking him to come there and 'they would set the crown on his head'; and that the servant of the Duke of Buckingham rode post-haste into the north, scattering copies of the alleged papers as he went, and 'desiring the postmasters at Royston and Huntingdon to publish it for the truth.'[1] It was further reported that 'some of the foot about Cambridgeshire give out that they will go for Holmby and fetch the King, which gives much offence and scandal.'

Mr. S. R. Gardiner (" Civil War," vol. iii, p. 52) quotes the following letter from Suffolk:—" The soldiers both in Norfolk and Suffolk sing one note, namely, that they have fought all this time to bring the King to London, and to London they will bring the King; some of the soldiers do not stick to call the Parliament men tyrants. Lilburne's books are quoted by them as statute law."

The Parliamentary newspapers indignantly denied an insinuation that the Army contained 4,000 Cavaliers, and declared that only one of the commissioned officers was ever on the King's side; and as to the common soldiers, they had fought in desperate engagements for Parliament. On the other hand, Sir William Waller declared that when he and the other Commissioners were at Saffron Walden a 'grave minister' of 'a poor contry village' in Suffolk, on the borders of Cambridgeshire, informed them that of twenty

---

[1] Perfect Diurnal.

soldiers quartered in his parish, nineteen had been in actual service against the Parliament.[1]

On May 7, Skippon, Cromwell, Ireton, and Fleetwood were sent down to quiet the distempers in the Army. A conference of the officers in Saffron Walden Church on that day set in motion a new system of ventilating grievances. The officers were directed to collect the views of the common soldiers. The latter at once set about the business of electing their delegates—ajutators or agitators [2]—two from every troop or company, and out of these a further selection was made, two or more from each regiment as spokesmen to lay their views before the officers. The rank and file of the Army was thus organized on the lines of a modern trades' union.

On Saturday, May 15, the spacious aisles of the parish church at Saffron Walden once more resounded with the clanking of swords, when upwards of 200 officers and a certain number of representatives of the private soldiers assembled for the convention at which the officers were to report the views of their regiments scattered over the Eastern Counties. The scene must have been a brilliant and impressive one.

Skippon, the veteran soldier, bearing the scars of Naseby fight, presided, and opened the proceedings in conciliatory tone—" Gentlemen, fellow soldiers, and Christian friends "—and, proceeding, he expressed the hope that the officers had "soe Christian-like, soe judiciously, soe impartially, soe faithfully discharged your duties as wee shall receive a very good account from you in relation to these things." The debate was, however, a stormy one, and did not end that day.

The great "Convention" reassembled in the church on Sunday. The speeches were sometimes loudly applauded and sometimes provoked angry signs of dissent. The veteran Skippon found it necessary to intervene with such words as—"I am sorry to observe that there should be such disagreement between you "—" I pray speake with moderation, or

---

[1] Waller's "Vindication," p. 120.
[2] The term should be understood not as incendiaries, but as agents to act for others.

else be silent!"[1] After sitting until a late hour Skippon wound up the stormy debate with a conciliatory speech, and "soe good night." As a result of it all, the next day the "Declaration of the Army" was drawn up and signed by 223 officers and sent up to Parliament. Its main purpose was to ask for more definite proposals for paying arrears.

The Commissioners reported to Parliament that they found "the Army under a deep sense of some sufferings, and the common soldiers much unsettled." The soldiers were, in fact, now fairly on strike, and the problem for Parliament was, whether it was prepared to redress their grievances or face an open quarrel with armed force. On May 25, the House resolved upon a disbanding of all the forces that would not go to Ireland. Fairfax's own regiment was to disband at Chelmsford on June 1; those who volunteered for Ireland were to march to Ingatestone, and receive two months' arrears of pay and a fortnight's pay in advance; those who did not volunteer were to deposit their arms in the church, receiving the two months' arrears, and have passes to go to their homes. Similar orders were passed respecting the other regiments, for disbanding at Bishop Stortford, Saffron Walden, Cambridge, Newmarket, Huntingdon, Bedford.

Simultaneously with these measures there was a movement in the City for organizing its Militia, which increased the ill-feeling of the Army towards Parliament. From Bury St. Edmunds the 'agitators' issued a circular letter to the various regiments—" Fellow souldiers, the summe of all this is, if you doe but stand and not accept of anything, nor doe anything without the concent of the whole army, you will doe good to yourselves, your officers, and the whole Kingdom. . . . . Resolve neither to take monie nor march from one another, but lett all your actions be joyn'd; and if any orders should come to your particular regiments to march from the rest of

---

[1] Clarke Papers.—Sir William Waller declares that "the debate grew so high that affronts passed between them, and there was a cry of 'withdraw!' which if it had taken effect would have produced a bloody issue among them."— "Vindication," p. 117.

the army, march not while you have consulted the rest of the army."[1]

On Saturday, May 29, a council of war was held at Bury St. Edmunds, at which 200 officers were present. The agitators, speaking for ten regiments of horse and six of foot, presented a petition to Fairfax, begging him to appoint a general rendezvous, and to use his endeavours against disbanding before their grievances were heard and fully redressed, which the Council agreed to do. Another Army news-letter from Bury at the same time declared—"the more they stirre to disunite the more we are cemented. A committee is appointed to come down on Tuesday next to disband the General's regiment. They may as well send them among soe many beares to take away their whelps."[2]

The Commissioners, however, set out upon their hopeless errand, travelling to Chelmsford on Monday, May 31, with £7,000, strongly guarded by a convoy of horse, for the appointed disbanding of Fairfax's own regiment. On their arrival they found the soldiers had revolted, and marched away for the general rendezvous at Newmarket appointed by the Council of Officers at Bury. On Tuesday morning Colonel Jackson and Major Gooday were sent after them, and overtaking about 1,000 of them at Braintree, the soldiers greeted them with, "there come our enemies!" and when the votes of Parliament were read, the soldiers retorted— "What doe you, bringing your twopenny pamphlets to us?" Taking their waggons and ammunition, they 'marched away towards Halstead and Heveningham, where they quartered for the night, and next day were to be at Sudbury and Lavenham.'

If this were done in the green tree what could be expected in the dry? If the General's own regiment could not be disbanded, would any attempt at Bishop Stortford, Saffron Walden, Cambridge, and Huntingdon be more likely to succeed? The Commissioners, finding their first efforts fail in attempting to separate the Army by drafting each regiment to a widely distant rendezvous, went back to Parliament,

---

[1] Clarke Papers, i, 87-8.   [2] Clarke Papers, i, 108-11.

leaving the various regiments of the Army drawing nearer together in spirit and in person. In fact, the state of things was daily getting nearer to two Parliaments—one at Westminster, wrangling with the City Guards and apprentices about its doors, and that of the Army, drawing together in the field, each with an eye upon the other, and the King with an eye upon both, watching to see if they would not extirpate one another.

In the event of a conflict, Parliament saw the importance of securing the train of artillery now for the most part at Oxford, and, while secretly negotiating with France and Scotland and for carrying off the King from Holmby, sent a force to Oxford. But the soldiers on arrival were opposed by the garrison, who fought them in the streets; and before Parliament knew what was happening, Cornet Joyce, sent down to prevent the seizure of the magazine at Oxford, had got his 500 horse together and marched to Holmby to carry off the King to the Army at Newmarket.

If Cromwell were responsible for this[1] he probably saw in it a counter-move, the lesser of two evils, and acted accordingly.

On Friday, June 4, the same day that Cromwell joined the Army at Newmarket, the King came in his coach to Huntingdon, to Hinchinbrook, the residence of Sir Sidney Montague, where His Majesty was 'nobly treated with much honour and affection, as were also the lords and other Commissioners.'[2] Fairfax, hearing at Newmarket of the King's arrival at Huntingdon, sent Whalley 'to induce the King to return.' The King declined to return, but came to Childerley, 'within four miles of Cambridge,' where quarters were taken for him 'at Sir John Cutts his house.'

The King stayed at Childerley[3] from Saturday, June 5, till Tuesday, June 8, flattered by visits from doctors, scholars,

---

[1] Sir William Waller says: "The egg was laid in Cromwell's own chamber, and brooded between him and Ireton, but they were too wise to cackle," and that "Cornet Joyce was employed as the man to hatch it."—Waller's "Vindication," p. 136.

[2] Sir Thomas Herbert's Narrative.—Harl. MSS., 7,396.

[3] There is a tradition handed down at Maddingley Hall that the King while at Childerley escaped and made his way across country to Maddingley, knocked at the door and asked if 'Jack' were in—meaning the then Sir John Cotton—that he was received into the house, wearing over his dress a countryman's

and graduates of the Cambridge University, to "most of whom his Majesty was pleased to give his hand to kiss, for which honour they returned humble thanks and 'Vivat Rex!'"

In Cambridge, the King's presence so near, and an expected visit from his Majesty, caused great excitement, of which the following news-letter makes graphic note :—

"Sir,—I believe you are big in expectation of receiving news from these parts. Thus, therefore, the King on Saturday was brought by a very small party, within four miles of this place, and all the noise was that he would be here; the harbingers in the meantime buying up the whole market. But we (who usually are not taken with the first reports of things) thought not fit to assemble together either in the head or body; whereas the Mayor and Aldermen (somewhat more credulous) fitted their saddles and foot-cloathes into their horses and had provided a present for his Majesty, which quickly after came as acceptable to his ears as if to his hands. The townfolk in all those streets through which it was conceived he would pass, decked their stalles and windowes with green boughs and whole rosebushes, and the ground all along with rushes and herbs. But the King turned aside to my Lady Cutts her house and there yet abides, whither people flow apace to behold him. He is exceeding cheerful, shows himself to all, and commands that no scholler be debarr'd from kissing his hand, and there the Sophs are (as if no further than Barnwell) in their gowns and caps; it was mirth to see how wett yesterday they were admitted into the presence. . . . . Then the King had a large table of diet, but this day (I believe) about to have a far greater, for

smock, and was conducted by a secret staircase to the roofs, when some troopers from Childerley came after him. Before he could escape from the roof he was retaken by the troopers and conveyed back to Childerley. The story, contributed by an esteemed correspondent, Mr. W. B. Redfern, of Cambridge, seems inconsistent with the condition in which the King was passing his time at Childerley; but it has at least the support of the facts that the King had sympathetic friends at Maddingley, that the tradition has been handed down there to the present time, and that until a few years ago a secret staircase to the roof could still be traced. Possibly the close association of the King with Childerley and the concealment of some Royalist at Maddingley—common incidents of the Civil War—may have got mixed in the tradition. The present Childerley Hall is a modern building, but in rebuilding care was taken to preserve the room in which the King was confined, and a small brass plate records the fact.

the General, Lieutenant-General Cromwell and others of the commanders and Council of War are gone to dine with him."[1]

Fairfax, Cromwell, Ireton, Hammond, Whalley, Rich, and other Officers of the Army went over to Childerley to the King's 'banquet.' There was witnessed the strange scene of the heroes of Marston Moor and Naseby kissing the King's hand; and the 'King had some discourse with the General, next with Lieut.-General Cromwell, and next with Commissary-General Ireton.' Compliments were passed, and the King 'was cares't and everywhere found civility from officers and soldiers.'[2]

From Childerley the officers returned to Cambridge, all of them highly extolling the King for his improvement. 'He argues his own and his subjects' case with each of them (one by one) to their no small astonishment.'

The Commissioners refusing to advise either way, and as the King objected to go back to Holmby, but wished to go to Newmarket, Whalley with his two regiments of horse was ordered to accompany His Majesty to Newmarket; the rendezvous of the Army being changed to Thriplow Heath, between Cambridge and Royston. The King was not allowed to pass through Cambridge lest the students should cause an uproar, but passed by Trumpington just outside Cambridge, bonfires making up for undergraduates' acclaim. Wednesday, June 9, was kept as a public fast in Cambridge, Fairfax and the Officers attending Great St. Mary's Church and hearing four sermons—by Hugh Peters, Dr. Hill, Mr. Saltmarsh, and Mr. Seaman—when 'Providence so ordered it that they all pitch upon one point, the reconciliation of things in love.'[3]

Meanwhile new Commissioners, the Earl of Nottingham, Skippon, and others, had been sent down with the votes of Parliament to the Army, and on this June 9 had got as far as Barley, near Royston, whence they wrote 'haste, post haste, with speed' to the Earl of Manchester, Speaker

---

[1] Papers from Cambridge, E. 395 (15), Brit. Mus. Lib.
[2] Sir T. Herbert's Narrative in Harl. MSS.
[3] They did not have the monopoly, however, even with their four sermons, for on the same day 'a fellow preached against Mr. Peters (or else against his way) on the Market Hill.'

of the House of Lords, giving an account of their progress and of letters sent on to the Army, concluding—"to-morrow we propose to make known your resolution to the Army."

These new Commissioners, sent down to the rendezvous at Thriplow by Parliament to present its votes to the Army—indemnity for acts done in the War and £10,000 more to be added to the sum already voted for arrears — had come from London, the inhabitants of which were on tenterhooks about what was to be expected from this army of 20,000 men[1] plus the King—an army which Carlyle has called "the remarkablest army that ever wore steel in this world; and an Oliver Cromwell at the head of it, demanding with one voice, as deep as ever spake in England, Justice! Justice! under the vault of Heaven."

On the morning of Thursday, June 10, this remarkable army was drawn up at the rendezvous upon Thriplow Heath —'upon a plain meadow within four miles of Royston'—and having been warned to be 'very silent and civil' towards the Commissioners, they listened to the votes of Parliament, read out, first, at the head of Fairfax's regiment of horse. Skippon, one of the Commissioners, 'spake to them to persuade a compliance.' One of the officers asked that the answer might be given after the votes had been perused by the Officers and Agitators chosen by the regiment. When asked if that were the opinion of the whole regiment, they answered with shouts of "All! All!" The same answer was given by the other regiments, and the defeated Commissioners rode away amidst cries of "Justice! Justice!"

The Army, on the same afternoon, moved slowly on to Royston, a movement which filled the City with alarm. The Lord Mayor and Aldermen petitioned Parliament, praying that all honourable means might be used, 'to avoid the shedding of more blood, to give just satisfaction to the Army'; and the disbanded soldiers in the City took advantage of the tumult to crowd about the doors of Parliament, and 'in a sort forced' the House to vote £10,000 for their arrears.

[1] According to the Clarke Papers, the Army at this time numbered 21,480 men; but as they had not all reached the rendezvous, the actual number appearing at Thriplow Heath was probably under 20,000.

While these strange ferments were working in London, the Army had encamped for the night around Royston, and Fairfax, Cromwell, and the chief Officers of the Army were sitting in Council at Royston, drawing up a letter, which was despatched the same night, " To the Right Honourable the Lord Mayor, Aldermen, and Common Council of the City of London." In this letter, which Carlyle attributes to Cromwell's own pen, the writers claimed 'satisfaction of our undoubted claims as soldiers'; reparation upon those who had sought the destruction of this Army, having no other way of escaping punishment themselves but by bringing about a new war. They claimed, not only their rights as soldiers, but as Englishmen who had made sacrifices, the right to ask for a settlement of the peace of the kingdom according to the votes and declarations made by Parliament itself, as inducements and arguments for them and their friends to take up arms, in the first instance. The letter concluded in these emphatic words :—

" These in brief are our Desires, and the things for which we stand, beyond which we shall not go. And for the obtaining of these things, we are drawing near your City ; professing sincerely from our hearts, that we intend not evil towards you ; declaring with all confidence and assurance, that if you appear not against us in these our just desires, to assist that wicked party which would embroil us and the kingdom, neither we nor our soldiers shall give you the least offence. We come not to do any act to prejudice the being of Parliaments . . . . in order to the present Settlement of the Kingdom. We seek the good of all. And we shall wait here, or remove to a farther distance to abide there, if once we be assured that a speedy Settlement of things is in hand—until it be accomplished. Which done, we shall be most ready, either all of us, or so many of the army as the Parliament shall think fit, to disband, or to go for Ireland, and although you may suppose that a rich City may seem an enticing bait to poor hungry Soldiers to venture far to gain the wealth thereof, yet if not provoked by you, we do profess, Rather than any such evil should fall out, the soldiers shall make their way through our blood to effect it. And we can say this for most of them, for your better assurance, that they so little value their pay, in comparison of higher concernments to a Public Good, that rather than they will be unrighted in the matter of their honesty and integrity (which hath suffered by the men they aim at and desire justice upon) or want the settlement of the Kingdom's Peace, and their own and their fellow-subjects' Liberties — they will lose all. Which may be a strong assurance to you that it's not your wealth they seek, but the things tending in common to your and their welfare. That they may attain these you shall do like Fellow-Subjects and Brethren if you solicit the Parliament for them, on their behalf.

"If after all this, you, or a considerable part of you, be seduced to take up arms in opposition to, or hindrance of, these our just undertakings—we hope we have, by this brotherly premonition, to the sincerity of which we call God to witness, freed ourselves from all that ruin which may befall that great and populous City; having thereby washed our hands thereof.

"We rest
Your affectionate friends to serve you,

Thomas Fairfax	Henry Ireton
Oliver Cromwell	Robert Lilburn
Robert Hammond	John Desborow
Thomas Hammond	Thomas Rainsborow
Hardress Waller	John Lambert
Nathaniel Rich	Thomas Harrison
Thomas Pride.	

"Royston, 10th June, 1647."

On Friday morning, while the great Army was getting on the move a stage nearer the City, the country-folk came crowding into the small town of Royston from Norfolk, Suffolk, and Essex. Fairfax and the other officers, with the new Parliamentary Commissioners, were returning from a sermon in church, when they were met in the street by "many persons, ministers, and others, about 100 in number, on horseback, stilinge themselves the peaceable and well affected inhabitants of the county of Norfolk, who meeting the General in the street, one of them after some time spent in a speech presented a petition to his Excellency."[1] The Norfolk men in their petition stated that "there is now an appearance of an abhorred design to ruin the native liberties and privileges of the subjects . . . . to the imminent danger of embroiling us yet again in blood"; and they appeal to his Excellency for the removal of all obstructions in the way of a peaceable establishment of "these our native liberties." Similar petitions came in from Suffolk and Essex.

As for the Parliamentary Commissioners, they had still the Parliamentary votes in their pockets, and promised in the above letter to endeavour to see them distributed amongst the Army, but acknowledged that 'we finde that they go off but slowly.' Finding that the quarters of the Army were to be removed to St. Albans, the Commissioners 'repaired to the General's quarters,' at Royston, and protested that St. Albans would be less than the twenty-five miles radius of the City, to which Fairfax replied that he would give them his reasons in writing, and marched on.[2]

When, on Friday morning, the letter from Fairfax and the Officers at Royston reached the Lord Mayor, the Aldermen and Common Councilmen rushed off with it to Parliament, which was sitting; they were called in and thanked for their care in 'a matter of so great consequence,' and the House at once put itself in communication with the Committee for the City Militia, and instructed Colonel Dalbier, whom we shall meet again, to prepare lists of fighting-men. When later in the day news arrived that the Army had left Royston, the City was thrown into the wildest tumult; shops were ordered to be closed, the Trained Bands were called out on pain of death to resist the great army believed to be marching on London, but they did not very readily respond. As soon

[1] Letters from the Commissioners, Royston, June 11, 1647: Add. MSS., 34,235, Brit. Mus. Lib.
[2] The reasons given by Fairfax for removing to St. Albans were soldierly and blunt—"for a nearer communication and intercourse with Parliament and the City, the more readily to obtain money for the satisfaction of the soldiers and keeping them under discipline, and to prevent the raising of any new war, and procure the speedy settlement of the Peace of the Kingdom."—Lords' Journals.

as Fairfax and the Officers reached St. Albans, three Guildhall coaches came down with four Aldermen and eight Common Councilmen to deliver 'the desires of the City,' that the Army would forbear quartering within thirty miles of the City; and having dined with the General and received 'infinite satisfaction' that the Army intended no hurt to the City, they drove back in their coaches to the realms of Gog and Magog, to reassure the citizens. They had scarcely departed when, on the same day, Monday, June 14, a procession of 100 knights, gentlemen, and freeholders on horseback from Buckinghamshire, and behind them a still larger procession of 200 from Hertfordshire, rode up and presented petitions demanding, before the Army disbanded, the condign punishment of the 'firebrands and incendaries' who had sought to create divisions. Fairfax sent up the petition to Parliament, with the assurance that there was nothing to fear if they would only send the Army a month's pay. There was, however, issued the "Grand Declaration of the Army," a sort of political programme recognizing the people as the source of political power. They also impeached eleven members of the House of Commons for defaming the Army, conspiring with the Queen, and seeking to bring the Scotch into the country and bring about a new war.

Meanwhile the King was spending his time cheerfully at his house at Newmarket, well guarded, yet 'more than regarded,' and waiting the turn of events. Here he was 'sometimes in his coach, other times riding unto ye Heath and taking fresh ayre, which is exceeding good there, and the place, both by the King and King James his father, much delighted in for pleasure.' The King was 'exceeding cheerful,' and during his stay at Newmarket many of the gentry and others, men, women, and children, came from most parts of Cambridgeshire, Suffolk, and neighbouring counties to see the King; 'so as the presence chamber was constantly thronged with people . . . . he never failed to dine in public . . . . and all of them prayed God to bless and preserve his person. Yet the King still observed his hours of devotion.'[1]

[1] Herbert's Narrative in Harl. MSS., 7,396.

Even a Parliamentary man like Colonel Russell, of Chippenham, was overcome by 'the splendour of his Majesty,' and other Officers made it their business to 'get the good opinion of the King,'[1] until some of the King's party began to think the Army was 'acting their game.' His Majesty, however, considered himself a prisoner, did not like the restraint, and declared that he came with the Army 'rather than be taken by the neck and heels.'

Parliament sent a request that His Majesty would remove to Richmond; and as His Majesty had arranged to leave Newmarket on Thursday, June 24, Fairfax sent Whalley instructions to attend him to Royston, where he was to lie that night. From this point, Presbyter, or 'old priest writ large,' and Independent struggled for supremacy in getting the King out of pawn. Respecting the first stage of the journey to Richmond, it is alleged that Cromwell's party came to a resolution that 'if the King would not be diverted by persuasion (to which His Majesty was very opposite) that they would stop him by force at Royston'[2]; and further, that the King had declared 'if any man should hinder his going, it would be by force, and laying hold of his bridle; which, if any were so bold to do, he would endeavour to make it his last.'

The King, in charge of Whalley's regiments of horse, set out from Newmarket to Royston on June 24, and on arriving at Royston a message arrived from Parliament desiring His Majesty 'to make a stay at Royston or go [back] to Newmarket, as he shall think fit, in regard to some things that are lately fallen out'[3]; and the Commissioners with the King were warned as to what persons were not to have access to the King. But all the details of His Majesty's journey had been arranged—from Royston to Theobalds, and Theobalds to Richmond; his belongings had been sent on in advance, and his dinner ordered at Ware.[4] So, as an alternative, His Majesty resolved upon going on by way of Hatfield.

[1] Ludlow's Memoirs.
[2] Major Huntington's Narrative in Thurloe Correspondence.
[3] Commons' Journals, June 24, 1647.
[4] Commissioners' Letter in Cary Memorials.

For two nights and one day His Majesty stayed in the house of King James I, his father, at Royston, and on Saturday, June 26, resumed his journey for Hatfield with something of the royal progress which tempered his condition of restraint. At the entrance to the town of Baldock, Herts, his Majesty met with an incident which deserves to be recorded.

"At Baldock .... there was at least one sincere friend of the Royal cause in its venerable rector, Josias Byrd [or Bird]. Deeply moved by the misfortunes of the King, the old parson, then in his 70th year or thereabouts, got together his parishioners; and in full canonicals marched at their head to the town's end, where the two strange processions met! Armed with the communion cup, from the Parish Church, filled with wine, the old rector saluted the King with a fervent ' May God bless your Majesty!' The King, touched at receiving such a demonstration of loyalty, inquired the name of his loyal subject, to which the old rector proudly replied—' I am Josias Byrd, the parson of Baldock, and I offer you this cup for your refreshment.' Whereupon the King drank and replied with ready wit—' Mr. Byrd, I thank you; I did not think I had so good a bird in all my kingdom.' "[1]

The King arrived at St. Albans amid the ringing of bells and throwing up of hats—for it was market-day—and shortly afterwards left for Hatfield, where, for five days and nights, His Majesty was entertained by the Earl of Salisbury, both Army and Parliament keeping a watchful eye upon the ecclesiastical side of His Majesty's conduct, when at Hatfield church next day he attended services conducted according to the Book of Common Prayer, at which Parliament was much shocked and talked loudly of sending His Majesty back to Holmby, and depriving him of his chaplains, but Whalley did not forward these rash proposals. On July 1 the King left Hatfield for Windsor, and thus ended His Majesty's last progress through the Associated Counties.

The remainder of the year 1647 was taken up mainly

[1] " Hertfordshire during the Great Civil War," p. 71.

with the movements of the Army around London, now drawing off with each move of Parliament on the subject of pay for the soldiers, now drawing nearer and alarming the City. Parliament fell under the rule of the mob; the Independent members and some Presbyterians, with the Earl of Manchester, Speaker of the Lords, and Lenthall, Speaker of the Commons, left the Houses in disgust, and made their way to the Army at Hounslow Heath, where 20,000 soldiers backed them up by throwing up their hats for 'a free Parliament,' and marched towards the City to put things right and remove the 'horrid force' at Westminster.

With Presbyterians in Parliament, Royalists in the country, Independents and 'Levellers'[1] in the Army, and the King now a prisoner in the Isle of Wight, the chances of a 'firm and lasting peace' seemed still remote. Cromwell was suspected by the Royalists because he had not supported the restoration of the King, and by the 'Levellers' because he had done too much.

On November 15, with plots hanging over them, Cromwell and Fairfax marched from their quarters at Hertford to a rendezvous at Corkbush-field, on the road to Ware. Here the Levellers in the Army met them with papers stuck in their hats, demanding 'England's freedom and soldiers' rights,' and the socialistic gospel of Colonel John Lilburne, or "Freeborn John," the 'stormy petrel of a stormy time,' who was quietly watching events in the neighbouring town of Ware. Fairfax addressed the regiments, and some of them removed the papers from their hats, but others, in Colonel Robert Lilburne's regiment, were obstinate and refused. Cromwell rode along the ranks, gave the order to the men to tear the papers from their hats, but finding no response sternly drew his sword and dashed into the mutineers, who now yielded to the force of military discipline, removed the offensive papers, and begged for mercy. Eleven of the mutineers were tried before a

---

[1] 'Men who declared that all degrees of men should be levelled, and equality established, both in titles and estates, through the kingdom.'

Council of War; three were condemned to death, but were allowed to draw lots for one of them to die, and one Arnald, upon whom the lot fell, was shot to death at the head of the regiment.

Christmas Day, 1647, was distinguished by a strange conflict of sentiment. Puritans, disregarding the day, kept open their shops; the Royalists forcibly closed them, and played football in the streets. Even the churches were decorated once more and theatres were reopened, only to be closed again 'under pains and penalties.' With bonfires and cries of "For God and King Charles," both in London and the Associated Counties, the last days of the year gave little hope of peace; and fears of a renewal of war in the year 1648.

CHAPTER XIII.

THE SECOND CIVIL WAR—RISINGS ALL OVER EAST ANGLIA — FIGHTING AT NORWICH, BURY ST. EDMUNDS, STAMFORD, CAMBRIDGE, LINTON, AND ST. NEOTS—THE SIEGE OF COLCHESTER—THE EXECUTION OF THE KING.

(1648-9.)

JUST as varying jets of flame sometimes burst forth, under a favouring breeze, and lick up unconsumed bits of the wasted surface after a great conflagration, so during the year 1648 there occurred here and there Royalist risings, fanned into flame by local discontent, in those very counties of the Eastern Association in which the Parliamentary cause had been supreme during the great struggle which ended at Naseby. The mismanagement of affairs by County Committees, which, minus the grip of Cromwell's presence, had been weakened by the doings of inferior men, the divisions in the Army, with the King a close prisoner in Carisbrooke Castle—these were not exactly the things for which some of the people of East Anglia had taken up arms. The popular idea with which they entered the War, that by daring to unsheath the sword and meet the King in overwhelming numbers in one great battle, the cause of the people would so impress itself upon the King, that he would yield to better counsel and sanction better laws, had been dissolved in the weary protracted struggle. Even the common people, the last element to be influenced by the original issues at stake, had their instincts. They listened over tankards of ale to rumours of harsh treatment, and of attempts to poison the King, and some of these men were found 'not to be trusted,' when next the Trained Bands were called out in Norfolk, Suffolk, and Essex, to suppress 'insurrections,' as the Royalist risings against the now triumphant party were called.

It is an interesting coincidence that Parliamentary East Anglia had its toughest struggle with the two extremes of its area—with the Lucases of Colchester at the beginning of the fray, and the Earl of Newcastle in the Fens. Margaret Lucas, of Colchester, was the wife of Newcastle, the commander of the "White Coats." Her brother, Sir Charles Lucas, had been Newcastle's Lieutenant-General, and was now in 1648 a force to be reckoned with among his own neighbours about Colchester.

The Grand Jury at Chelmsford were the first to stir, at the Spring Assizes in March, 1648, and the result was a proposal to hold a great meeting at Stratford Langthorne in the beginning of May, which Parliament declared 'prejudicial to the peace of the Kingdom in these distracted and tumultuous times.'

A tragic incident occurred in the city of Norwich in the early days of April, which ended in an awful disaster. Parliament had sent down its messengers to bring up Mr. Utting, the Mayor, for somewhat done 'against its dignity'; 'the disaffected to Parliament opposed his going up, while the well affected endeavoured to further it.' The Royalists locked up the gates, to prevent the Mayor from being taken off in the night-time. Noisy crowds hung about the market-place till past midnight, and in the morning they mustered again in great force, openly shouting "For God and King Charles!" and threatened to "pluck the Roundheads out of the Common Council."[1] The messenger barely escaped with his life, and was glad to get back to Parliament without the Mayor. The city was soon involved in a tumult, shops were plundered, arms seized whenever they could be found, and

---

[1] Blomfield, "History of Norfolk."

for the moment the attempt to vindicate the Parliamentary cause in Norwich was in a bad way. Dotted over the county were the troops of Colonel Fleetwood's regiment, some as far away as Dereham ; but the ominous news set them all on the move under orders to meet at Norwich. Galloping into the city about four o'clock in the afternoon, the troopers 'fell desperately on several parties of the mutineers, who were most resolute in their engagement.' They had, however, possessed themselves of the Committee House, 'wherein was the great magazine.'[1] In this Committee House with its magazine—where the Hospital now stands—the rioters were scrambling for the possession of gunpowder, of which there were ninety-eight barrels in store. Outside, the troopers were battering the gate, inside loose powder was being spilt all over the place, ready for the inevitable spark.[2] With an awful crash, 'which did shake the whole city,' the magazine and the Committee House were blown up, 'ninety-eight barrels of gunpowder going off at one crack'! Forty persons who were inside were 'spoyled by the powder,' and the shock 'threw down part of some churches.' 'Not many that were killed as yet found or can be found, for many were torn in pieces, and carried limb from limb, several legs, arms, etc., being found in the streets ; there are already missing and mortally wounded at least one hundred and twenty persons, besides as many more which received slight wounds and hurts.'[3]

The mutineers, to the number of 108, were brought to trial, and several of them were executed in the Castle Ditches ; Parliament ordered all others who had taken part in the tumult to be disabled from voting in the election, or being elected as Mayor on May-day. Mr. Utting, the Mayor, 'of his own accord,' accompanied by some of his officers and friends, rode to Parliament; while the following Tuesday was a day of thanksgiving for deliverance from the mutiny, when Mr. Collins had 20s. for preaching in the Cathedral

[1] Perfect Diurnal.
[2] "One man swore afterwards that he swept up a hatful from the stairs."—Rye's "History of Norfolk."
[3] Letter to Fleetwood.

to the Aldermen in their scarlet gowns; and £250 was afterwards granted to the troopers for their services.

Parliament having appointed as Deputy-Mayor the venerable Christopher Barrett, that worthy, with a Pepys-like frankness and simplicity, wrote to the Speaker acknowledging the honour—" I have ever had a young heart, but my great age and many other unfitnesses," etc., etc. But until May-day Mr. Barrett upholds the honour and then tells how, by means of Colonel Fleetwood's troopers drawn up in the Castle-yard, the election of Mayor passed off 'with that quietness and peaceableness as was wonderful.' He adds some graphic details of the late blowing up of the magazine, from which it appears that some adjoining houses were demolished and some of the neighbours buried alive for above four hours, but 'all miraculously preserved.'[1]

On the 3rd of May there was a tumult in Colchester, and on the 4th, the day appointed for the great meeting at Stratford Langthorne, the Grand Jury and the thousands of Essex freeholders, instead of proceeding thither, marched up to Westminster. A cavalcade of 2,000 persons on horseback and on foot, representing thirty thousand of the inhabitants of the country, presented a petition to Parliament praying that 'the King might be satisfied, with the Army disbanded.' Mr. Speaker informed them in diplomatic phrases that the House was in debate concerning the settlement of the Kingdom, and 'did not doubt they would give satisfaction to the county and to the rest of the Kingdom.'[2] Parliament, however, found it necessary to advise the Earl of Warwick to be careful in assembling the Trained Bands, so as not to prejudice the peace of the county 'at this juncture of time and of ill-affected humours.'

The next Royalist rising occurred at Bury St. Edmunds. There, in the ashes of past popular risings, the smouldering fire had kindled around the daring act of setting up of a may-pole, when about 600 got together and cried out, "For God and King Charles!" They laid hold upon some

[1] Letter in Cary Memorials.
[2] Commons' Journals.

of the Trained Bands, set guards in several places and assembled 'in the church and other strong places,' and were joined by 'divers from Colchester and those parts.' The House of Commons ordered the County members to go down to Bury 'to use their endeavours to appease the tumult there.' Fairfax was informed of the state of affairs at Bury 'and into what a height of distemper they are grown there. The business may prove of very dangerous consequence if not effectually stopped in the beginning.' Colonel Whalley was ordered to march 'within some few miles of that town with such troops as are most conveniently quartered for that service.'[1]

On the arrival of Colonel Whalley's troops near Bury St. Edmunds, a curious conflict arose. The scouts of the Trained Bands came into conflict with the scouts of Whalley's forces, and the outcome was a letter from the Parliamentary Authorities in Bury to the officers in command of the parties lying near their town—" Your party has taken some offence at ours, and our party has been offended by the scouts on both sides." Whalley's forces were blocking up the town, thinking the whole town was against them, and the letter continues—" I beg you will interpret matters fairly and desist from hindering provisions coming to our town till you know the resolution of Parliament."

Inside the town Sir Thomas Barnardiston and Sir William Playters, who had been sent down by Parliament to Bury St. Edmunds, had instructions to let the leaders of the insurrection know that in case they laid down their arms and restored the powder magazine which they had seized, and submitted themselves to Parliament, they should be indemnified for all acts done in 'the late tumult.' The report sent up to Parliament was as follows :—" We are now in quiet possession of the town. We had the assistance of two troops of my Lord General's Regiment, and three of Colonel Fleetwood's, with three of the Trained Bands of Sir Thomas Barnardiston's regiment. We cannot yet discover the bottom of this design. There was not much

[1] State Papers, Charles I.

blood-shed, but upon a skirmish in a sally out, there were two of the town killed, and none of ours, only two horses." In the communications which passed between the party outside the town and the Royalists within, it was stipulated that the latter should lay down their arms in the market house. So the arms were laid down, the magazine restored, and Sir Thomas Barnardiston and Major Desborough were allowed to enter the town as described in the report to Parliament.

But this was not the end of the risings in these parts. At Thetford, in Norfolk, there were 'drums beat up and many tumultuously assembled, but were soon suppressed by the Mayor's power.' A similar state of things arose at Stowmarket, in Suffolk, and Colonel Dodson, Governor of Crowland, was ordered to repair to his post to hold that place against malignants 'secretly lurking' ready to fall upon it, and Colonel Walton, Governor of King's Lynn, was ordered to give his assistance.

The Jermyns of Rushbrooke Hall kept the spark alive around Bury, and on June 3, Sir Thomas Barnardiston wrote to Sir Nathaniel Barnardiston and other Suffolk Committeemen :—" This enclosed I received just now from the aldermen of Bury St Edmunds, by which you will see there are grounds for fear. The disaffected in these parts keep still their meetings at Newmarkett, under pretence of horse racing, Rushbrooke Hall, near Bury, the place of their general rendezvous, and there feasted by the Jermyn family. . . . . This day seven night we are to have a general meeting at Stowmarket. . . . . We are mustering our forces, both horse and foot and auxiliaries. Many of them, I fear, are disaffected ; we shall endeavour to mend them by a new modelling of them."

The letter he enclosed was as follows :—

" Sir,

"This morning before I came out I was informed that the Duke of Buckingham and divers others came yesterday to Rushbrooke Hall, where was a great feast and present divers gentlemen, and this day also since I came to Newmarket I understand that all those captains which were at Bury in the time of the mutiny are now at Newmarket, which makes me and others much fear that there is some ill suddenly intended to our town; how we shall oppose them, I know not. . . . . Yesterday our soldiers did muster with us, and we had about seven score that we dare trust, but they want experience. We conceive that horses would be very useful."[1]

The significance of these doubts concerning the trustworthiness of the Trained Bands will be understood from what was coming to pass in Essex and the Fens.

When, at the end of May, the Royalist rising in Kent was coming to a head, it was confidently predicted that the 20,000 Kentish men who were to assemble at Blackheath would be joined by an equal number of men from across the river in Essex. These anticipations were not, however, realized. Fairfax crushed the Kentish rising; and about 500 of the defeated Kentish men crossed the Thames by a bridge of boats into Essex. On June 4 the Essex Committee for Parliament were meeting at Chelmsford for the purpose of 'appeasing and suppressing the ill-affected humours,' when a tumultuous scene occurred. The crowd, at the instigation of Colonel Farr, an officer of the Trained Bands, forcibly entered the Committee-rooms and carried off the members of the Committee as prisoners. News of the event reached Parliament the same night, and next day both Houses in a panic passed an ordinance offering the "white feather," in the form of an indemnity for all the inhabitants of the county for what they had done, providing that all persons should disband and go peaceably to their homes within twelve hours of the publication of the Ordinance at Chelmsford, and the imprisoned Committee-men to be liberated. On June 6 the Ordinance of Indemnity was published at Chelmsford, and most of the people gathered to hear it were willing to accept the offer of Parliament, but the old Earl of Norwich hastened to Chelmsford, where he

[1] Lords' Journals.

was joined by Sir Charles Lucas, and their influence caused many of the Trained Bands and others to alter their minds and remain in arms.

By June 9 the united Royalists from Kent and Essex came together at Chelmsford, where they were joined by Lord Capel, who had, much to the concern of Parliament, got together a body of his Hertfordshire neighbours and others. At Chelmsford the Royalist party remained, where supplies came 'from all parts of the Kingdom,' until Saturday the 10th, when they marched from Chelmsford, in sight of Colonel Whalley. In their march the Royalists entered the Earl of Warwick's house in Leighs' Park, where they took away a quantity of arms and ammunition.[1] The same evening (Saturday) the growing force marched to Braintree and there rested for the night, and on Sunday they 'disgested' the volunteers into several troops under Lord Norwich, Lord Capel, Lord Loughborough, and Sir Charles Lucas. To shape their future movements was not so easy. There is evidence that the intention was to march through and recruit in the Associated Counties as far as the Isle of Ely, and then march up 'to the very walls of London,' to be joined by their friends there 'in plundering that rebellious city.'[2] Indeed, so widespread were the plans for a fresh rising that letters sent out to old East Anglians in Massachusetts reflect 'the great design of the King's party throughout England to rise together and so seize upon Parliament and the Army.'[3]

Parliament warned Suffolk, the Isle of Ely, and Huntingdonshire to block up the passes, and assured them that Fairfax would follow with the whole force of Parliament in the rear.

It was fortunate for Parliament that some of the Essex commanders were absent from the Committee meeting at Chelmsford at which their colleagues were taken prisoners —Sir T. Honeywood, Colonel Harlackenden, Colonel Cooke, Colonel Sparrow, 'and other firebrands of that county,' who

[1] Beaufort MSS.
[2] Rushworth, viii, 1160.
[3] "Life and Letters of John Winthrop, Governor of Massachusetts," ii, 383-4.

got together a regiment of horse and two of foot, had sent over for the magazine at Braintree, before the Royalists got there, and took up their position at Coggeshall; which, on the direct road to Colchester, the Royalist army would have to pass. On the other hand, Fairfax was hourly expecting to join Whalley in the rear; and so, "apprehending they might fall on us on both sides of the toune [Braintree], we drew out in the night on the highway towards Suffolke, as if we had designed our march towards the Isle of Elye." After continuing their march some little distance out of the town, they, by a stratagem, returned sharp back into Braintree, turned to the north-east and marched to Halstead, a few miles beyond Coggeshall, round which and its force of Trained Bands they wheeled, and so 'deceived the enemy by this stratagem.' At Halstead they remained until the rear came up, and then marched towards Colchester. Meanwhile, Fairfax, with characteristic swiftness, though tormented with gout to the extent of being described in Royalist prints as "King Gowty-leggs," had crossed the Thames, joined Whalley, and personally rode forward to see how the Essex troops fared at Coggeshall, just as the Royalists were completing the detour in the direction of Colchester.

Drawing near to Colchester, the Royalists found there a divided sentiment, for while they were met with 'neere a thousand of the townsmen' who had broken through their guards to welcome them, the advanced party were opposed by some horse of the town, and of Bardfold and Dedham, but Sir Charles Lucas rode to the front and counselled his neighbours to admit them. "The gates were opened and wee marched through the towne in greate order, and drew our men into the lower courte of my Lord Lucas his house, which having been formerly an abbey was capable of receiving them all. . . . . But the inhabitants of the towne . . . . were so distracted with the noveltie of their busines—having never seene an army before—that they suffered our souldiers to want, which created soe great a mutinie that it was above the skill and authoritie of the officers to appease. . . . . Soe we were forst to let them march into the towne before their quarters were made, where wee reposed that night."[1] The Royalist Army was thus installed in quarters which, by the fortunes of war rather than by the choice of the people, became the scene of one of the most terrible experiences of the Civil War.

The next day, June 13, Fairfax reached Colchester, where Sir T. Honeywood and the Essex Trained Bands had arrived from Coggeshall, making a total force of 5,000 disciplined troops, against about 4,000 new levies only partly armed within and about the town of Colchester. Ireton compared the town and those therein to 'a great beehive, and our army to a small swarm of bees sticking on one side of it'[2]; while Whalley wrote to Fairfax: "Our friends report the enemy to be 5,000 horse and foot; and, like a snowball, increasing."[3]

The Suffolk Trained Bands marched towards Colchester to block up the bridges over the Stour at Nayland, Stratford, and Catawade, but at first showed 'a strange averseness to the service.' Fairfax sent a trumpeter to the Earl of Norwich summoning him and those under his command to lay down their arms in order to prevent 'much blood that is like to be spilt' and 'the town preserved from plunder and ruine.' This summons the Earl slighted by asking the trumpeter 'how his general did, telling him that he heard he was ill with the gout, but he could cure him of all diseases.'[4] This answer highly enraged the soldiers, and both sides prepared for an attack on the outskirts of the town.

'About two of the clock in the afternoon' the Parliamentary forces were alarmed by the enemy's drummers, and at once drew out, says the writer already quoted, "a considerable partie of our foote and some horse and lyned the hedges." Across the approach to the town by the London Road, Sir Charles Lucas drew up his defending force. Three times the Royalist infantry in the centre repulsed the attack of the Parliamentary foot, but their cavalry routed the right wing of

[1] Narrative in the Beaufort MSS., Hist. MSS. Rep., xii., App., pt. ix, p. 24.
[2] Ludlow's Memoirs, i, 255.
[3] Fairfax Correspondence.
[4] Morant, "Hist. Colchester," i, 59.

the Royalist horse, who were in full gallop for the town, and the whole body were soon forced to retire and get into the town in the best manner they could. At the narrow entrance through the Head Gate of the old Roman walled city there followed an act of valour not unworthy of Macaulay's lines—

> In yon straight path a thousand
> May well be stopped by three :
> Now who will stand on either hand
> And keep the gate with me ?

"The enemie, advancing boldly upon us, forced our men to retreate and pursued them to Head Gate, where stood the Right Honourable the Lord Capell with a partie of horse to receive the enemie, but justly apprehending that the disorder of our men retreating and the narrowness of the place would render his horse unserviceable—like himselfe, that is a man of incomparable honour and presence of judgment in the greatest danger—hee alighted and tooke a pike, who was presently seconded by Sir Charles Lucas, Sir George Lisle, and two or three others, and there these worthies —like Horatius Cocles—oposed themselves to the furie of the enemie, whilst under cover of their courage the remains of our men saved themselves within the porte. Then those bucklers of their partie retreated with their faces to the enemie, selling every foote of the ground they parted with at the price of the invaders' lives: an action without flatterie to the living or the memories of the dead, that would be thought as worthy of place in a chronicle as any that is legible in ancient storie."[1] According to a more definite and slightly different account of the same thing, the front ranks of the Parliamentary infantry were allowed to get inside the gate, and there entrapped, at the bottom of the roadway sloping down from within to the gate, were charged by the Royalist horse, and, taken in flank by Royalist foot coming out of the lane from St. Mary's Church close by, were driven through the 'Head Gate,' quite into the street of the suburb, and most of them

---

[1] Narrative of the Siege of Colchester in the Beaufort MSS.

that had so rashly entered were cut in pieces,' when Lucas ordered the gate to be closed, and fastened the bar with the cane he carried in his hand.[1]

By the hurried closing of the gates, a considerable number of the Royalists were left outside and were made prisoners. The walls 'being too high to be stormed,' pieces of ordnance were brought into requisition, and around the angle of the wall near the Head Gate and St. Mary's Church, there were brave deeds performed. The walls were stoutly defended, but taking advantage of some houses near St. Mary's Church, the Parliamentary soldiers leaped from these into the town, 'as if . . . . it had been their only business to seek— what they found—their graves in that churchyard.' An attempt was made by Fairfax to fire the gate by setting fire to the houses adjoining, but this failed. From afternoon till night the attempt on the walls continued, and at midnight or soon afterwards the attacking forces drew off, and according to the Royalist version leaving their cannon with their dead, but according to the outside account getting the cannon away 'with difficulty and danger.'

The losses on both sides were considerable; those of the Royalists before they entered the town, those of Fairfax afterwards. While the forces within and without the walls of Colchester are settling down to a bitter struggle of endurance, we may turn with interest to what was happening elsewhere.

Once more on the Lincolnshire borders of the Fens, the spirit of Royalism asserted itself, and again Mr. Styles, the parson of Crowland, was a leading spirit. Michael Hudson, rector of Uffington, near Stamford, the King's plain-dealing chaplain, who accompanied His Majesty in disguise through the Fens to Newark, had twice escaped from prison, this time in disguise carrying a basket of apples on his head. After making his way to the King at Hampton Court, he went into Lincolnshire, where he was joined by Mr. Styles, of Crowland. Colonel Wayte came in from Northampton side, and, finding that Hudson and Styles intended to

---

[1] Diary in the Round MSS.

beat up recruits at Stamford Fair on the Thursday, he marched to Stamford. Here he was joined by Major Underwood with 100 men from Crowland garrison, and next day, June 6, they 'fell upon the rogues,'[1] drove them into Woodcroft House, stormed the house, and 'gave no quarter to the better sort.' In this adventure Michael Hudson came to a tragic end. The following is the account given by Bishop Kennett :—

"I have been on the spot and made all possible inquiries, and find that the relation given by Mr. Wood may be a little rectified and supplied. Mr. Hudson and his beaten party did not fly to Woodcroft, but he had quietly taken possession of it and held it for a garrison with a good party of horse, who made a stout defence, and frequent sallies against a party of the Parliament at Stamford, till the Colonel commanding there sent a stronger detachment under a captain, his own kinsman, who was shot from the house; upon which the Colonel himself came up to renew the attack and demanded surrender, & brought them to capitulate upon terms of safe quarter. But the Colonel, in base revenge, commanded that they 'should not spare that rogue Hudson.' Upon which Hudson fought his way up to the leads, and when he saw they were pushing in upon him, threw himself over the battlements, and hung by the hands, as intending to fall into the moat beneath, till they cut off his wrists and let him drop, and then ran down to hunt him in the water, where they found him padling with his stumps, and barbarously knocked him on the head."[2]

Wood, in his "Athenæ," states that one Walker, a chandler or grocer of Stamford, cut out Hudson's tongue and carried it about the country as a trophy, but afterwards lost his trade through poverty and 'became a byword to the boys when he passed through the streets of Stamford.' As for Mr Styles, the parson of Crowland, he escaped the fate of Hudson and lived until after the Restoration.

About the same time there was hard fighting in Cambridge, which is thus recorded by an eye-witness :—"You would not

[1] Rushworth, vii, 1145.
[2] Printed in Peck's "Desiderata Curiosa," lib. ix, 44.

imagine to what a great height we are grown unto here; we who, upon little or no alarms, were used to ride and run are become the sons of Mars. The last week grew a quarrel between the Parliamentiers and Royalists, occasioned by some disgraceful expressions in the schools against the Parliament and Army, and their friends, not enduring, pull down the Orator and Moderator, there upon fell to blows, both parties increase, the Royal townsmen assisting the schollers of their party which drew into a body, charged with much gallantry, and after a long and hot dispute, the victory first on one side and then on the other, at last the Parliamentiers prevailed, and the other left the field. About which time Captain Pickering came in with a troop of Horse to assist the Parliamentiers, who . . . . made proclamation, that if any person or persons whatsoever should presume to raise any insurrections or tumults . . . . he would use his utmost endeavours to suppress them, and to bring them to condign punishment.

"Then he marched into the country, where he understood some were, and finding, charged and routed them, killed about nine, and took three or four of the chief actors prisoners. The next day there was another great skirmish near this city, which continued some time in a very hot dispute, divers falling and the number great."[1]

Another account says that in this action at Cambridge "the schollers of Trinity did gallantly."[2] The College authorities backed them up by purchasing ammunition.[3] In this action Mr. John St. George was taken prisoner by Captain Pickering.

The other 'hot dispute' referred to happened at Newmarket and at Linton. The meetings at Newmarket 'under the pretence of horse-racing' had already come to a head. Colonel Thornton, of Soham, and two or three other Colonels in the King's Army assembled at the "King's Arms," Newmarket, whence they sent out a proclamation that 'all gentlemen whatsoever that had a desire to serve his Majesty

---

[1] "An Exact Relation of Another Great Fight in the City of Cambridge, etc."
[2] The Moderate Intelligencer, Brit. Mus. Lib.
[3] "Spent £10 : 0 : 0 for amunicion."—Bursar's Accounts, Trin. Coll., 1648.

.... should repair to the King's Arms, there to receive present entertainment and advance money ; whereupon divers resorted thither protesting to live and die in the cause.' But Captain Pickering, fresh from his victory over the 'schollers' in Cambridge, arrived upon the scene at Newmarket with his troops, and there was a scattering of the crowd of recruits around the door of the "King's Arms." The troops made a rush for the commanders, but they got inside the house and 'maintained the doors,' and 'shot out of the windows.' Captain Pickering, with twelve men, forced an entrance, but the Colonels 'fought it out very resolutely' in the rooms of the inn, and killed one of Captain Pickering's men, but at last 'submitted to mercy.'[1] The four Colonels were made prisoners, including Colonel Sir Bernard Scudamore and Colonel Thornton.

This was only part of a greater rising of a strong force of men and horse for the purpose of joining the Essex rising. Captain Reynolds, a deputy-lieutenant for Cambs, Captain John Appleyard, and others were entrusted with commissions, and a rendezvous was appointed at Linton between Cambridge, Saffron Walden, and Newmarket. Men and horse came in freely from villages ten miles round—from Sir Anthony Cage, of Burrough Green, to the smaller men who joined in the rising. John Curd, or Crudd, of Ickleton, high constable, sent out warrants to the petty constables of his hundred ; Giles Jocelyn, the stout farmer of Babraham, who had resisted Sheriff Pychard's Ship-money collectors, with 'unlawful weapons,' was constable for his parish, and raised men 'by forging their names and his own on the warrants'; Francis Frost, of Brinkley, and William Symons, of Ickleton, were other constables who sent out warrants. From Newmarket, Dullingham, Exning, Sawston, Horseheath, Linton, Saffron Walden, and Bishop Stortford, and all the country round, came in 500 horse and foot, to the rendezvous at Linton, where Barnaby Richmond was appointed Quartermaster. But although Captain Reynolds was in actual command of the 'Linton Insurrection,' as it is styled in the

---

[1] Letter from Newmarket, E. 448 (10), Brit. Mus. Lib.

old documents, the leading man was Mr. John Appleyard, of Dullingham, who entertained some of the officers at his own house, and, assisted with horses and arms, rode over to Stetchworth and to Weston and roused the villagers there; and, when a considerable body had been got together at the rendezvous, he urged them on with a stirring speech 'to play their parts like men; for if they should lose the day now, they should be overthrown for ever.'

Hearing of this rising, on his arrival before Colchester, Fairfax despatched two troops of his own horse and three troops of Colonel Harlackenden's regiment in command of Colonel Sparrow. About the same time that the scene at the "King's Arms" at Newmarket occurred, or a day later, Colonel Sparrow's force reached Linton, came in conflict with the Royalists, routed them, and took prisoners 'Major Reynolds, a colonel with a wooden leg, and Major Mustamp, and others they killed.'[1]

The fire still smouldered in Suffolk, where Sir Thomas Peyton, 'a great stickler in the Kentish engagement,' had got back, and, with Mr. Swan and others, was captured at Bury St. Edmunds, and sent a prisoner to Windsor Castle. Fairfax, unable to get away from Colchester, was concerned about the safety of the Isle of Ely, especially the inner parts about Wisbech adjoining 'Marshland.' The result was that Colonel John Hobart, of Outwell, patrolled the Isle with a troop of 50 horse.

[1] An Exact Narrative, E. 448 (18). That the actual date of this incident was nearly that which is here assigned, is indicated by entries in the Linton Parish Register, which, under date June 16, 1648, contains these particulars of soldiers' interments:—
"John Sendall, of Brinkley, gent., slain in a skirmish by the Parliament forces.
"Robert Giles, of Newport, slain at the same time & upon the same occasion."
—Bowtell MSS., ii, 136.

Among the active partisans in the rising were:—Edward Bridgeman, Oliver Bridgeman, and H. Morden, of Exning; —Bridgeman and Edward Galway, of Newmarket; John Morden ('who entertained Hudson and plotted with him in the last war'); Thomas Appleyard of Dullingham, John Crudd of Ickleton, Giles Jocelyn of Babraham, Francis Frost of Brinkley, Lawrence Myriott of Horseheath, Barnaby Richmond of Linton, Wm. Bridge of Weston, Wm. Symons of Ickleton, Thomas Firn of Wood Ditton, Jas. Floyd of Brinkley, John Isatson of Dullingham, — Smith of Whittlesford Bridge, Mich. Westwood of Ickleton, Geo. Blundell or Blunden, and John Byatt of Sawston; John Humphrey, sen., of Brinkley, Widow Trowles of Hildersham, and others, who all sent men and horses or took part in the rising, and figure in the Royalist Composition Papers.

On June 21, Colonel Walton informed Parliament of designs to surprise Lynn and Crowland, and that the enemy had 'an eye especially upon the Isle of Ely.' He adds that he had 'spent the last week in putting the Isle of Elye—the south part—into a posture of defence, caused breastworks to be made upon other places, and all great boats upon the fresh rivers.' He summoned in the auxiliary forces, 'who made a good appearance of about 400 men.' In the north of the Isle he was met with opposition of the disaffected, at Wisbech, March, and Whittlesey, but expressed his intention of disarming them and 'arming honest men if they may be found.'[1]

But with all their disadvantages the troops of Cambridgeshire and the Isle, and of Lincoln and Northampton, saved the crisis in the Fens for Parliament, just at the time when the arrival of Fairfax in Essex had checked the design of the Royalists to march into the Fens, and back on London.

Meanwhile, Fairfax, 'weary with last night's work,' on June 14 had settled down before Colchester on the same ground where he had first faced the Royalists, the previous afternoon. All the bridges towards Suffolk were now filled up, and the Suffolk forces were sent over to make good the part of the siege on their side, and Sir Thomas Honeywood and the Essex forces in their part; 'this way being better than to cast away such excellent men against walls and bulwarks.' The enemy, it was declared, 'must betake themselves to sea, for there is no escape, and we hear the country will come in very freely to block them up.'[2]

Inside the walled town, says the Royalist narrative, "like the Jews in Jerusalem, with our swords in one hand and our trowells in the other, began to repaire the ruines of our walls, which were many; this towne being one of the antientest foundations in the kingdome. There were above five hundred places without any fortification at all." As to the other means of defence the writer adds:—

"Wee looked into the magazine of the towne, where wee found 70 barrells of powder with some match, and in private

[1] Letter in Portland MSS., Hist. MSS. Rep., xiii.
[2] Portland MSS.

houses neare a thousand armes; then we searched the stores for provision, and at the Hithe, a parte of the east suburbs where a small river runns into a creeke of the sea, wee found two thousand quarters of rye with a greate proportion of salte and wine, which wee brought into the towne. . . . . The inhabitants were as much amaz'd at this plenty as our selves, for the market day before wee enter'd the towne the poore were complayning in the streets that they could not gette corne for their money; those bowell-lesse merchants having ingross'd it to enhanse the price."[1]

By June 19 the beleaguered Royalists in Colchester received the unwelcome news that their 'friends at Linton were defeated by the enemy, and Major Muschamp, a loyal gentleman, killed,'[2] and all hope of the expected support from that quarter was practically cut off. Their hopes of aid from the sea had, however, been rising through the revolt of part of the ships to the King. There was an attempt to force the passage of the Colne by these ships laden with provisions for the beleaguered town, but they were driven back by the garrison on Mersea Island, aided by ships which had come up from Harwich.

The Suffolk men on the banks of the Stour were still halting between divers opinions, whether to fight for the King, for Parliament, or to block up their own borders. The Royalists were not yet completely cut off on the east and north-east side, and after taking possession of the house of Sir Harbottle Grimston at Bradfield, they sent the following communication to the Suffolk men across the river:—

"Gentlemen, we are commanded by Sir Charles Lucas, commander in chief of his Majesty's forces in Essex, to desire your positive answer whether you do declare yourselves to be our enemies or no. Likewise, we desire to give you notice that our coming hither is to preserve this hundred from plunder; nor to act in anything against you in Suffolk, upon your declaring either to be our friends or to stand as neuters, and that your intentions of drawing

[1] Beaufort MSS.
[2] Diary in MSS. of J. H. Round, Esq., M.P.

together are only to secure your own county; hoping you will be so tender of spilling any more blood, especially of your so near neighbours, as we Essex men that have associated with you, as that you will take away all just occasions, by coming no more into our county, and sending back those men, horses, and arms which you have taken from us, or forcing us to declare ourselves to be what we loath to think of, your enemies; whereas our wishes and studies shall be to subscribe ourselves, gentlemen, your friends and loving neighbours. June 22, 1648."[1]

Two days later, the news-letters were declaring that although the Essex soldiers 'had stood so many cannon shots that they deserved to be called Essex lions,' yet the Suffolk forces were still at their rendezvous. But on June 25, the bridge over the river was finished, and the Suffolk men, consisting of about 2,000 foot and five troops of horse, crossed over, threw in their lot with the besieging army, and entrenched themselves before the East Gate on the Suffolk Road.[2]

In a few days Colonel Barnardiston reported to Parliament that their forces had "behaved themselves so gallantly that after a hot dispute, where some of them lost their lives and many of them much blood, yet in the conclusion they beat the enemy out of their houses in the suburbs . . . . so far as the East Bridge, which doth much straiten those within the town by hindering their sallies into Tendering Hundred."[3] The House thanked them for 'their gallant and valorous service.'

The share of the Essex men before Colchester is also reflected in letters from their commanders. On June 26 Colonel Sparrow wrote to Sir Harbottle Grimston:—"Our country now begins to be so exhausted of provisions that it may well be doubted that the poor will be compelled to

[1] Rushworth, vii, 1163.
[2] "The Suffolk forces under the command of Colonel Barnardiston, Colonel Gourdon, Colonel Fotheringill, Captain Moody, and others, were persuaded to quit their passes at Stratford and Hayland, where at first they pretended only the securing of their own county."—Narrative in the MSS. of the Duke of Beaufort.
[3] Letter to the Speaker in the Portland MSS.

rise for want of bread. And I cannot see any other remedy unless some pay may be advanced for the pay of the General's army; and . . . . then we should be supplied by way of markets here, and other countries would readily send in for our money, whereas now all provisions are raised in our country."[1]

The Suffolk commanders were able to bring provisions for their own men, but Essex, with its County Committee shut up in Colchester, suffered from the hardships of a year of famine. If those within the walls of Colchester were enduring all the horrors of the siege, the besiegers without were suffering the misery of camping on the soddened ground during one of the wettest summers of the century.[2] So desperate was the condition of the soldiers from this cause, that Warwick says: "The weather being very rainy, it rotted divers of Fairfax's men, and had cost him more had not the provisions and shelter the country brought in to him made him so well struggle with that difficulty."[3]

The efforts made to secure the release of the Essex Committeemen were continued by Parliament. A temporary committee for the County, made up of members of the Hertfordshire and other Committees, was appointed to look after the affairs of Essex, with power to seize twenty individual Royalists to be sent to the General to have such treatment as the imprisoned Committee had.[4] One of the persons to be seized was 'young Mr. Capell, son and heir-apparent of the Lord Capell,' and 'in case of opposition to break open locks and doors to search for the said Mr. Capell,' who was then at Hadham Hall, Herts. The result is reflected in the particulars which follow:—

"At 16 years of age, in the middle of June, 1648, when his father Lord Capell defended the town of Colchester against the rebels, a seargent with two men came to Hadham to carry him to the General at the league before Colchester. He was then very sickly and had scarce rid ever on

[1] Portland MSS., Hist. MSS. Rep., xiii, pt. 1, 467-8.
[2] "Mending ye Great Walk, washed down with ye G^t Flood."—Bursar's Accounts, St John's College, Cambridge, 1648.
[3] Memoirs, p. 314.
[4] Commons' Journals.

horseback, or been out of the family, and from the time that Cromwell took away the horses,[1] there never could be one kept, soe that he was forced to hire horses for himself and one man, which was all that would be allowed him, and was soe ill-used that he was forced sometimes to lye in a cabin, and sometimes in a little thatchet house, with two soldiers lying by him in straw, and every day was carried round the works. The first day they sent my Lord word that his son was there and whether he would not surrender, which he answered that 'if his wife and all his children were there he would doe his duty.' However, on the 6th of July he had leave to return."[2]

It was said in the diary of a lady of the time, that the incident so affected Lady Capel, that she was 'brought abed of a son with the grief of it.' The circumstance is further illustrated by the following letter, from one of the Capels to Mrs. Sadler, of Standon, Herts:—"Noblest Madam Sadler, I humbly thank you for your letter, and for the contents; wee were acquainted with them before. This day they are (by order of ——) carrying my young nephewe Arthur Capell to the Lo : Fairfax, to the great and extraordinary grief of his blessed mother, who was on Monday night delivered of a brave lusty boy, but takes this great iniustice with so deep a rescent [resentment] as I very much fear it will hazard her life. Madam, I am your most humble servant, Arthur Capell. For the most noble Mrs. Sadler."[3]

Sir Thomas Honeywood, writing to the Speaker from the Leaguer before Colchester, on July 11, says:—"The sad condition of our worthy friends in Colchester . . . . doth every day heighten our compassion . . . . besides such is the policy, or rather cruelty, of the enemy, that they place them just under the mouth of our only advantageous battery. A bullet within these few hours, notwithstanding all our care, passed through the room where they are all in

---

[1] See "Hertfordshire during the Civil War," p. 18.
[2] Hist. MSS. Com. Rep., xii, App., pt. ii, MSS. of the Duke of Beaufort.
[3] Collection of letters to and from Mrs. Sadler, of Standon.—MSS. R. 5, Trinity College, Cambridge.

durance."[1] Fortunately, Parliament had Mr. Ashburnham a prisoner, and he was exchanged for Sir William Masham ; and as to the rest of the Committeemen, the House ordered that "it be referred to the General to make convenient exchanges for all the rest of the Committee of Essex, now in restraint in Colchester."

With Fairfax unable to move from before the walls of Colchester, and Cromwell away besieging Pembroke Castle in Wales, Royalists had a fair chance of rising wherever commanders could be found to lead them. On July 4 the House wrote to Colonel Rossiter that 'the enemy hath taken Lincoln,' and that adjoining counties had been directed to send in forces to assist him in Lincolnshire. In Huntingdonshire there were, on July 4, tumultuous meetings, in which Colonel Montague was taken prisoner and carried to Washingley House, and for suppressing which Colonel Walton sent troops out of Norfolk. At Elstree, Herts, there was a skirmish ; but a more important rising was that under the Duke of Buckingham and the Earl of Holland, who, after being defeated near Kingston-on-Thames, were driven into Hertfordshire 'into the lion's den,' with Sir Michael Livesey in pursuit. While these Cavaliers, with 400 or 500 horse, were crossing Hertfordshire, the Earl of Holland having 'a bullet in his shoulder,' the news reached Fairfax before Colchester, and he sent off Colonel Adrian Scroope with seven troops of horse upon a forced march to intercept the Royalists, whose presence in the county had so alarmed Hertfordshire that the 'well-affected' mustered in strong force to guard Hatfield House.

Marching day and night, Colonel Scroope almost came up with the Cavaliers on Sunday, July 9, when a Committeeman from Hertford accompanied him to Hitchin, where 'six good guides' were obtained to direct them in their march during Sunday night to St. Neots, on the borders of Beds and Hunts, towards which the Royalists were known to be marching. Sir Michael Livesey's advanced guard had lost trace of the Cavaliers apparently, though

[1] Portland MSS.

they had fallen upon a small party of them indulging in a revelry at an inn at Luton, 'with their hats on the table and their swords stuck in the ceiling.'[1]

On the arrival of Buckingham and the wounded Earl at St. Neots, on the Sunday evening, a council of war was held for the purpose of deciding the line of march for the next day. Dalbier, the old soldier, who 'was esteemed an eminent officer amongst them, to whose advice they much adhered,' stoutly maintained that St. Neots itself could be held without the necessity for renewing their march next day. He 'engaged to make good the town of St. Neots against any party that should pursue them, and that he would engage his life, which he would lose rather than see them surprised.' The Council of War having adopted Dalbier's advice to remain at St. Neots, the Duke of Buckingham and the Earl of Holland addressed themselves to the magistrates and principal inhabitants of the town in conciliatory speeches, as they had done in other towns. Here is the speech of the Duke of Buckingham :—

"Gentlemen, we come not hither to carry anything from you; but have given strict orders that neither officers nor soldiers carry what is now yours away. Nor are our intentions to make a new war; but to rescue the kingdom from the arbitrary power of the Committees of the several counties that labour to continue a bloody war to destroy you. Our resolution for peace is by a well-settled government under our royal King Charles; and we do bless God that He hath made us instruments to serve the King, the Parliament, and the Kingdom in the way to peace."[2]

The Earl of Holland also made a speech, 'at which the Earl had a better faculty than at the sword,' in similar terms, and the St. Neots people seem to have accepted the situation without demur. The Duke of Buckingham 'slept at a gentleman's house two or three miles out of the town'; and the Earl of Holland, 'so weary and shaken in his joynts that he had better well to his bed than to his horse,' went to one of the inns in the town.

[1] "Hertfordshire during the Great Civil War," p. 83.
[2] "A Great Victory at St. Neots," London, 1648.

Just before sunrise on Monday morning, July 10, 100 dragoons, forming the forlorn hope of Colonel Scroope's force, arrived at the town end at Eaton Ford. The Royalists on guard cried "To horse! to horse!" and those who were already under arms disputed the bridge warmly, but on account of the suddenness of the attack, and the few who had assembled, were 'overpowered and driven into the town.' There the Earl of Holland's forces were out of their beds and drawn up in three companies on the Market Hill. The other officers had speedily assembled, but the Earl of Holland, 'if the enemy did not slander him, took more deliberation to dresse him.' The main body of Colonel Scroope's force dashed into the town, and 'six troops were instantly brought into action.' Dalbier and Colonel Legg fought with great bravery, but the force they commanded was soon overpowered; and the young Duke of Buckingham, who had got into the saddle and into the town in time to see which way things were going, set off along the Huntingdon road with about sixty of the horse. As for the Earl of Holland, who had taken so much pains about his toilet, he either had not got out of his room, or was forced back partly dressed by his own men, who fell back upon the old inn yard where the Earl had slept. Here a brief, sanguinary conflict ensued; the great gates of the inn next the street were closed, and the Earl's body-guard sought to defend him by firing pistol shots upon the attacking force in the street.

But here they were in a trap from which there was no escape; for in front were troops enough to take a small garrison, and in the rear of the premises flowed the turgid waters of the Ouse. The great gates were forced; the courtyard swarmed with the Parliamentary troopers, who soon 'made short work' of the Earl's party, many of whom were drowned in the Ouse in attempting to escape at the rear. A rush was then made for the Earl of Holland's chamber in the inn, the door was broken open, and the fastidious young Cavalier surrendered himself in the following graceful speech :—

"Gentlemen, souldiers, I am a gentleman and desire you

that I may be used as a gentleman. I pray you let me have quarter for my life; I am your prisoner and desire that I may be civilly used, and that you will show yourselves souldiers and gentlemen towards me. I offer you no opposition, but freely surrender myself your prisoner."[1]

The soldiers gave him quarter, used him civilly, and delivered him to Colonel Scroope.

Dalbier, the former Parliament Quarter-Master-General, although he 'drank sack stiffly,' had done his best to justify his advice to hold the town, by fighting to the death, and the Parliamentary troopers, 'to express their detestation of his treachery, hewed him in pieces.' The Royalists afterwards declared that their assailants at St. Neots 'fought more like devils than men.'

In a hurried dispatch sent off to the Committee at Derby House, the same day, Colonel Scroope wrote :—

"The enemy when we entered the town were drawn up into three bodies, which my forlorn hope charged and routed before the rest of my horse entered, but when the rest came up the dispute was quickly at an end, for then they got out at all the passes and ran for it, but divers of them fell, and some of the chief ones, and we have taken divers prisoners. . . . . The Duke of Bucks escaped with about three score horse, who is gone, as I understand, towards Lincoln. I had marched all day Saturday and all night that my horse was unable to pursue further than Huntingdon, but I hope if he goes that way that he will be met with by Colonel Rossiter's forces. He is not at all considerable, and unable to do anything."

He then gives particulars of the prisoners taken, who included the Earl of Holland, and Sir Gilbert Gerard, Colonel Dalbier, and a son of Sir Kenelm Digby being killed.

More definite particulars which followed showed that the prisoners included 30 officers, 120 troopers, and 200 horse, besides arms 'and of gold and silver clothes a store.' The spoil included the Earl of Holland's white charger, 'with splendid caparison,' £600 in gold taken from the Earl's

[1] "Bloody Newes from Bedfordshire," E. 452 (32).

private chest, and 'his blew ribbon and his George taken from his person.' The soldiers declared 'they never met with such golden bootie; fine cloathes, gallant horses, and bags full of coin.'

The prisoners were, for greater security, taken into St. Neots church, where they remained well guarded until the following day, when they were sent on to Hitchin, and thence to London. The Earl of Holland was sent off in a coach, and with other officers was secured in Warwick Castle; the Duke of Buckingham, who had fled towards Lincolnshire, eventually found his way back to London and escaped to France.[1]

Two days before this affair at St. Neots, Hamilton with his Scottish forces had crossed the border and seized Carlisle; and Cromwell, having taken Pembroke Castle, was, a few days later, marching northwards to meet him. Nearer home Parliament was anxious about the marine population of Yarmouth, who were ready to burst out in sympathy with the crews of the revolted ships, and the Deputy-Lieutenants of Norfolk earned the thanks of the House for promptly sending their forces to Yarmouth. Meanwhile the siege of Colchester was, day by day, becoming more desperate, as the old narratives which have already been quoted clearly indicate.

On Friday, July 7, about the time that Colonel Scroope set out upon his forced march to St. Neots, there was a 'grand sally upon the east suburbs with 600 foot and 150 horse,' which resulted in a severe engagement with the besiegers. Gradually the line of communication was drawn closer, taking in 'my Lord Lucas his house'; then the Hithe church was taken in, and, adds the narrative, "then we were

---

[1] Particulars of this victory at St. Neots are to be found scattered over a number of the old newspapers, news-letters, and pamphlets of the period, the principal being :—
"A Great Victory at St. Neots": London, 1648. "A letter from Isaac Puller & William Plomer (Mayor of Hertford), dated Hertford, past five in the morning, July 11th, 1648" (King's Pamphlets, Brit. Mus., E. 452). *Mercurius Britannicus*, *Moderate Intelligencer*, *Perfect Weekly Account*, etc., etc. These are reprinted for the most part in Gorham's "History of Fynesbury and St. Neots." Other authorities are: Sanderson's "Charles I"; the Welbeck MSS.; Rushworth; Whitelock; the Journals of Parliament, etc.

wholly invested. We must needs acknowledge our besiegers wrought hard and not irregularly, but in truth they began at the wrong end; for had they first possessed St. John's they had cut us off from the Hithe, and that provision which fed 7,000 mouths for 11 weeks, & without it we could not have subsisted five days.

"Being cut off from our forage, and having no provision of hay and oats in the town, on Saturday the fifteenth of July, about ten at night, we attempted to break away with part of our horse, ordering them to march northward, and join with the Scotch Armie, who, as we were informed by private letters, were upon their march to our relief. . . . . But the enemy having blocked up all the passes, we failed in our attempt, which upon second thoughts we thankfully acknowledged to Providence preserving us against our design. For had the horse passed we had wanted their flesh, upon which we fed six weeks; and their riders whom as we ordered, made the strongest part of our defence; for as their horses were slaughtered for our provision, they were armed with halberds, brown bills, and scythes, straightened and fastened to handles, about six foot long, weapons which the enemy strongly apprehended, but rather of terror than use, for they required such distances to manage them, that they could not be brought to fight in a gross. These were divided into three companies and commanded by my Lord of Norwich, the Lord Capell, and Sir Charles Lucas, who took their posts and hutted themselves upon the line, where they fed and lodged with their souldiers, a wise and worthy undertaking to revive the antient discipline; for though we humbly confess our sins, the primary cause which hath pulled down these judgments upon us, yet we look upon our luxuries and remissness in discipline as the proximate causes of our ruin. For many of our general officers in the former wars had such indulgence for their debaucheries that they adopted none to preferments but the companions of their pleasures.

"The enemy began their approaches on the east part of the town, called Berrie fields, which we suffered with great silence from our cannon, for besides our want of ammunition we desired an assault, as the likeliest means of our relief; only to free us from surprise we were forced to fire some of the neighbouring houses of the suburbs, where the enemy might have lodged their whole army within pistol shot of our walls. . . . .

"The last month passed quietly, for the enemy knew that we must be reduced by our wants, and we allowed them to make their approaches unchecked for lack of ammunition."

The besieged were at last compelled to reduce the allowance of bread to seven ounces a day. "It was received without murmuring by the souldiers, though being made of mault, oats, and rye which had taken salt water, it was not only distasteful, but such unwholesome food, that many chose to eat their horse and dog's flesh without it. But the greater suffering was of the poor inhabitants, who were reduced to that extremity that they ate soape and candle, which they endured with notable resolution. . . . . But upon review of our magazine and the provisions of private families, we found our store so little, that it was thought fit time to send a letter to Fairfax, wherein we proposed that if he would grant a truce for twenty days, and a pass for a messenger to find out Sir Marmaduke Langdale, if we were informed that in that interim he were not in a condition to relieve us, then we would treat with him upon a surrender. But the insolent enemy refused it, whereupon we resolved to·continue our defence, hoping that the justice of our cause and the temper of our proceedings might in some degree make us worthy of the protection of Providence and our friends." [1]

It was alleged that the soldiers and inhabitants were deliberately deceived by the Royalist commanders as to the chances of relief from outside,[2] and there can be no doubt that the Royalist prints in London had kept up the delusion. One of them appealed to the Earl of Norwich and Capel "and the rest of the renowned captains in Colchester"—

[1] Beaufort MSS.
[2] Fairfax Correspondence.

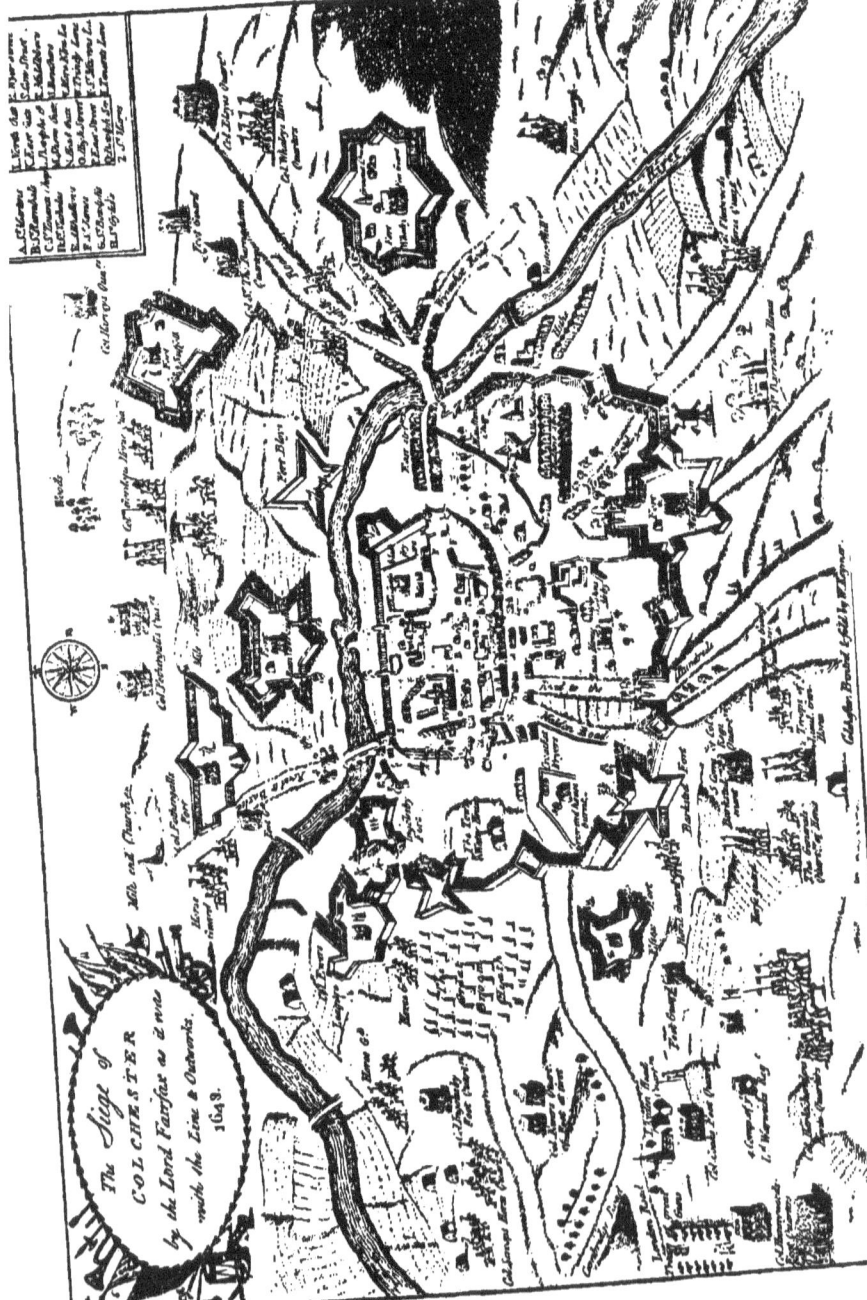

> Shrink not, brave heroes, be you not dismaid ;
> Things work apace, be patient and ere long
> Unto your rescue come three armies strong.

Outside the leaguer this sort of thing fell flat, with the victories at St. Neots and of Cromwell in Wales; and to counteract it, Fairfax shot papers over the wall to undeceive those inside of any false hopes concerning what was happening without.

At last the situation became too desperate to live on hope: the townspeople and the women with their children appealed to the humanity of Norwich, but the commanders still held on to the hope of Langdale and the Scots reaching them. The Mayor of Colchester appealed to Fairfax to allow civilians to pass the lines of communication, but like Norwich inside, Fairfax without had to set aside private feelings, and while pitying their condition found that 'it did not stand with his trust to permit it.' Again a famished crowd of women and children appealed to Norwich, and rather than give way he threw open the gates and told them ' to go to the enemy with their complaints.'

In their dire extremity it is said that a woman and five children, one sucking at her breast, came outside the fortifications. 'She fell down at our guards, beseeching them to let her pass beyond the lines; the people in the town were watching to see if the woman and children were allowed to pass, and resolving to follow them. But the guards were necessitated to turn them back, or otherwise hundreds would come out, which would prejudice the service. The woman said that could they but get dogs and cats to eat it were happy for them, but all the dogs and cats and most of the horses are near eaten already.' No wonder the writer adds—"Some sad thing of necessity must befall the town suddenly [presently]."[1]

Towards other women who came out, the sentries could only fire shots over their heads to frighten them back ; and at last were obliged to threaten to strip them of their clothing and send them back naked. In the face of this threat they

---

[1] Rushworth.

retired, but huddled themselves together, and took shelter in a mill just outside the walls for the night.

At last, on August 22, says the Royalist narrative inside the walls, "all hope was cut off by the news of Cromwell's victory over the Scots [at Preston], of which the enemy sent in a printed account by trumpet. At first we refused to believe it, but after two days further news convinced us, and a Council of War was called, which decided that overtures should be made to the enemy."

Two of the imprisoned Essex Committeemen were induced to address a letter to the Commanding Officer to allow them, 'out of their tender bowells to the starving inhabitants of the towne,' to wait upon Fairfax and mediate an accommodation. Fairfax, knowing that it was the defeat of the Scots that had prompted the device, sent back answer that they had held out and defied his summons so long that the best conditions they could expect would be to submit to mercy. Between the cries of the townspeople and the difficulty of keeping the starving soldiers together any longer, the commanders, finding the terms offered would be heaviest upon themselves, in desperation resolved upon an attempt to save themselves by mounting their half-starved horses and breaking through the lines in the night-time. Those having a horse left to mount, fell in with the project; but the common soldiers naturally demurred to a plan which would leave them behind, and, threatening to kill their officers rather than they should go out in this way, declared in favour of giving themselves up to Fairfax rather than continue the hopeless struggle.

Under these circumstances there was nothing for the Royalist Commanders but to submit, and on August 27 terms of capitulation were signed; a Council of War decided that Sir Charles Lucas and Sir George Lisle should suffer death, and they were led out to be shot. Lucas was the first to fall, justifying his action in his last words by 'all the laws of the kingdom,' and his commission from his sovereign. Lisle caught his body in his arms and 'kissed the dead man's face.' Then, taking his fallen comrade's place, Lisle called to the firing party to come nearer, to which one of the soldiers replied: "I'll warrant you, Sir, we'll hit you." "I have been nearer you when you have missed me," Lisle smilingly replied, and then fell as the bullets pierced his body.[1]

Much controversy has been carried on around the question whether the execution of Lucas and Lisle was justifiable or not—whether its inhumanity can be condoned by any question of parole given by compounders, or of the difference between the first and second wars—a controversy into which it would be profitless to enter here. Capel and Norwich, being peers, were left to be dealt with by the civil power.

From the starved, empty shell of a town now in ruin and in ashes,[2] with only 'a barrel and a half of powder left in it,' but 'plenty of the enemy's great shot' in place of food, 65 gentlemen, 72 lieutenants, 69 ensigns and cornets, 183 sergeants, and 3,067 private soldiers, with gaunt, hungry looks, filed out in charge of their captors, and on August 28 Fairfax was in possession of the town.

Many of the prisoners were marched across the county into Hertfordshire, and there for a time were accommodated in the churches, revelling in the new-found luxury of the bread and cheese doled out to them,[3] but with the harder fate in store for many of them of being shipped off to the West Indies. For the inhabitants of Colchester an equally rigorous punishment was meted out by the victors in the £12,000 exacted from them for the soldiers in lieu of plunder, of which £2,000 was returned by Fairfax to be given to the poor. The Essex and Suffolk Trained Bands received £2,000 as their share, the other £8,000 going to Fairfax's soldiers.

While the tragedy at Colchester was being enacted,

---

[1] There is a belief prevalent in Colchester that around the stone upon which Lucas was shot the grass refuses to grow, upon which Mr. S. R. Gardiner has this comment—"Possibly there are stones from the old walls buried at no great distance from the surface."

[2] Rushworth says that when riding round about the wall of the town "it was a sad spectacle to see so many fine houses burnt to ashes, and so many inhabitants sickly and weak with living upon horses and dogs." It appears that 800 horses were eaten during the siege, and 300 houses burned.

[3] See "Hertfordshire during the Civil War," p. 87.

a curious little adventure was happening in the corner of Norfolk on the Wash. That threatened irruption into the Isle of Ely and the Fens had actually come to pass on a small scale; and, out of the mists and shadows which a few small fragments of fact illuminate for us, there is visible to the imagination a short, sharp tussle with some hundreds of the King's men. The outcome of that tussle was one which probably charged the memory of the longshoremen of the Wash with the material for many a fireside tale, not unworthy of other tales of the sea. The King's men were hustled out of the Fens on to the muddy strand of the Wash about King's Lynn, and there placed on board one of the harbour craft, with directions to the keelman to take his cargo of prisoners across the Wash to Boston. But finding themselves once on the free, tossing waves, the captured turned upon their captors, after the approved fashion of all sea stories, lay about them in earnest, got the upper hand of the Parliament men in charge of them, bound them hand and foot; and then, also in the approved manner of fiction, made the keelman their servant, and bade him navigate his vessel according to their own will, which was that he should shape his course for Scarborough, right away from this fighting region of East Anglia and its memories of old "Ironsides."

The keelman, with his flat-bottomed craft, protested that it was impossible; but he promised them that he could land them on the coast at Heacham, near which place there lived one Sir Hamon Le Strange, a man who after the War began, held the town of Lynn for the King until my lord of Manchester besieged and took it. This they agreed to, and the keelman coasted along the Wash to Heacham, where the party landed, with the Parliament convoy who had now become the prisoners. On a hot day, the thirsty party made their way to Hunstanton Hall, where Sir Hamon Le Strange was pondering over the turn of events. One of his sons, Roger, had escaped hanging for his attempted recapture of Lynn, and had now fled the country after a futile effort in writing proclamations for the Kent and Essex rising of the second Civil War. But Sir Hamon, though he could no longer use his sword as he would like to do, was not the man to see the King's soldiers in want of a stoup of ale, and so they get at least that comfort. Unfortunately, there lived at Hunstanton one Toby Pedder, now chief constable of the hundred, who was too zealous for Parliament to remember that it was through Sir Hamon's influence that he obtained his office: so the affair got wind; and this is the best face Sir Hamon himself is able to put upon the story, when called upon for an explanation two months later.

"Sir Hamon L'Estrange to ———, understands that Toby Pedder, of Hunstanton (whom he made not chief constable to repay him with malice and ingratitude), has given information concerning some clandestine favour shown by him [Sir Hamon] to some soldiers of the King's party lately landed at Heacham. The facts are these. About two months since there came to his house a keelman of Lynn and two gentlemen in the outer court, who wanted to see him. He sent his servant, who was told that many hundred of the King's party had been sent as prisoners from Lynn to Boston. They overmastered their convoy, and wanted the keelman to take them to Scarborough. He said he was not able, but would land them at Heacham, and that Sir Ham. L'Estrange, who lived near, had appeared for the King and would show them favour, and they now desired to speak with Sir Hamon. He refused to see them, and so they departed." He admitted, however, that afterwards "some of the prisoners and their convoy came to his outer court, and the weather being very hot, asked for drink, which his butler gave them without his direction (tho' I might safely justifye that charity to a Turk), and this is the sum of all that buysiness."[1]

From this point the thirsty Royalists and their convoy vanish completely from our view, like many another fragment of a thrilling story. It may be that some of the Norfolk 'blades' came to the rescue of the helpless convoy, and got the original prisoners back across the Wash to Boston after all.

[1] L'Estrange Papers, Hist. MSS. Com. Reps.

How completely the attempted renewal of the War in East Anglia had failed, before the end of the year 1648, is shown by the Cambridge Colleges returning to their peaceful academic life. At Trinity College the authorities even dared to venture upon a little function of peculiar interest. The College was wealthy, was its own banker, and amid the din of arms the precaution had been taken of hiding away its money until the evil day had passed. As soon as it was considered safe to do so the treasure was taken up, and there was an interesting little ceremony of counting the money which had been hidden, and when the task was finished there was a supper given, apparently, to the workmen.[1] The same kind of thing was happening on every hand, in public institutions and in private houses where secret places had been found or made in which to put away such treasure as could be hidden.[2]

At St. John's College, too, there had been a peaceful transformation—sycamore-planting in the "New Walk," the laying out afresh of the Bowling Green, for which the charges for the mole-catcher exceeded all previous records, and plumber's and glazier's work on roofs, leads, and windows swell the Bursar's yearly accounts, both in this and other Colleges.

The last notable action of the now all-powerful Army within the Associated Counties was the gathering of Fairfax's officers in St. Albans Abbey over the final question of determining the fate of the King. While Parliament was attempting its treaty-making with the King in the Isle of Wight, the officers of the Army, embittered by the experience of the past few months, were engaged in November, 1648, in St. Albans Abbey, drawing up the great Remonstrance, which, though covering the whole field of the War, was yet well summed up in these two paragraphs :—

"That capitall and grand Author of our troubles, the

---

[1] "Att ye takeing up and telling of ye hid money, 00–14–06 ; Jo. Staggs' bill for ye supper then, 00-15-00."—Bursar's Accounts, Trin. Coll., 1648.

[2] At Gorhambury, near St. Albans, Lady Sussex, having concealed her plate, packed up her 'hangings and best stuffs' and hid them away in one of the round turrets above her bedchamber, and then had the place walled up.—Verney Papers.

person of the King, by whose commissions, commands, or procurement, and in whose behalfe and for whose interest only (of will and power) all our warres and troubles have been (with all the miseries attending them), may be speedily brought to justice for the treason, blood, and mischiefe he is therein guilty of.

"That for further satisfactions of publique justice. Capitall punishment may be speedily executed upon a competent number of his chiefe instruments also, both in the former and latter warre, and (for that purpose) that some such, of both sorts, may be pitcht upon to be made examples of justice in that kind, as are really in your hands or reach, so as their exception from pardon may not be a mockery of justice in the face of God and men."[1]

When this emphatic document reached Parliament the House was thrown into great alarm, but after prolonged debating courageously voted, by a majority of 90, that it 'will not take the Army's Remonstrance into consideration'! So the Army marched to London to enforce its Remonstrance, got rid of the majority of 90, and at the same time brought the King away from the Isle of Wight to London. Cromwell had by this time marched back from the north, and arrived in time to share in the final tragedy of the trial and execution of the King, which closed the year 1648 and opened the year 1649. The tragic story needs no retelling in these pages, except to notice presently the consequences to some of the individual actors therein.

Although the King adhered to the original notion of divine right to the last—"For the people truly I desire their liberty and freedom as much as anybody whatsoever; it is not their having a share in the Government; that is nothing appertaining unto them; a subject and a sovereign are clean different things"[2] — and 'lost his head for his kingcraft,' yet he 'gained the hearts of his people by his bearing as a man.'

There was a great revulsion of feeling over the execution

---

[1] "A Remonstrance of his Excellency, Thomas Lord Fairfax, and of the Generall Counsell of Officers, held at St. Albans, the 16th of November, 1648."
[2] Speech of Charles I on the scaffold at Whitehall.

of the King. In Hertfordshire a former Parliament-man declared that 'it was the most horrid murder that ever any history made mention of,' and 'if he had thought the Parliament would have gone in that way he would never have drawn his sword for them.'[1] This feeling, increased by the publication of the "Eikon Basilike," detailing the sufferings and fate of the King, was prevalent in other counties of the Association.

In the Summer months of 1649, there was a remarkable instance of this divided feeling on the borders of Hertfordshire and Cambridgeshire. In July, Commissary-General Ireton's Foot, quartered at Braughing and adjacent villages, sent a recruiting party to Royston fair, with the result which has been thus graphically recorded :—

"The inhabitants, being somewhat troubled thereat, resolved to make opposition, and immediately gathered to a head, which being done, about 150 marched to the Market Place, fell upon the Parliamentary party, cut and mangled them exceedingly, laid many for dead upon the place, broke their halberts, arms, and drums, wounded Captain Stewart, the commander-in-chief, Lieut. Smith, and some others; and in a most barbarous and inhumane manner, slit their fingers, the palms of their hands, cut their wrists, and wounded them even from the crown of the head (almost) to the sole of the foot, calling them rebels and traitors for murthering of their King, and saying that they would make rogues of them before they had done with 'em. The conflict being ended, these blood-thirsty villains departed, leaving some gallant spirits gasping on the ground, and their inveteracy was so great that if they did but see any of them stir, presently they made at them again with clubs and other weapons vowing to leave not a man of them alive."[2]

Captain Steward, in his own dispatch to Ireton, says : "After my drummer had beaten some short time, the townsmen (who are very malignant) and others rose in mutiny about six score of them, fell upon my sergeants and drummer,

[1] Cobb's "Hist. Berkhamsted." p. 46.
[2] "A Bloody Fight in Hertfordshire."—King's Pamphlets, E. 565 (73), Brit. Mus. Lib.

broke my drum, and beat my men most lamentably, upon which the Captain, to appease the crowd, told them that 'what was done was by authority of Parliament,' and they replied by telling him he was a rebel and a traitor, and fell upon him, cut his hand from the fingers to the wrist, and wounded his head most desperately; and when they had gone in and we endeavoured to stand on our legs, which we could not do without help, they came again, knocked us down, and thought they had made their intents sure, which was to kill us."

A Royalist print,[1] describing the same incident, says:— "The Royston crowes have already taught you the way to take revenge on Prince Ireton's owly birds; for one Stewart's son of Braughing, Cromwell's cousin, was beating up drums for recruits, and had gained some loose idle fellows that had rather rob and be hanged than take pains to work and earn their livings, which the loyal-hearted townsmen understanding, seized on them, yet nobly spared their lives, but cut a-too the sinews of their right hands to make them unserviceable for fighting against their King. I would all towns and cities in England would do the like."

In Norfolk, Cambridgeshire, and Hertfordshire, there are further glimpses of disturbances over the execution of the King, and of an inclination to rise in support of Charles II, afforded by depositions taken at a later date and preserved in the Portland MSS. But in these later developments East Anglia found that that peculiar identity which had given it such a prominence as the one great historic unity of the Civil War, dissolved into the broader issues of the Commonwealth, leaving behind it a harvest of unhappy memories in the religious, social, and family life, the origin of which must be sought, for any clear idea of the full purpose and effect of the great struggle.

[1] "The Man in the Moon; discovering a World of Knavery under the Sunne."—King's Pamphlets.

CHAPTER XIV.

TAXING THE ROYALISTS—THE FORTUNES OF COMPOUNDERS
—SEQUESTRATORS AND THEIR WAYS.

ONE of the most far-reaching effects of the
Civil War upon social life was that arising out
of the efforts and methods adopted by the
respective parties for raising the sinews of war. At the
commencement of the strife contributions both to King
and Parliament took the form of voluntary acts by the
supporters of either side. When the quarrel had reached
the stage of actual war, these sources of supply were
inadequate, and other measures were of necessity adopted.
The King, for whom county families and wealthy corporations like the Universities had in the beginning of the
quarrel furnished substantial contributions of plate and
arms, found himself obliged when these were exhausted
to levy contributions by such means as were open to him;
while Parliament was constrained, through its Committee for
the Advance of Money, to convert the system of voluntary
contributions into a sort of forced loan, with, at first, the
security of the "Public Faith" of the Kingdom for repayment with interest at 8 per cent. per annum; a security
which under stress of war soon lost what little value it ever
had. For enforcing this new principle of making all
contribute alike, willing or unwilling, Parliament had
the great advantage of official machinery—from its own
votes down to the warrants of the parish constable wherever

the baton of that worthy still remained supreme; and with this, through its Committee, a machinery for distributing the money so raised, in different parts of the field of war according to the necessities of the moment. On the other hand, the King found himself reduced to the necessity of taking supplies wherever they were to be found, and hand them over direct to the officers in the field to meet the needs of the moment.

Parliament's first assessment of a lump sum was to take one-twentieth of the real estate and one-fifth of the personal estate of each contributor. The exacting of this original assessment was a source of much trouble in many families, those who refused being carried off to prison until the money was paid or security for it provided; as in the case of Sir William Cowper, of Hertford Castle. As the War proceeded and the demands for money became more pressing, Parliament ordered weekly assessments from time to time upon the Counties, for which precepts were issued to the chief constable of each hundred, and by him to the parish constables of the hundred. Defaulters in this case were punished by way of distraint made upon their goods and chattels by the collectors, backed up by the parish constable, and if necessary the soldiers of the Trained Bands—a frequent source of irritation in the civil life of non-combatants. The result was a constant stream of traffic in goods and chattels carried up from the Home Counties to the Guildhall in London and sold by auction, 'by the candle'; an arrangement out of which the fraternity of brokers and dealers made a good harvest.

History has been careful to record how much the triumph of the Parliamentary cause was due to the valour of Cromwell's Ironsides, and has said less of how much was due to the financial weapon by which Parliament was able to squeeze out its weekly assessments from counties practically untouched by the ravages of the War, and to exact substantial contributions from the very men who hated the name of Parliament. The strength which the Parliamentary cause derived from the Associated Counties was not confined solely to the forwardness of the people to fight for that cause. The fact that the tide of war flowed, and that its operations were for the most part kept, outside the borders of the Association, had this peculiar effect, that it drew away every zealous fighting Royalist from his ancestral estates. These were at once sequestrated for Parliament, which took the rents and profits, and, for the necessities of the War, often impoverished the estate of its timber, etc. Where the estates of 'malignants,' as Royalists were called, were sequestrated, their farms were sometimes let, their rents collected by the County Sequestration Committees; and where the farms were unlet, or tenants could not be found upon such lease as Parliament and its Committees were justified in giving, the County Committee through an agent would farm the land itself, giving an account to Parliament of the crops, etc.

If the method of levying contributions adopted by the Cavaliers was, in the hands of unscrupulous agents, known as "plunder," a name which it very often deserved; the Parliamentary sequestrations were, in the eyes of those who suffered by them, only saved from the same description by the formal procedure which accompanied them. But, allowing for the conditions under which some such pressure became a necessary corollary of war, there was a certain element of judicial fairness, if the word be admissible, in the way Parliament set about its levies, which was absent in the foraging expeditions of the Cavaliers. If Parliament seized the 'delinquent' Royalist's estate, it did not leave him to starve, but allowed him one-third of it to live upon, or in the case of a clergyman, the sequestration of whose living involved the necessity of finding another man to do the work, the allowance for his wife and family was one-fifth. The family of the Royalist squire or clergyman, if it came to the worst, was thus secured certain rights, under rules which they could demand to have enforced; and were generally, though not always, safe from the violence of the first marauding troop of soldiers which came along; an exemption which could not always be secured from their friends the Cavaliers, who did not distinguish much between friends and foes.

The County Sequestration Committees for Parliament, the members of which were paid for their attendance, and were required to sit two days in each week, combined the work of an assessment committee and of the sheriff and his officers; and that the functions of both were unpopular with all having the misfortune to come under the rod, goes without saying. Large sums of money were raised, and it was a part of the irony of this old weapon of paradox which Parliament was able to wield, that the counties in which Royalists were the most numerous, contributed most to the ultimate success of the Parliamentary cause, and to the defeat of their own, if only Parliament once got a sufficient hold to keep the constable's head above water. Of the seven counties of the famous Association, Lincolnshire, which was only won and retained for the Association by repeated engagements and the most obstinate fighting, contributed by far the largest share to the Parliamentary treasury from Royalist estates. Next to Lincolnshire, Cromwell's own county of Huntingdon, for a small county, paid the largest penalties for its divided allegiance. Then came Norfolk, Suffolk, Herts, Essex, and Cambs.

Wherever detailed accounts of household expenses upon Royalist estates have been preserved, they afford clear testimony to the grip of the Parliamentary tax-gatherer, and show how, after the first flush of excitement of the clash of arms, many a country Royalist was reluctantly contributing with almost prosaic regularity to the defeat of his own cause. The most interesting evidence of this character which has come under my notice from the Eastern Counties, is that afforded by the household accounts of Sir Hamon Le Strange, of Hunstanton Hall, whose attempt to hold the town of Lynn for the King has been already referred to. These accounts have an additional interest from the fact that they were regularly and methodically kept by, and are in the handwriting of, Lady Alice Le Strange, wife of Sir Hamon, a capable woman, whose opinion of men and things, one feels, would have been worth having. The accounts show not only the regular draining of the wealth of the Association for maintaining the War, but also how the process of impoverishment of Royalist estates went on, and how hard it was when a rich man had once offended against Parliament, so openly as Sir Hamon had done, to 'purge' himself and his estate of that offence. After that notable attempt at King's Lynn, Sir Hamon went back to Hunstanton Hall, and apparently tried hard not to offend Parliament. He paid the taxes levied by Parliament, for 'Sr Thomas Fayrfaxe,' 'for the Eastern Association,' 'to the rate for all the garrisons,' 'for the reducing of Newark,' 'money for the Skotts,' 'for a rate for alarums,' and even 'advance money for a troop of horse raysed in this hundred'; and all these as well for Hunstanton as for his estates at Heacham, Ringstead, Sedgeford, and elsewhere, with the regularity of a law-abiding citizen in a time remote from the distractions of war.[1] Yet again and again the consequence of that act at Lynn overtook him with exhausting effect, from which the estate never recovered, and until even Lady Alice lost patience and called the Parliament's doings hard names.

Lady Alice Le Strange, who speaks of her husband, not as Sir Hamon, but as 'Mr. Strange,' faithfully records only such of their experiences as led to expense, but these were frequent enough in all conscience. A very suggestive entry is one for July, 1643, when Sir Hamon was getting possession of King's Lynn—

	£	s.	d.
For a barrel of powder which was cast overboard, weight 50 lbs.	2	1	6

and the next entry is more significant still—

	£	s.	d.
Layd out as appeareth by a bill of Mr. Strange's, when he travailed to avoid the troopers	5	5	0

Then there are charges for messengers going to and fro with letters, and others which show that Sir Hamon and his lady managed to get into Lynn despite the troopers.

---

[1] Some idea of the cumulative effect of these contributions may be inferred from the fact that for one contribution, 'the greate subsidy' of £400,000 for Ireland, paid Jan. 4, 1643, Sir Hamon's quota was, for ' Hunstn,' £6 11s. 0d. ; for Sedgeford, £10 15s. 7d. ; Ringstead, £2 2s. 7d. ; and Heacham, £9 5s. 7d., or nearly £30, at one call of the collector.

	£	s.	d.
August, 1643. For horse meat at Linne for 6 horses, 3 weekes and 5 dayes ...	3	16	8
for our owne dyett for 3 weekes & 5 dayes ...	8	0	0
for our 3 men for their dyetts for 3 weeks at 10s. ...	4	10	0
for washing of our Linnen	0	7	0

Then the good lady has to lament the loss of household stuff—'spiritt of saffron,' 'spiritt of mint,' 'a box of cash left to pay workmen'—total, £10 8s., which Captain Thomers' men 'did plunder with other things.' The attempt to hold King's Lynn and its failure were only the beginning of Sir Hamon's and Lady Alice's monetary troubles, for when the bombardment had ceased Parliament fixed upon the man who had called the tune to pay the piper. The Ordinance passed in December following the siege "enforced malignants to satisfy damage done to the well affected," and Sir Hamon, being the chief 'malignant,' the effect of the Ordinance is reflected in Lady Alice's accounts, which bristle with claims charging Sir Hamon with the damage of his fortifications, and possibly by the Parliament's own artillery. In April, 1645, Lady Alice makes these entries:—

	£	s.	d.
April 14, to Mr. May, mayor of Linn, upon an uniust order made by Mr. Miles Corbett, Mr. Valentine Walton, governour of Linne, and Thomas Toll, Alderman of Linne, for the pretended losse sustayned, as they falsely suggest, by the command of Sr Hamon le Strange	47	13	4
April 16. To Bartholomew Wormell upon the same Order	34	17	0
to William Johnson, upon the same order, for fyering of his mill	37	15	0
to the towne of Lynne for the towne Houses which were pulled downe & the Governour tooke away all the materials: yet by his order wee pay...	95	13	10
to Mr. Nelston for Sechy Bridg by the same Order	2	10	0
to others at Lynn	11	0	7

Four years after the siege, Robert Clarke obtained an execution against Sir Hamon upon which he paid £10, 'upon a pretended fyering of his stacks of hey in the siege of Linn, proved by a false witnesse.' This was followed by a still more serious claim. During the short time Sir Hamon had the upper hand at Lynn, in August, 1643, he seems to have found it necessary to exercise some control over Mr. Toll and Mr. Percivall, the members for the town, for which he had to answer afterwards. In May, 1643, there is this entry:—

Payd to Mr. Toll and his wife upon a Tryall for their
supposed imprisonment, beside £40 before deposited
in his hand £50 0 0

Sir Hamon also had to compensate Mr. Percivall, the other member for Lynn, and other persons, upon similar claims; and in less than a year Mr. Toll sought to annul his first action in order to claim 'larger damages.' Smaller men followed the example, and William Johnson for the firing of his mill obtained another £12 11s. 8d. 'upon an uniust order, being formerly payd all that he could demand.' In February, 1649, Sir Hamon was saddled with £30 'to John Johnson for his house that was taken downe in the Siege of Linne.' Finally, Lady Alice sums up the demands made upon Sir Hamon and his estate in the following interesting particulars entered at the end of her accounts :—

1643. We payd to the Rebells for our 5th & 20th part
[ordinary assessments for the War]... ... ... 300 0 0
1643. We were plundered by the Rebells of 1600 sheep,
all our corne and divers horses.
1644. We payd to the advance of the Skottish Rebells ... 200 0 0
1645. Payd to May, Wormell, etc., for their pretended
losses 225 11 2
1646. Payd to Stileman upon a sute pretending the false
imprisonment of his Father when he refused to
pay the money appoynted for him to pay by my
Lord Martiall in the Court of Honour 385 0 0
1647. To Mr. Percivall for pretended
imprisoning... ... ... 86 0 0 ⎫
to Mr. Toll for the like in part ... 40 0 0 ⎬ 334 4 10
payd for the Almes House ... [sic] 883 4 10 ⎭
1648. To Mr. Toll upon his pretended
imprisoning... ... ... 50 0 0 ⎫
to William Johnson upon a second Order... 12 11 8 ⎬ 92 11 8
to John Johnson for composition ... ... 30 0 0 ⎭
1649. To Mr. Toll for Mr. Jegon's part, uniustly 136 8 0

Upon another page are entered, 'among losses in my husband's estate,' this little summary :—

Payd and spent in sute by the uniust and tirannicall op-
pression of Mr. Toll and others of his faction in Linne
concerning the seige 1088 0 0
Received by Stileman in an Uniust Sute, being overpowered
by the times 385 0 0
besides our greate losse when we were plundered of all our sheepe
and corne.[1]

[1] Household accounts preserved in the Muniment Room at Hunstanton Hall, from which the foregoing and other extracts have been courteously furnished by Hamon Le Strange, Esq., the present representative of a historic house.

Powerful though this grip of the Royalist's estate by Parliament was, as a factor in the struggle, the interest of it centres chiefly in the effects of it upon individual lives and fortunes, in the vicissitudes of families, the humours and the sharp practices of the County Sequestrators themselves, and in the ingenious resorts and excuses of the 'delinquents' in their desire to get their estates out of the clutches of Parliament on the easiest terms. With little further hope of serving the King with the sword, with their estates in the hands of others, they were ready even to submit to the process of paying a heavy fine, fixed according to scale by Parliament, or even to part with some of their estate to redeem the rest, if they could only get back something to call their own. The fine was assessed by the Committee sitting at Goldsmith's Hall, and was confirmed by Parliament, and a pardon given upon its discharge. The ground of the fine was generally 'for being in arms against the Parliament,' 'for absenting himself from his home and going into the King's quarters,' 'going to the King at Oxford,' etc., etc.; and the fines varied as much in amount as in the circumstances, often curious and sometimes romantic, under which they were imposed.

Among the heavy fines imposed upon Royalists of great wealth and position may be mentioned, Viscount Camden, whose exploits about Stamford made the name of the 'Camdeners' a terror in the Spring months of 1643, who was allowed to compound upon a fine of £14,000; Sir Edward Hussey, of Honnington, Lincolnshire, who executed the King's Commission of Array for calling his neighbours to arms, fined £8,750; Sir William Thorold, of Lincolnshire, Commissioner of Array, £4,160; John Russell, of Shingay, Cambs, brother of the Earl of Bedford, £7,000; Mr. Thomas Jermyn, of Rushbrooke Hall, Bury St. Edmunds, £2,800; Sir John Hewitt, of Waresly, Hunts, £3,000, reduced to £2,158; Sir Anthony Cage, of Burrough Green, Cambs, who was prominent in the Linton Insurrection in the Second Civil War, £2,440; John Newton,[1] of Haver, Lincolnshire,

---

[1] This was a remarkable case, if his story is to be believed. His offence was for being in the King's quarters; and his defence, that he was a lad of 16 years

£3,000; Edward Pelham, of Brockley, Lincolnshire, £2,250; Edward Aylmer, of Akenham, Norfolk, £1,900; Sir Benjamin Ayloffe, of Essex, £2,000; George Newell and his son, Sir Gervase, of Awber, Lincolnshire ('in Newark garrison'), £1,737; Sir Sutton Coney, of North Stook, Lincolnshire, £2,648.

These examples of large fines are, perhaps, more than matched in interest by the smallness of some of the fines, and the peculiar circumstances under which others were exacted. There was a nominal limit of £100 value of estates, below which persons were supposed to be exempt, but this was not always observed, and occasionally the delinquent who had only his hat to throw up for the King, found his wearing apparel assessed and a fine placed upon him. Among the smaller offenders who failed to get through the sequestrators' net, the following examples may be given:— Lionel Walden,[1] junior, of Huntingdon, escaped with a fine of £6; Edward Whitchcot, of Dunston, Lincolnshire, paid only £5; Anthony Cubbit, of Hobbies, Norfolk, got off with a fine of £2; John Smith, of Winford, Cambs, for being in Worcester while it was a garrison for the King, for 'only two nights and one day,' paid a fine of £1 10s. 0d.; Rob. Turner, of Westley, Cambs, apparently one of Captain Appleyard's men at the Linton Insurrection, was fined £1; and a like sum sufficed to purge the delinquency of Anthony Garley, of The Close, Lincoln, assessed upon 'his books and apparel.' Akin to John Smith's fine for spending two nights and a day in Worcester, was that of Sutton Dalton, a Lincolnshire man, who ventured to go into Newark garrison and stayed for two days only, but having some estate was fined £100. The most extraordinary fine of this character met with in the Reports of the Committee

of age at school in the Parliament's quarters, when his mother was plundered by the King's soldiers of £4,700 of his money, and she was carried away prisoner. He followed her into Newark and Belvoir garrisons to procure her enlargement and obtain restitution; but as he appears to have been long enough about it to have come of age, Parliament concluded that he was a voluntary 'Newarker,' and fined him £3,000.

[1] There is, I am told, still a Walden House in Huntingdon which preserves the connection of this family with the town.

for Compounding[1] was perhaps that of Henry Docwra, of Pirton, near Hitchin, Herts, concerning whom there is this entry in April, 1649: "Compounds for his delinquency in being twelve hours in company with the forces raised against Parliament last summer, fine £66."

Sometimes the efforts of the compounders to get themselves and their estates free from the grip of the Sequestrators disclose curious effects and vicissitudes in domestic life. A Royalist might find himself declared a delinquent, and yet had no estate upon which he could raise anything to purge himself. In such a case it was a relief to a young impoverished Cavalier to find a wife with some estate and willing to make a sacrifice at the altar of love. A young Cavalier of this type was John Jacklin, of Cambridge, who "confessed that he had taken up arms for the King, but laid them down again, that he had no estate, but a horse, which was sold for the benefit of the Commonwealth, but he had now married and expected to get an estate." A fine of £40 was imposed upon his improved estate. Sometimes the advice of the elder Mr. Weller in respect to widows, had that been available, would have saved curious complications of which the following was one :—

In the Royalist risings in Essex which led up to the Siege of Colchester, a number of men took up arms from the neighbourhood of Saffron Walden and Bishop's Stortford. Among these one Simon Slaughter, of 'Starford,' had the misfortune to be slain in Colchester. Slaughter, being a man of substance, had, while in Colchester, with death by famine and the sword staring him in the face, settled his estate in lands upon his wife. It so happened that John Cockson, another Stortford man, was also in arms in the Siege of Colchester, and after Slaughter's death Cockson found his way back to Stortford, and, probably knowing of the settlement, married the deceased Slaughter's widow. But as an old soldier he knew that money would be more

---

[1] The Reports of the Committee for Compounding, from which the extracts in this chapter are chiefly taken, are preserved at the Public Record Office, and are familiar to the student as State Papers, Interregnum, Series G, or as the Royalist Composition Papers.

valuable than land, and so the dead man Slaughter's lands in Herts and Essex were sold 'at great under value' to one Woolley. Information reached the Sequestrators, who came down upon the lands ; and upon the ground that both Mrs. Slaughter's husbands, Slaughter who was slain and Cockson who got possession of the widow and the lands, were delinquents, the lands belonged to the State, and out of them the delinquency of Mrs. Slaughter's two husbands had to be satisfied.

Thomas Dereham, of Dereham Grange, Norfolk, says that he was obliged ' by the sickness of his child ' to go to King's Lynn just at the time when it was held for the King. Here he was detained during the siege. When the town was surrendered the Earl of Manchester gave order that his estate, real and personal, was to be preserved from sequestration, and he had a pass for his protection. The affair was inquired into, and Dereham, who had his horse taken for the King, and yet was called to account for being a Royalist, was able to get his discharge.

Sir William Clarke, of North Scarle, Lincolnshire, according to his own showing, only went to Newark 'on market days' while it was the King's quarters. But market-days were notorious occasions for Commissions of Array and for beating up recruits. Parliament took this view of it, Sir William was 'imprisoned six months for it,' and having so signally repented of going to Newark market as to afterwards 'take the National Covenant' he was let off with the small fine of £21. John Rous, of Stow, Hunts, went to Oxford, and afterwards pleaded that he was detained there 'by sickness and never took up arms against Parliament.' But Oxford was the Mecca of Royalism, and a fine of £144 had to be paid. William Tonge, a Lincolnshire man, was almost able to plead Hobson's choice for his Royalism, being "forced by Major Kaye either to serve himself or send his servant, which latter he could not do, having but two out of eight left." Richard Wyche, or Weeke, of Crowland, 'was compelled to take up arms against Parliament,' when the enemy possessed Crowland.

Sometimes the 'unruly member' brought the individual

into the clutches of the Sequestrators as much as the sword. Nich. Tabor, of Cambridge, had the temerity to call Mr. John Lowry, member for Cambridge, 'an ass and a fool,' and got into prison for it. Captain Anthony Bourne, of Thriplow, Cambs, another old soldier, whose loose Wildrake speech got him into trouble at the beginning of the fray, put in this original plea, that "after being a soldier in Foreign service he refused to take up arms again on either side, but being treated by Parliament as a Malignant [instead of mustering the Horse he had denounced the "*infanum Parliamentum*"!], he was forced to leave his home and take refuge in Oxford, where he confesses he bore arms."

Wheathill Audley, of Woodhurst, near St. Ives, Hunts, on the eve of the War had the curiosity to go with the crowd along the Huntingdon Road towards Cambridge to see the University plate carried off for the King, and though he pleaded he only went with the sheriff 'to the edge of the county,' he was fined £223. As for the sheriffs on that occasion, Sir John Cotton, of Landwade, Sheriff for Cambs, who played the milder part, was let off with £350, but Sir Richard Stone, High Sheriff of Hunts, who raised the *posse comitatus* of his county, to convey the University plate away, was fined £1,500. Sometimes the ladies were called to account, as in the case of Jane Pritchard, an adventurous lady Royalist of Uffington, near Stamford, who played a conspicuous part in the risings of that neighbourhood, 'going several times to the Belvoir and Newark garrisons when held for the King.'

Not unfrequently the Royalist found himself between the Scylla and Charybdis of creditors and Compounding Committee. The case of Lord Rich, son of the Parliamentary Earl of Warwick, of Leighs, Essex, presents a remarkable complication of Royalism, money-lending, imprisonments for debt, and curious turns in the wheel of fortune. Before the war began young Rich had outrun the constable, and mortgaged his annuity, allowed by the Earl, to a City money-lender named Gosse. For a £600 loan Lord Rich and two sureties gave £1,000 bonds. Being unable to recover either principal or interest, Gosse, in the time of the War, arrested one of the sureties, who was, however, rescued by Lord Rich and other officers, who beat and wounded Gosse 'to his great damage.' Sticking on like the proverbial leech, Gosse, 'thinking that Lord Rich had not the privilege of a peer,' caused him to be arrested for the debt. But Rich was released by order of the House of Lords, and the unfortunate Shylock, Gosse, was himself cast into the Fleet Prison, and four of the Sheriff's officers into Newgate for causing the arrest! They were detained fourteen days, and poor Mr. Gosse 'by reason of his ill-accommodation contracted such a weakness that he was constrained to keep his bed,' and died shortly afterwards; but not without casting up the costs and damages, which by now had swelled the original £600 into £6,300! Rebecca Gosse, his widow, next comes upon the scene, pressing her suit for the debt, and lamenting that "there hath not any progresse beene made, unlesse to ye unhappiness of y^r pet^r." Unfortunately, the young Lord Rich had been fined £2,000 for going to the King at Oxford; and, notwithstanding that the Earl of Warwick, his father, 'believed in the reality of his repentance for his errors,' and pleaded for him, the Committee thought it reasonable that he should pay something out of his annuity to widow Gosse before his fine could be remitted.

John Pigott, of Morden, and Abington juxta Shingay, Cambridgeshire, pleaded in defence of leaving his home and going into the King's quarters at Oxford, that he went because he was pressed by his creditors. A wife and seven children, with a fine of £540 to pay out of an estate of £203 a year, left him little chance of improving his condition. Mr. Thomas Chichley, of Wimpole Hall, Royalist member for Cambridgeshire, who was fined for his delinquency in going to Oxford and sitting in the King's Parliament there, pleaded that his debts amounted to £5,000; and he also complained that he lost £3,000 worth of timber cut down 'since these troubles and by reason thereof,' and his loss in goods was to the value of £500.

When after the K:ng's death delinquents were required to compound within a certain time, there were curious searchings of heart among the doubtful ones, who, though they had escaped actual sequestration, were conscious of some little act which might be construed to their disadvantage. There was an extraordinary rush of small county people up to London, crowding about Goldsmith's Hall to get their cases heard within the specified time, and an amount of 'conscience money' tendered which must have astonished the Committee. Even among the Parliamentary Russells of Chippenham, Cambs, Gerard Russell 'compounds on his own discovery,' doubting that he may be 'impeached for delinquency'; Edward Thompson, of Boothby, Lincolnshire, also 'discovered himself,' and although never sequestered, 'doubts he may be liable for something said and done in the first war,' and pays his £200 conscience money; Henry Huddleston, of Sawston, made a similar discovery, which cost him £16; while the case of Edward Greene, of 'Hoggington' [? Oakington], Cambs, affords a glimpse of a busy scene at Goldsmith's Hall. Mr. Greene did not get in by the time allowed, and urged in extenuation that when he presented his petition there were '100 others before him.'

Curious complications arose sometimes upon the death of a person whose estate was in the hands of the Sequestrators, of which the case of Thomas Lacey, a Suffolk recusant, is an example. He was 'a very antient feeble creature, much given to solitariness, and his abode in no place certain.' He was allowed his one-third of the sequestered estate for his maintenance. For six years he did not apply for it, and his Protestant heir appealed for the discharge of the estate, on the ground that he was believed to be dead. The Sequestrators acknowledged that there was a 'violent presumption' that Lacey was dead, but there was not sufficient proof of the death. It was two years more before the Protestant heir to the estate was allowed even his recusant father's third part, and not until four years afterwards, or eleven years from the time when ancient Mr. Lacey was last heard of, that the taint of recusancy got purged from his estate, and his son entered into full possession.

The difficulties attending the sale and transfer of land

which had been seized are illustrated by the case of one Francis Patten, of Barley, Herts, who purchased a farm from a Royalist named Curtis at Bassingbourn, Cambs (where Cromwell's mother's estate lay). Curtis had compounded, paid half his fine, and given security for the other half upon the land. Patten bought the farm and 'knew not but that it was absolutely discharged of the sequestration.'; he placed his cattle on the farm, and the Sequestration Committee for Cambridgeshire seized them for the non-payment of the remaining half of Curtis' fine.

The burden of sequestrations and the fine were not the only inconveniences which sometimes followed. The County Committees and the Committees in London had power to examine witnesses, and the chance of mitigating a heavy penalty was sufficient inducement to bring up large numbers from long distances and at great expense. Thomas Withering, postmaster, of Hornchurch, Essex, being maliciously accused by one Wilkes, went before the County Committee at Chelmsford, and 'after seven months debate, during which petitioner carried 30 witnesses to Chelmsford from London,' the Committee discharged him and imprisoned Wilkes for sending horses to the enemy. As soon as he was free Wilkes again instigated proceedings against Withering, this time before the Committee at Haberdashers Hall in London, and got twenty to fifty witnesses to swear against him, but he was again discharged.

A curious story told by Vicars of the way in which a Royalist's property was sometimes intercepted and dealt with is that of a Mr. Neville, of Cressing Temple, Essex. In 1642, at the beginning of the strife, Mr. Neville had some fat beasts to send up to the London market, twenty in number. But Mr. Neville had declared himself as a Royalist, and it leaked out that the twenty fat beasts were being sent up to Smithfield to raise money 'to supply the Cavaliers, his comrades.' Ten of them were actually sold to a butcher for £100, when some of the agents for Parliament appeared upon the scene, and compelled the butcher to bring the £100, and instead of paying it to Mr. Neville, to pay it into the Guildhall, to help on the cause of Parliament, and the other ten oxen were conveyed to the victualling department of the Navy. Akin to this was the dispatch of Lord Capel's letter from Hertfordshire in a hollow stick, giving to the Cavaliers in Cornwall power to receive and gather up all his rents in the West country. The messenger entrusted with the stick was detained, and 'by great accident this hollow stick and the concealed letter were intercepted and brought to the Parliament,' who promptly saved all trouble in collecting the rents by sequestering all his rents there.[1]

The ways of the sequestrators themselves were not always models of fair dealing or of competent work. Parliament, by selecting men from all parts of a county, did its best to secure a tribunal free from local favouritism or local prejudice, but in practice the work of the sequestrators often drifted into the hands of a small minority of the Committee. The best men on these Committees were drawn away on the more urgent business of the War, others became half-hearted in the work, and the task of carrying off the Royalists' goods and chattels was performed by agents who had not always Cromwell's wholesome grip of the elementary principles of order, or by well-meaning Committeemen without the capacity for properly dealing with the confusing succession of ordinances issued by Parliament, and with what was really a most complicated business of account-keeping. The difficulties and the hazards of the sequestrators in getting their business done; the journeys, the interviews, and the persistent canvassing of the agents of the Guildhall Committee in London to keep the County Committees up to time in rendering their accounts; the crooked ways of some of the local agents intrusted with the carrying out of sequestrations; and the vexation and contempt of the Royalists towards the 'mean men' who did not spare them in their humiliation —these were the common experiences of county life within the Eastern Association during and after the War. The county of Cambridge, after Cromwell had left it for more

[1] Perfect Diurnal, Nov. 7, 1642.

stirring scenes elsewhere, was especially notable in this respect, and some of the documents in which local experiences are recorded afford striking examples of the legacy of ill-feeling which was left to the Commonwealth and broke out afresh in efforts to set right old grudges after the Restoration.

This is shown by the letters from the sequestrators to the Guildhall Committee in London, in which in 1643 and 1644 they declare they found men who were 'truly malignant' under protection orders from the Earl of Manchester, having 'abused the Earl's good nature.' In those stormy months of 1648, when the Second Civil War was raging in East Anglia, John Davies, messenger from the Guildhall Committee, had an unpleasant time in looking after sequestration accounts. On September 4, 1648, he writes thus from Ipswich to the Guildhall Committee :—

"In pursuance of your instructions, I have delivered two letters, the one at Chelmsford, the other at Colchester. For the first I desire to make a particular but brief relation by reason of contemptible language I received at the delivery of it. On Friday last, being market day there, I made inquiry of some for the Committee, and I was informed that Mr. Whitcombe, of Ingatstone, and Mr. Sorrell, of Much Waltham, members of it, were in town. I presently went to them, where I found Colonel Mildmay, alias Sir Henry Mildmay (then unknown to me), another member of that Committee, lying cross the bed. I, with my hat in my hand, desired to know which was Mr. Whitcombe and Mr. Sorrell, for I had a message to deliver to them, on which Mr. Whitcombe came to me, received the letter ; on breaking it open he took one of the ordinances to read, gave the other to Mr. Sorrell, and the letter he delivered to the Colonel, who (having scarcely read it) burst into a passion, saying : 'What are these fellows that write thus peremptorily? I know them not:' here are better men in company than themselves.' To which I replied : 'Sir, they are the treasurers at Guildhall, sitting there for sequestration.' At which he arose from the bed and told me I was too saucy, and deserved a box on the ears, and should be laid by the heels if I had nothing besides my letter to protect me. Then I showed him my commission, and taking my leave of the Colonel in a great hurry, he said that they had earnester employment, now Colchester was taken, than to give up accounts. At Colchester he saw Mr. [Sir] Thomas Barrington, who treated him very courteously."[1]

Again, he writes on September 17, this time from Cambridgeshire and Huntingdonshire:—"I came to Ely on Wednesday, September 13, where I delivered a message I had in charge to Mr. Luke Voyce and Richard Ponsonby, the one a draper and the other a servant to Leuit. General Cromwell, both living in Ely. They cheerfully received it, and promised a fair accompt. They say they must bring divers eminent persons on the stage for their transactions, and I do believe they will discover some foul passages of Mr. Basse, sequestrator for Suffolk, and some others. They have about £1,000 to bring up with them. I thence repaired to Cambridge, where I delivered one of my letters to Mr. Stephen Fortune, haberdasher there, sequestrator to the University. The other I delivered to Mr. John Taylor, he lives at Cotnam [Cottenham], four miles from Cambridge, one of the sequestrators for the whole Co. Mr. Fortune has in part discovered to me some passages of Col Mildmay (that litigious gentleman), now one of the Committee for Essex and formerly governor of Cambridge, which I shall tender on my return. Mr. Taylor is a plain, but active man, and I think will do much good in the service. I am now at Huntingdon, endeavouring to procure an answer there."[2]

After John Davies, the messenger from the Guildhall Committee, had received that cheerful assurance from Mr. Voyce, the draper, and Mr. Ponsonby (Cromwell's servant), at Ely, these gentlemen and Mr. Cole, only a month afterwards, wrote to the Committee in London a very different

[1] Add. MSS. 5,494, Brit. Mus. Lib.
[2] Ibid.

and offhand account, that they had no money, the lands of the Bishop and the Dean and Chapter being no longer in their hands. To this the Committee at Guildhall appear to have written a sharp reply, with an ultimatum demanding an account and £270 from each person within three days; a demand which elicited a graphic recital of the trials and dangers of a man appointed, even with the authority of Parliament, to seize his neighbour's goods. On December 16, John Cole, Richard Ponsonby, and Luke Voyce write from Ely to the Committee at Guildhall in the following extraordinary tone:—

"We have received yours of the 9th December wherein your threatnings are so very harsh and severe against us. You charge us to be indebted to the State upwards of £270 per perse. We do, indeed, acknowledge we have received about that sum in the Isle of Ely towards our charge & travayle for ourselves & horses ever since July 1643 at which time we first entered on the State's service as commissioners of sequestration; namely, 20s. per week. But not that we are indebted or have in our hands one penny of the State money, it being spent and more in the State's service. The letter of ordinance says we shall have our charges, but it does not say how much. Indeed, Mr. Maddyn said well that we should have bargained with the Parliament before we began what we should have, for then we should surely have been worthy of £50 per annum besides our riding charges, as well as Mr. Maddyn. Sure we are, our service hath been as dangerous to ourselves as any in the kingdome, in regard to the opposition we have found, and the detestation of the opposite party, besides the extreme hazard of our persons and estates in case the wheel should turn, by seizing and sequestrating men's goods, which danger is greater than that of any solicitor; yea, than of any soldier that hath fought against the other party. Are we then, in your judgments, thought worthy of nothing? It is a very hard measure, and we beseech you to do as you would be done unto. But you say you are not to be the judges of what is necessary for us to have; therefore we don't appeal to you, but to them that imployed both you and us. Whereas you require the money to be paid forthwith within three days after the receipt of your letter, we cannot pay it in your time limited ; no, not if for three days you had said three years ; for we have expended more money in the State's service than we are worth . . . . neither can we pay it, some of us, if we were to sell all we have. Gentlemen, we desire nothing from you but what is just and reasonable, and according to the trust imposed on you, and as it is not yet determined by those who are to be judges in this case, whether we have any monies in our hands or not, we desire you will suspend this business till we can get it resolved by the House . . . . and we hope we shall not find you more harsh and unreasonable than those who, having the greatest interest in it, appear well satisfied with us." [1]

It was alleged by the Royalists who suffered at the hands of the sequestrators that the latter took care to feather their own nest out of the business. Proceedings during the War formed the subject of an Inquisition, held at the " Red Lion," Petty Cury, Cambridge, twenty years afterwards, 'when the wheel had turned.' It was sworn by the witnesses that from Sir Anthony Cage, who had supported the rising at Linton, horses, oxen, sheep, and effects were taken to the value of £8,000 ; that from the Bishop of Ely's park and house at Downham, £700 in value was taken, and not more than £140 accounted for ; that the sequestrators sold the goods distrained upon to one another. The chief persons against whom these charges were brought were John Taylor, the 'plain, but active man' already referred to, and John Wright, both of Cottenham. The old Royalist rector, Dr. Manby, who was ejected by them, put in evidence against them that they seized or caused to be taken from him, grain, malt, hay, grass, horses, milch cows, and other cattle, sheep, swine, bricks, boards, timber, household stuff, brewing vessels, and other goods to the value of £600. It

---

[1] Add. MSS. 5,494, Brit. Mus. Lib.

was further suggested, or rather sworn to by old men from Cottenham, that Wright was at the commencement of the War only a collar-maker, working at his trade and earning eighteenpence a day, and had a small estate of two houses at Cottenham, bringing in £16 a year, but then (1664) he was 'seized of an estate in lands worth £100 per annum at least.' The evidence for the defence was, that they had the authority of the Association Committee for what they did. There are glimpses of the finding of some of the old Committee books in a cupboard at the "Bear" at Cambridge, and witnesses came forward to say that the signatures to letters therein were authentic and 'had not been forged.' Another defendant at the same time was Richard Harrison, treasurer of the Isle of Ely, during the later years of the War, concerning whose actions old men were brought up from Wisbech who remembered the money and men raised by that town for 'reducing of Crowland' when it was besieged. It was suggested among other things that Harrison offered to repay the town of Wisbech by a sort of composition of 5s. in the pound.[1]

Generally, the account-keeping of the sequestrators was in a hopeless muddle, due as much to the incapacity of the men to whom in stress of war a puzzling succession of conflicting and overlapping ordinances was entrusted, as to their wilful default. When, at the close of the War, new Commissioners came on the scene in Cambridgeshire, meeting twice a week, Tuesday and Friday, at the "Cock," on 'the Peas Market Hill,' they reported —"We are now taking the old sequestrators' accounts, which occupy much time, as most of them cannot tell how to make up accounts, and therefore we are glad to have the sequestrators by us to express their meaning."[2] In Huntingdonshire new Commissioners were also appointed, with Mr. John Leet, of Southoe, as Chairman, and met every Saturday at the "Falcon." Here and also in Suffolk there was considerable

---

[1] Particulars of these cases are to be found in Exchequer Depositions, 18 Charles II.
[2] Letter of Commissioners to Guildhall Committee, Hist. MSS. Reps.

delay over the state into which the accounts had drifted. In some cases the old sequestrators resented their dismissal and 'turned counsel for malignants,' and in others they still had 'great sums of money in hand which they keep for allowances as they report.' At best it was a thankless task when done conscientiously according to order of Parliament, and when done ill, by inferior and unscrupulous agents, it was the cause of as much ill-feeling between individuals as was set up in a parish between the parson and his flock.

CHAPTER XV.

A RELIGIOUS REVOLT—THE PURITANS AND THE CLERGY
—UNHAPPY RURAL ENGLAND.

NO modern attempt to rehabilitate Archbishop Laud as a cultured High Churchman upon those Anglican lines which have found a wide acceptance to-day, can alter the view with which history must regard the Puritan revolt against the abuse of human authority in religion which was largely responsible for the Civil War. Laud may or may not have meant to Romanize the Church of England, but judging by the standard of the times—the only safe rule for the student of history—he did exactly that which was calculated to make the people think that he intended it.

In order to understand how the system of things ecclesiastical presented itself to the people of East Anglia, certain general facts of early seventeenth-century life have to be remembered. The relation of the individual to the State came very largely through the contact with the Church. One effect of this contact had been throbbing through recent history in the memory of funeral pyres lit up around those who had dared to die for their faith in Norfolk, Suffolk, and Essex, in the thrill of patriotic fire which ran through these shires over the Spanish Armada and the Gunpowder Plot. With the memory of these things, the fact of the King marrying a Catholic, and the more recent massacre of Protestants in Ireland, the inhabitants of a region which was dominated by Calvinism, and its capacity for sturdily hating the Pope and all his ways, had no choice but to revolt against a tendency which reminded them and seemed likely to revive the bitter experiences of the past. They had before their eyes men in the pulpits of the Church who were out-Lauding Laud, and the cast-iron creed of Calvin had come too recently out of the fire to admit of any very broad views of life amongst its adherents. The very scruples of the parishioners against alterations in the Church service may perhaps seem trivial in these days, until one remembers the strange divorce there was between that human authority in religion which had been so blindly cruel in the day of its power, and the tenacious hold of the individual conscience upon such spiritual authority as each individual found or thought he found in the Word of God.

The part which the men of the Eastern Counties played in the struggle teaches emphatically the lesson that the quarrel between King and Parliament was above all things a religious quarrel. So completely did the religious element and the "No Popery!" cry predominate over the civil differences, that the same men who had exacted Ship-money later on stood up for Parliament on religious grounds, as in the case of Mr. Pychard, Sheriff for Cambridgeshire, who first levied Ship-money and afterwards signed the petition against the Bishop of Ely. As in the pulpit and the Church, so in the field. The people of East Anglia, being pre-eminently Puritan, came into the field just at the point where the conflict was the hottest, where their zeal was fanned through being called upon to fight on their own borders with an army largely in the pay of the Catholic Queen—with the 'white coats' under Newcastle, so frequently referred to as an 'Army of Papists.' Here, then, in East Anglia, the extremes of the two hostile halves of the nation met; here was the secret of the immense impetus which the religious zeal of Puritan East Anglia gave to the Parliamentary arms, a zeal of which such personal factors as an Oliver Cromwell were at once cause and effect.

In one respect, in its earlier stages, the religious followed the same line of cleavage as the political revolt; if, indeed, the two principles can ever be separated, for the former was then no more a revolt against a State Church than the latter was a revolt against the Kingship. It meant a temporary nonconformity which in the end had no choice left but to become a separatism. The logical extreme of the revolt against Episcopacy in the Church and human authority in religion was, of course, to be found in Independency, and the trend that way received its greatest impetus from the Eastern Counties, whose famous Association Army became absorbed, and its methods continued, in the all-powerful Army of Independents under Cromwell.

Although Puritanism and the Parliamentary cause were divided between Presbyterianism and Independency, yet the former was distinctly the lesser factor in the Eastern Counties, and at best a mild compromise which the greater zeal of the Independents could not brook.[1]

In the earlier stages of the Civil War, Puritanism was, however, one solid factor at the point where it came in conflict with the King and with the Royalist clergy. By the end of 1643 that conflict had assumed an acute form: the powerful influence of the Bishop of Ely in and around Cambridge was no longer of any avail, and the Earl of

[1] An interesting example of this in the family life is afforded by the Norths of Kirtlington, near Newmarket. Sir Dudley North, son of the old Lord North, married one of the Montagues of Boughton; Sir Dudley was a rigid Presbyterian, and his wife was a not less rigid, but more zealous, Independent. She was 'head of the Church in her house,' both over her 'carnal' husband and her children. She 'used to instruct her babes in the gift of praying by the Spirit, and all the scholars were made to kneel by the bedside and pray'; or 'poure out themselves in spiritual prayer.' One of them, the future Lord Guilford, and Lord Keeper of the Great Seal to Charles II and James II, was only a 'babe' in truth, and 'this petit spark was too small for that posture.' So he was 'set upon the bed to kneel with his face to the pillow,' and go through his little exercise there. Poor little fellow! Tired and sleepy after the activities of the day, he seems to have been hard put to it for a theme, and in after life all that he could remember of his infantile attempts at extempore prayer was, that 'he prayed for his distressed brethren in Ireland.' Considering that he was only four years of age when the Irish massacres occurred, the incident has a peculiar and almost pathetic interest, and shows how the subject had burned itself into the very soul of the Puritans, and how severe was the mental discipline which enabled them to 'hold forth' and to 'testify' against the Papacy. Lady North, however, brought her husband fourteen dutiful children, and has been described as a lady of noble and lofty character. That her children were fine types of English gentry, the splendid portraits in the "Lives of the Norths" are eloquent testimony.—See "Lives of the Norths," by the Hon. Roger North; also Baker MSS., vol. xxxvii, ff. 29, 30; Dict. Nat. Biog., etc.

Manchester, now settled at Trinity College for the Winter, turned his attention from the routine of quartering soldiers, until active operations could be renewed in the Spring, to another kind of routine devised for calling to account the clergy who had followed the Bishop's example, or who were 'scandalous' in their life and conversation.

On January 22, 1644, the Lords and Commons issued the following Ordinance for regulating the University of Cambridge, and for removing 'scandalous ministers' in the seven Associated Counties :—

"Whereas many Complaints are made by the well-affected Inhabitants of the Associated Counties of Essex, Norfolk, Suffolk, Hertford, Cambridge, Huntingdon, and Lincolne, That the service of the Parliament is retarded, the Enemy strengthened, the peoples Soules starved, and their mindes diverted from any care of God's cause, by their idle, ill-affected, and scandalous Clergy, of the University of Cambridge, and the Associated Counties; and that many that would give Evidence against such scandalous Ministers are not able to travell to London, nor beare the charges of such a journey: It is Ordained by the Lords & Commons assembled in Parliament, That the Earle of Manchester shall appoint one or more Committees in every County, consisting of such as have been nominated Deputy Lieutenants, or Committees by any former Ordinance of Parliament, in any of the said Associated Counties, every Committee to consist of ten, whereof any five or more of them, to sit in any place or places within the said Associated Counties where the said Earle shall appoint, with power to put in execution these instructions following, and in pursuance thereof, to give assistance to the said Committee."

The Earl or the Committees were given power to call before them heads of colleges, students and members of the University, ministers in any counties of the Association, and all schoolmasters 'that are scandalous in their lives or ill-affected to Parliament, or fomentors of this unnatural war, or that shall wilfully refuse obedience to the ordinances of Parliament, or that have deserted their ordinary place of residence'; also to send for witnesses and examine them upon oath; also to administer 'the late Covenant.' The Committees were to report to the Earl of Manchester, and he had power to eject 'such as he shall judge unfit for their places.'

During the month of February, 1644, the Earl of Manchester commenced his task of the 'reformation of the University of Cambridge,' and to deal with 'scandalous ministers' in the Associated Counties. Warrants were issued by his Lordship calling upon the Cambridge Colleges to send in their statutes, lists of members, and certificates of those in residence and those absent; and by another warrant all Fellows, scholars, and officers were required to be in residence by the 10th of March. On the appointed day there were still so many absent, that another warrant called for a list of those who had returned and of those who were still absent.[1]

The Commission for dealing with the University and the ministers of Cambridgeshire appears to have been somewhat different from the rest of the County Committees, and consisted of Cambridgeshire Committeemen with members from each of the Associated Counties added. The minutes of the Committee's proceedings in this case show an average attendance of five or six, including at different times nearly forty different names; fresh members dropping in at different sittings according to personal convenience or the pressure of business elsewhere; the most regular attendants being the Cambridgeshire Committeemen proper—Robert Clerk (Meldreth), Samuel Spalding (Cambridge), Thomas French (Cambridge), Robert Robson (Cambridge), Thomas Duckett (Steeple Morden), John Sherwood (Cambridge)—and those most frequently on duty from other Counties on the Association Committee for the general purposes of the War.

With the formation of the Earl of Manchester's 'reforming' Commission, the Grand Committee for the Associated Counties, which had formerly sat at the "Bear," appears to have removed its quarters to Trinity College, and the Earl's Commission for dealing with 'scandalous ministers' sat at

[1] Baker MSS., vols. xlii and xlvii.

the " Bear," situate in the corner block of buildings connecting Market Street with Sidney Street, in the corner of Market Passage, near the site of the present Conservative Club.[1] Around this spot some strange scenes were witnessed as the Puritan folk came forward with hot zeal to impeach their parson, or the latter attempted to justify before the Commissioners some act of ritual, some slighting words concerning the Parliament, or regard for the proclamation of the King.

The separate County Committees appointed for each of the other counties were empowered to divide into smaller Committees of five, and to fix certain days for sitting at different places. It appears to have been a general rule that the accused clergyman was not allowed to be present, when the depositions of witnesses against him were being taken, 'lest it should discourage the witnesses'; but he was entitled to have a copy of the depositions, upon paying for the same, in order that he might answer them in writing and make his defence at another meeting. The Committeemen were to receive 5s. per day, out of which a clerk had to be paid 'that he may not discourage informers by taking fees.'

An analysis of the offences charged against the Royalist

---

[1] It is stated in a local book ("The Cambridge Portfolio," p. 389) that "the Commissioners under the Earl of Manchester sat at the ' Bear ' Inn, in a yard which communicates with Sidney Street and with the Market Street, nearly opposite the entrance into the church of the Holy Trinity. The large room, which about sixty years ago was divided into three, is an upper story looking into the inner yard through three bow windows connected by a long series of narrow lights; the two fireplaces with their carved oak mantelpieces and the oak wainscotting remain, Oct. 4, 1839." From a satirical rhyme printed in 1642, entitled "The Cambridge Royalist Imprisoned," it appears that the " Bear " was used by the Parliamentary party from the commencement of the War ; and that the Town Hall was the Court of Guard. At any rate, the narrative, coarse and unsparing towards the Parliamentarians, represents the " scholler " being

" Marcht to the Town-Hall, where being straight let in,
Such company, such smoake, such stinke, such dinne,
Three tedious houres amongst these hell-hounds wee
Bravely endured, when coming in we see
A spruce young Rebell, who scarce yet did know
Whether he fought against the King or no."

From the Town Hall he was hurried to the " Beare," and brought before

" A veryer Beast then that which hung at doore."

A copy of this tract, which does not clear up the fortunes of the Royalist "scholler," is in the possession of Mr. Robert Bowes (No. 2,912 in his Catalogue of Cambridge Books).

clergy would distinguish them as (1) Ecclesiastical, (2) Moral and Social, and (3) Civil and Political. Indeed, it was something in this order that the evidence in support of the cases against the offending clergyman was presented to the Court—'that he was an innovator, a common alehouse haunter, and hath spoken malignant words against the Parliament.'

Around the conduct of the parson and his position in the parish was fought out on a small scale the conflict between King and Parliament, and the strife inevitably mingled even with the elements of public worship. At the baptism of an infant, if the clergyman used the sign of the Cross, some one would be sure to protest or register the act against him; if he asked a communicant to come up to the rails within the chancel to receive the Communion, the individual would perhaps sit stolidly in the body of the church and argue openly before the congregation and show that it was 'against his conscience and received no warrant from Scripture.' On the other hand, the parson would reply with threats of excommunication. Even when the constable delivered to the churchwardens, and the latter delivered to the parson, copies of proclamations from Parliament, the parson had at the same time most likely received from the emissaries of the King copies of proclamations to a contrary effect.

The position of the clergyman was not an enviable one. If he cherished notions of 'divine right' and yet desired to keep the peace, he would read the King's proclamation 'with seeming joy,' and the Parliament's in 'so low a tone that no one could hear it'; if he were a strong Royalist he would read the 'King's book' defiantly and 'throw away that of Parliament in contempt.' Then, if his sermon contained any references to the bitter controversies of the hour, which it was hard to avoid; if he encouraged the youth of the village to play bowls and other games on the Sunday afternoon, or visited the alehouse himself in the evening—all this was taken note of to be used against him hereafter, not merely by a bigoted person here or there, but by many of his parishioners, and, likely enough, his own churchwardens. It must not be understood, however, that the clergy in general were of the character of those who were brought up before the Earl of Manchester's Commissioners, but these were sufficiently numerous for their cases to disclose a most unhappy state of things in rural England as a background to the horrors of the Civil War.

The charges against the Royalist clergy which occurred most frequently were the following :—

(1) Ecclesiastical. That he was a strict observer of the late illegal innovations—bowing at the name of Jesus, bowing towards the altar, standing up at the Gloria Patri, reading the second part of the service at the communion table in the chancel, making the sign of the Cross in baptism, requiring the communicants to come up to the rails to receive the Sacrament, preaching in his surplice and hood. Also that he was very forward in reading the Book of Sports; was non-resident; employed curates who were superstitious and malignant; and that he denounced those who went away to hear sermons elsewhere.

(2) Social and Moral. That he is a common haunter or frequenter of alehouses and taverns, a common gamester, a common drinker, an outrageous swearer and tippler, a singer of profane songs, etc., etc.

(3) Civil and Political. That he is a fomentor of this unnatural war, hath often expressed great malignancy against Parliament, refused to read the declaration that came from Parliament, but was very forward in reading those that came from the King; spends much of his time in company of those who are disaffected to Parliament, and associates with the Cavaliers; refuses to take the Covenant, and never prayeth for Parliament.

The foregoing made up the general run of charges preferred against the most notable of the Royalist clergy, but these were varied, of course, in individual cases, and sometimes worse charges were made.

By the first sweep of the new broom of the reforming Commission most of the Colleges in Cambridge lost their masters—Trinity, St. John's, Jesus, King's, Queen's, Clare Hall, Gonville and Caius, Catherine Hall, Pembroke Hall,

Magdalene, and even the Puritan fold of Emmanuel; while Trinity, St. John's, and others had a large number of their Fellows excluded.

The strength of Puritanism and Parliamentary sympathy in a county did not always coincide with the proportion of clergy on the one side or the other. There might be, and often was, as in Hertfordshire and Cambridgeshire, a strong Parliamentary feeling and yet a very high percentage of Royalist clergy; a proof in itself that the clergy did not represent the people. On the other hand, a small percentage of sequestered clergy is evidence of the Parliamentary cause being triumphant all along the line. Norfolk, judged by this standard, was the most exclusively Parliamentarian county in the Association, with only 81 sequestered clergy out of 500 parishes; Suffolk had 129 out of nearly the same number sequestered; Essex about the same number, or rather more; Hertfordshire had about 40 per cent. of its clergy sequestered; and Cambridgeshire and the Isle of Ely, with all their Puritan strength, had the highest percentage, viz., of 173 parochial clergy, only 53 conformed to Puritan rule, about 70 were sequestered, and the rest are doubtful. The inference seems to be that the influence of the Bishop of Ely was more powerful among the clergy nearest to where the Bishop lived,[1] and that here the breach between parson and parishioners was the most marked.

Space will only admit of a few glimpses of the proceedings before the Earl of Manchester's Commissioners, but these will be sufficient to show the part which the clergy were sometimes tempted to take in the fray, and the unhappy state of things under divisions which tore asunder the ordinary relations of parochial life.[2] Some of the clergy left their cures, went to Oxford with the King, or in some cases were

---

[1] The parish of Fowlmere, Cambs, is an instance of the general sentiment of East Anglia in associating Bishop Wren with Archbishop Laud. Thus, Mr. Morden, the parson, was reported to have said : " They are about to settle religion, but they dare as well eat their fingers' ends as dispute for it, for there is two men that if they might have their liberty would lay them flat upon their backs; that is, the Bishop of Canterbury [*sic*] and the Bishop of Ely."—Minutes of Committee for Scandalous Ministers, Add. MSS. 15,672, B.M.

[2] The authorities for the cases which follow are to be found in the Minutes of the Committee for Scandalous Ministers; White's "First Century of Malignant Priests"; Walker's "Sufferings of the Clergy"; the Baker MSS., etc.

with the Royalist Army in the field or in garrisons; while others who remained in their parishes did not hesitate to accumulate arms and ammunition, or in other ways to play a militant part for the King.

Dr. Rowe, Fellow of Trinity College, Cambridge, and rector of Orwell, Cambs, according to the evidence of witnesses, 'sent Alderman Rose, of Cambridge, to buy thirty muskets in London for Trinity College,' and was the chief means of procuring the College plate to be sent to the King, manifesting his zeal by 'going round to the Fellows' chambers with the College servants to fetch their plate to the end it might be in readiness.' Mr. Nicholas Felton, parson of Stretham, in the Isle of Ely, against whom there were also charges of getting drunk, gambling, and paying too much attention to Mrs. Hogg, the wife of his curate, persuaded a parishioner not to join Cromwell's regiment, and when the soldiers came for the Bishop of Ely they took 'some arms and a barrel of powder' from Mr. Felton's house. Richard Watts, parson of Mildenhall, Suffolk, and Chesterton, Cambs, after telling the men who were threshing his corn at five shillings a week 'to make haste and get done, and they would receive six shillings a week to kill men,' sent two soldiers towards Banbury with his servant with them to guide them so that they did not meet with Parliament troops. Roger Ashton, parson of Linton, Cambridge, and Fellow of Pembroke Hall, associated with the Cavaliers, left his parish, it was believed, to join the King's Army, and when he had gone his house was searched, and a box containing 'about 200 musket bullets' was found. Mr. Baker, parson of Bartlow, Cambs, one of the most notorious brought up at the "Bear" in Cambridge, if only half the charges were true, is alleged to have gone out with his gun into the village at night, fell to quarrelling with some young men, and then finding the constable at his post keeping watch, began to rail at him, adding, "You will never be quiet until I drop a brace of bullets in your sides."[1]

---

[1] Of Mr. Baker's drunken freaks, John Butcher, an old man of Hadstock, was summoned to give evidence, but could not appear, and sent in the following sworn declaration:—" Mr. Baker forced me to drink at his house so long that

At Furneaux Pelham, in Hertfordshire, the clergyman, Mr. Hancock, walked about the churchyard with his sword during the night-time, declaring that he would rather lose his life than suffer the communion rails to be pulled up; and in the pulpit rejoiced that God should have put it into the heart of the King 'to fight the Lord's battil' at Edgehill on the Lord's day. Edward Aston, parson of Pentelow, Essex, came out boldly in the pulpit by declaring that "now that every child lifted up its sword to shed innocent blood it was high time for him to lift up his voyce like a trumpet," and he did so by reading the King's declaration instead of that of Parliament.[1]

The relation of the clergy to the Puritan conscience, and the Puritan habit of going out of the parish to hear sermons, formed another phase of the divisions in parochial life. For instance, when Mr. Morley, parson of Little Eversden, Cambs, presented his parishioners at the Ecclesiastical Court for leaving the church when he went up to the altar to read the second part of the service there, one of them pleaded that he "could find no warrant in God's Word for him to continue in church while the minister read the second service at the altar." Dr. Gray, of Castle Camps, Cambridgeshire, refused to 'church' the wife of one of the witnesses, because she would not come up to the altar rails, and she 'being satisfied in her conscience that it was more than God required, she did not go up, but went away without being churched.'

Wherever the clergyman was not often to be heard in the pulpit, or was not a particularly 'edifying' or long-winded

when I could take no more he poured the rest upon my head. I am an old man and at this present sicke and not able to appear before you, but before two witnesses I have solemnly declared to be very true, and have hereunto set my mark."

[1] As to utterances in the pulpit, Dr. Hurst, of Barrowby, preaching at Lincoln from the book of Daniel on the four Horns, compared the Earl of Essex to the horn of the south, Fairfax the horn of the north, Sir William Waller the horn of the west, and Cromwell was the great terrible horn. Thomas Pickhard, of St. Mary's, Stamford, was scandalous in frequenting inns and 'tobacco shops,' and, being quarrelsome, was carried off to Rockingham Castle. The clergy of Stamford appear to have been pretty solid for the King: the parson of St. Nicholas and another Mr. Salter were found in Burleigh House when it was taken, while Mr. Holt, of All Saints, fled to Newark and Oxford.

preacher, the Puritans were hard upon him in their evidence ; and, on the other hand, against the habit under such circumstances of going out of the parish to hear Puritan sermons elsewhere, the Royalist clergyman was constantly railing. Against the parson of Rockland, in Norfolk, it was alleged that he could not preach 'by reason of an impediment in his mouth'; against Mr. Underwood, of Bartley, in Lincolnshire, that he preached but seldom, and when he did preach 'he did it very meanly and is not above half an hour in the pulpit.' But if the Puritans had a poor opinion of the 'malignant' clergyman as a preacher, the latter had an equally poor opinion of the habit of going to hear long sermons and much preaching. Henry Osbaldeston, D.D., of Much Parndon, Essex, declared that "it was never a merry world since there had been so much preaching," and taunted his parishioners who went elsewhere to hear sermons that they "stanke of two sermons a day." Mr. Exeter, parson, of Soham, Cambs, 'caused warrants to be served upon parishioners to appear at the Assizes for going abroad to hear sermons on Sunday in the afternoon when they had none at home'; and at Fen Ditton, some of the parishioners, finding it impossible 'to edify by his doctrine,' were excommunicated for four years by Dr. Collins, the parson (and provost of King's College, Cambridge), for going to hear sermons elsewhere.

The publication of the King's "Book of Sports," and encouraging sports on a Sunday afternoon, by the parson, and in a few cases charges of drunkenness even while discharging or attempting to discharge ministerial duty, were laid to the account of the clergyman. Mr. Page, of Hemingford, Hunts,[1] Mr. Felton, of Stretham, Isle of Ely, and Mr. Morden, of Fowlmere, Cambs, were examples of the former ; and of the latter, Mr. Good, of Hatley, Cambs, of whom Walker says he 'ought rather to have been hanged than sequestered' if the charges against him were true,

---

[1] It was alleged against Mr. Page that he encouraged the young people on the Sabbath-day in 'foot-ball play and cudgel play'; and that he would go and see the same himself, and said 'well done !' as he looked on.—Lords' Journals.

Mr. Baker, of Bartlow, Mr. Sone, or Soan, of Aldenham, Herts, and a few others.

Among the general charges, Mr. Cherry, parson of Much Holland, Essex, was accused of 'bowing twelve times to the East when he goeth into the chancell'; Mr. Nicholas Lowes, of Great Bentley, Essex, 'hoped to see them all hanged that set their hands against Bishops and pulpits'; Mr. Evans, of Sandcroft, Suffolk, read the King's declaration instead of a sermon; Mr. Cuthbert Dale, of Kettleborough, in the same county, visited his anger upon a stranger who sat in his church with his hat on, calling him 'a sawcy unmannerly clown, a scabbed sheepe, and none of his flock'; while John Wells, of Shimpling, Suffolk, the parish which responded so well for Parliament when the quarrel began, was accused of too much regard for the ladies, and that 'he sold his calves for kisses with them.'

With the exception of 'alehouse haunting,' actual charges of immorality, though they were made the most of where they did arise, were comparatively few; and, putting aside mere partisanship of 'malignancy against the Parliament,' perhaps the worst that could be said of these Royalist clergy, from the standpoint of to-day, when High and Low Church are equally orthodox, is that, thinking more of the Church and its authority than of the people for whom churches should exist, they had lost their influence for good over the very people to whom they were appointed to minister; because these were not always charges by individual fanatics, but often proceeded from their own churchwardens, and from responsible men of sufficient influence and numbers in the parish, to make it clear how complete was the divorce between parson and people in many parts of these Puritan counties. In all the cases to which reference has been made and in many others, the clergyman was ejected from his living and a Puritan installed in his place.

Where the sequestered clergyman and his family had no friends to go to, or, what was more likely, where he either refused to give up the parsonage to the nominee of Parliament or preferred to remain in the parish and pose as a martyr, the execution of the orders of Parliament and its

Committees was sometimes attended with painful scenes. One of these occurred at the parish of Woolley, near Huntingdon, where the rector, Alphery Mikepher (if Walker has given the name correctly), had been sequestered from the living in 1643, and apparently had given the sequestration authorities some trouble over the business. "On a Lord's day as he was preaching [apparently in defiance of the orders of Parliament] a file of musketeers came and pulled him out of his pulpit; turned him out of the church, and his wife and children with their goods out of the parsonage. The poor man then ejected out of his house, built an hutt or booth over against the parsonage house in the street, under the trees growing in the verge of the churchyard, and there lived for a week with his family. He had procured three eggs, and gathered a bundle of rotten sticks, and was about to make a fire in the church porch to boyl his eggs, but some of his adversaries came thither, broke the eggs and kicked away his fire."[1]

Two other Huntingdonshire parishes are mentioned by Walker, who says that Mr. Baker, rector of Wistow, "was imprisoned at Huntingdon jeyl, where he was abused and barbarously treated. His goods were also plundered and exposed to public sale, but his neighbours were so generous that none of them would buy them." In the case of Mr. Brook, of Ripton Regis, he says " he was so harassed and abused that he was forced to quit his living in the beginning of the Revolution; being assaulted in person, having his horses hamstringed, and suffering other insults and indignities."[2]

Mr. Barnabus Oley, vicar of Great Gransden, who had guided the party with the Cambridge plate through the byways of Huntingdonshire towards the King, though not actually sequestrated, was harassed and threatened, and obliged to quit his living, says Walker; and in order to escape discovery 'changed his habit to a cloak and grey clothes'; and for almost seven years 'had not wherewith to support himself,' though a man of profound learning,

[1] Walker's " Sufferings of the Clergy," pt. ii, p. 183.
[2] Ibid., ii, 202.

'as eminent for his piety and charity as any man in the Church of England.'

Two of the most notable of eviction scenes in clerical life were afforded by the parishes of Soham and Cottenham, Cambridgeshire ; the one having a typical interest as an example of the squire and the parson pulling together for the King, and the other a personal interest from the marriage and residence of a sister of Cromwell in the parish.

The old Royalist Vicar of Soham, Mr. Exeter, had been replaced by Mr. John Fenton. After Mr. Fenton had officiated for about three years, in 1647, the old vicar, Mr. Exeter, "in combination with, and with the assistance of, Samuel Thorneton and Israel Thorneton, Esquires, Thomas Gin, senior, Robert Lambert, William Ellsden, Andrew Bainard, John Peacher (alehouse keeper), Edward Dockery, George Mensham, William Pamment, Jeremy Canon, Thomas Cheaveley, junior, Robert Prime, Henry Carlton, Peachie Clarke, Robert Amner, and divers others, disaffected persons, thrust the said Mr. Fenton out of the possession of the premises and possessed the same himself, and officiated the cure of the said church. Divers of the aforesaid persons, being the Lord's day, did in a violent and riotous manner and by force keep the said Mr. Fenton out of the desk and pulpit. The said Mr. Exeter, and one Grymer, a sequestrated minister, officiated the same day, the said Exeter reading the Book of Common Prayer, and the said Grymer publishing a proclamation in the name of the King, and a pretended declaration from the Army for reinvesting of such scandalous ministers as are sequestrated into their livings. The confederates above named, with divers others, turbulent and ill affected persons, did with weapons and other instruments, in a riotous and hostile manner, beset and assaulted the said Mr. Fenton, his house, and by force broke open and entered the same and possessed themselves thereof, beating and ejecting such as kept the same, and spoiled and cast forth out of doors most of the goods and household stuff of the said Mr. Fenton, and settled the said Mr. Exeter in possession of the said house, who still keepeth and possesseth the same."

Complaint was made to the justices, but Mr. Thorneton and his following appeared before the justices "with swords and clubs, and staves, to justifie their aforesaid insolent practices." Samuel Thorneton, who was under a previous order of Parliament for contempt, was sent for in safe custody to appear before the Committee for Plundered Ministers. But when the officers came down for him "the said Thorneton, in further contempt of the authority of Parliament being arrested by Nathaniel Denham, deputy of the serjeant-at-arms of the House of Commons, did fall upon the said serjeant's deputy and beat him, refusing to submit unto the order of Committee, and hath committed other outrages in manifest contempt of the authòrity of Parliament."

The Justices of the Peace, Mr. M. Dalton, Mr. Story, and Mr. Clark, appear to have been overawed by the demonstration of 'swords, clubs, and staves,' and certified to the Committee for Plundered Ministers in London that, " in regard to the threats, boldness, and turbulent carriage of divers malignants in the said countie, questioning the said Justices authority to their face, they durst not at present without further course and direction assist the deputy of the sergeant-at-arms of the House of Commons in the execution of the order of July 29th last for bringing Samuel Thorneton and Thomas Eaton before the Committee in safe custody." [1]

The Committee for Plundered Ministers renewed their order for Thorneton's arrest, and the sheriff was ordered to see that it was carried out; but how they fared is not clear. Disturbances of a similar kind, though less violent, occurred at Girton and Teversham.

In 1643 Dr. Manby was sequestrated from the living of Cottenham. His goods were seized by the local sequestrators appointed to the work—John Wright, then a collar-maker at Cottenham, and John Taylor, a husbandman of the same place—who, according to Dr. Manby's sworn depositions made twenty years afterwards, took, or caused to be taken, " in moneys, graine, malt, hay, grasse, horses, milch cows, and other cattell, sheep, swine, bricks, boards, timber, household

[1] Add. MSS. 15,671, B.M.

stuffe, brewing vessells, and other goods of this deponent, to the value of six hundred pounds or thereabouts, and did sell or otherwise dispose of the same as they pleased."[1] He also states that "they took away ten milch cowes, one calfe, and a bull," the goods of Hester Manby, a relative. As for Dr. Manby, he had been carried off a prisoner to St. John's College, Cambridge, then 'converted into a jayl,' where he remained for a year and a half, and while there escaped from a pistol shot discharged at him. It was while he was in durance that his estate was seized by Wright and Taylor, who were destined to be called upon later for an account of their proceedings. Walker, in his account, says that "Dr. Manby was plundered of all his goods, his sickly wife and five small children were turned out of doors by a party of soldiers under the command of Major Jordan, then Governor of the Castle of Cambridge . . . . they entered the house with their pistols cocked and swords drawn, and took Mrs. Manby by the arm, with a suckling child at her breast, and turned her and her other four children out of doors into the open street."[2]

The living was given to Dr. Peter French, who married Oliver Cromwell's sister Robina ; or, as Walker puts it : "The rich parsonage was given to Oliver Cromwell's daughter [sic] Robina, who soon after bestowed both it and herself upon Peter French." He adds that Dr. French, Dr. Manby's 'gaping successor,' was in the yard, a 'spectator of the barbarities and insults of the soldiers' who came to take possession of the parsonage, and alleges that Mrs. Manby and her children were harshly treated in the parish. Dr. Manby, upon his release from Cambridge Castle in 1644 or 1645, appears to have gone into Yorkshire for a year, and coming to Cottenham just as Walker alleges they were going to take off his wife prisoner, he went in her stead and remained a prisoner for some time in London.

Such incidents as the foregoing only arose in parishes in which there was a resistance to the orders of Parliament, and must not therefore be taken as an indication of the

[1] Exchequer Depositions, Charles II (March 22, 1664).
[2] "Sufferings of the Clergy," pt. ii, 303-4.

spirit in which Parliament set about its work, so much as one of the inevitable results of sequestering that which on the one hand was naturally regarded by the clergy as their private rights, and that by Parliament on the other hand as a privilege attached to a responsible position which had been abused. Harsh as the sequestrations must have been, Parliament did not allow the ejected clergyman to starve; but required the minister put in his place to allow him and his wife and family one-fifth of the emoluments.

To get rid of the 'malignant' parson was not enough; there was the Church itself and its ceremonial to be stripped of the things which 'put upon it the face of Popery.' One of the first acts of the Westminster Assembly of Divines appointed in the Summer of 1643 was to petition Parliament in favour of reforming things amiss, 'where God is especially dishonoured,' and among them that 'all monuments of idolatry and superstition' should be abolished, but 'more especially the whole body and practice of Popery.' The Commons responded by framing an Ordinance, to which the Lords after some delay assented on August 26, 1643. By this Ordinance it was ordered that 'in all Cathedrals, Churches, and Chapels, all altars and tables of stone, shall be utterly taken away and abolished.' Communion tables were to be removed from the east end to the body of the church, and the chancel levelled where it had been raised round about the altar. Tapers, candlesticks, basins, crucifixes, crosses, all images and pictures of any one or more persons of the Trinity, or of the Virgin Mary, and images and pictures of saints, or superstitious inscriptions, were all to be removed and done away with by the 1st of November, 1643, or a fine of 40s. was to be paid to the poor. In all cases of default by the 1st of December any Justice of the Peace was to order the work to be done at the cost of the defaulting authorities. Coats-of-arms, put up to any King, prince, nobleman, or other dead person, 'not commonly reputed or taken for a saint,' were not to be interfered with. There had already been a great inroad made upon the ceremonial of public worship. In many parish churches mutilated copies of the Book of Common Prayer were in use,[1] and in October Parliament was ordering the surplices to be 'taken from the Parish Churches and applied to the relief of the maimed soldiers,' and parsons were enjoined not to wear them during divine service.[2]

By the month of December it was found that in many parishes the Ordinance for demolishing 'idols,' images, pictures, etc., had not been complied with, and the task of sweeping away these offensive objects from the churches was entrusted to William Dowsing, the record of whose proceedings is familiar enough. The entries in Dowsing's Journal have too much of a sameness to be very interesting reading in detail. They are chiefly of interest as showing what kind of an interior the churches presented at the time of the Puritan revolt, and what was the temper of the iconoclasts and the *modus operandi* of the paid agent employed upon the business.

"We brake down 10 mighty great angels with wings."

"We brake down the pictures of the Seven Deadly Sins."

"We brake down above 600 superstitious pictures and 8 Holy Ghosts, 3 of God the Father and 3 of the Son."

"We brake down 2co pictures, one Pope and divers Cardinals, Christ and the Virgin Mary."

"We brake down . . . . some Popes and crucifixes,[3] and God the Father sitting in a chayre and holding glasses in His Hands."

"We brake down St. George and the Dragon, and St. Catherine and her wheel," etc.

These are the kind of entries for parishes in Suffolk, and in the town of Cambridge, where Dowsing had a busy

[1] "The Booke of Common Prayer from ye beginning of it to David Psalms was cut out and torn in pieces in all our churches in the Isle of Ely, not by any order or command of Parliament, but by private directions and command, and the ministers referred to their own conceived prayer for Divine Service, administering ye sacrament, marrying, churching of women, burials," etc.—Extract from Wilberton (Cambs) Parish Register, Jan. 13, 1643, in Baker MSS., xxxvii, 446.

[2] Commons' Journals.

[3] Wherever a cross appeared the Puritan saw the Pope. In one Suffolk parish it was made matter of complaint that an Irishman was seen by the High Constable to 'bow and take off his hat at the cross on the steeple'; and at St. John's College, Cambridge, 6*d*. was paid to a man to climb up and take the cross off the Bell Tower, as the Bursar's accounts of the College still testify. The parish churches invariably lost the cross off their steeples as the entries for Cambridgeshire show.

fortnight from December 20, 1643, to January 3, 1644. Often, as at Pembroke Hall, the rude strokes of the workmen were accompanied by long arguments and the bandying of texts of Scripture between Dowsing himself and the Fellows of Colleges, or the clergyman; or the latter may have stood in the despoiled building uncovered as a reverent and silent protest on the one hand against the irreverence of the destroyer on the other, as at Queen's College, Cambridge, where Dowsing 'brake down 110 superstitious pictures besides cherubim,' while the Fellows of the College stood by 'refusing to put on their hatts.'[1]

On December 29, 1643, the Earl of Manchester issued a warrant to Dowsing to bring before him all who had in Cambridge and the Associated Counties refused to comply with the Ordinance, or who had opposed Dowsing in his work.[2]

It is no part of the purpose of this book either to join in the commonplace execrations which have fallen upon the head of William Dowsing, or to defend what was done in the name of Parliament under the above Ordinance. The mere facts of the existence of such a vast amount of ornate imagery left behind after the Reformation in the churches on the one hand, and on the other the issuing by Parliament of such a sweeping ordinance for its destruction, and the callous disregard of sentiment shown by Dowsing in his work and his Journal—these things represent the two extremes which came into conflict, neither of which can very well be defended from the standpoint of to-day.

The attitude of the Puritans towards cathedrals rests upon a somewhat different footing from that of the parish churches. The cathedrals they looked upon as centres of the objectionable side of things ecclesiastical, without the merit of the parish church of being essential as a place for public worship,

---

[1] The only records now extant of Dowsing's work are those for the counties of Suffolk and Cambridgeshire. The Suffolk "Journal" is the one most familiar to the student. It has been carefully edited, with notes on the personal life of Dowsing, by the Rev. C. H. Evelyn White. Of the less known Cambridgeshire record a transcript is preserved in the Cambridge University Library portion of the Baker MSS., vol. xxxviii, ff. 455-8 and 471-3.
[2] State Papers, Charles I.

and so were prepared to suggest their application to secular purposes. On March 3, 1648, there was, for instance, this Order made by the House of Commons :—
"Ordered that it be referred to the Committee for sick and wounded soldiers to consider of and examine the structure of the Cathedral Church in the Isle of Ely, in relation to the ruinous condition of the same ; and what other churches there are in the same place for the people to meet together in, for the hearing the Word of God, and communicating in the Ordinances of God, and to bring in an Ordinance as they shall find the business, for making sale of the materials of the said Cathedral, that out of the proceed thereof provision may be made for the relief of sick and maimed soldiers, widows and orphans."[1]

A more extreme proposal was that made with regard to Norwich Cathedral, in a petition from the Bailiffs and Aldermen of Great Yarmouth. They asked Parliament to "be pleased to grant us such part of the lead and other useful materialls of that vast and altogether useless Cathedral in Norwich, towardes building of a workshouse to employ our almost sterued poore, and repairing our peeres, or otherwise as you shall thinke fitt and sufficient."[2] It is something to be devoutly thankful for that this utilitarian view of things, and the absolute poverty of any historical sense which it discloses, did not prevail.

[1] Commons' Journals.
[2] Yarmouth Corporation Records, Hist. MSS. Com. Reps.

CHAPTER XVI.

CROMWELLIANA AND BIOGRAPHY — EVOLUTION OF THE
IRONSIDES — CONCLUSION.

WHEN Oliver Cromwell had succeeded by almost unparalleled exertions in raising that 1,000 horse and 3,000 foot—'three score men out of one poor petty village in Cambridgeshire' and the like—and by forced marches had joined Fairfax and been received with a 'mighty shout' on the hills of Naseby, the resolute farmer of St. Ives and the man of affairs who had controlled the head of the Eastern Association, and led its forces to victory passed beyond the view of his neighbours. Henceforth the name of Oliver Cromwell belongs to the history of England and the world. To follow the broader issues of Cromwell's life in their national bearing, is neither necessary nor, indeed, possible within the limits of this book. But there remains the duty of recalling something of the spirit and influence of his work, and of the features and the deeds of a few of Cromwell's neighbours and others who shared in his herculean labours or suffered in person or estate through taking sides in the War. To give a place to all whose career might be worthy of mention would require a separate volume. Such a volume would show hòw superficial, if not absurdly inaccurate, are the conventional labels of the school-books respecting the Civil War—"the gentry for the King and the common people for Parliament"—for, even in these Puritan Counties of East

Anglia many of the best families were on the side of Parliament. All that is possible, however, within the limits of a chapter is a passing reference to a few interesting careers in Cromwell's own and other counties of the Association.

It is part of the fate of leaders of all great movements such as that of the Puritan Revolution of the seventeenth century to become identified with the extreme views and actions of lesser men.

> From kings to cobblers 't is the same,
> Bad servants wound their master's fame.

Perhaps no leader of men has been more unjustly treated in this respect than Oliver Cromwell by most of the historians who wrote of this period until within the last fifty years. Yet Oliver Cromwell, with all his faults, was above all a great Englishman of an intensely practical turn of mind, standing head and shoulders above all the narrow fanatical sectaries which grew up around him. In the wide field of national affairs he was tolerant of all sorts of fantastical dreamers and theorists who swarmed around him, in almost incredible numbers, in the day of his power; and yet he was firm as adamant in keeping them in check directly they began to use their theories for the subversion of law and order—great sacred watchwords which Cromwell, like Alfred the Great, made all men reverence. For upwards of two hundred years the older historians played the Philistine part of first depriving Cromwell of his locks—first ignoring the central fact and grip of the man in his strong element of personal religion and his insistence upon its connection with public policy in national government—and then denouncing him as a hypocrite for his audacity in pretending to execute the judgments of God upon a perverse generation. At last we are getting a little beyond the temporary limitations of the sects, which hampered rather than inspired Cromwell's genius; beginning to hear, out of the discords, that 'bridal dawn of thunder peals' in which faith for once, verily, 'wedded fact,' and to recognize those universal elements in which Cromwell's great Protestation stands, not for an age, but for all time.

For the reader of these pages it is not unlikely that the

most interesting traits of Cromwell's character may be those which were displayed in that part of his career when, at the beginning of the fray, he was rousing his neighbours for the great service to which circumstances were so loudly calling them. From these traits we may judge how he presented himself to his neighbours, and, to some extent, what they must have thought of him. Enthusiasm was with Cromwell, as with other great leaders of men in the world's history, felt to be almost a God-inspired faculty. "Verily I do think the Lord is with me. I do feel myself lifted up by a strange force, I cannot tell why." This was Cromwell's spirit, if not, as given by the writer of the "Squire Papers," his actual words. Then his superabundant energy carried all before it—"Throw off fear ; be as a bundle of sticks : I shall be with you ! It is no longer disputing, but out instantly all you can !" His sense of justice was a part of the stern discipline which moulded his victorious Ironsides —" Tell Captain Russell my mind of his men drinking the poor man's ale and not paying. I will not allow any plunder, and so pay the man and stop their pay to make it up. I will cashier officers and men if such is done in future." Cromwell's self-denial and consideration for those serving with him was a quality which distinguished him as a general as well as a man—" I ask not your money for myself, but others will not be satisfied. . . . . You have had my money ; I hope in God I desire to venture my skin."

Cromwell, the stern rugged Ironsides, was not without his gentler moods; as in that touching interchange of brotherly sympathy with Colonel Valentine Walton, of St. Neots, on the loss of his boy at Marston Moor. Both men had faced the greatest trials that could come to a man, but only a great heroic soul could have met the demands of a trying situation, and stepped aside out of the full flush of victory to pour balm into a private sorrow as Cromwell did—"You know my own trials this way. . . . . He was a gallant young man, exceedingly gracious. Let this drink up your sorrow ; seeing these are not feigned words to comfort you, but the thing is so real and undoubted a truth. Let this public mercy to the Church of God make you forget your private sorrow."

This sinking of private sorrow and private interest in the public good was characteristic of Cromwell, and no one can rightly understand him who fails to notice the intense devotion and almost consuming passion for what he believed to be the public good, as distinguished from private ends, in the presence of a great national emergency. Sometimes his pressing this upon his neighbours may have seemed overbearing and irksome, but if so it was because the occasion was one for heroic measures, the immense importance of which Cromwell realized more keenly than they. That he was a man of strong passion is certain, and before the severe discipline of his later years, he sometimes gave way to it in notable fashion, as in the quarrel with his neighbour, Mr. Barnard, of Huntingdon, about the town charter; but he had even then the good sense to ask that words spoken in 'heat and passion' might be forgotten.[1] Oliver Cromwell has, at least, this vindication in history, that just as no man ever demanded more to be given up for the public good, so no man was ever more willing to sacrifice himself and his means for the promotion of the same end.[2]

That a man should fight courageously and make sacrifices for his own honour and his Sovereign's service, even a Cavalier could understand; but that he should do this for an abstract principle of justice, the privileges of the people, or profess to do it for that Scriptural righteousness which 'exalteth a nation,' without having some ulterior motive, they could not believe; nor, after the sacrifice of the King and the Protectorate of Cromwell, could the historians to whom the genealogical tree is sacred, ever quite understand it. "His personal endowments were such, especially in martial courage and conduct, that had they been employed for his own honour and his Sovereign's service, probably no man in that respect would have deserved a greater name, but,"[3] etc., etc.

[1] See "Court and Society from Elizabeth to Anne," by the Duke of Manchester, i, 340–1.
[2] In 1648 Cromwell had £1,500 due to him as Lieutenant-General to the Earl of Manchester, and two years' pay as Governor of the Isle of Ely, which he gave up for the benefit of the State, and received the "hearty thanks" of the House of Commons "for his free and liberal offer, to the good example and encouragement of others."—Commons' Journals.
[3] "Magna Britannia," ii, 1,048, published in 1740.

—this was the kind of estimate of Cromwell which was destined to prevail so long as loyalty was regarded as a virtue only for the subject and not for the Prince.

Of Cromwell's family relations there are some few points of interest which are deserving of notice in these pages. Mrs. Cromwell, Oliver's wife, when at Court, as in the old house at Ely, was still the excellent housewife, 'and as capable of descending to the kitchen with propriety as she was of acting in her exalted station with dignity.' It is even asserted that she 'as deeply interested herself in steering the helm as she had done in turning the spit,' and among the stories which have gained some credence it is said that she tried to influence her husband to become reconciled to

NORBOROUGH HOUSE. the seat of the Claypooles.

the King's family on the ground of the dangers to which his (Cromwell's) situation exposed him, 'and the certain ruin of his family at his death,' to which, it is alleged, she got the unlikely answer: " You are a fool: Charles Stuart can never forgive me his father's death, nor the injustice he has suffered from me; and if he can, he is unworthy of the Crown." After the Protector's death, his widow retired to live with her son-in-law Claypole, at Northborough Deeping, Lincolnshire, where she died and was buried, but no memorial of her exists there.

Mrs. Claypole was Cromwell's favourite daughter. In her last illness at Hampton Court, where she died, it is said she so impressed her father the Protector by representing to him the 'blood that he had spilt,' and placing his policy in an unfavourable light, that he was 'exceedingly perplexed,' and either from this cause or the death of his daughter became very melancholy afterwards. She was buried in state in Westminster Abbey. Bridget, his eldest daughter, like her first husband, Ireton, deputy-governor of the Isle of Ely, was as strong-minded a republican as her sister Mrs. Claypole was chivalrous towards the Royal Family. To

BRIDGET (IRETON) FLEETWOOD

Bridget, whose portrait is here given, belongs the distinction of marrying two of her father's generals — Ireton and Fleetwood.

Concerning Cromwell's son Oliver, who died in the wars, the entries in a paper folio admission book, "Daniel Mill's Register," at St. Catherine's College, Cambridge, for the year 1640-1, contain that of Oliver, second son of Oliver

Cromwell, who was admitted as a pensioner at this College : a fact which, as Mr. Riley, in reporting upon the College MSS., states, does not appear to have been anywhere mentioned. Of the other two Oliver Cromwells who took sides in the War, Sir Oliver of Ramsey, and formerly of Hinchinbrook, in 1645 gave his age as 84, and three years later he was still living, stating his age as '90,' and urging the ruin of his estates at the hands of the sequestrators "for some opposition he should make against the Parliament's forces, under the command of Lieutenant General Cromwell at Ramsey."[1] The other Oliver, son of Sir Philip, of Biggin House, was killed in Ireland in 1649 under circumstances not without their pathetic side. In June of that year he was urging his claims to £2,138 arrears of pay, that he had raised 80 horse at his own charge, that his creditors were very urgent, and he was in daily danger of arrest, and that he had engaged to serve under Lieutenant-General Cromwell in Ireland. Parliament ordered his arrears to be satisfied, but before this could have been accomplished he was killed in action.

The numerous Olivers in the Cromwell family suggest that the colloquial name of "Old Noll," applied by the Cavaliers to Cromwell, was not so much a name of contempt as might be supposed. It was but taking a liberty with the common appellation for Oliver in the Cromwell family. Thus, Major Thomas Cromwell, of Great Staughton, writing to Ann Cromwell, administratrix of the Major Oliver Cromwell just referred to, says that "his brother Noll owed him two several twenty pounds, one on a bond and the other on a bill of exchange."[2]

Of the two Henry Cromwells, Colonel Henry Cromwell, son of Sir Oliver of Ramsey, who marched with his men to help get away the Cambridge plate, was fined £1,882 5s. 8d. for his delinquency.[3] Cromwell's own son Henry, to whom

[1] Reports of the Committee for Compounding, in which his fine is put at £841.
[2] MSS. of Duke of Marlborough, Hist. MSS. Com. Rep., viii.
[3] Among the papers at Ramsey Abbey is this letter addressed to Colonel Henry Cromwell:—"For Colonell Cromwell or the chief officer of his regiment at Hinton or elsewhere. Sr, you are immediately after sight hereof to march with your whole Regiment of Horse to my Lord Hopton, wheresoever, from whom you shall receive further orders. And hereof you may no faile as you will answer it.—Rupert."

that precocious letter about the Camdeners and Newcastle's broom for sweeping the Fens is attributed in the "Squire Papers," is said to have entered the Army under his father at the age of sixteen. At the age of twenty he was made a captain, and two years later, in 1649, went to Ireland and served with distinction under his father. His subsequent career as Lord-Deputy of Ireland gained for him much credit under great difficulties. On his return to England he lived in retirement with the Russells of Chippenham, near Newmarket, a daughter of which house he had married, and was favourable to the restoration of the King. He afterwards removed to Spinney Abbey, near Soham, 'descending from the toilsome grandeur of governing men to the humble and happy occupation of husbandry.'[1] He died in 1674, and was buried within the communion rails of Wicken church.

Of Richard Cromwell, who became Lord-Protector in succession to his father, there is only this that need be said here, that he was nominated by his father's old friend and landlord, Henry Lawrence, of St. Ives, and that his accession to the high office of his father elicited flattering and fulsome addresses from his neighbours in Huntingdonshire, which were not justified by events.

From these family details which naturally cluster around the name and fame of Cromwell,[2] and so demand a passing notice, it is fitting that we should turn to some other

---

[1] In this connection there is the well-known story of Charles II, when returning from Newmarket, seeking hospitality and finding the former Lord-Deputy of Ireland in his farmyard occupations, with the doubtful addition that his brother-in-law, Lord Inchiquin, took up a muck fork and walked in front of Mr. Cromwell as he had formerly done as mace-bearer in Ireland.—See Noble's Memoirs, i, 212.

[2] Mr. W. B. Redfern, of Cambridge, has in his possession two very interesting Cromwellian relics : a pair of leather gloves, which belonged to Cromwell, as well authenticated as anything could possibly be in such a case, which have only changed owners once since they were in the Russell family, Cromwell's daughter's husband, of Chippenham ; and a pair of spectacles, which have been handed down through the Desborough family as Cromwell's. Another old family estate which had, until recently, a visible link associating the house with Oliver Cromwell, is the manor of Offord Cluny, Hunts, which was for many generations, and still is, in the possession of the Sismey family, one of whom appears to have served on the Parliamentary side. This link of association was a tapestried bedroom and a state bed, in which it is believed Cromwell passed a night or two in one of his many ridings to and fro. Until the room was at last dismantled by a late owner, it was often visited by persons staying at Kimbolton Castle, the Duke of Manchester's seat.

individual careers whose heroic deeds belong to East Anglia, or by old associations were connected with Cromwell.

Of the seven counties of the Eastern Association the county of Hertford was the most notable for the heroism and romance which belonged to individual careers in the War, and of these the valiant Lord Capel occupied the foremost place. 'As plain Mr. Arthur Capel, member for Hertfordshire, he was 'the first to stand up for grievances'; but, like many others, could not follow Parliament far enough to fight against the King, by whom he was created a peer before the War began. His exploits in the siege of Colchester have been already referred to. After the summary execution of Sir Charles Lucas and Lisle, Lord Capel was committed a prisoner in the Tower. In an effort to escape by a cord let down from his window in the night-time, he had to wade through the deep muddy ditch which surrounded the Tower, where, 'if he had not been by the head taller than other men he must have perished, since the water came up to his chin.' He was again taken prisoner, tried and sentenced to death with other noble lords, including the unfortunate Earl of Holland, whom the reader has met with at St. Neots; and, despite the efforts of Lady Capel, he was appointed to be executed on March 9, 1649, only a few weeks after the execution of the King. His letters to his wife in his last moments display a remarkable combination of tenderness and fortitude. "My dear life! my greatest care in relation to the world is for thy dear self. I pray remember that the occasion of my death will give thee more cause to celebrate my memory with praise rather than to consider it with sadness." Again, on the day of his execution he wrote to his wife these last words:—"Let me live long here in thy dear memory to the comfort of my family and our dear children. . . . . God be unto thee better than an husband, and to my children better than a father. God be with thee, my most virtuous wife; God multiply many comforts to thee and to my children!"[1]

At the execution before Westminster Hall his fortitude is thus described by Whitelock: " Next was my Lord Capel

[1] Excellent Contemplations, etc., 1,416a (27), Brit. Mus. Lib.

brought to the scaffold, much after the manner of a stout Roman." Having asked if the other noble lords had 'spoken with their hats oŋ,' and being told that they were bare, he gave his hat to his servant, and, speaking in a clear strong voice, addressed the great crowd assembled. He declared that he was brought thither to die for doing that which he could not repent of, and was now condemned to die against all the laws of the land, to which sentence he did submit.

In accordance with Lord Capel's request his heart was taken from his body and deposited in a silver box with a view to its being presented to Charles II, when he came home, and buried at the feet of Charles I wherever he should be buried. As there were no funeral rites to Charles I the box containing Capel's heart was restored by Charles II to Capel's son, the Earl of Essex, and was preserved at Hadham Hall, until its removal to Cassiobury, Watford, Herts, where on the wall of the inner Library of the Palace is this inscription: "Within this stone is deposited the heart of Arthur Lord Capel, who was beheaded by the Rebels, March 9th, 1649."[1]

Another Hertfordshire hero was the great Lord Falkland, of Aldenham, a prince among the learned, poet, philosopher, and statesman; and, like Hampden, a moderating influence when moderate men were only too rare. He became a soldier by necessity, and not by choice. Going into the fight at the first battle of Newbury on September 20, 1643, with the prophetic words on his lips—"I am weary of the times and foresee much misery to my country, but I believe I shall be out of it ere night"—he placed himself in the front rank of Sir John Byron's regiment, and was struck by a bullet as he was riding through a gap in the hedge. Only a few hours after he had left his inn in the morning, dressing himself carefully that the enemy 'should not find his body in a slovenly condition,' he was brought back, 'slung across a horse,' to the Town Hall, where his body was identified.'[2]

[1] The bibliography of Capel covers a number of interesting and rare pamphlets and books in the British Museum Library.—See "Hertfordshire during the Great Civil War," pp. 103-112.
[2] A handsome granite monument to his memory now occupies the site of the battle where Falkland fell.

The romance of love and war has never received a more interesting illustration than in the careers of Sir Richard and Lady Fanshawe, of Ware Park, Herts, around whose lives quite a halo of romance was thrown by the fortunes of war, and a wedded love which rose superior to all misfortune. The handsome and accomplished young courtier went to the King at Oxford, and Sir John Harrison, of Balls Park, Hertford, and his beautiful daughters, went there too. The two young lovers, near neighbours at home, came together in the strange medley of city, camp, and court, in which highborn dames were sharing mean lodgings and indifferent food, little comforts and fewer luxuries. But love threw a gossamer veil over all the distractions of war, and young 'Dick' Fanshawe and Anne Harrison, a young girl only nineteen years of age and exceedingly beautiful, met at the village church of Wolvercot, two miles outside Oxford on the road to royal Woodstock, and there, defying all the discordant notes of war, were made man and wife, though their entire capital at the time, as the lady frankly admits, was only twenty pounds. Fanshawe had to follow the Prince to Bristol, leaving his young wife behind at Oxford, just after her confinement, and a short time afterwards a perilous journey to Bristol brought husband and wife together once more; and of the delight at meeting she writes: "Now I thought myself a perfect Queen, and my husband so glorious a crown that I more valued myself to be called by his name than a born princess." Driven away from Bristol by the plague, and plundered of what goods they had by the person with whom they were left, the young wife and mother went through peculiar hardships in the Scilly Isles, and in 1648 was brought once more in contact with the King, not long before his trial and execution. Of this interview Lady Fanshawe writes:—

"The last time I ever saw him was on taking my leaf. I could not refrain from weeping, and when he saluted me I prayed God to preserve his Majesty with life and happy years. He stroked my cheek, and said: 'Child, if God pleaseth it shall be so, but both you and I must submit to God's will, and you know in what hands I am.' Turning to

Mr. Fanshawe he said: 'Be sure, Dick (a term by which his Majesty generally spoke to Mr. Fanshawe), to tell my son all that I have said, and deliver those letters to my wife. Pray God bless her. I hope I shall do well'; and, taking him in his arms, observed: 'Thou hast ever been an honest man, and I hope God will bless thee, and make thee an happy servant of my son, whom I have charged in my letter to continue his love and trust in you'; adding: 'I do promise you that if ever I am restored to my dignity, I will bountifully reward you both for your services and sufferings.' Thus did we part from that glorious sun that within a few months afterwards was murdered, to the grief of all Christians that were not forsaken by God."

Soon after this she was in Ireland with her husband, and, while the latter was away at Kinsale, she was lying with a broken wrist at the house of Dean Boyle, when the town was taken by Cromwell's soldiers. Waking up in the night and hearing the guns going off, she despatched a letter to her husband at Kinsale to warn him, and made her way by the light of a taper, 'in that pain I was in,' into the market-place. There, with only a man and a maidservant, she passed through the tumult, and the soldiers with their swords in their hands. From the chief officer Jeffries, who had received civilities at another time from her husband, she obtained a pass, and so got away, and little by little made her way to Kinsale garrison, where she found her husband 'the most disconsolate man in the world for fear of his family, which he had no possibility of assisting.'

Fanshawe was with Prince Charles in his march from Scotland, and was taken prisoner at the battle of Worcester, and when with other prisoners he was brought up to London, his wife was allowed to see him in a room at Charing Cross. Of their meeting she writes:—" Taking my hand and kissing me, he said: 'Cease weeping; no other thing on earth can move me! Remember we are all at God's disposal.'" The effect of a long imprisonment at Whitehall told upon the health of the young courtier, and again his wife stood nobly by him; and in her memoirs, written for her children, there is this crowning touch of heroic womanhood:—

"During the time of his imprisonment I failed not constantly, when the clock struck four in the morning, to go with a dark lanthorn in my hand, all alone and on foot, from my lodging in Chancery Lane to Whitehall, by the entry that went out of King's Street into the Bowling Green. There I would go under his window and call him softly. He, excepting the first time, never afterwards failed to put out his head at the first call. Thus we talked together, and sometimes I was so wet with rain that it went in at my neck and out at my heels."[1]

Eventually the noble woman got the ear of Cromwell, and her husband was released from his imprisonment. He escaped to Paris, and his wife, by a stratagem, got a passport to follow him. At the Restoration they were not forgotten, and Sir Richard met with a brilliant reception as Ambassador to the Court of Spain. The record of their adventures, written by Lady Fanshawe to her children, is one of the most beautiful examples of perfect wedded love, strengthened by peculiar joys and sorrows, to be found either in actual life or literature.

Heroism of another kind was abundantly shown on the Parliamentary side. The extremes of revolution generally do violence to human nature, and when the 'wheel turned' at the Restoration, the trial and execution of the Regicides were not surprising, but the brutal revenge shown in carrying them out was at once a lasting stigma upon the Royalist cause and the occasion for heroic fortitude on the part of the victims.

Among the foremost of these was Colonel Axtell, of Great Berkhamsted, Herts, who, although only acting under orders, was so prominent at the trial and execution of the King, as the officer in command of the Guards, that he shared the fate of the other Regicides—was sentenced to be hung, drawn, and quartered, a fate which he met with undaunted courage. Returning from his trial and sentence 'with a cheerful countenance,' and his wife coming to him 'full of trouble,' Axtell said: "Not a tear, wife! What hurt have

[1] Memoirs of Lady Fanshawe.

they done me to send me sooner to Heaven? I bless the Lord I could have freely gone from the bar to the gibbet!" To a friend he said: "Tell them that for the good old cause, which we were engaged in under Parliament, I am now going to be their martyr, and as for the King I wish him as well as my own soul." To other friends he said: "I am now going to my bed of roses; my last bed. If I had a thousand lives I would lay them down for the Good old Cause!"

The public, who had witnessed almost a surfeit of executions and quarterings at Charing Cross, turned up at Tyburn to witness the execution of Colonels Axtell and Hacker in a more favourable mood towards the victims. They had witnessed the brutal displays of the executioner over the other victims; had seen Cook, the Solicitor-General, dragged on the sledge from Newgate to Charing Cross, with the severed head of Harrison placed in front of him during his 'dismal progress'; they had seen the attitude of Hugh Peters, the Army Chaplain, who when the executioner, having finished quartering Cook, held up his gory hands and tauntingly said: "Come, Mr. Peters, how do you like this work!" undaunted, made this courageous reply: "I am not, thank God, terrified at you; you may do your worst!" Although as a matter of policy, the venue was changed to Tyburn for the execution of Axtell and Hacker, yet the scene was a remarkable one.

Axtell, addressing the Sheriff, said: "Mr. Sheriff, I am now, as you see, come to the place of execution according to my sentence. I desire your leave that I may speak freely and without interruption, first to these people and then to God; for it is the last that I shall speak in this world, and I hope it will redound to your credit." He then addressed the people, declaring, with the Bible in his hand, that "the very cause for which I have engaged is contained in this book of God, both in the civil and religious rights of it." Having finished his speech and given his Bible to the Sheriff, Axtell prayed fervently and in a loud voice before the people, begging as 'the last request this side of Heaven' that 'this poor people might have the pardon of a dying

Saviour.' Turning to his companion, Colonel Hacker, they "saluted and embraced each other in their arms and said: 'The Lord sweeten our passage and give us a happy meeting with Himself in glory.'" The crowd was much affected, and it was alleged that the man in charge of the cart refused to draw it away [to leave them swinging], declaring that "he would lose his cart and horse before he would have a hand in hanging such a man"; and that the hangman himself had at last to come down out of the cart and pull the horse forward.[1] After his death Axtell was 'drawn and quartered,' his head placed upon Westminster Hall, and his 'quarters exposed to public view in other parts of the city.'

"So passed away one of the stout old praying, fighting Ironsides, the Berkhamsted boy who learned to pray as an apprentice in Laurence-lane, and to wield the sword on many a hard fought field. . . . . His life and work may have had in them all the defects as well as the virtues of the extreme party to which he attached himself . . . . but through it all the side of Parliament had no braver soldier, Protestantism no stouter champion, and the great drama of the Civil War no more courageous man in the face of its awful development, than Daniel Axtell."[2]

Miles Corbet, member for Yarmouth and a member of the Norfolk Committee, was another example of that fortitude which enabled men to face the ordeal of death on the scaffold and the ignominy intended thereby. The studious, dark swarthy-faced man of affairs was fired with heroic courage in the face of such a death; for, although he at first had scruples about sitting at the trial of the King, he came round to that point, took his seat in the Court upon the last day of the trial, and before his death assured his friends that he was so fully convinced of the justice and necessity of the action for which he was to die, that he could not refuse to do it again if necessary.

When preparing for his execution, in company with Colonel Okey and Colonel Barkstead, on April 19, 1662, he took his Bible in his pocket 'as a companion on the sledge to the

[1] State Trials, vol. v : "Trial of the Regicides," etc.
[2] "Hertfordshire during the Great Civil War," pp. 139-40.

gallows.' He put on his clean linen, bands and cuffs, with his cloak clean brushed, and also a new pair of gloves which his wife had provided for him, and which he called his 'wedding gloves.' When told that the Sheriff was ready for him he replied, "and I for them." He then took leave of his wife, 'commending her to the Lord,' and bade her farewell; but she, clinging to him, cried out: "Oh, my dear husband, my precious husband, what an husband shall I now lose! Oh, what will become of me!" With tears ready to burst from his eyes he conquered himself, and taking his wife by the hand, said: "Oh, my dear wife, shall we part in a shower! Be contented, God will be a husband and a father to thee and thine"; and 'with other such like good words and so kissing her, turned to his son Miles, whom he took by the hand and blessed him also.' Then he hastened to the sledge on which he was to be drawn to the scaffold, 'desiring a friend to stay with his wife and son to comfort them.' To a friend who had done him some kindness, who came and took him by the hand and asked him how he did, Corbet, looking up into the bright blue sky from his position on the sledge to which he had been bound, replied: "Methinks I begin to see the Lord appearing; farewell, and the Lord requite you for all the civilities that I have received from you." He was then drawn along from Newgate to the place of execution at Tyburn, carrying his Bible in his hand. Replying to inquiring friends how he was, he said: "I am well now, but I shall be better anon, when I am gotten yonder, above that place," pointing up to the heavens above him. When nearing the end of the journey he was told of efforts being made to get his body for burial, to which he replied: "What care I what becomes of my body when I am dead! Let them do what they will with it!" On the gallows with Colonel Okey and Colonel Barkstead, he made a speech to the crowd, in which he said: "We are now dying men and upon dying ground, and we are in the presence of the great God to whom we are now going. . . . . I will only say this (Mr. Sheriff), both the levying of the war and that act we are now accused and condemned for, if they had been done without authority that had been abominable, and to justify that authority, I do not come here to do it." He urged submission to the law, and that God must be the judge of those who made the law. He prayed for the King, Charles II, 'as for his own soul, and that he might reign in peace and righteousness to the glory of God, and the good of the people of the nation.' In conclusion he added: "And now we have done speaking to men, we may now speak unto our God." He then poured out his soul in a long and earnest prayer.[1]

Colonel Valentine Walton, of Great Staughton, near St. Neots, member for Huntingdon, neighbour, brother-in-law, and companion in arms of Cromwell, who took the risk of open conflict at Cambridge when the strife began, had a chequered career in store. Taken prisoner and carried to Oxford in 1643, exchanged and released, made Governor of King's Lynn, he became an active member of the High Court of Justice formed for the trial of the King, and was one of those who signed the warrant for the King's execution, and so belonging to the Regicides had to face their risks. He became a member of the Council of State, but was less in sympathy with Cromwell, and lived in comparative retirement during the Protectorate of Cromwell. Upon Richard Cromwell succeeding, he came, says Noble, to Admiral Edward Montague, at Hinchinbrook, "to take off prejudices and to let him know that his principles were not such as they might be represented," and "in diverse other particulars discoursed very orthodoxly." After the dethronement of Richard Cromwell, Walton became very active for Parliament, and was appointed with General Monk and three others for governing the Army. Finding Monk had designs for bringing back the exiled Charles II, Walton retired to the Continent and became a burgess of Hanau, in Germany. Fearing, however, that, like others of the Regicides, he might be delivered up, he left that place just in time to escape, and spent the short time remaining to him 'in the greatest privacy in Flanders'; going under an assumed name in the disguise of a gardener. Finding himself ill and at the point of death,

---

[1] Howell's "State Trials," Cobbett's Collection, v, 1,315 et seq.

he 'discovered himself, and desired that after his death his relations in England might be acquainted of it.' He died in Flanders in 1661; his end being probably, says Noble, 'occasioned by disappointment, anxiety, and dread of a violent and ignominious death.'[1]

Among the King's Judges who were nominated to that office, and sat at the trial, but did not sign the warrant for the King's execution, was William Heveningham, of Heveningham, Suffolk, whom the reader has already met. When brought to trial at the Restoration, he pleaded that in 1648 'they were under a force, under the tyranny of the Army,' who were their masters; but 'a malicious and traiterous heart he had not.' He further pleaded that he protested against sealing the King's warrant and did not sign it. He admitted that he might have sat at the trial of the King, and now threw himself upon the mercy of the Court in rather abject fashion. He was sentenced to death, but was not executed.[2]

Of Cromwell's neighbours the most conspicuous figures in the War were the Earl of Manchester, young Edward Montague, of Hinchinbrook, and John Desborough, of Eltisley, Cambs.

The Earl of Manchester, 'a man of gentle, generous nature,' was, as Clarendon suggests, hardly fitted by temperament for the rough parts of the times; "insomuch as he was never guilty of any rudeness towards those he was obliged to oppress, but performed always as good offices towards his old friends and all other persons . . . . as the nature of the employment he was in would permit." Sir Philip Warwick, who knew him well, says: "The Earl was a gentleman of debonair nature, but very facile and changeable." The Earl's indifference to the prosecution of the War after his forces had triumphed at Marston Moor, may have deserved some of the reflections of Cromwell and other officers, but the Puritans of East Anglia owed him this acknowledgment, that he lent to their cause the weight of his great influence in their time of sorest need, just when the Parliamentary cause

[1] Memorials of the House of Cromwell, ii, 225-6.
[2] State Trials, vol. v.

was trembling in the balance, and thus materially helped to make the subsequent victorious career of Cromwell and his Ironsides possible.[1]

Edward Montague, son of the Royalist, Sir Sidney, of Hinchinbrook, was the brave young officer who, as Noble says, "when little more than eighteen years old raised one thousand men in Cambridgeshire and the Isle of Ely, with which he distinguished himself in the most important sieges during the Civil War, and in other battles. Cromwell, who well knew the strength of every one's abilities, employed him much." He became one of the Protector's Privy Council, afterwards, as an Admiral, went over with the fleet and brought Charles II back to England at the Restoration, and was created Earl of Sandwich.

Of the Desboroughs of Eltisley, Cambridgeshire, John, the famous Major-General, was first brought up to the law, then cultivated his farm at Eltisley, and in 1636 married Cromwell's sister Jane. As one of the captains of the Fenmen under Cromwell, and as Colonel and Major-General, he distinguished himself on many occasions, notably at the storming of Bristol. He fought at the battle of Worcester, and in his romantic flight Charles II encountered Desborough, near Salisbury, and narrowly escaped recognition.[2] Desborough afterwards became one of Cromwell's Major-Generals, and was in charge of the Western Counties. He was opposed to the idea of his brother-in-law Cromwell taking the title of King, and after Cromwell's death became a thorn in the side of poor Richard. At the Restoration he was arrested on the coast of Essex when attempting to leave England; was liberated, and again arrested on suspicion of a plot to kill Charles II; was again liberated, and escaped to Holland; and

---

[1] The Earl married five times, the last time to Lady Sussex, of Gorhambury, near St. Albans, whose letters have been quoted, and whose taking four husbands —a baronet and three earls—gained for her the name of "Old men's wife."— See Verney Papers.

[2] "The ways were full of soldiers. . . . . Thereupon he [the King] resorted to his old security of taking a woman behind him, a kinswoman of Colonel Windham, whom he carried in that manner to a place not far from Salisbury. In his journey he passed through a regiment of horse, and presently after met Desborough walking down a hill, with three or four men with him, who had lodged in Salisbury the night before."—Clarendon's "History of the Rebellion."

in July, 1660, obeyed a proclamation requiring him to return to England, and was committed a prisoner to the Tower. He remained there until 1667. After this he lived in retirement until his death at Hackney in 1680. At the time of his death he still possessed the family manor at Eltisley.[1]

But the heroism of the Puritan Revolution was not all on the side of those who threw themselves into the bitter struggle which divided the nation into hostile halves. In the great Protestation of Puritan England there was an offshoot which was taking root beyond the seas under conditions scarcely less heroic, and yet full of promise of almost boundless possibilities for the future. Some of the best traits of Puritan England are those which connect families from East Anglia with their friends who had gone out to New England settlements. John Winthrop, a Suffolk man, had gone out to become the first Governor of Massachusetts, and Samuel Stone, a Hertford man, to give a name to Hartford, the capital of Connecticut. But more intimately connected with Cromwell than these were the two young men already referred to— —William Leete and Samuel Desborough—who went out from England just before the Civil War began.

The departure of William Leete is an illustration of how great events from little causes spring. From his legal training in the Bishop's Court at Cambridge, the conviction he formed there that the Puritans were being oppressed, and his throwing in his lot with them, there arose the possibility of a great career; and from the interesting fact that he had just been married to Anne Payne, daughter of the minister of Southoe, Hunts, and took out his young bride to share his fortunes in the unknown land, there was to follow a remarkable dispersion of the name of Leete all over the New England States.[2] On his arrival with Samuel Desborough Leete drew up the deeds of the purchase from the Indians

---

[1] A portrait of Cromwell's sister, Mrs. Desborough, an indifferent print, and a small medallion portrait of Major-General Desborough, are now in possession of Mr. C. J. Desborough, of Hartford House, Huntingdon.

[2] In "The Family of William Leete, Governor of Newhaven and Connecticut Colonies," by Edward L. Leete, the names of 1,074 of his descendants bearing the name of Leete are entered, many of whom, says Judge Ralph D. Smith, the historian of Guilford, have been distinguished in New England.

of the land for the settlement upon which the town of Guilford now stands, and his son John was the first white child born in the settlement.

After Desborough's return to England, Leete rose to the rank of a Colonial Statesman ; in 1676 he became Governor of the State of Connecticut, and was re-elected until his death in 1683 at the age of 70. He was laid to rest in the burial-ground of the first church established at Hartford, the capital of Connecticut, the town founded by Samuel Stone, of Hertford. That the citizens of Connecticut, at the modest funeral of their State Governor, took leave of a great man worthily, is still attested by this entry in Treasurer John Talcott's Account Book, preserved in the State Library of Hartford, Conn., under date April 18, 1683 :—

"To 11 pound of powder for the Great Guns at Gou^r leet's funerall."[1]

Governor Leete had kept in touch with affairs in England, had obtained the advice of Cromwell at critical times in the colony, and when the great reaction came at the Restoration in England, and Whalley and Goffe fled to New England to escape the fate of the Regicides, Leete sheltered them for days in the cellar of his store and fed them from his table.[2]

Samuel Desborough, brother of John Desborough, the Major-General, who went out to New England with Leete before the War, also gained distinction. Samuel Desborough became first magistrate of Guilford, Connecticut, and filled other high offices in the colony. Upon the advent of the

---

[1] Particulars of Leete and Desborough in New England are to be found in these authorities: " History of Guilford, Connecticut," by the Hon. Ralph D. Smith ; Dr. Trumbull's " History of Connecticut "; "The 250th Anniversary of the Settlement of Guilford, Conn. "; "The Family of William Leete," by Edward L. Leete, of Guilford, Conn.

[2] There were Leetes left behind in England during the War—a captain in the New Model Army, and Governor Leete's brother John, who became Chairman of the Parliamentary Sequestration Committee for Huntingdonshire. The Irish branch of the family of Leet, or Leete, traces its descent from an ancestor who went over to Ireland with Cromwell. The handsome genealogical record of the descendants of Governor Leete, whose names now permeate the New England States, had a worthy precursor in a record of the Leete family in England, chiefly in Hunts and Cambs, from the thirteenth century to the present time. This is compiled by a descendant of the Eversden branch, Mr. Joseph Leete, of South Norwood Park, Surrey. He is a Knight of the Legion of Honour, and a successful merchant in the City of London.

Commonwealth he returned to England, became Member of Parliament for Edinburgh, and Keeper of the Great Seal for Scotland. At the Restoration he accepted the King's declaration of pardon, came back to his old home in Cambridgeshire, and bought the manor of Elsworth, in the parish church of which place there is a monument erected to his memory.

The interesting association of the two Puritans, Henry Lawrence and Oliver Cromwell, the quondam landlord and tenant at St. Ives, was renewed under very different but not less interesting circumstances at a later date. Lawrence went abroad during the War, sat for Westmoreland in 1646, and is said to have disapproved of the proceedings against the King; but, if so, he was reconciled during the Commonwealth, when he became Lord President of the Council of State under the Protector Cromwell, and at the latter's death had to perform the office of declaring Richard Cromwell as the Protector's successor. It was of Lawrence's son Henry that Milton wrote his twentieth Sonnet—

Lawrence, of virtuous father virtuous son.

Stephen Marshall, born at Godmanchester, a few years before Oliver Cromwell saw the light at Huntingdon, became as famous with the tongue in the pulpit as Cromwell was with the sword in the field. The son of a poor glover, it is said that as a boy he went gleaning over the Cromwells' fields. If so his father's fortunes improved, for his son graduated at Emmanuel College, Cambridge, became Vicar of Finchingfield, Essex, and famous as a Puritan preacher. In 1640 he preached the first of a long series of sermons before the House of Commons, in St. Margaret's, Westminster, with a 'fervid eloquence which seemed to spurn control.' A famous member of the Westminster Assembly of Divines, he was appointed to wait upon Archbishop Laud in the interval between sentence and execution. He preached before the Commissioners at the Uxbridge treaty-making; and was with the King at Holmby, though it is said the King never attended his sermons and said grace himself, and commenced dinner while Marshall was 'at inordinate length' invoking a blessing. He died in London in 1655, was buried in Westminster Abbey, and his remains were taken up on September 14, 1661, by a royal warrant and cast into a pit at the back door of the Prebendary's lodgings in St. Margaret's churchyard. Of his fame as a preacher, a writer has said that "he was listened to because no man could rival his power of translating the dominant sentiment of his party into the language of irresistible appeal."[1] He was, says Fuller, "their trumpet by whom they sounded their solemn fasts, preaching more public sermons on that occasion than any four of his function."

Another of the Puritan band in Huntingdonshire who surrounded Cromwell was Philip Nye, minister of Kimbolton, who married a daughter of Stephen Marshall. He and Marshall went to Scotland and brought back the Solemn League and Covenant. At first, like his patron, the Earl of Manchester, Nye was a Presbyterian, but later went over to the Independents, and with Marshall was sent to the King at Carisbrooke Castle. Both these men, connected with neighbouring parishes in Hunts, were members of the Westminster Assembly of Divines.

It is an interesting fact that the present Lord-Lieutenant of Cambridgeshire, Alexander Peckover, Esq., of Wisbech, with others of that name, is a direct descendant of Edmund Peckover, of Fakenham, a trooper in Colonel Fleetwood's regiment, and now possesses among other relics the original discharge of his ancestor from Fleetwood's regiment. The document, in its seventeenth-century spelling, reads as follows :—

"Thes are to sertyfey home it may concern that Edmund Peckover, Gentillmane, served as a Solger in the troupe of Will. Collman, major : after him Joseph Blisitt capting had and hath still the Comand of the same troupe under the Comand of the Right honorabull Leftennante General Charles Fletewod whom is Colonell in the service of the Comonwellth, both in England and Scotland, from the yeare of our Lord

[1] "Dictionary of National Biography."

on thousand six hundred forty six untill the yeare on thousand six hundred fiftey and five: during which time he behaved him selfvef faithfull ley and honesley, as becom a Solger, in witnes whareof we have here Uonto set our hands and Seels this Sixen of Aguste, 1655.

           Joseph Blissett ☉
           Hugh Parrye   ☉ "

After his discharge, Edmund Peckover settled at Fakenham, became attached to the Society of Friends, and frequently suffered with them for his religious principles. The Peckovers came from Fakenham to Wisbech about 120 years ago, and the house at Fakenham purchased by Edmund Peckover, the trooper, after his discharge, is now owned by Alexander Peckover, Esq., the Lord-Lieutenant of Cambridgeshire.[1]

Other East Anglians, who figured on the stage in the drama of the Civil War, might be mentioned did space permit, but in the foregoing typical examples there is enough to show that the heroic spirit was not lacking on either side; that among the Royalists there was a fine, chivalrous devotion to the King, and among the Puritans a strength of conviction and a stimulus to high endeavour of which Cromwell and his Ironsides were the natural product. Still, it is not always remembered as it should be that, while, practically, all Puritans were Parliamentarians, all the Parliamentary soldiers were not Puritans in the religious sense of the word. What did distinguish the Parliamentary Army in this direction was the presence of a decided leaven of religious conviction among the officers, and to some extent among the soldiers, and the pre-eminence of this class of men in certain regiments such as Cromwell's. In times of urgency the rank and file of that Army had, of necessity, to be made up of those who were but average men of their day and generation, with human feelings and human failings. That there was, however, a distinct leaven among the rank and file which restrained them even where their memory has been

---

[1] Letter from the Lord-Lieutenant to the writer. Edmund Peckover's trade token bears on the obverse his name and the Merchant Tailors' Arms, and "In Facnham, grocr, 1667" on the reverse.—Boyne's "Tokens."

most slandered, there is the testimony of those who saw them when in contact with the refinements of Cambridge University life. When assembled in the Chapel of Trinity College, the College authorities were so impressed with the devout behaviour of some of the soldiers that a gratuity was bestowed upon them from the funds of the College ; and on another occasion a similar acknowledgment was made when some of the soldiers defended the Chapel from others of their number who would have laid violent hands upon it.[1]

If the officers were not always able to find the godly men with a conscience in their work, who were so dear to Cromwell's heart, it was clearly the aim of some of them to do this, as appears by Sir Samuel Luke's letters. The bluff old Knight was himself in sympathy with Cromwell's method of looking after the godly men for his soldiers, as the following little certificate still bears witness :—

" By reason of ye disaffection of Robert Nicholls, of Potton, to this service, and his perverseness to all religious exercises, these are to certifye all whom it may concerne that I have released him from being a soldier in the garrison of Newport, March 15, 1644 [5].—S. L."[2]

The testimony of others concerning Cromwell's methods and discipline was unanimous. " He had a brave regiment of horse of his countrymen, most of them freeholders and freeholders' sons, who would as one man stand firmly and fight desperately. . . . . At a general muster in 1644 no men appeared so full and well-armed, and civil, as Colonel Cromwell's horse."[3]

" Cromwell used them daily to look after, feed and dress their horses, and when it was necessary to lie together on the ground, and besides taught them to clean and keep their arms bright, and have them ready for service, to choose the best armour and to arm themselves to the best advantage. Trained up in this kind of military exercise, they excelled all

---

[1] " To divers souldiers at severall times that behaved themselves very devoutly in ye chapell, 5*s*. To some of Major Scot's souldiers who defended ye chapell from ye rudeness of ye rest, 5*s*."—Bursar's Accounts, ' Extraordinaries,' Trinity College, Cambridge, 1644.
[2] Luke's Letter-book, Egerton MSS., 787, f. 94, Brit. Mus. Lib.
[3] Whitelock, pp. 72, 131.

their fellow soldiers in feats of war, and obtained more victories over the enemy. These were afterwards preferred to be commanders and officers in the army, and their places filled up with lusty strong fellows, whom he brought up in the same strictness of discipline."[1]

"The officers of the army are such as knew little more of war than our own unhappy wars had taught them. Except some few. They were better christians than soldiers, and wiser in faith than fighting, and could believe a victory sooner than contrive it. And yet I think they were as wise in the way of soldiery as the little time and experience they had to make them. These officers with their soldiers were much in prayer and Scriptures, an exercise that soldiers till of late have used but little; and thus they went on and prospered. Men conquer better as saints than as soldiers, and in the countries where they came, they left something of God as well as of Caesar behind them, something of piety as well as pay."[2]

But nothing can give so clear a conception of Cromwell's rise to power and of the evolution of the Ironsides, as Cromwell's own account of himself and the men who fought under him :—" I was a person that from my first employment was suddenly preferred and lifted up from lesser trusts to greater. From my first being captain of a troop of horse I did labour (as well as I could) to discharge my trust, and God blessed me as it pleased Him. I had a very worthy friend then, and he was a very noble person, and I know his memory is very grateful to you all. Mr. John Hampden [was the person]. At my first going out into this engagement, I saw our men were beaten on every hand. I did indeed, and desired him that he would make some additions to my Lord Essex's army of some new regiments. . . . . 'Your troops,' said I, 'are most of them old decayed serving men and tapsters, and such kind of fellows. And their troops are gentlemen's sons, younger sons, and persons of quality. And do you think that the spirit of such base and mean fellows will ever be able to encounter gentlemen that

[1] Bates, p. 239.
[2] Sprigge's "Anglia Rediviva," p. 323.

have honour and courage and resolution in them! You must get men of a spirit, and (take it not ill what I say) of a spirit that is likely to go on as far as gentlemen will go ; or else I am sure you will be beaten still.' I told him so. He was a wise and worthy person, and he did think that I talked a good notion, but an impracticable one. I told him I could do somewhat in it. And I raised such men as had the fear of God before them, and made some conscience of what they did. And from that day forward they were never beaten; but wherever they were engaged against the enemy they beat continually."[1]

One of the most interesting things, perhaps, in all our military history was this evolution of the famous Ironsides, chiefly from those plain, tawny-coated yeomen of the Fens, who, without any idea of ever becoming soldiers, sent up to King and Parliament their contribution to that thundering "No" against Ship-money and things ecclesiastical when the struggle began. Without any previous acquaintance with the arts of war, such as the Royalist sons of knights and gentry who followed the King may have acquired, these brown-coated husbandmen left their ploughs, their maltings, their grazing-lands and dykes; and, armed with no panoply, but the musket, sword, and pistol, with Cromwell's Soldiers' Bible in their pockets, and enough practical common-sense to see that success in war, as in peace, meant discipline and preparation, they wielded so stoutly the "Sword of the Lord and of Gideon," that their brown coats, and strong, sinewy arms were ere long, seen by all England emerging from the mists and shadows of their native Fenland, which they had wrested from the Earl of Newcastle's invading army as they had before wrested it from the inroads of the sea. Standing there on the borders of the great marshland which they had swept with a stiffer "broom" than that with which they had been threatened, they, not without some murmuring here and there, exchanged their tawny coats for the red coats of war ; and, with an outward bearing in harmony with the militant spirit within them, marched under the leadership

[1] Speech on the offer of title of King to Cromwell.

of a born commander into the broader issues of the strife at Marston Moor and Naseby. Inured to the hardships and discipline of war on many a hard-fought field, and finding the power of the Army the only real power in the nation, they took into their hands the notion of governing as well as fighting, with all the defects which must follow where an executive instrument sets about determining questions of policy, aggravated by the application of military sternness to civil life.

All fanciful accounts, such as have sometimes been placed on record, of any actual enrolment of the famous Ironsides, or the assignment of any particular period of time at which such a force became a recognized part of the Parliamentary Army, may be dismissed as inadequate and misleading. The Ironsides, as we apply the term now, were neither a definite territorial regiment, nor a distinct regiment at all perhaps in the ordinary sense of the term. It would be sufficiently near the mark to say that they were that part of the Parliamentary Army which came under the immediate personal influence of Cromwell and his methods of selection and discipline of the men who were to serve under him. It would, therefore, be almost the literal truth to say that the modest Slepe Hall troop in their tawny coats who left their grazing-lands on the banks of the Ouse, about St. Ives, and rallied around their neighbour Mr. Cromwell at the very beginning of the struggle, was the actual nucleus of the famous Ironsides, and that the force grew with the widening influence of Cromwell's methods of recruiting and discipline.

The Puritan freeholders and farmers whom Cromwell selected from the Eastern Counties were to be found chiefly in the cavalry; the Civil War was largely a war of cavalry, and the Puritan horsemen were led by one of the greatest cavalry officers whom England, if not the world, has ever seen. Thus, forces were working both for the evolution of Cromwell's military genius, and for the triumph of his Ironsides in a field where the impelling force of religious enthusiasm covered the ground of the quarrel much more effectually than the solitary motive of a chivalrous devotion to the King's person which animated the Cavaliers. The evolution of the famous Ironsides, from a small and unpromising beginning, thus became a monument to the effect upon a receptive people of the commanding force of personal character, and the inspiration of a great principle. It was a clear case of the survival of the fittest, the fittest to carry to its logical issue that famous protest, with which all England had set their faces against the abuses of the royal prerogative. If Cromwell persisted in keeping the Army supreme, when his neighbour of Kimbolton would have given up the game, and continued to fight when many moderate men felt that the sword should have been in its scabbard, it was because from the first he had a clearer insight of the Stuart policy, and, like Martin Luther, kept his stand with that solid background of irresistible conviction as to the thing which in England should not be. It was the strength of the Ironsides that, unable to recognize the subtle distinction between those who fought merely for the Kingship, and those who would re-establish the policy which had been so emphatically declared to be intolerable to the English people, they swept away with such irresistible force this "right divine of kings to govern wrong." It was their weakness that, having swept that away, they attempted a task for which they were unfitted, of governing the country themselves; an attempt which, but for the practical statesman's instinct of Cromwell, must have led to hopeless confusion. But the Ironsides under Cromwell will always be judged as soldiers, or rather as men who in a great crisis first taught the English people to say "No"; who gave us the germ of a standing army, the instinct of the professional soldier, and left behind them one of the most brilliant and enduring of fighting records in the annals of British warfare.

To the unknown rank and file of the Ironsides who followed Cromwell with Spartan firmness and with Spartan fame, there is due this final tribute. Above all their excess of zeal or their lack of culture, which their best friends may have had reason to condemn and their enemies to despise, they were men of whom England has still reason to be proud. Of them it may be said that where they trod, there sprang up a harvest of liberty for other men to gather in happier times, when the bigotry and the bitterness of the strife had passed away. With almost unexampled valour these homely Fenmen cut, with sword instead of pen, in letters of imperishable clearness the maxim that he ever fights best whose cause is for the right. In their unknown graves we may leave them. Their bones lie scattered, but their place in history is assured. With the valiant men who have dared to risk all for what they believed to be right; and with soldiers in the foremost rank of the great phalanx enrolled with the iron pen—from Marathon and all succeeding deeds of valour—having earned the laurel wreath, they now rest beneath the epitaph of all brave men—

> On Fame's eternal camping-ground
> Their silent tents are spread,
> And Glory guards, with solemn round,
> The bivouac of the dead.

APPENDICES.

I.

SOCIAL AND PUBLIC LIFE DURING THE CIVIL WAR.

THAT the effect of the Civil War in the domain of social and domestic life was an ever-present terror to many, may very well be imagined. That the omens of coming woe pressed upon the popular mind even more than the actual realization, can also be understood when it is remembered how the popular imagination was stirred on the one hand by the familiar repetitions of Scripture prophecies and the fear of Roman Catholic persecutions, and on the other how the popular mind was, at the same time, bound by superstitions. The belief in witchcraft, for instance, was so general that while the Ironsides were marching to the triumph of the faithful at Naseby, and Essex was bringing up its reserves, the Essex magistrates—the Parliamentary Earl of Warwick and the rest of them—were trying for witchcraft eighteen women—'poore, mellencholic, envious, mischevous, ill-disposed, ill-dieted, atrabilus constitutions'—who were condemned and sentenced to be hung at the Chelmsford Midsummer Quarter Sessions of 1645.[1] The Huntingdonshire magistrates were condemning others to death in 1646, and next year the magistrates at Ely were engaged in similar trials.[2]

[1] Wilson's Narrative in Peck's "Desiderata Curiosa."
[2] See Ely Episcopal Records by Gibbon.

The terror of pestilence also stalked abroad, as at Cambridge, where in 1646 and 1647 tents were erected on Jesus College Green and on the Commons for receiving patients, to which reference may be found in Sancroft's letters (Carey Memorials) and in Cooper's "Annals of Cambridge." Strange signs were seen, or related as being seen, in the heavens above, which the reader may attribute partly to an excited imagination. The narratives of these are, however, so precise, that an example may be given, in the "Strange signes from Heaven seen and heard in the ayre" in Cambridgeshire, Norfolk, and other counties—

"Near Newmarket there were seen by divers honest, sober, and civil persons, and men of good credit, three men in the ayre, striving, struggling, and tugging together, one of them having a drawn sword in his hand. . . . . Betwixt Newmarket and Thetford a pillar of cloud ascended from the earth with a bright hilt of a sword towards the bottom of it ; and there descended also out of the sky the form of a pike or lance, with a very sharp point to encounter with. . . . . At Brandon, Norfolk, the inhabitants were forced to go out of their houses to behold so strange a spectacle of a spire and steeple ascending up from the earth, and a pike or lance descending downward from Heaven. . . . . At the same place also were seen semblances of a fleet or navy of ships in the ayre, swiftly passing under sail, with flags and streamers, as if they were ready to give encounter." At Comberton, near Cambridge, where the Trained Bands had mustered, "the form of a spire or steeple with swords set round about it" appeared in the sky. In Marshland, Norfolk, within three miles of King's Lynn, "a captain and lieutenant with divers other persons of credit" heard "in the time of thunder the sound of a whole regiment of drums beating and calling, with perfect notes and stops much admired at of all that heard it ; and the like military sound was heard in Suffolk upon the same day" and in several parts of the Eastern Counties.

It is further added that "in all these places there was very great thunder with rain and hailstones of extraordinary bigness"; and the narrative concludes with these words:

"The Lord grant that all the people of this kingdom may take heed of every warning trumpet of His."[1]

Behind the confusion and the strife, the sound of drums and trumpets, and the marching and counter-marching of men in arms, there was ever present in the social life of the people that unfailing stimulus—in sermons, fastings, thanksgivings, protestations, and the like—by which Parliament kept up the zeal of adherents to its cause. In the early months of 1644 there was pressed upon the belated parishes which had not already complied with it, the Solemn League and Covenant, the taking of which was one of the conditions of the marching of the Scots over the borders towards the issues of Marston Moor. It had been taken by Members of Parliament in the previous Autumn, and was to be taken by everyone in office, down to the parish constable, and to be tendered by the minister to the inhabitants generally of every parish at church on the Sunday. In some cases the clergyman flatly refused, and had to answer for his conduct to Parliament; in others it was delayed; but gradually it was taken in most of the parishes in the Associated Counties; and interesting glimpses of it survive here and there, of which the following is the clearest :—

In the parish church of Swineshead, Huntingdonshire, on a Sunday in June, 1644, just before the battle of Marston Moor, the minister, Mr. Whitehand, at the close of the morning sermon, unrolled his copy of the Solemn League and Covenant. As he commenced to read the solemn vow, 'that we shall sincerely, really, and constantly, through the grace of God, endeavour, in our several places and calling, the preservation of the Reformed Religion,' etc., every man in the church above sixteen years of age, in obedience to previous directions, took off his hat, and so remained uncovered while the solemn vow was read. At the conclusion of the reading fifty-one men in the congregation stood up, held up their right hand,[2] and then walked into the

---

[1] "Signes from Heaven," etc., King's Pamphlets, Brit. Mus. Lib., E. 340 (3).
[2] The instructions for taking the Covenant provided that the minister was ' to read the whole Covenant distinctly and audibly in the pulpit; and during the time of reading thereof the whole congregation to be uncovered, and at the end of reading thereof all to take it standing, lifting up their right hands bare; and

chancel, while the womenfolk looked on, and there, following the example of their minister, the parish constable, and the churchwardens, subscribed their names or made their marks, as the list at the end of the old document still testifies. " Tho. Whitehand, min." and "William Pentlow, const." lead off, and the rest of the fifty-one in columns after them.

The old rector of Swineshead lived to see many changes. After the Restoration he renounced the Covenant he had signed, but still there was the unfortunate document itself in his own possession a witness against him. So the old man, with one eye on the political weather-vane and one on the future, took up the old document once more, and mounting a table or chair, made a hole in the ceiling of his room, coiled up the document, thrust it through the hole, dabbed it over with moist clay, and descended to his daily round of duty. Six years later, in 1666, Mr. Whitehand was gathered to his fathers and buried in the little churchyard ; but that secret contribution to the history of Swineshead by the fifty-one Covenanters, still rested on the rafters, while many succeeding rectors paced the room below through all the changeful times.

In 1846 the late Rector of Swineshead, the Rev. W. Airy, brother of the Astronomer Royal of that name, found it necessary to take off the dilapidated roof of the rectory house. On exposing the rafters to view there lay the rolled-up document which Mr. Whitehand had concealed, now mouldering and crumbling away from the effects of rain penetrating the roof, at the end of it which projected beyond the rafter, but in other parts clear as when it received the names of fifty-one of Swineshead who with uplifted hand encouraged each other and their neighbours for the fight two hundred years before. The ruined part of the old document, extending when unrolled all down one side, was carefully restored and the missing words added, and it was then neatly framed in wood from the rafter upon which it had rested so long. In

then afterwards to subscribe it severally, by writing their names or marks, to which their names are to be added, in a parchment roll or book, whereunto the Covenant is to be inserted, purposely provided for that end, and kept as a record in the parish.'

this handy form it was presented to the Library of Trinity College, Cambridge, where it may still be seen by the visitor, near by the relics of Sir Isaac Newton, Byron, and the famous Scottish Covenant signed with the Covenanters' blood. The Swineshead document is prefaced with this introduction: "The solemn vow and covenant taken by us, minister, constable, churchwarden, and inhabitants of Swineshead, in the county of Huntingdon and hundred of Layghtonston, June, 1644." The signatures, names and marks, are all left intact, and fourteen Thomases, nine Johns, and seven Williams attest the popularity of those Christian names.

The writers of the University's Complaint mention that some of the scholars at Cambridge were thrown into prison 'for not being old enough to take the Covenant.' They also made bitter complaint of the soldiers breaking into their Colleges, of their libraries and treasuries being 'ransackt and rifled,' and that pictures from the Colleges—'were they but paper prints from the Twelve Apostles'—were carried to the market-place on market-day, and there burned as the 'Popish idols of the University'; a proceeding which made the scholars 'hated by the common people.' Besides the conversion of the Old Court of St. John's College into a prison 'for His Majesty's loyal subjects,' there is this reference to the other Colleges:—"Their malice has since extended itself to all the rest in quartering their soldiers in those glorious and ancient structures . . . . nor was it one whit strange to find whole bands of soldiers training and exercising in the Royal Chapel of King Henry the Sixth [King's College Chapel]. Nay, even the commanders themselves, being commanded to show their new Major-General how well they understood their trade, choose that place to train in." In conclusion, the writers of the "Querela," to whom the great cause for which Parliament and the people had taken up arms had little meaning outside those personal experiences which came to them chiefly through the fortunes of war, reach a fitting climax of pathos set in a classical form befitting its origin—

"If posterity shall ask who thrust out one of the eyes of the kingdom, who made eloquence dumb, philosophy sottish, widdowed the arts, and drove the muses from their ancient habitations .... they are quickly answered—those who have transformed this kingdom into a large gaol to keep the liberty of the subject, they who maintained 100,000 murderers by sea and land to protect our lives and the propriety of our goods, that have gone a-king-catching these three years, hunting their most gracious Sovereign like a partridge on the mountains in his own defence."[1]

Some of the rough use of College buildings here complained of was involved in the larger question whether the War itself was justifiable. If it were, then, with Cambridge full of soldiers from all parts of East Anglia, the occupation of College Halls was for the time being a military necessity. The stripping them of their ornament was a part of the reforming zeal of the Commission sitting at the "Bear"; and against any excesses from that quarter, lamentable as they may have been, it will always be remembered that although Cromwell's horses may have been stabled in the nave, the magnificent series of stained glass windows of King's College Chapel were spared—it is said through Cromwell's friendship for the Provost. That there were those among the Puritan soldiers who would defend the Colleges from violence, we have seen from the records of the Colleges themselves; and that those in authority were not altogether the foes of learning and philosophy that the "Querela" has represented, posterity will, in fairness to both sides, acknowledge from the following resolution of Parliament, passed on March 24, 1648, just on the eve of the Second Civil War, when it had no cause to befriend the Cambridge scholars:—"Resolved, &c. that the sum of Two Thousand Pounds be forthwith advanced and bestowed upon the University of Cambridge, to be employed towards the building and finishing of the Public Library there, and that this Two thousand Pounds do issue and be paid out of the estates and lands of the Dean and Chapters, and that it be referred to the Committee for the University of Cambridge to consider and take care that this Two thousand Pounds be forthwith raised and issued accordingly."[2]

[1] "Querela Cantabrigiensis."   [2] Commons' Journals.

It was also ordered that the sum of £500 be paid out of the receipts of Goldsmiths' Hall "for the purchase of Mr. Thomason, a Library or Collection of Books in the Eastern languages, of very great value, and that the said books be bestowed upon the Public Library in the University of Cambridge."[1]

Surprising as it may seem, peaceful operations in the midst of war were possible during most of the time. The Judges on circuit did, upon one or two occasions, suspend the business of Assizes; yet preachers of endowment sermons in connection with St. John's College, Cambridge, appear to have travelled to Hatfield and Stamford to discharge the trust; and their charges, and the keeping and sweeping of the Library of that College, are regularly accounted for in the Bursar's Accounts. But the most remarkable instance of attending to local needs during war—even to the outward shell of religious systems which Puritanism was condemned for neglecting—was perhaps that afforded by the parish of Barholm, a small village situate about four miles from Stamford in Lincolnshire. Here the western tower added to the parish church bears the date "1648," and a stone below the date bears this inscription, which makes further comment unnecessary:—

> WAS . EVER . SVCH . A THING
> SINC . THE . CREATION
> A . NEW . STEEPLE . BVILT . IN
> THE . TIME . OF . VEXATION.

Another church in the same part of Lincolnshire which preserves a reference to the Civil War is that of Moulton St. James, near Spalding, which, rebuilt in 1722, bears an inscription attributing its former ruinous condition to the Civil War. "Fanaticorum sacrilego furore Civili Bello," says the inscription; but it is not always safe to accept an eighteenth-century view of motive in the Civil War. It is interesting, however, to note that Moulton St. James was in the thick of the fighting in South Lincolnshire; and in the crowding of prisoners into churches and the fortification

[1] Commons' Journals.

of such buildings which often took place, it probably suffered enough to account for the tradition and the inscription.

In the belt of Fenland, lying between Stamford, Crowland, and Spalding, where the advance-guards of the Ironsides so frequently met those of the Whitecoats of Newcastle, the severity of the struggle left traces to which my attention has been called by a correspondent.[1] 'Here in every village are one or more good houses (now sometimes getting more or less dilapidated) that were built, or almost rebuilt, between 1660 and 1700. Many of them are dated.' My correspondent adds:—" I think this shows that when the times became settled people began to repair the ruins caused by the fights." But, alas! he might have added, they were not always the same people who had formerly owned them. Forces economic as well as military were at work in these rebuildings. That these houses were fortified there is no doubt; that many of them must have been injured by military assault and battery seems equally certain; but it is much less certain that their owners had the means of rebuilding them when peace returned. In too many cases the hard necessities and sacrifices of the War had brought them to the end of their fortunes, and so a great many estates changed hands; and the large amount of post-Restoration rebuilding is, in too many cases, to be put down to the passing of country estates into the hands of wealthy City men who had helped to make their fortunes in provisioning the armies for the necessities of the War.

Letters of the time show how much family estates, the collection of rents, etc., had to be left to others, and how difficult it was in those times to get accounts rendered of the stewardship, owing to the way in which such claims were prejudiced by the urgent demands of the War.[2]

Robert Burton, bailiff for Sir Thomas Barrington for estates in Lincolnshire, writes to Sir Thomas:—"By reason of the

---

[1] The Rev. W. D. Sweeting, vicar of Maxey, near Market Deeping, and the Editor of "Fenland Notes and Queries." For Royalists about Deeping, see Reports for Advance of Money, part ii, 1,173.
[2] See Letters of the Cromwell Family in the Ramsey Papers, vol. xix, Add. MSS. 33,463, Brit. Mus. Lib.

Earl of Newcastle's forces coming together all men's estates are weakened and decayed, that I fear few men will be able to pay any rents ; for all our horses, beasts, and sheep are driven away, and most of our houses plundered ; our corn lost in the fields, our hay devoured—2,000 load lost in one lordship—some of it devoured by the great number of their troop horses, and other horses and oxen which they brought with them to bring their guns and other provisions along with them ; another great part cast into the ditches for making their highways, and another great part of it used about their works, tents, and huts." He adds that they carried off the plate from one of the churches, " carrying themselves more like Turks and Pagans than like Christians."[1]

The recovery of debts justly due was attended with difficulty and risk. Sir Arthur Jenney, a Suffolk man, arrested one George Martin for debts, only to find that the man had on him an old commission from the Earl of Warwick which protected him, and Sir Arthur and his bailiffs were thrown into prison on the score of privilege, and had some trouble to get released. Widow Browne, of Bourn and Spalding, adopted the same tactics for meeting the Parliamentary levies as did Sir Arthur Jenney, and Mrs. Brown had much trouble in consequence, 'being spoiled of all that she had by the adverse party at Bourn.'

Members of Parliament and Committeemen made personal sacrifices in order that the Parliamentary finances might not suffer. A member would forego his wages for attending in Parliament,[2] as in the case of Mr. Abraham Burrell, member for Huntingdon, who in 1646 took the place of Edward Montague, and the town returned him on the condition that 'he will serve as Burgess in Parliament without requiring or demanding any manner of wages or pay.'[3]

We think of the issues of the great battles in which Cavalier and Roundhead fought for King or Parliament, but forget the harvest of woe which, during three years of the maddening

[1] Hist. MSS. Com. Rep., 7.
[2] The Records of King's Lynn showed that the members for that town were paid 5s. a day each for their attendance in Parliament, and the Cambridge Corporation Records contain frequent entries of such payments.
[3] Carruthers' "History of Huntingdon," pp. 163-4.

strife, was reaped in the domestic and social life of England, and especially by women and children, 'waiting to hear the step that never comes.' The vivid picture of the fiery sword in the heavens above was but a symbol of the cutting asunder of family ties, when, in the words of a famous orator of a later day, "the angel of death passed over the land until you could almost hear the beating of his wings." The terror of it was intensified by the knowledge of the fact that neighbour was fighting against neighbour, and it might be even father against son and brother against brother. After the final triumph of the Parliamentary cause at Naseby it became possible to 'slight' garrisons, and to gradually cover up the outward signs of the War, but there were deeper scars in the social life, and a legacy of objects of pity moving through the villages of England, whose footprints are still visible here and there in old Churchwardens' accounts, as at North Elmham in Norfolk; Cratfield in Suffolk, and other places, in which are repeated entries of gifts to 'maimed souldjers and their wives.'

Happily, the Civil War, with all the implacable animus which called it forth, and the bitter memories which followed in its train, had this distinguishing characteristic, that non-combatants in the sphere of social and domestic life, and especially women and children, rarely met with personal violence. That many a family was rudely disturbed by the quartering of soldiers in their houses, and alarmed by rumours and actual experiences of plundering, is undoubted, but the bitterest complaint of this rarely, if ever, suggests such a thing as personal violence, and there is frequent testimony to the civility of an officer charged with a disagreeable duty.[1] It is, therefore, a pleasure to acknowledge that, in the main, the soldiers of the Civil War deserved something of the eulogium passed upon both sides by Warburton in his "Memoirs of the Cavaliers."

---

[1] Lady Elizabeth Wiseman, writing in September, 1643, from Canfield Hall to Sir Thomas Barrington, says :—" I had last night at my house a troop of horse, which added great affrightment to my late griefs [the loss of her husband], although I must needs commend the civility of the captain. The demand was for the twentieth part."—Barrington MSS.

"Through all these stormy times shines steadily the heroic character of English nature, nobly manifesting its grave earnest power, terrible and unsparing on the battlefield, self-controlled and considerate in all intervals of peace, compared with the great German War generous and gentle as a tournament—

"England's war revered the claim
Of every unprotected name,
And spared amidst its fiercest rage,
Childhood and womanhood and age."

II.

PAYING AND FEEDING THE ARMY.

WHEN, after the first few months of the Civil War, voluntary contributions became inadequate, the machinery for the creation of a National Debt, carrying 8 per cent. interest, collapsed, and Parliament attempted to pay its way by a direct war-tax, the experience of the Eastern Counties affords at once an example of the heavy financial burden which was imposed, and of the enormous contributions which these Eastern Counties made towards the prosecution of the War for Parliament. About the beginning of 1644 there are frequent recitals in the old Ordinances of the fact that the Associated Counties had raised 14,000 horse and foot and dragoons, and 'intend to raise a far more considerable force.' This flattering preamble was accompanied by an order for a weekly assessment of the following amounts upon the Associated Counties :—

Essex	the weekly sum of	£1,687	10 0
Suffolk	,, ,,	1,875	0 0
Norfolk	,, ,,	1,875	0 0
Lincolnshire ...	,, ,,	1,218	15 0
Hertfordshire ...	,, ,,	675	0 0
Cambridgeshire...	, ,,	562	0 0
Huntingdonshire	,, ,,	330	0 0
The Isle of Ely ...	,, ,,	221	5 0

Here, then, in this one Ordinance, to say nothing of others for special purposes, such as for the Scottish Army, was a demand for nearly £8,500 a week, or £442,000 a year, from the Associated Counties. Before, however, this sum could reach the Army it was subject to various deductions, and some of it could never be collected at all.[1]

The best example of this part of Parliamentary finance for the Eastern Counties which is known to me is that contained in the Duke of Manchester's Papers in the Record Office, which gives one complete year's amounts collected in weekly assessments from the Associated Counties, and paid over to the two Treasurers for the Association. The dates are in the old style, the actual year being 1644, in which the Association forces under Manchester were sent to York and fought at Marston Moor. The totals, it will be observed, are not in all cases exact.

"An accompt of monies received by us, William Leman and Gregory Gawsell, treasurers appointed and chosen by the Right Hon. Edward, Earl of Manchester, Major-General of the Association, and the Committee for the Association, sitting at Cambridge, from the first day of January, 1643, until the first of January, 1644."

From Suffolk.	£	s.	d.
Rec^d out of 5th and 20th part … … …	240	0	0
Rec^d of sequestration money … … …	1,632	7	6
Rec^d for fines imposed upon men… … …	20	0	0
Rec^d in full of the 1st 4 mos assessments from Jan 1 1643… … … … …	30,000	0	0
Rec^d in part of the 2nd 4 mos assessments …	27,069	18	5½
,, ,, ,, 3rd 4 ,, ,, …	9,730	14	2
	68,693	0	1½

From Norfolk.	£	s.	d.
Rec^d out of ⅛ & 1/16 part … … …[1] …	3,630	0	0
Rec^d of sequestration money … … …	1,300	0	0
Rec^d of 1st 4 mos assessment in part … …	20,782	4	3¾
,, 2nd ,, ,, ,, … …	26,379	18	7¼
,, 3rd ,, ,, ,, … …	7,227	0	0
	59,319	2	11

---

[1] Threepence in the pound was allowed for collecting, of which the overseers and petty constables received twopence.

	From Essex.	£	s.	d.
Rec^d out of ⅕ & ¹⁄₂₀ part	... ...	1,806	1	1½
Rec^d of sequestration money	... ...	3,606	6	8
Fines imposed	... ...	190	0	0
Rec^d for 1st 4 mos assessment in part	... ...	24,117	5	1
,, 2nd ,, ,, ,,	... ...	23,814	0	0
,, 3 ,, ,, ,,	... ...	7,130	0	0
		60,664	6	10

	From Cambs.	£	s.	d.
Rec^d out of ⅕ & ¹⁄₂₀	... ...	230	0	0
Rec^d of sequestration money	... ...	450	0	0
For a horse	... ...	4	0	0
Rec^d in part 1st 4 mos assessment	... ...	8,616	9	0
,, ,, 2 ,, ,,	... ...	8,502	8	4
,, ,, 3 ,,· ,,	... ...	1,855	5	0
		19,685	2	4

	From Huntingdon.	£	s.	d.
Received of sequestration money	... ...	1,999	6	0
Rec^d in full 1st 4 mos assessments	...· ...	5,280	0	0
,, part 2 ,, ,,	... ...	4,365	0	0
,, ,, 3 ,, ,,	...· ...	0	0	0
		11,645	0	8

The return from Lincolnshire is imperfect; but these figures are sufficient to show that in the form of weekly assessments alone five of the Associated Counties raised about a quarter of a million sterling for the purposes of the War in one year. But there is evidence that the amount of work they did, in defensive operations, garrisons, meeting alarms, etc., was in excess of the money raised, and in the same class of documents there is a representation from the Association Committee at Cambridge submitting reasons why the weekly assessments were not sufficient to meet the emergencies of the times, by about £12,000 for the year. They further urged that "much of the money assessed cometh not to the treasury at Cambridge, partly in regard it cannot be collected by reason of plunderings by the enemy, depopulations and other difficulties, and partly because· being collected, it is charged by superior powers and particular Committees. . . . . By these means a great debt is contracted upon the Association, and there must be some provision made for the discharge thereof. Therefore, is not the Committee for the Association at Cambridge to be blamed, if after five months soliciting for relief the soldiers still cry out for want of cloathes, food, and pay, and contract diseases and die upon the guards, to the daily grief of all that are true hearted and well affected."

Parliament, recognizing the value of the Association Army, allowed one-third part of the money raised by the sequestration of Royalists' estates within the Associated Counties to go direct to that Army, less £100 per month which was at a later date allowed for the Association Committee at Cambridge 'for their salary and their clerk.'

Under the new model in 1645, the assessments upon the Associated Counties were made a monthly charge at the following rates :—

	£	s.	d.
Essex	6,750	0	0
Suffolk	7,070	0	0
Norfolk	7,070	0	0
Norwich	366	0	0
Lincolnshire	2,070	0	0
Herts	2,432	10	0
Cambs	2,171	6	8
Hunts	1,020	0	0
	28,949	16	8

In addition to this the same Counties were ordered to raise for the Scots Army a total per month of £8,223 10s. 9¾d., making a levy of £37,000 a month. In order to get in these vast sums of money, or as much of them as was possible, Parliament, with its brand New Model, depended less upon the old expedient of sending down the members for the Counties to whip up the contributions, and appointed canvassers of its own.[1]

But though these canvassers, or Parliamentary agents, were less likely to be influenced by local circumstances, it

---

[1] "Resolved that there shall be persons employed in the several Counties to solicit the bringing in of the assessments charged upon the several counties and cities by the ordinance for raising and maintaining the Army under Sir Thomas Fairfax." Mr. Edward Herbert was appointed at 10s. per day for his own services, with five deputies at 5s. per day, in the Earl of Manchester's Association.— Commons' Journals.

sometimes happened that the complaints of the unpaid soldiers were as much due to the agent as to backwardness on the part of the inhabitants of the Counties. The Parliamentary system of trying to be exact with its finances and audited accounts in the field, sometimes found an agent who could turn it to his own advantage. There are traces of one Captain James Pinckney who served Parliament well with his tongue, and himself out of the moneys entrusted to him. He was employed in canvassing and getting in the proportions from the Associated Counties for maintaining the garrison of Newport Pagnell, under the Governor, Sir Samuel Luke. Here is his own account of his riding and talking powers. He had previously, in writing to Cambridge, painted the condition of the soldiers in Newport Pagnell in vivid colours, if the enemy should attempt to surprise this "ye bulwark of the Association."

"From Captain James Pinckney, Ware, Jan. 27, 164$\frac{4}{5}$.— Honoured Sir. Be pleased to take notice that I have not in the least procrastinated. I rode first to Cambridge with three or four stout men to give ye better luster to ye business. I found as much opposition as was possible from men who would be thought friends to ye Parliament; to tell you the particulars would be to trouble you with tedious discourse. But I, considering they were the great Levyathan with whom I had then to deal, I resolved neither to be repulsed nor exasperated with harsh usage, but to demean myself as to gain (not give) advantage. I obtained advantage in words, and by that means drew a consent and promise to further it, and to prepare monies as ye week now coming; in breife of enemys I made them friends. This last week I rode to Chelmsford notwithstanding the floods, where I found no less opposition; but here also gaining advantage in words, and they sent out 24 warrants for two months tax."

The next day after Captain Pinckney's eloquent letter from Ware, Sir Samuel Luke's deputy at Newport Pagnell was writing to his chief:—"We are hearty and well resolved, but much straightened for want of pay. Captain Pinckney hath promised it again and again. *I conceive you may do well to have an eye on him, for I much doubt him.*" On the same day this was sent off Pinckney was at Stevenage, looking after the Hertfordshire money and writing to Sir Samuel: "Expect to supply you with at least £1,000 next week. Am now going into Isle of Ely and Norfolk issuing warrants." The next day another warning goes up to Sir Samuel from Newport—"I fear Captain Pinckney will deceive your former good opinion of him." Just a week after this, Pinckney had got as far as Royston, and writes asking that Mr. Harrison, the treasurer, should "repaire to Royston with a party of horse to Mr. Jo. Glover's, high constable, where he had left £800 for the service of Sr Samuel Luke." Next day, February 6, Henry Oxford writes to Sir Samuel these significant words:—" Looke to Pinckney ; he hath £2,000 at least. He is suspected to be false."

By this time Sir Samuel Luke had got back from London and to his post ; and then Pinckney made his way to London,[1] Sir Oliver Luke being there writes :—" Having interviewed Captain Pinckney, I find no reason to trust him longer. So entered an action of £4,000 against him in the Counties, and gave an order for him to be arrested. He paid £400, and afterwards confessed that he had received £1,000 more, which he had paid to satisfy some debts of his own, but hoped to make it up soon. He remains in custody." [1]

Parliament was also obliged to have a keen eye for anything like "jobbery" in connection with its Army contracts. Thus when the Cambridgeshire money assigned for pistols for Cromwell's regiment was to be paid over to the gunsmith somebody wanted a little private commission of 4d. in the pound out of the transaction, but Parliament became aware of it, put its foot down, so to speak, and required the parties to pay the money over forthwith, to " Mr. Watson, gunsmith, without his paying 4d. in the pound for the same." [2]

As to the money finding its way to the soldier, this is how the vexed question of arrears of pay sometimes began :— " Every captain, both of Horse and Foot, and every other superior or inferior officer, or other, in the Army of the said Earl of Manchester, or belonging to the said Associated

---

[1] Luke's Letter-book, Stow MSS. [2] Commons' Journals.

Counties, whose pay comes to Ten Shillings a day or above, shall take but half the pay due to him, and shall respite the other half upon the Public Faith until these unnatural wars be ended ; and every officer or other that is to have Five Shillings a day or above, or under ten shillings, shall accept of two-thirds of the pay due to him, and shall respite one-third part upon the Public Faith . . . . and when there is three months pay due to any of them, or more, a certificate thereof from the said Earl, or two of the Committee, shall be sufficient to demand the said monies owing upon the Public Faith." [1]

The question of clothing the soldiers raises an interesting point as to the colour of their coats. When the two great armies of the King and Parliament faced each other at the beginning of the Civil War, there was very little in the uniforms of the different forces to distinguish friend from foe, excepting the red sash worn by the Royalists and the orange sash worn by the Parliamentarians. When the various regiments were brought together at a rendezvous, the effect was therefore pretty much like that of a gathering of Volunteers from different counties of England to-day, only that the diversity was much greater. Vicars describes "red-coats, blew-coats, purple-coats, and gray-coats" at the battle of Edgehill, but even these did not complete the diversity, which embraced coats of many colours—red, white, blue, green, purple, gray, and brown or tawny. This diversity of colours often led to confusion and the slaying of 'friends by friends.' The evolution of the red-coat was in fact a part of that strict discipline which made the Eastern Counties' forces the predominant factor in the strife. Carlyle's comment 'red coats for the first time' upon the entry in the "Squire Papers" concerning the objections of soldiers to wearing the red coats about the time of Marston Moor, is a little too sweeping. There were red coats worn even before the War began. Certainly the Suffolk men raised to march against the Scots in 1640 wore red coats ; Essex men who came up to Cambridge, coatless, tattered and torn, a few months after the War began, in the Summer of 1643,

[1] Ordinance in Lords' Journals, Jan. 20, 1644.

were provided with red coats,[1] and without the testimony of the "Squire Papers" it is safe to assume that the red coats became general among the Association forces apparently in time to afford an example for the New Model Army.

For the purposes of feeding the Army, and especially the Association Army, Parliament was able to draw upon these same counties which had furnished it with its 'coslets and muskets,' 'stout Norfolk blades,' and valiant yeomen of Puritan stock, as appears by the following :—

A particular of provisions assessed upon the several counties by the Commissioners of Parliament for the accommodation of the Scottish Army now before Newark :—

Norfolk. Per mensem to go to Boston.

600 quarters of oats at 14/- per qr.	£420	0 0
30,000 lb cheese at 2½ᵈ per lb	312	10 0
77 qrs, 5 strikes, 1¾ pecks of oatmeal at 4/8 per strike	145	0 0
114 qrs, 6 strikes, 2½ pks. pease or beans at 2/8 per strike	112	10 0
	£990	0 0

Cambs & Isle of Ely. To go to Boston.

400 qrs, of oats	£288	0 0
400 qrs malt at £1 6 8 per qr	533	6 8
8322 lbs cheese at 2½d.	86	13 5
	£908	0 1

Hunts. To go to Grantham.
100 qrs of oats
150 qrs „ pease
3520 lbs of cheese
100 qrs malt.   Total   £400 0 0

Lincolne. To go to Gainsborough.
Lyndsey.
20,000 lb beef at 2½d.
12,000 lb mutton at 3d.
150 qrs. malt
10,000 lb cheese
3,000 lb butter at 4d.
82 qrs. 1 peck pease or beans   £800 0 0

---

[1] "Red-coats Field," applied to the site of the battle of Gainsborough, fought in July, 1643, is a local survival bearing upon this point.

Kesteven.
90 qrs malt
5,000 lb cheese
1600 lb butter
3600 lb of pork
38 qrs 5½ strikes of pease   £300 0 0

Holland.
20,000 lb beef
10,000 lb mutton
24,000 lb bread
4,000 lb cheese
1,500 lb butter   £500 0 0

As to means of communication, it would be impossible to over-estimate the enormous advantage to the Parliamentary Army and to the Parliamentary cause which was derived from an almost uninterrupted command and use of the great thoroughfares leading from London towards the ever-shifting seat of war in the north and west. With one or two exceptions it was possible during the whole period over which the struggle extended for the Parliamentary transport to pass along without much risk of serious interruption between the Metropolis and the Parliamentary outposts, such as Cambridge and Newport Pagnell, which marked off the Home Counties and the Eastern Counties as a recruiting base.

The same advantage enabled the City of London in its turn to draw regular supplies for its markets and raw material for its trade, from just those counties least affected by the ravages of the War. As a mere matter of communication the command of the first fifty miles out of the Metropolis was often of the greatest possible moment at a crisis in the War, and this the Parliament could nearly always hold along these great thoroughfares leading towards or bordering upon the Associated Counties of East Anglia. The Grand Committee for the Associated Counties sitting at Cambridge was thus within four or five hours' communication of the Committee in London, and it was no uncommon thing at a crisis such as that in the Summer of 1644 on the eve of Marston Moor, for a dispatch to pass between these Committees in the morning and a reply be received during the afternoon, as the following will show :—

STAGES OF THE POST BETWEEN LONDON AND HULL, BY WAY OF LYNN REGIS.

	miles.
From London to Waltham	12
From Waltham to Ware	8
From Ware to Barkway	12
From Barkway to Witchford [? Whittlesford][1]	10
From Witchford to Newmarket	12
From Newmarket to Brandon	14
From Brandon to Lynn Regis	22
From Lynn Regis to Boston	22
From Boston to Horncastle	14
From Horncastle to Castor	16
From Castor to Barton [on Humber]	12

154[2]

III.

THE EASTERN ASSOCIATION COMMITTEES.

THE discarding of the wretched 'tapsters and decayed serving men' in favour of men having a conscience in their work, by which Oliver Cromwell built up the solid fame of his Ironsides, was not the limit of his influence in this direction. In the selection of men for administrative work, from the composition of a committee for Parliament down to the parish constable, there are traces of Cromwell's practical methods of working with select tools. The student who is bewildered by the innumerable ordinances of Parliament, and the number of committees appointed to meet special local difficulties as they arose—until ordinances and committees appear to overlap one another in almost inextricable confusion—cannot hope to unravel their real meaning except by reading the Parliament's executive work upon this Cromwellian principle of the survival of the fittest. Whenever a County Committee was failing to work together through the disaffection or half-heartedness of any of its

---

[1] Whittlesford was the nearest point to Cambridge on this route.
[2] State Papers, Dom. Ser. Charles I.

members, or any special duty was to be added to a Committee, down came a fresh ordinance from Parliament to be read in church on Sunday, reappointing most of the old Committeemen, and adding new and more vigorous men who had given evidence of fitness for the special duty required, or of zeal for the cause of Parliament. In this way the process of reappointments continued from time to time until the whole body of Committeemen who are named for any given county had been brought together by no end of different appointments, all made for the same purpose of seeing that the Parliamentary cause did not suffer from its enemies or from lack of whole-hearted workers amongst its friends. In this way, from the individual troopers to the great and powerful organization of the Eastern Counties' Association and its invincible army, the Parliamentary cause was held together in the field by men who believed in their work, and the famous Eastern Association owed a large measure of its pre-eminence to the man who never spared himself in his incessant riding to and fro in the interests of unity of spirit as the great secret of effective strength.[1]

Besides the original appointment of a County Committee for each of the seven Associated Counties, there were special appointments of Committees for sequestrating Royalists' estates, of Committees named in the Ordinances for levying and collecting weekly assessments; and then another special appointment in the Ordinance placing the Associated Counties under the Earl of Manchester in 1643, with special instructions for the choice, from amongst their numbers, of the Grand Committee to represent the Association at the headquarters at Cambridge. Then, again, when the Earl of Manchester himself became half-hearted after Marston Moor, and the New Model Army came under the direct command of Fairfax and Cromwell, in February, 1645, there was a general sifting of Committees, and reappointments, with men added who

[1] The only qualification to these observations indirectly confirms the view here taken. Cromwell's influence over County Committees is traceable from 1641 to 1644; but from 1645 to 1649, when he was away in other fields, there was among County Committees a relaxing of that grip of fair dealing which Cromwell had enforced; and there was a renewed strictness of control and investigation of finances and accounts as soon as the Commonwealth came in.

would support Fairfax and the New Model. In addition to the above, there were various minor appointments all tending to the same end, and making it almost impossible to reproduce the separate lists here; moreover, as the same names turn up again and again in different lists it will suffice to accept, with slight modifications, the plan adopted by Carlyle[1] of putting all the principal Committeemen for each county into one list:—

CAMBRIDGESHIRE.

Aldmond, Edward (*t.*).
Becket, Thomas.
Bendish, Thomas.
Blackley, James (*t.*).
Browne.
Browning, Edward.
Butler, Henry.
Butler, Nevill.
Castle, Robert.
Castle, Thomas.
Chennery, John.
Clapthorn, George.
Clark, Edward.
Clark, Robert.
Clench, Edward.
Clopton, Walter.
Cooke, Thomas.
Cromwell, Oliver.
Cutts, Sir John, Kt.
Dalton, Michael, sen.
Dalton, Michael, jun.
Desborow, Isaac.
Diamond, Tristram (*e.*).
Ducket, Thomas.
Eden, Dr.
Fiennes, Ald. (*t.*).
Fisher, William.
Foxton, Richard.
French, Thomas (*t.*).
Hobart, John.
Hynde, Robert.
Janes, William.
Leeds, Edward.

Lowry, John (*t.*).
Male, Edmund.
March, Humberston.
Marsh, William.
Martin, Sir Thomas, Kt.
Mayor of Cambridge, The (*t.*).
North, Sir Dudley, Kt.
Parker, Thomas.
Partridge, Sir Edward, Kt. (*e.*).
Pepys, Samuel.
Pepys, Talbot (*t.*).[2]
Pope, Dudley.
Raven, John.
Reynolds, James.
Reynolds, Sir James.
Robson, Robert (*t.*).
Russel, Francis.
Russel, Killiphet.
Sandys, Sir Miles, Kt.
Sherwood, John (*t.*).
Smith, Henry.
Spalding, Samuel (*t.*).
Staughton, Robert.
Stone, Richard, M.D. (*e.*).
Story, Philip.
Symonds, Thomas.
Thompson, James.
Towers, John.
Walker, Thomas.
Welbore, John.
Welbore, William (*t.*).
Wendy, Francis.
Wright, John.

[1] Appendix to Cromwell's Letters and Speeches.
[2] Talbot Pepys, of Impington, Recorder of Cambridge, and great-uncle of Samuel Pepys, the diarist, who in 1661 visited the old man at Impington, and found him, "sitting all alone, like a man out of the world: he can hardly see; but all things else he do pretty livelyly."

e. These sat for Ely only; *t.* for the town and University of Cambridge only.

ESSEX.

Adams, Thomas, of Thaxted.
Allen, Isaac, of Haseley.
Alliston, John.
Atwood, John.
Atwood, William.
Aylet, Jeremy.
Aylett, Thomas, of Kelldon.
Bacon, Nathaniel.
Barnardiston, Arthur.
Barrington, Henry.
Barrington, Robert.
Barrington, Sir John, Kt.
Barrington, Sir Thomas, Bart.
Berkhead, Edward.
Bourn, Robert.
Brook, John.
Burket, John.
Buxton, Robert.
Calthorp, Robert.
Cheeke, Sir Thomas, Kt.
Clapton, Thomas.
Cletheroe, Captain.
Collard, William.
Cook, William, Ald.
Cooke, Thomas.
Cooke, Thomas.
Crane, Robert.
Eden, John.
Eldred, John.
Everard, Sir Richard, Bart.
Farr, Henry.
Fenning, John.
Friborne, Samuel.
Gambeil, James.
Goldingham, William.
Grimston, Harbottle.
Grimston, Sir Harbottle, Bart.
Harlackenden, Richard.
Harlackenden, William.
Harrison, Ralph, Ald.
Harvey, John.
Hawkin, Richard, of Harwich.
Herne, James.
Hicks, Sir William, Bart.
Holcroft, Sir Henry, Kt.
Honywood, Sir Thomas, Kt.
Jocelyn, John.
Johnson, Thomas.
Kemp, Sir Robert, Kt.
Langley, John, of Colchester.
Langton, John.

Lumley, Sir Martin, Bart.
Luther, Anthony.
Maidstone, Robert.
Martin, Sir William, Kt.
Masham, Sir William, Bart.
Masham, William.
Matthews, Joachim.
Mayor of Colchester, The.
Mead, John.
Middleton, Timothy.
Mildmay, Cary.
Mildmay, Henry, of Graves.
Mildmay, Sir Henry, of Wanstead, Bart.
Nicholson, Francis.
Palmer, Edward.
Pike, John.
Plume, Samuel.
Raymond, Oliver.
Reade, Dr., of Birchanger.
Rowe, Sir William, Kt.
Sayer, John.
Shaw, John, jun.
Sheffield, Samson.
Smith, Robert.
Sorrell, John.
Stonehard, Francis.
Talcot, Robert, of Colchester.
Talcot, Thomas.
Thomas, Captain.
Thorogood, George.
Thorogood, John, of Walden.
Tindall, Deane.
Topsfield, —.
Turner, William, of Wimbish.
Umphrevill, William.
Vesey, Robert.
Wade, Thomas, Ald.
Walton, George.
Ward, Ald.
Watkins, John.
Whitcombe, Peter.
Williamson, Francis, of Walden.
Wincall, Isaac.
Wiseman, Henry.
Wiseman, Richard.
Wiseman, Robert, of Mayland.
Wright, John.
Young, John.
Young, Robert.

HERTFORDSHIRE.

Atkins, Edward, Sergeant-at-Law.
Barber, Gabriel.
Carter, William, of Offley.
Cecil, Robert.
Combes, Toby.
Cranborne, Charles, Lord Viscount.
Dacres, Sir Thomas, Kt.
Fairecloth, Litton.
Freeman, Ralph.
Garret,[1] Sir John, Bart.
Harrison, Sir John.[2]
Heydon, John.
Humberston, John, sen.
Jennings, Richard.
King, Dr. John, M.D.
Leman, William.
Litton, Rowland.
Litton, Sir William, Kt.
Lucy, Sir Richard, Bart.
Marsh, John.

Mayor of Hertford, The.
Mayor of St. Albans, The.
Meade, Thomas.
Mewtys, Henry.
Norton, Graveley.
Pemberton, John.
Pemberton, Ralph.
Porter, Richard.
Priestly, William.
Puller, Isaac.
Read, Sir John, Bart.
Robotham, John.
Sadler, Thomas.
Scroggs, John.
Tooke, John.
Tooke, Thomas.
Washington, Adam.
Wilde, Alexander.
Wingate, Edward.
Wittewrong, Sir John, Kt.

HUNTINGDONSHIRE.

Armyne, Sir William, Bart.
Bonner, John.
Bulkley, John.
Burrell, Abraham.
Castle, John.
Cotton, Sir Thomas, Bart.
Cromwell, Oliver.
Desborow, Isaac.
Drury, William.
Fulwood, Gervaise.
Harvey, Robert.
Hewet, Sir John, Kt.

Ingram, Robert.
Joceline, Terrill.
King, William.
Montague, Edward.
Montague, George.
Offley, John.
Petton, John.
Temple, Thomas.
Vintner, Robert.
Walton, Valentine.
Winch, Onslow.[3]

LINCOLNSHIRE.

Anderson, Edmund.
Archer, John.
Armyne, Sir William, Bart.
Ashton, Peter.
Askham, Thomas.
Ayscough, Sir Edward, Kt.
Ayscough, Edward.
Bernard, John.
Bowtal, Barnaby.
Brassbridge, Ald.
Browne, John.

Brownlow, Sir John, Bart.
Brownlow, Sir William, Bart.
Broxholme, John.
Bryan, Richard.
Bury, William.
Cave. Morris.
Cawdron, Robert.
Cholmley, Montague.
Coppledike, Thomas.
Cornwallis, Thomas.
Cust, Samuel.

[1] Or Garrard. [2] Sir John Harrison afterwards went over to the King at Oxford.
[3] There were also amongst the Hunts Committeemen Apollo Pepys, one of the Pepys of Brampton, from whom Samuel Pepys, the diarist, sprang; and John Leete, of Southoe, brother of Governor William Leete, of Connecticut, was at one time Chairman of the Sequestration Committee for this county.

Davison, William.
Dawson, Stephen, Ald.
Disney, John, sen.
Disney, Mollineux.
Disney, Thomas.
Disney, William.
Ellis, Edmund.
Ellis, William.
Emmerson, Alexander.
Empson, Charles.
Empson, Francis.
Erle, Sir Richard, Bart.
Escote, Captain.
Filkin, Richard.
Fines, Francis.
Fisher, Francis.
Grantham, Thomas.
Godfrey, William.
Hall, Charles.
Hall, —, of Kettlethorp.
Hall, Thomas.
Harrington, James.
Harrington, John.
Hatcher, Thomas.
Hickman, Willoughby.
Hitchcott, Edmund.
Hobson, John.
Hobson, William.
Hudson, Christopher.
Irby, Sir Anthony, Kt.
Irby, Thomas.
Johnson, Martin.
King, Edward.
Knight, Isaac.
Leigh, Samuel.
Lister, Thomas.
Lister, William.
Luddington, William.
Marshal, William, Mayor.
Massinbeard, Draynard.
Massinbeard, Henry.
Massingden, —.
Mayor of Boston.

Mayor of Lincoln.
Miscendyne, Francis.
Moorcroft, Robert, Ald.
Munckton, Michael.
Nelthorp, Edward.
Nelthorp, John.
Nethercote, Thomas.
Owfield, Sir Samuel, Kt.
Owfield, William.
Parkins, Wyat.
Pelham, Henry.
Pierpoint, Francis.
Rawson, Nehemiah.
Rossiter, Edward (Colonel).
Rossiter, Thomas.
Samuel, Arthur.
Savile, Thomas.
Savile, William.
Sheffield, John.
Skipworth, Edward.
Thompson, William.
Thorrald, Nathaniel.
Tilson, Edmund.
Trollop, James.
Trollop, Sir Thomas, Bart.
Walcott, Humphrey.
Watson, William, Ald.
Welby, Thomas.
Welcome, John.
Whitchcot, Edward.
Whitchcot, Sir Hamond, Kt.
Whiting, John.
Willesby, John.
Williamson, Richard.
Williamson, Thomas.
Willoughby, Hickman.
Willoughby, Lord Francis, of Parham
Wincopp, John.
Woolley, William.
Wrath, John.
Wray, Sir Christopher, Kt.
Wray, Sir John, Bart.
Wray, John.

NORFOLK.

Ashley, Sir Edward, Kt.
Ashley, Sir Isaac, Kt.
Bailiffs of Yarmouth, The.
Bainham, Robert.
Baker, Thomas.
Barkham, Sir Edward, Bart.
Barret, Christopher.
Barret, Thomas, Sheriff.
Beddingfield, Philip.
Berkham, John.

Berney, Sir Richard, Bart.
Blofield, Jeremy, of Alby.
Brewster, John.
Brewster, Samuel.
Brown, John, of Sparkes.
Burnum, Edmund, Ald.
Buxton, John.
Calthorp, James.
Calthorp, Philip.
Chamberlain, Edward.

Church, Bernard, Sheriff.
Clarke, of Gaywood.
Collier, John.
Collyns, of Blackborne Abbey.
Coney, William.
Cooke, John.
Cooke, William.
Corbet, Miles.
Dagley, Robert, of Alsham.
Day, Sucklin.
Doylie, Sir William, Kt.
Earl, Erasmus.
Felsham, Robert, of Sculthrop.
Fountain, Briggs.
Fryer (Friar or Frere), Tobias.
Gasley, William, of Holcan.
Gawdy, Edward.
Gawdy, Framlingham.
Gawdy, Sir Thomas, Kt.
Gawsell, Gregory.
Gibbon, John.
Gibbon, Sir Thomas, Kt.
Gooch, Robert, of Elham.
Gower, Robert, of Yarmouth.
Greenwood, John, Sheriff.
Grey, James de.
Grey, John.
Harman, Richard.
Harvye, Richard.
Heveningham, William.
Heyward, Edward.
Hobart, Sir John, Bart.
Hobart, Sir Miles, Kt.
Holland, Sir John, Bart.
Houghton, John.
Houghton, Robert.
Hogan (Huggen, etc.), Sir Thomas, Kt.
Hunt, George.
Jaye, John, of Ersham.
Jermy, Francis.
Jermy, Robert.
Johnson, Thomas.
Ket, Robert, of.Wicklewood.
Kettle, Henry, of Thetford.
King, Henry.
Lincoln, Thomas, of Thetford.
Lindsey, Matthew.
Long, Robert.
May, John, of Lynn.
Mayor of Lynn, The.
Mayor of Norwich, The.
Money, Samuel, of Binnam.
Mountford, Sir Edmund, Kt.
Owner, Edward.

Palgrave, Sir John, Bart.
Parkes (or Parker), Samuel.
Parmenter, Adrian.
Paston, Sir William, Bart.
Peckover, Matthew.
Pell, Sir Valentine, Kt.
Percivall, John, of Lynn.
Potts, Sir John, Bart.
Raymes (Reimes, etc.), John, of Oxtron.
Rich, Robert.
Rower, Robert.
Russell, Thomas.
Salter, John.
Scamler, Adam.
Scamler, James.
Scottow, Timothy.
Sedley (Sidley, etc.), Martin.
Sheppard, Robert.
Sheriffs of Norwich, The.
Sherwood, Livewell.
Shouldham, Francis, of Fulmerston.
Skippon, Philip.
Smith, Samuel.
Sotherton, Thomas.
Spelman, John.
Springall, Thomas, of St. Mary's.
Steward, —.
Swalter, John, of South Creek.
Symonds, William, of Norwich.
Taylor, Henry.
Thacker, John.
Thoresby, Edmund.
Tofts, John.
Tofts, Thomas.
Toll, Thomas.
Tooley, John.
Townsend, Roger.
Utber, Thomas.
Vincent, John, of Crinisham.
Walpool, John.
Walter, —, of Dereham.
Ward, Hamon.
Warner, Richard, of Little Brand.
Wasted, Thomas.
Watts, Henry.
Webb, John.
Weld, Thomas.
Wilton (or Wilson), Robert.
Windham, Sir George, Kt.
Windham, Thomas.
With, —, of Brodish.
Wood, Robert.
Woodhouse, Sir Thomas, Bart.
Wright (or Weight), Thomas.

SUFFOLK.

Aldermen of Bury St. Edmunds, The.
Aldus, John.
Appleton, Isaac.
Bacon, Sir Butts, Bart.
Bacon, Sir Edmund, Bart.
Bacon, Francis.
Bacon, Nathaniel, of Freeston.
Bacon, Nathaniel, of Ipswich.[1]
Bacon, Nicholas.
Bacon, Thomas.
Bailiffs of Aldeburgh, The.
Bailiffs of Ipswich, The.
Baker, Thomas.
Barnardiston, Sir Nathaniel, Kt.[2]
Barnardiston, Sir Thomas, Kt.
Barrow, Maurice.
Bass (Base or Bates), John.
Bence, Alexander.
Bence, Squire.
Blosse, Thomas.
Bloyse, William.
Bokenham, Wiseman.
Brandling, John.
Brewster, Francis.
Brewster, Robert.
Bright, —.
Brook, Sir Robert, Kt.
Brooke, John.
Cage, William.
Chaplin, Thomas.
Chapman, Thomas.
Cheney, Henry.
Clinch, John, sen.
Clinch, John, of Culpho.
Cole, Thomas.
Cotton, John.

D'Ewes, Sir Simond, Bart.
Duke, Sir Edward, Kt.
Duncombe, Robert.
Fisher, Peter.
Gale, Jacob.
Gibbs, Thomas.
Gurdon, Brampton.
Gurdon, Brampton, jun.
Gurdon, John.
Harvey, Edmund.
Heveningham, William.
Hobart, James.
Hodges, John.
Johnson, Thomas.
Lawrence, William.
Lucas, Gibson.
Moody, Samuel.
North, Henry, sen.
North, Henry, jun.
North, Sir Roger, Kt.
Parker, Sir Philip, Kt.
Parker, Sir William, Kt.
Pemberton, Joseph.
Pepys, Richard.
Playters, Sir William, Bart.
Puplet (Pupler, Pulpit, etc.), Richard.
Read, Edward.
Reynolds, Robert.
River (or Rivet), William.
Rous, Sir John, Kt.
Sicklemer, John.
Soame, Sir William, Kt.
Spring, Sir William, Bart.
Terrell (or Tirrell), Thomas.
Vaughan, Theophilus, of Beccles.
Wentworth, Sir John.

[1] Recorder of Ipswich, and said to have acted as Chairman of the Grand Committee of the Association at Cambridge.

[2] The strong representation on the Committees of such great families as the Bacons and the Barnardistons is an example of the hold which the Parliamentary cause had among the gentry of these Puritan counties. Sir Nathaniel Barnardiston is said to have been the twenty-third Knight of the same family ;.and a Sir Samuel Barnardiston was conspicuous among the London Apprentices, and in the riots over Lunsford's appointment as Constable of the Tower he was noticed by the Queen, who, looking out from a window, exclaimed, "See what a handsome young Roundhead is there!"

IV.

A LIST OF THE DEPRIVED ROYALIST CLERGY OF CAMBRIDGESHIRE, DURING THE CIVIL WAR.

[By W. M. Palmer.]

AN examination into the condition and conduct of the clergy in the county of Cambridge during the Civil War, is especially interesting from the circumstance that Matthew Wren, the Laud of the Eastern Counties, had been at the time of the assembling of the Long Parliament over two years Bishop of Ely. He would no doubt during that time endeavour, as far as he was able, to fill all vacant benefices with men of his way of thinking. In this he was not always successful, for many of his appointments remained permanent during the War, their holders preferring Puritan forms to losing their livings. But the majority of the clergy accepted his teaching, and the evidence against scandalous ministers consists largely of complaints about the persistent manner in which the Popish innovations of Bishop Wren were thrust on the people.

Wren had been translated from Norwich to Ely in May, 1638. He had brought with him the reputation of being an uncompromising enemy of Puritanism to a county where many of the inhabitants were of that way of thinking. Rigid and sincere in his belief, he did not, however, shrink from reforming the arrangement of the churches, such as removing the altar from the body of the church to the eastern end of the chancel, and making other alterations which the Puritans stigmatized as rank Popery. These things had to be endured, but were not forgotten, and as soon as Parliament showed its spirit by impeaching Archbishop Laud, a numerously signed petition was sent up by the county of Cambridge, charging the Bishop with having, amongst other things, endeavoured to set up idolatry and superstition. The original signatures to this petition, several hundreds of them, may still be seen in the British Museum. Amongst the signatures are Thomas Pychard, of Trumpington, the High Sheriff, appointed by the King, Hasilden Bury, of Meldreth, Robert Castell, of East Hatley, Thomas Bendish, of Barrington, John Lynne, of Bassingbourn, William Hitch, of Melbourn, John Nightingale, of Kneesworth, Isaac Disborow, of Eltisley, and many other gentry, besides two vicars, John Lawson, vicar of Bassingbourn, 1626–1660, and Stephen Wilson, vicar of Shepreth, 1612–1640. As a result of this and other petitions, the Bishop was promptly lodged in the Tower, where he remained for eighteen years, narrowly escaping the fate of Laud.

All these proceedings had tended to inflame the minds of the people against episcopacy; and when the Earl of Manchester came down to Cambridge in 1643, armed with a commission to inquire into the character of scandalous ministers, there was no lack of witnesses to testify against such unfortunate clergy as had carried out the orders of their Bishop. In almost every parish there was some extreme Puritan who was smarting under the refusal of his minister to administer the sacrament to him unless he walked up to the rails to receive it; and if that unfortunate minister had been known to speak against the Parliament, publicly or privately, or had been in the habit of taking a little too much wine or beer, his tenure of his living was a precarious one.

At the time of the Civil War there were about one hundred and fifty-five livings in Cambridgeshire, including fourteen in the town of Cambridge. Of this number we have direct evidence that from sixty-eight the clergy were ejected, chiefly for their Royalist opinions. Sixty-five parochial clergymen accepted the Solemn League and Covenant, or at least conformed as regards outward show to Puritan forms; and of these more than a third lived to see and participate in the restoration of monarchy and episcopacy. There remain twenty-two livings, twelve of which were in Cambridge town, and perhaps were not all filled at this period, for no mention of them occurs in the ordinary sources of information. Concerning ten livings, it has not been possible to decide whether there was an ejection or not. The names of these places are Great Abington, Barton, Caxton, Eltisley, Ickleton,[1] Kirtling, Littleport, Litlington, Sawston, Triplow. Such information as has been collected about these doubtful places will be found in *East Anglian Notes and Queries*, vol. vi, pp. 353-5, 372-6. It may be here mentioned that the proportion of clergy ejected is much the same as it was in the neighbouring county of Hertford.

In the following list, all the ejections have been verified from the original authorities, with the exception of four instances, which are taken from Walker's "Sufferings of the Clergy." These authorities are far too numerous to mention in detail, but the principal are as follows : The Proceedings of the Earl of Manchester's Committee sitting at Cambridge, some of which are in the British Museum, Additional MSS., 15,672 ; the Proceedings of the Committee for Plundered Ministers in the same library, Additional MSS., 15,669-71 ; the Parliamentary Surveys of Livings in 1650 and the Augmentation Books, both in Lambeth Palace Library ; the Exchequer Bills and Answers for the Commonwealth period, and the Institution Books in the Public Record Office. Of these the Proceedings of the Committee sitting at Cambridge are the most interesting. The Museum MS. is a contemporary copy of the original minute-book of the committee. It gives the names of the witnesses against scandalous ministers, and what appears to be a verbatim report of the informations to which they swore. The greater part of the informations refers to 'popish practices' which the unfortunate minister had been guilty of, and to his expressions of friendliness towards the King and unfriendliness to Parliament. In only a few cases is immorality alleged. An example of these informations will be found in *East Anglian Notes and Queries*, vol. vi, p. 122, where the record concerning Mr. Mapletoft, parson of Downham, is printed in full.

During the researches necessary for the production of this list, much interesting information has been gained concerning

---

[1] The incident of the soldiers and the minister of Ickleton referred to on p. 25 is suggestive that he may have been amongst those who were ejected.

nearly every rectory and vicarage in the county. There were few livings which were not affected in some way or other during the period 1642–62. At some future time the author hopes to publish the whole results of his researches into the lives of the Cambridgeshire clergy at this period.

Abington Pigots.—Edward Lynne was appointed rector in 1631, and was buried in 1655. In 1645 Isaac King was appointed. But it is not certain that Lynne was ejected.

Barrington.—Anthony Marshall was ejected in the early part of 1646. A Fellow of Emmanuel College named Wenham was here in 1650, and he was followed by Robert Carr.

Bartlow.—John Baker was ejected in 1644.

Bottisham. — Theodore Crossland was ejected in 1644. He was followed by Thomas Walker and Richard Britten.

Burrow Green.—Thomas Wake was ejected in 1644. He was followed by William Stephenson.

Burwell.—William Brearley, Fellow of Christ's College and vicar here, was ejected from both benefices according to Walker. But the rector, Dr. Robert Metcalfe, stayed on from 1618 to 1650.

Caldecote.—Thomas Saunders was ejected in 1644. He was followed by George Biker, who was not in holy orders, as we learn from an entry in the church register by his successor in 1650, Thomas Smith, Fellow of Christ's College.

Cambridge.—The only notices which have been obtained of ejections from livings in Cambridge town are from Walker. He states that Charles Bussey was ejected from All Saints in 1644, and Peter Gunning from St. Mary the Less.

Carlton.—Thomas Greeke, Fellow of Trinity College and rector here, is stated by Walker to have lost both his life and his living through the Civil War. But he was here as late as April 3, 1645. He was followed by Robert Sendall.

Castle Camps.—Nicholas Gray was ejected in 1644. He was followed by Nahum Kenitie, who died in 1649. Faithful Theate, Walter Ellis, and Martin Francis succeeded in turn. Francis was properly inducted on the death of Gray in 1660.

Chatteris.—George Otway was sequestered in 1644. Thomas Dearsley was here during the Commonwealth.

Cherryhinton.— Isaac Barrow, who had been appointed to this living in 1641, was deprived of his fellowship at Peterhouse, and probably of this living also. He was succeeded by Walter Ellis. In 1660 Barrow came back.

Chesterton.—Richard Watts was ejected in 1644. Francis Tallance was here in 1650, but Watts returned at the Restoration.

Cheveley.—Robert Levitt was ejected in 1644, and was very troublesome in 1646 to one of his successors, Abraham Wright. Levitt died in 1659, but Wright was deprived by the Act of Uniformity.

Connington.—Edward Martin, Master of Queen's College, was ejected for political reasons in 1643. He was followed by John Yadley and

William Whitfield, the latter of whom stayed until the Restoration, when Martin returned, and Whitfield, having conformed, was promoted to another benefice.

Cottenham.—John Manby was ejected in 1644. Peter French and John Nye followed. In 1660 Manby came back.

Coveney cum Manea.—John Hill was ejected in 1644, having been vicar for 26 years. A minister was then supplied to each place.

Doddington.—Algernon Peyton, the rector here, was in prison in 1647, but he was back again in his living in 1649.

Downham.—Edmund Mapletoft was ejected in 1644. Thomas Giles was here in 1653.

Duxford St. Peter.—George Chamberlain was ejected in 1646. A man named Swan followed, after whom came Samuel Mills, who stayed until 1660, when Chamberlain came back.

East Hatley.—Thomas Goode was ejected in 1644. He was followed by Robert Pepys and Richard Kennet, the latter being deprived by the Act of Uniformity.

Elm.—William Allanson was ejected from the vicarage in 1645, and Thomas Petit appointed.

Eversden Parva.—Thomas Marley was ejected in 1644. He was followed successively by Richard Britten, John Howorth, Oliver Sell, and James Spering. At the Restoration Marley returned.

Fenditton.—Samuel Collins, Provost of King's, was ejected in 1644. William Retchford followed, and after him came Robert Allington.

Fordham.—Stephen Hall was ejected in 1645. Hugh Floyd or Lloyd followed and remained vicar 45 years.

Fowlmere.—John Morden was ejected in 1644. He was followed by a minister named Watson, who had been driven from his benefice in Lincolnshire by the Royalist forces. When he regained possession of his former living, Ezekias King came to Fowlmere, and remained until the Act of Uniformity.

Fulbourn St. Vigors.—Thomas Wilson, D.D., Chaplain to the King, was ejected in 1644. He was followed successively by Robert Dacie, John Alders, and John Masterson.

Gamlingay.—Charles Gibbs was ejected from the rectory, and John Worlich, or Woldridge, from the vicarage about 1644. John Heringe succeeded to both, but Esdras Marshall was here in 1650.

Girton.—William Ling was ejected in 1644, and gave his successor, John Wilson, a good deal of trouble when the second Civil War was brewing in 1647.

Granchester.—Thomas Whatton was ejected in 1644. Isaac Dobson, Fellow of St. Benet's, was here in 1650, and in 1660 Whatton returned.

Gransden Parva.—John Tolly was ejected in 1645, and Thomas Perry succeeded him. Bishop Wren, whilst in the Tower, appointed Joseph Beaumont, but he did not gain possession of the living until the Restoration.

Guilden Morden.—Thomas Anscell was ejected in 1644. He was followed by John Peacock, John Wilson, and Andrew Strode. In 1660 Anscell returned.

Hardwick.—Edward Mapletoft was ejected in 1644. He was followed successively by Francis Creswick, Francis Johnson, and John Fidoe.

Harlton.—Richard Sterne was ejected about 1644. He was followed by Jonathan Allen. In 1660 Sterne came back. He became Archbishop of York in 1664.

Haslingfield.—Griffith Hatley was ejected about 1646. In 1650, Robert Quarles was being paid ten shillings a day for officiating here.

Histon.—John Slegg was ejected shortly before July, 1647. John Ashley followed, and remained for nearly 50 years.

Isleham.—Nathaniel Whitlow was ejected in 1645, and was followed by Roger Peachey.

Kingston.—Cuthbert Pierson was ejected in 1644. Robert Brand followed. The living was again under sequestration in 1647, and Phillip Johnson, the minister in 1650, was found by the Parliamentary Commissioners to be "insufficient."

Knapwell.—John Staunton was sequestered in 1646 because he held also the living of Longstowe.

Leverington.—George Bailey was sequestered in 1645. He was followed successively by—Stukeley, Tristram Dimond, William Sheldrake, and Richard Reynolds.

Linton.—Roger Ashton was ejected in 1644. Thomas Punter followed. In 1660 Ashton came back.

Lolworth.—Thomas Whincoppe had to resign in 1644, because he also held the living of Elsworth.

Longstanton All Saints.—John Goche, or Gothe, seems to have been displaced about 1650 in favour of Henry Gray.

Melbourn.—Francis Durham was sequestered in 1644. William Wells followed. Durham returned in 1660.

Meldreth.—Thomas Elton was obliged to have an assistant in the person of Isaac Worrall, of St. John's College.

Milton.—Edward Johnson was ejected from the vicarage in 1644. George Thomasson followed.

Newton in the Isle.—Thomas Lee was ejected in 1644. He was followed by John Pawson.

Oakington.—Daniel Chandler was ejected in 1644. He was followed successively by — Selby, James Spering, and Andrew Paschall.

Orwell.—Cheney Rowe was ejected in 1644. He was followed by — Brooks.

Pampisford.—Michael Selbie resigned in 1646, and William Johnson was appointed.

Soham.—Roger Hexteter[1] was ejected in 1644. John Fenton succeeded, but was very much troubled by Hexteter, and in the latter part of 1647 soldiers had to be sent to keep the ejected vicar quiet.[2]

Steeple Morden.—Thomas Kitchener was ejected in 1644, and Richard Flower appointed.

Stretham.—Nicholas Felton was ejected in 1644. Matthew Clark followed. After him came Robert Carr, who was deprived by the Act of Uniformity.

Swaffham Bulbeck.—William Isaacson was ejected in 1644. Israel Shipden followed. After him came John Idle, Eli Bentley, and Daniel Foote, the last-mentioned being deprived by the Act of Uniformity.

[1] Or Exeter.   [2] See pp. 326, 327.

Swaffham Prior (St. Cyriac).—Richard Peacock was ejected in 1644. The living was afterwards united to that of St. Mary's, of which Jonathan Jephcok was vicar.

Swavesey.—The Vicar (whose name is not mentioned; perhaps it was Thomas Knight) was sequestered in favour of William Sampson in 1648.

Teversham.—Daniel Darnelly was ejected in 1643 or 1644, and was succeeded by William Sharp, who did not get on well with his parishioners in the matter of tithes. Darnelly caused a good deal of trouble in the parish in the Autumn of 1647.

Toft.—Henry Downhall was ejected in 1644. John Ellis followed.

Trumpington.—Nathaniel Welis resigned in 1643. He was followed by Thomas Giles.

Wentworth.—Daniel Wigmore was ejected or sequestered in 1646, and Richard Wethered appointed.

Whaddon.—William Pickering was sequestered in 1645, and Henry Lilly appointed. After him came John Yong.

Whittlesford.—Robert Clarkson was ejected in 1644. He was followed by John Swan.

Wicken.—Robert Grimer was ejected in 1644. William Walker was here in 1650, but in 1656 Grimer was back again.

Wilbraham Parva.—John Munday was ejected in 1644. He was followed successively by William Rhett, Peter Harrison, and Thomas Whitehead.

Wimpole.—Joseph Loveland was ejected in 1644. He was followed by John Gibson and William Scarlett. In 1660 Loveland came back, and died here in 1695, aged 92.

Wisbech (St. Mary and St. Peter).—Edward Furnace was ejected in 1645, and Thomas White appointed. He was followed by William Sheldrick.

V.

THE "FIRST CENTURY OF SCANDALOUS AND MALIGNANT PRIESTS."[1]

OF this list of Royalist clergy who were among the first to lose their benefices at the outbreak of the War, on grounds of alleged misconduct, 'superstitious' innovations in worship and 'malignancy against the Parliament,' White has taken 58 of the 100 from five of the Associated Counties named below. The list is not, of course, representative of the Royalist clergy generally, but

[1] By John White, published by authority of Parliament, 1643.

Great Civil War. 397

only of those who were most notorious for the conduct which brought them in conflict with Parliament. The paragraph number refers to the position of the names in the "Century."

Cambridgeshire.
Paragraph 40, the case of John Manby, D.D.   Cottenham.
„   58   „   Thomas Goode   East Hatley.
„   85   „   Edward Marten   Dunnington and
                                         [Houghton Conquest, Beds.

Huntingdonshire.
„   47   „   John Reynolds   Haughton & Witton.

Suffolk.
„   20   „   Robert Cotesford, D.D. Hadleigh.
„   30   „   Edward Brewster   Lawshall.
„   31   „   Richard Hart   Hargrave.
„   36   „   Alexander Clarke   Bredfield.
„   52   „   William Evans   Sandcroft.
„   57   „   Cuthbert Dale   Kettleburrough.
„   59   „   Nicholas King   Friston & Snape.
„   61   „   John Wells   Shimplyn.
„   62   „   Thomas Geary   Beddingfield.
„   69   „   John Ramew   Kettlebaston.
„   71   „   Miles Goultie   Walton.
„   72   „   Samuel Alsop   Acton.
„   77   „   Matthew Clay   Chelsworth.
„   86   „   James Buck   Stradbrooke.
„   94   „   Robert Shepard   Hepworth.
„   99   „   Samuel Scrivener   Westhropp.

Essex.
„   3   „   Charles Forbench   Henny.
„   4   „   Stephen Withers   Kelvedon.
„   5   „   Emanuel Vty, D.D.   Chigwell.
„   6   „   Edmund Cherry   Much-Holland.
„   9   „   Lawrence Washington Purleigh.
„   14   „   Edward Thurman   Hallingbury.
„   15   „   Robert Sell   Matching.
„   32   „   Edward Jenkinson   Panfield.
„   33   „   Joseph Plum   Black Novelty
                                         [or Notley].
„   38   „   Nicholas Wright   Theydon Garnon.
„   44   „   Thomas King   Chesill Magna.
„   45   „   Edward Aston   Pentlow.
„   51   „   Nicholas Lowes   Much Bentley.
„   55   „   Richard Nicholson   Stapleford Tawney.

Essex (cont.).

Paragraph 56, the case of Francis Wright — Witham.
" 60 " Edward Turner — St. Lawrence.
" 63 " Thomas Darnell — Thorp.
" 66 " Erasmus Laud — Little Tey.
" 73 " Robert Senior — Feering.
" 76 " Clement Vincent — Danbury.
" 80 " Henry Osbalston, D.D. — Much Parndon.
" 81 " Humphrey Dawes — Mountnessing.
" 89 " Thomas Staple — Mundon.
" 90 " Peter Allen — Tollesbury.
" 91 " John Hurt — Horndon-on-Hill.
" 95 " John Woolhouse — West Mersea.
" 97 " Samuel Southen — Malendine [?].
" 98 " Thomas Heard — West Tukely [? Takeley].
" 100 " Ambrose Westrop — Much Totham.

Herts.

" 10 " Philip Leigh — Redburn.
" 13 " John Gorsuch, D.D. — Walkern.
" 17 " Joseph Soane — Aldenham.
" 24 " James Mountford, D.D. — Tewin.
" 27 " Griffith Roberts — Ridge.
" 35 " Henry Hancock — Furneaux Pelham.
" 46 " Christopher Webb — Sawbridgeworth.
" 68 " John Sydall — Kensworth.
" 82 " Richard Taylor — Buntingford, Westmill, & Aspenden.

INDEX.

Agitators, The, 235, 238.
Alpheton (Suffolk), 84, 85.
Appleyard, Capt. John, 266, 267, 298.
Appleton Hall (Norfolk), 185, 186.
Army, The Parliamentary, and the City, 243; and the King, 236, 286, 287; arrears of, 234; at St. Albans, 286; declarations of, 238, 247; order to disband, 238; refuses, 239; paying and feeding the, 373; contracts of, 378; colour of coats of, 379, 380.
Armyne, Sir William, 19, 22, 23.
Ashburnham, John, 224 et seq.
Ashton, Mr. (of Linton), 321.
Assembly of Divines, The, 329.
Association of Counties, 77. See also Eastern Counties' Association.
Astley, Sir Jacob, 72.
Aston, Edward (Essex parson), 322.
Audley End, 23; threatened, 66.
Audley Wheathill, 301.
Axtell, Daniel, 197; career and trial of, 345, 346; execution of, 347.
Aylesbury, 155.
Aylmer, Edward, 298.
Ayloffe, Sir Benjamin, 298.

Bacon, Francis, 193.
Bacon, Nathaniel, 193, 201, 389.
Bacon, Thomas, 193.
Baker, Mr. (of Bartlow), 321.
Baldock, Charles I at, 225, 249.
Barholm (Lincolnshire), 369.
Barley, Letters from, 243.
Barnard, Mr., 88.
Barnardiston, Sir Nathaniel, 257; descent of, 389; colonel, 270.
Barnardiston, Sir Samuel, 389.
Barnardiston, Sir Thomas, 256, 257.
Barrett, Christopher, 255.
Barrington, Sir Thomas, 64, 114, 132, 146, 307, 370.

Bassingbourn, 5, 304.
Beale, Dr., 37, 68.
Beccles, 24.
Bedford, seized by Cavaliers, 145; retaken by Parliament, 147; Cromwell at, 205.
Bedford, Earl of, 68.
Bedfordshire, Petition of, 32, 76.
Bellasize, Lord, 231.
Berry, Captain, 116.
Bishop's Stortford, 238, 239, 299.
'Bishops' War,' The, 23-6.
Book of Common Prayer, The, 329, 330.
Boston, 51, 69, 120, 131, 143, 177.
Bottisham, 74; King at, 226.
Bourchier, Sir James, 6.
Bourn, 371.
Braintree, 239, 260.
Brampton Gurdon, Colonel, 201.
Brampton Gurdon, jun., Mr., 193.
Bramston, Sir John, 60; his sons' ride to York, 60, 61.
Brandon (Suffolk), 364.
Brentford, 74, 75.
Browne, John (of St. Ives), 227, 230, 231.
Browne, Major-General, 157, 158.
Brownlow, Sir William, 193.
Buckingham, Duke of, 273, 274, 276.
Buckinghamshire, Petition of, 31, 76.
Bunyan, John, 13, 196.
Burghley House, 117, 118, 153.
Burgoyne, Sir John, 99.
Burrell, Abraham, 371.
Bury St. Edmunds, 51, 66, 130, 201, 238; Army Conference at, 239; New Model Conference at, 192-5; Royalist risings at, 255-8; Royalists seized at, 267.

Cage, Sir Anthony, 266, 297, 309.
Caistor (Lincolnshire), 45.

Calamy, Edmund, 126.
Cambridge, Riotous soldiers at, 24; signing the Protestation at, 27; plague at, 34; Charles I and the Prince at, 36-8; rival Proclamations in the Colleges, 47; sending arms to, 50; carrying off the College plate from, 55-9, 301; the Castle seized by Cromwell, 59; Commission of Array at, 67; full of soldiers, 89; fortifications of, 91, 95, 98, 115; bridges demolished and Castle strengthened at, 95; the "Bear" inn at, 99; threatened by Prince Rupert, 145; Royalists in, 146, 147; condition of the Castle at, 198; East Anglian forces at, 201-3; rejoicings at, after the battle of Naseby, 209; Cavaliers approach to, 220; Fairfax at, 234; fighting at, 264, 265; digging up hidden treasure at, 286; sequestrators at, 307; inquisition at the "Red Lion" at, 309; Committee Books at, 310; Committees at, see Eastern Association Committee; Reforming Commission sitting at, 316, 317; Dowsing, William, at, 330, 331.
Cambridge Colleges—Clare Hall, 95; Emmanuel, 36; Jesus, 37, 67, 148; King's, 36, 38, 57, 58, 95, 367, 368; Magdalene, 59; Pembroke, 178, 331; Queen's, 67, 95, 331; St. Catharine's, 338; St. John's, 37, 38, 56, 67, 95, 328, 367, 369; Sidney Sussex, 6; Trinity, 37, 51, 56, 95, 148, 149, 172, 180, 182, 213, 234, 265, 286, 316, 357, 367; Trinity Hall, 51.
Cambridge University and the King, 29; students' petition, 34; reception of the King and Prince by, 36-8; petition to Parliament from, 62; arrest of heads of Colleges, 68; the "Complaint" of, 95, 96; the Vice-Chancellor of, sent to the Tower, 96; soldiers and the, 97, 98, 149, 357; students and the King, 240, 241; students of, and the Second Civil War, 265; Ordinance for reforming the, 315, 316; Association Committee at Trinity College, 316; Colleges losing their masters and fellows, 319; troops exercised in King's College Chapel, 367; burning of pictures of the, 367, 368; Library of, 368, 369.
Cambridgeshire, 24, 39, 71, 74, 87, 88; Ship-money riots in, 21, 22;

Quarter Sessions of, and the crisis, 33; petitions from, 41, 42; members of, taking sides, 43; Sheriff of, 57; Militia of, 66; Protestation of, 76, 77; sequestrators for, 304, 307; Reforming Commission for, 316; Royalist clergy in, 320; contributions of, 373, 375, 376; supplies from, 380; Committee of, 384; deprived Royalist clergy of, 390-6; malignant priests of, 397.
Capel, Lord, 27, 68, 88, 89, 259, 262, 279, 305; his career and heroic death, 341, 342.
Capel, Arthur, the younger, 271, 272.
Capel, Lady, 69, 272, 341.
Carr, Sir Robert, 177.
Cave, Mr., and the King, 227, 228, 230.
Cave, Mrs., 230, 231.
Cavendish, Viscount, 116, 120.
Charles I and the Puritans, 14; and the Scots, 26; his return from Scotland, 29; and the Militia, 35, 37; departs from his Parliament, 35; his reception at Cambridge, 37, 38; his letter from Huntingdon, 40; at York, 60; the raising of his standard, 62; his speech to his soldiers, 71, 72; his designs upon the Associated Counties, 204; defeated at Naseby, 206; his approach to the Associated Counties, 213; takes Huntingdon, 214; leaves Huntingdon, 220; at Newark, 223; escapes from Oxford, 224, 225; his passage through the Fens in disguise, 226-8; carried off from Holmby, 240; at Childerley, 240; at Newmarket, 242, 247; his trial and execution, 287; his execution resented by the counties, 288, 289.
Chelmsford, 238, 239, 253, 258, 259, 304, 306.
Chicheley, Thomas, 43, 302.
Childerley, 66, 240, 241, 242.
Chishall, Little, 28.
Churches, Images, etc., demolished in, 330, 331.
Clarke, Sir William, 300.
Claypole, Mrs., 337, 338.
Clergy and proclamations, 51, 52; reforming of the, 315-7; offences of, 318, 319; and the Puritans, 322-4; scenes at ejections of, 326-8.
Coggeshall, 260, 261.
Colchester, 32, 95, 109, 261, 299; tumult at, 25; scenes at, 63, 64; Fairfax's

attack upon, 261, 262; valorous Royalist defence of, 263; siege of, 269 et seq.; condition of besiegers, 271; desperate condition of the besieged in, 281; surrender of, 282, 283; sequestrators at, 306.
Commission of Array, 62, 63, 300.
Communion rails pulled down, 25.
Compounders, 303, 304.
Compounding Committees, see Sequestrators.
Coney, Sir Sutton, 298.
Coningsby, Thomas, 19, 87.
Coppingford, The King at, 226.
Corbet, Miles, 229; his trial and execution, 347–9.
Cottenham, 307, 309, 310, 327, 328.
Cotton, Sir John, 38, 59, 301.
County Committees, see separate counties.
Cowper, Sir Wm., 291.
Crane, Mr., Sheriff of Cambs, 33, 34.
Crane, Sir Robert, 65, 66.
Cratfield (Suffolk), 47, 372.
Crawford, Major-General, 152, 175.
Crimplesham, 226, 229.
Cromwell, Bridget, 338.
Cromwell, Sir Henry, 5, 44.
Cromwell, Henry, 116, 117, 339, 340.
Cromwell, Henry (son of Sir Oliver), 58, 217, 220, 339.
Cromwell, Henry (of Biggin?), 212.
Cromwell, Jane, 351.
Cromwell, Oliver, Birth, education, and marriage of, 6; at St. Ives, 7, 8; his removal to Ely, 8; early life of, 13; confessions of, 14; member for Cambridge, 15; Hampden's prediction of, 17; his resolution concerning the Grand Remonstrance, 29; seizes College plate at Cambridge, 56–9; authorized to hold Cambridge, 61; Captain of Horse, 71; at Edgehill, 72; arrests the Sheriff at St. Albans, 87; Colonel of a Regiment, 90; his ride into Norfolk, 93; suppresses Royalists at Lowestoft, 93, 94; at King's Lynn, 94; relieves Crowland, 106, 107, 108, 109; his strict discipline, 110, 111; charge of inhumanity against, 111; in Lincolnshire, 113; meets, "Ca'ndishers," 116; takes Burghley House, 117, 118; defeats Cavendish at Gainsborough, 119, 120; his rousing letters, 121; appointed to the command of Cambs and Hunts Horse, 124; at the siege of Lynn, 135; his regiment of 1,000 horse, 139; joins Fairfax at Hull, 142; at Winceby fight, 144; at Ely Cathedral, 149, 150; his tolerance of opinions, 152; loses his son Oliver, 154; at Marston Moor, 159–61; letter to his brother-in-law, 162; his quarrel with Manchester, 168–76; charge against, 175, 176; his attitude towards the New Model Army and unity, 188–90; takes the Queen's colours, 197; in the Isle of Ely, 198; at Cambridge, 200; riding through the Fens, 202; rousing his neighbours, 203; made Lieut.-General of Horse, 204; his march to Harborough and welcome by a 'mighty shout,' 205; his victorious charge at Naseby, 206; his dispatch from the battlefield, 207; 'Old Ironsides,' 208; his valour recognized by Parliament, 209; marches into the west, 211; with the army at Saffron Walden, 235; meets the King at Childerley, 241; with the army at Thriplow Heath, 243; and the Levellers, 251; his victory at Preston, 282; his character, 334–6; in Ireland, 344; character of his troops, 356–8; his own account of himself and his troops, 358, 359; his policy, 361; his administrative methods, 382, 383.
Cromwell, Mrs., 337.
Cromwell, Oliver, junior, 106, 338, 339; death of, 154, 169.
Cromwell, Sir Oliver, 5, 44, 111, 139.
Cromwell, Oliver (son of Sir Philip), 44, 339.
Cromwell, Sir Philip, 44.
Cromwell, Richard, Protector, 340, 351.
Cromwell, Robert, 5.
Cromwell, Robina, 328.
Cromwell, Thomas, 339.
Crowland, 100, 222, 263, 264, 268, 300, 370; first siege of, 101 et seq.; captured by Parliament, 107; retaken by the Royalists, 177; Eastern Counties' troops march to, 178; again besieged, 179; Royalist relieving force defeated, 179; special ordinance for, 179, 180; forts erected around, 180; surrounded by boats and recaptured by Parliament, 181; fortification of the church at, 197; ordinance for securing, 212.
Croyland, see Crowland.
Cutts, Sir John, 34, 66, 74, 240.
Cutts, Lady, 241.

Dacres, Sir Thomas, 68.
Dalbier, Colonel, 275; slain at St. Neots, 277.
Dallison, Sir Charles, 48, 49.
Deeping, Market, 200.
Denton (Lincolnshire), 179.
Dereham (Norfolk), 254.
Dereham, Thomas, 300.
Desborough, John, Major-General, 14, 113, 169, 174, 212, 257; his career, 351, 352.
Desborough, Samuel, 14, 352-4.
D'Ewes, Sir Symonds, 20, 70.
Docwra, Captain, 57; Henry, 299.
Dodson, Major, 53, 106, 118, 141; Colonel and Governor of Crowland, 197, 212, 222.
Downhall, Mr. (of St. Ives), 8.
Downham (Isle of Ely), 67, 309.
Downham (Norfolk), 135; Charles I at, 225-32.
Dowsing, William, 330, 331.
Dunstable, Cavaliers at, 157, 158.

Earith, 223, 226.
East Anglia and Bishop Wren, 26; and 'No Popery,' 27; the Compact of, 79; popular rising of, 81-5; recruiting in, 164; Puritans of, 191, 196; Royalist risings in, 252; Puritan revolt of, 312-14; Puritan horsemen of, 360.
Eastern Counties and Puritanism, 2; proclamations in, 52; troops of, at Edgehill, 72; forces of, march to Cambridge, 88-90, 99, 100; Royalist designs upon, 115; reorganizing forces of, 125, 126; the King's design to march through, 140; forces of, again march to Cambridge, 147; "Remarkable Mercies" in, 153; Royalist advance towards the, 157; troops of, at Marston Moor, 159, 164; forces mustering for Naseby, 202; forces at Naseby, 206; reserves of, 208; final triumph of their forces, 209; alarms in the, 215; sending forces to Newark, 223; thanksgiving in, 224; Fairfax's army in, 237; 'scandalous ministers' in, 315; committees for reforming them, 317, 396-8; contributions from the, 373-5; supplies from, 380, 381; communication with, 383, 384.
Eastern Counties Association, The formation of, 78, 80; subscribing to it in the counties, 81-5; ordered to raise 20,000 men, 130; army of 15,000 strong, 153; jealousy of, 155;
army of, at Marston Moor, 165; army of, at Huntingdon, 167; against marching westwards, 172, 173; the King's designs upon, 183; integrity of the, 190; conference of, and the New Model, 192-5; Trained Bands of the, 198; Grand Committee of the, 90, 98, 99, 125, 130, 177, 198; letters from and to the Committee of the, 118, 119, 121, 132, 145, 172, 200, 201, 213; finances of the, 375, 376; lists of County Committees in the, 382-9.
Edgehill, Battle of, 72.
Elm, 139.
Elmham, North (Norfolk), 372.
Eltisley (Cambs), 169.
Ely, 11, 13, 113, 115, 203, 363; Cromwell's house at, 10; Great Tithe Barn at, 11; scene in Marketplace at, 53; Cromwell at, 133; Cromwell and the Cathedral service at, 149; Royalist plot to secure, 158; Charles I at, 226; Parliamentary Sequestrators at, 307; letters from, 308, 309; orders as to the Cathedral, 332.
Ely, Isle of, 72, 77, 112, 113, 124, 284; petition from the, 41; soldiers in the pulpits of, 175; defence of the, 197; Cromwell to be Governor of, 198; ammunition sent into the, 199; Cromwell recruiting in, 202; ordinance for securing, 212; Charles I passing through, in disguise, 226; passes into the, 259; safety of the, 267; sequestrators in, 308; contributions of, 373; supplies from, 380.
Emneth, 139.
Essex, Sheriff of, and Ship-money, 20; soldiers of, 25; petitions from, 31, 46; soldiers of, and their Captains, 74; how the men came in from, 131, 132, 134, 143, 379; the King's forces to march into, 140; forces of, for Naseby and at Cambridge, 208, 221; the County and the Army, 233; the Clergy and the Army in, 235; petition from, 246, 255; Royalist rising in, 258, 259; Committee of imprisoned, 258, 271-3, 282; Trained Bands of, 261, 283; soldiers of, at the siege of Colchester, 268; the 'Essex Lions,' 270; Puritanism of, 312; Royalist clergy in, 320; contributions of, 373, 375, 376; list of County Committee of, 385; 'Malignant Priests' in, 397, 398.
Essex, Earl of, 73, 115, 122; appointed

Lord General for Parliament, 69; his march against the King, 70, 71; his speech to his soldiers, 71; his Army in the West, 155; defeat at Lostwithiel, 168.
Exeter, Mr. (of Soham), 326.
Eynesbury, 223.

Fairfax, Sir Thomas, in Hull, 140; defeats the Royalists at Selby, 155; at Marston Moor, 162; appointed commander-in-chief for Parliament, 195; asks for Cromwell to have command of the Horse, 203; welcomes Cromwell at Market Harborough, 205; with the Army at Saffron Walden, 235; in Essex, 260, 263; besieging Colchester, 268; takes Colchester, 282.
Falkland, Lord, 29, 142, 342.
Fanshawe, Sir R. and Lady, 343-5.
Farre, Captain, 47; Colonel, 258.
Fen Drayton, 91, 92.
Fenmen, The, 77, 126; valour of, 122.
Fens, The, 113; defending passes, etc., in, 115, 125; the 1648 rising in, 268.
Fleetwood, 113, 237, 256.
French, Dr. Peter, 328.

Gainsborough, Battle of, 119, 120.
Gawsell, Gregory, 174, 374.
Godmanchester, 220, 221; bailiffs of and the King, 215; plunder of, by Cavaliers, 218.
Gransden, Hunts, 325.
Grantham, 180.
Graveley (Herts), The King at, 225.
Grey, Lord, of Wark, 96, 97, 100, 125.
Grimston, Harbottle, 27, 64, 269, 270.

Hacker, Colonel, 179; execution of, 347.
Hadham Hall (Herts), 68, 271, 342.
Halstead, 239, 260.
Harlackenden, Sir William, 132, 134, 259.
Hampden, John, 10; death of, 114; influence of, 115, 142; Cromwell and, 358, 359.
Harrison, Sir John, 343.
Harwich, 269.
Haselrigg, Sir Arthur, 174.
Hatfield, Charles I at, 249.
Hatfield House, 273.
Hemingford (Hunts), 323.
Hertford, 27, 53.
Hertfordshire, Scenes in the churches of, 25; petition against grievances from, 27; Charles I in, 31; petition from, 32; arrest of Sheriff of, 87; forces of, at Hitchin, 147; Committee's letters from, 157; Charles I in, 224, 249; pursuit of Royalists through, 273; Colchester prisoners in, 283; contributions of, 373, 374, 376; Committee of, 386; "Malignant Priests" in, 398.
Heveningham, Sir Wm., 80, 350.
Hewitt, Sir John, 297.
Hill, Dr. (of Coveney), 53.
Hinchinbrook, 5, 43, 44, 169, 240.
Hingham (Norfolk), 28.
Hitchin, 145, 147, 171, 273, 299; yeomen rising at, 157, 158.
Hobart, Sir John, 63, 267.
Hobart, Colonel Sir Miles, 106, 107, 117.
Holdsworth, Dr., 28, 96.
Holland, Earl of, 273, 275; taken prisoner at St. Neots, 276, 277; his execution, 341.
Honeywood, Sir T., 259, 261, 268, 272.
Horncastle, 144.
Horsey Bridge, Pass of, 177.
Hudson, Michael, 224, 225, 227; his tragic end, 264.
Hull, Siege of, abandoned, 145.
Hunstanton, 184, 284, 285, 293, 294.
Huntingdon, 61, 88, 98, 148, 177, 197, 307, 371; Mayor's speech, 29; Charles I at, 40, 58; Cromwell at, 110, 119, 120, 129, 199, 200; Committee's letter from, 117; Association Army at, 168, 170, 171; King's forces opposed at, 214; His Majesty's entry and reception, 215; his letters from, 216; plundering of, by the Cavaliers, 218, 219; the King's departure from, 221; his return to, with Cornet Joyce, 240.
Huntingdonshire, Sheriff of, and Shipmoney, 19, 22, 23; petitions from, 28, 42; divisions in, 43, 44; the Montagues and the Cromwells in, 44; publishing the King's proclamation in, 52; Royalists in, 58; added to the Eastern Association, 113; defending the passes into, 115; plundered by Cavaliers, 219; alarms in, 223; tumults in, 273; sequestrators in, 307, 310; contributions of, 373, 375, 376; supplies from, 380; Committee of, 386; "Malignant priests" in, 397.
Hussey, Sir Edward, 297.

Ickleton, 25.
Independents, The, 171, 175, 176, 189, 224, 234, 248, 250, 314; army of, 314.
Ipswich, 109, 389; scenes in the churches at, 26; letter from, 306.
Irby, Col. Sir Anthony, 107.
Ireland, Massacres in, 29.
Ireton, Quarter-Master-General, 170, 171, 237, 288.
Ironsides, The, 113, 131, 223; at Marston Moor, 160, 161; Captains of, 212; evolution of, 360, 361; final tribute to, 361, 362.

Jermey, Sir Arthur, 371.
Jermyn, Thomas, 297.
Jermyns, The, of Rushbrooke Hall, 257.
Jocelyn, Giles, 20, 266.

Kimbolton, Lord, 31, 35, 42, 58.
King, The, see Charles I.
King's Lynn, 32, 51, 61, 69, 112, 122, 131, 133, 153, 177, 197, 212, 215, 229, 268, 284, 294, 295, 364; Cromwell disarming Royalists at, 94; siege of, 134; capture of, from Parliament, 138; plot to recapture, 184-6; strengthening the garrison of, 198; imprisonment of members for, 296.
Kirtlington, 314.

Laud, Archbishop, 96, 312.
Lavenham (Suffolk), 239; contributions and soldiers furnished by, 81-3.
Lawrence, Henry, 7, 340, 354.
Leete (or Leet), John, 310, 386.
Leete, William, 14, 352, 353.
Leigh's Park, 259, 301.
Le Strange, Lady Alice, and her account-keeping, 293-6.
Le Strange, Sir Hamon, 113, 131, 284, 293-6; secures King's Lynn, 131; befriends the Royalist prisoners, 285.
Le Strange, Roger, The King's commission to, 184, 185; his plot to retake King's Lynn, 186; his trial and defence, 187.
Lilburne, John, 250.
Lincoln, 120, 177; the King at, 48, 49; taken by the Earl of Manchester, 156; Association Army at, 167; Royalists at, 273.
Lincolnshire, The Militia of, 45, 46, 48; the King's visit to, 48, 49; Volunteers training in, 51; Cavaliers of, 101; joined to Eastern Association, 143; Danes landing in, 148; Royalist petition from, 151; Cavaliers overrunning, 214; Royalist rising in, 263; effects of the War in, 370, 371; contributions from, 373, 374, 376; supplies from, 380, 381; Committee of, 386, 387.
Lindsey, Earl of, 48, 72.
Linton (Cambs), Royalist rising at, 265; Parliamentary victory at, 267.
Lisle, Sir George, 262; execution of, 283, 341.
London, City of, and the Army, 238; excitement in, 246; letters to and from, in Guildhall Committee, 305-8; Goldsmiths' Hall Committee of, 303.
Loughborough, Lord, 259.
Lowestoft, Skirmish at, 93, 94.
Lowry, John, 161, 301.
Lucas, Sir Charles, 132, 140, 259-62, 269, 279; execution of, 282, 341.
Lucas, Sir John, 63, 140.
Luke, Sir Oliver, 378.
Luke, Sir Samuel, Governor of Newport Pagnell, 181; letters from and to, 176, 178, 179, 182, 183, 190, 191, 196, 204, 357, 377, 378.
Lynne, Elizabeth, mother of Cromwell, 5.

Maddingley (Cambs), 241.
Manchester, Henry, Earl of, 44, 75.
Manchester, Edward, second Earl of, 75; Commander of the Association forces, 123, 125, 130; at the siege of Lynn, 134; joins Cromwell and Fairfax in Lincolnshire, 143; at Winceby fight, 144; at Cambridge, 147, 148; besieges Lincoln, 155; at Marston Moor, 159-64; his quarrel with Cromwell, 168-76; his letter from Huntingdon, 168; his defence to the charges of apathy, 173, 174; his absence in the West, 178; his view of the Association forces, 190; apathy of, 191; resigns his Commission, 197; as Speaker of the Lords, 243; his good-nature, 306; reforming the clergy, 315-7; his character and services, 350, 351; proceedings of his Commission, 392.
Manchester, Countess of, 148.
Mandeville, Lord, see Kimbolton.
Marshall, Stephen, 15; his career, 354, 355.
Marston Moor, 159.
Martin, Dr., 68.
Maynard, Lord, and the soldiers, 24, 25.

Melbourn, Cambs, Riots at, 21, 22.
Melford, Long, 65 ; riots at, 66.
Mildmay, Sir Henry, 179, 193, 201, 306, 307.
Militia, The King's refusal of, 35, 37 ; Parliament's Ordinance for, 44.
Montague, Edward, 15, 44, 71, 169, 174, 212, 273, 350, 351, 371.
Montague, Sir Sidney, 44, 75.
Moulton, St. James, 369.

Needham Hall, Cromwell at, 138.
Newark, 112, 179, 195, 199, 209, 211, 214, 223, 300 ; the King at, 228, 231.
Newbury, Battles of, 141, 173, 342.
Newcastle, The Earl of, 99, 113, 115, 120-2, 141, 191 ; the 'Whitecoats' of, 101 ; holding of Lincolnshire by, 140 ; his defeat at Marston Moor, 160 ; his army, 359.
Newell, George and Sir Gervase, 298.
Newmarket, 114, 200, 257, 258 ; Charles I at, 37, 225, 242, 247 ; Fairfax's army at, 239, 240 ; skirmish at, 265, 266 ; signs and wonders near, 364.
New Model Army, The, 189, 190, 192, 196.
Newport Pagnell, 145, 147, 176, 181, 182, 204, 377, 378 ; John Bunyan at, 196.
Newton, John, 297.
Nicholas, Sir Edward, 30.
Norfolk, Sheriff of, and Ship-money, 20 ; watching the bridges in, 63 ; prisoners taken in, 94 ; petition from, 172 ; Charles I in, 226 ; petition of, 246 ; Royalist prisoners in, 284, 285 ; Puritanism of, 312 ; contributions from, 373, 374, 376 ; supplies from, 380 ; Committee of, 381, 388.
Norris, Sir John, 145.
North, Sir Dudley, 43, 45, 50, 66, 74 ; his wife and children, 34.
North, Henry, 192.
North, Lord, 33.
North, Sir Roger, 118.
Northborough Deeping, 337.
Norwich, 80, 93, 94, 130, 131 ; clerical utterances there, 27, 28 ; held for Parliament, 61 ; Volunteers of, 88 ; Maidens' Troops of, 130 ; arresting the Mayor of, 253 ; fighting and tragic scenes at, 253-5 ; orders as to Cathedral, 332.
Norwich, Earl of, 258, 259, 261, 279.

Offord Cluny (Hunts), 340.
Oley, Barnabus, 56, 325.
Osbaldeston, Henry, D.D., 323.
Oxford, Charles I at, 85 ; his Parliament at, 152 ; his escape from, 224 ; seizing the artillery at, 240.

Packer, Colonel, 152.
Page, Mr., Royalist parson, 323.
Palgrave, Colonel, 116, 117, 192.
Parliament and Militia, 40 ; first army of, 70 ; reverses of, 122 ; and Cromwell's successes, 123 ; and the Army, 234, 246, 287 ; Commissioners of, 242, 243 ; assessments by, 291 ; and the Royalists, 292 ; agents of, 376 ; finances of, 377.
Parliamentary cause, The, 4.
Peckover, Edmund, 355, 356.
Pelham, Furneaux (Herts), 73.
Pelham, Edward, 298.
Peterborough, 41, 106, 109, 116, 131, 199, 203 ; Cromwell and the Cathedral, 109, 110 ; Cromwell at, 122.
Peters, Hugh, Execution of, 346.
Pickering, Captain, 151, 170, 174, 265, 266.
Piggott, John, Royalist, 302.
Pinckney, Captain, 184, 377, 378.
Popish innovations, 196.
Presbyterians, 189, 224, 234, 248, 250, 314.
Pritchard, Jane, 301.
Priests, "First Century of Scandalous and Malignant," 396-8.
Prince Charles at Royston, 35 ; at Cambridge, 36-8 ; at Worcester, 344, 351.
Protestation, The, 27.
Puritans, The, 4 ; first victorious charge of the, 112 ; singing psalms in battle, 144 ; their joy at Naseby, 206 ; the revolt of, 312 ; the conscience of, 322 ; of New England, 352.
Puritanism and Parliament, 320, 356.
Pychard, Thomas, 19, 20, 391.
Pym and the petitions, 32.

Queen, The, 72, 99, 115, 128, 197, 247 ; and the Catholics, 313.

Ram, Mr., parson of Spalding, 102 et seq.
Ramsey, Cromwell at, 111, 112.
Recruiting for Naseby, 202.
Red coats for soldiers, 132, 379, 380.
Remonstrance, The Grand, 29.
Rich, Lord, 301, 302.
Ripton Regis, Parson of, 325.

Rival proclamations, 44, 51-3.
Rivers, Countess, 64; her adventures, 65, 66.
Romford, 133.
Rossiter, Colonel, 178, 221, 273.
Rowe, Dr., 26, 321.
Rowe, Sir William, 145; his letters from Cambridge, 146.
Royalists, Taxing the, 292-4, 297 et seq.
Royston, Charles I at, 35, 225, 248, 249; Prince Charles' letter from, 35, 36; Cromwell at, 205; Army at, 243, 244; Army's letter to the City from, 244, 245; resenting the King's execution at, 288, 289.
Rupert, Prince, 115, 145, 158; his challenge to Cromwell, 159; at Marston Moor, 160, 161; at Naseby, 206; defeat at Bristol, 223.
Russell, Frank, 169, 201, 212, 248.
Russell, John, 67, 297.

Saffron Walden, 208, 299; Army conferences at, 234-7.
St. Albans, 34, 70, 147; Mayor of, arrested, 53; Sheriff arrested at, 87; Earl of Essex's army at, 148; Charles I at, 225, 249; Fairfax's army at, 247; Army officers in Council at, 286, 287.
St. Ives, 28, 98, 223, 227; Cromwell at, 7-10, 199; Cavaliers at, 181.
St. John, Mrs., 13.
St. Neots, 169, 220, 223, 273; defence of, 148; battle of, 275-8.
St. Osyth, 64.
Scots, The, 26, 151, 195.
Scroope, Col. Adrian, 273, 276, 277.
Scroope, Sir Jervase, 48, 73.
Self-denying Ordinance, The, 189, 197, 209.
Sequestrators, 293, 297, 299-301, 303, 310.
Shimpling (Suffolk), Contributions and soldiers from, 83, 84.
Ship-money, 18, 21, 22, 88, 93.
Skegness, 69.
Skippon, Major-General, 45, 206, 237, 238.
Skipworth, Ralph, 226, 229, 230.
Soham (Cambs), 265, 323; parson ejected from, 326.
Soldiers, Condition of, 190, 191; arrears of pay, 213.
Solemn League and Covenant, The, 142, 151; instance of taking the, 365-7.
" Souldiers Pocket Bible," The, 126-9.

Southwell, 225.
Spalding, 102, 105, 107, 112, 122, 369, 370; seizing the parson of, 104.
Sparrow, Colonel, 259, 267.
Stamford, 39, 41, 60, 99, 116, 183, 369, 370; Mayor's speech to Charles I at, 29; taking of Burghley House, near, 117, 118; seized by Cavaliers, 177; Cavaliers defeated at, 211; Alderman of, made prisoner, 212; Charles I at, 214, and again in disguise, 227, 228, 230; Hudson and Styles' rising at, 264.
Stanstead, 133.
Staughton, Great, 169.
Sterne, Dr., 68.
Steward, Sir Thomas, 8.
Stilton (Hunts), 214, 221.
Stone, Richard (Sheriff), 39, 57, 301.
Stowmarket, 257.
Strafford, Execution of, 27.
Stretham, 321.
Styles, Mr., of Crowland, 102 et seq., 263; his escape, 264.
Styles, Captain Thomas, 103, 109.
Sudbury, 100, 201, 239; scenes at, 65.
Suffolk and Ship-money, 20; prisoners taken in, 94; Cromwell's letter to, 134, 143; letter to deputy-lieutenants of, 200; sends troops to Naseby, 201; cost of forces of, 223; petitions of, 246; passes into, 259; trained bands of, 261; and the Second Civil War, 268; forces of, at the siege of Colchester, 268-70; sequestrators of, 310; Puritanism of, 312; Royalist clergy in, 320; contributions of, 373, 374, 376; Committee of, 389; malignant priests in, 397.
Suffolk, Earl of, 23.
Sussex, Lady, Letters of, 34, 70, 75, 297.
Swineshead (Hunts), 365-7.
Symonds, Richard, 220.

Taylor, John, sequestration agent, 307, 309, 327.
Thetford (Norfolk), 257, 364.
Thornton, Colonel, 265.
Thorold, Sir Wm., 297.
Thriplow Heath, 242, 243.
Trollop, Sir Thomas, 193.
Trumpington, Charles I at, 242.

Uxbridge, Treaty of, 189.

Vermuyden, Colonel, 199, 200.
Verney, Sir Edmund, 72.
Verney, Sir Ralph, 34.
Volunteers, 51, 62.

Walden, Lionel, 298.
Waller, Sir William, 115, 155, 158, 167, 235, 236.
Walton, Captain. 162.
Walton, Colonel Valentine, 15, 56–9, 62, 71, 118, 162, 169, 229, 268, 335; Governor of Lynn, 186; Cromwell's letter to, 162; his escape and death, 349, 350.
Ware, 68, 248, 377; Charles I at, 30; mutiny at, 250.
Waresley, 297.
Warwick, Earl of, 25, 65, 74, 255, 259, 301, 302.
Watford, 342.
Welby, Captain, 119.
Wentworth, Sir John, 93.
Whalley, Major, 113, 119, 242, 256, 259.
Wheathampstead (Herts), 225.
Whittlesea, 116, 268.
Willett, James, 28.
Willoughby of Parham, Lord, 45, 46, 48, 120, 143, 144; quarrel of, with Manchester and Cromwell, 151.
Wilson, Arthur, Narrative of, 65, 66.

Winceby, Battle of, 144.
Windham, Thomas, 20.
Winthrop, John, 352.
Wisbech, 100, 106, 113, 115, 139, 197, 267, 268; Royalist prisoners in the church at, 141.
Wistow (Hunts), 325.
Witchcraft, 353.
Witham (Essex), 28.
Wolph, Mr. (of Stamford), 227, 228.
Woodcroft House, 264.
Woolley (Hunts), 325.
Wren, Matthew, Bishop of Ely, 11, 26, 54, 196, 313, 314; information against, 26; sent to the Tower, 30; charges against him, 31; pursuit and re-arrest of, 66, 167; his influence with the clergy, 390, 391.
Wright, John, sequestration agent, 309, 310, 327.

Yarmouth, Great, 63, 93, 332; Volunteers of, 88; disturbances at, 278.
York, Mayor's speech, 29; Association Army before, 156.

For County Committeemen, whose names are mentioned in the text as such, and for Parishes from which Cambs Royalist clergy were ejected, see alphabetic lists in the Appendices.

Elliot Stock, 62, *Paternoster Row, London.*

www.ingramcontent.com/pod-product-compliance
Lightning Source LLC
Chambersburg PA
CBHW050843300426
44111CB00010B/1113